The
Identity ? Question

The Identity ? Question

Blacks and Jews in Europe and America

Robert Philipson

University Press of Mississippi
Jackson

To Craig Werner
In gratitude

www.upress.state.ms.us

Copyright © 2000 by University Press of Mississippi
All rights reserved
Manufactured in the United States of America

08 07 06 05 04 03 02 01 00   4 3 2 1

Library of Congress Cataloging-in-Publication Data

Philipson, Robert.
  The identity game : blacks and Jews in Europe and America / Robert
Philipson.
    p. cm.
  Includes bibliographical references and index.
  ISBN 1-57806-292-6 (cloth : alk. paper) — ISBN 1-57806-293-4
(pbk. : alk. paper)
    1. Blacks—Europe—Social conditions. 2. Jews—Europe—Social con-
ditions. 3. Europe—Ethnic relations. 4. Blacks—United States—Social
conditions. 5. Jews—United States—Social conditions. 6. United States—
Ethnic relations.   I. Title.
D1056.2.B55 P45 2000
305.89604—dc21
                                                    00-035196

British Library Cataloging-in-Publication Data available

Crammed with riches, Europe accorded human status de jure to its inhabitants. With us, to be a man is to be an accomplice of colonialism, since all of us without exception have profited by colonial exploitation. This fat, placid continent ends by falling into what Fanon rightly calls narcissism. Cocteau became irritated with Paris—"that city which talks about itself the whole time." Is Europe any different? And that super-European monstrosity, North America? Chatter, chatter: liberty, equality, fraternity, love, honor, patriotism, and what have you. All this did not prevent us from making anti-racial speeches about dirty niggers, dirty Jews and dirty Arabs. High-minded people, liberal or just softhearted, protest that they were shocked by such inconsistency; but they were either mistaken or dishonest, for with us there is nothing more consistent than a racist humanism since the European has only been able to become a man through creating slaves and monsters.

—Jean-Paul Sartre

Contents

Introduction

Flight from Egypt

"Are you not like the Ethiopians to me, O people of Israel?" saith the Lord. "Did I not bring up Israel from the land of Egypt, and the Philistines from Caphtor and the Syrians from Kir?"

—Amos 9:7

Let us start by unraveling an American cultural tangle. The Reverend Al Sharpton, African-American gadfly of New York politics, has led scores of protest marches against assaults and injustices perpetrated on the Black community. This man's name has become anathema to many Jews for what they perceive to be his inflammatory role in the Crown Heights riots of 1991 and the 1995 arson that killed eight people in a Jewish-owned clothing store in Harlem. Yet when Al Sharpton published the autobiography that has become the standard accessory of American celebrity, he gave it the title *Go and Tell Pharaoh* (1996). The reference, as anyone familiar with the African-American religious tradition would know, is to the spiritual, "Go Down, Moses," which retells the biblical story of Exodus. Although no member of the Judeo-Christian world could miss the grandiose comparison to Moses, Sharpton prefaces his book with the following lines from the spiritual.

Go down Moses
Down to Egyptland

> *Go and tell Pharaoh*
> *Let my people go.*

The irony of a Black leader considered by many Jews to be an anti-Semite appropriating a narrative of Jewish origin to explain his role in the world is the result of the peculiar positioning that Western—and specifically American—culture has imposed on Jews and Blacks, and, collaterally, upon their interrelations.

We recognize the cultures we belong to by the myths we consume within those cultures. British citizens are familiar with the stories of King Arthur; Ibos tell each other about how Mbe, the trickster turtle, got cracks in his shell; Americans know all about the boy Washington and the cherry tree; and Israelis refer to Masada when they wish to invoke a history of militant resistance. Within nations, ethnic cultures operate by similar rules. Jews know about the thirty-six Just Men who watch over the conscience of the world, and Black Americans are as familiar with Stagger Lee as White ones are with Billy the Kid. As Roland Barthes pointed out in his 1957 essay on the subject, "what allows the reader to consume myth innocently is that he does not see it as a semiological system but as an inductive one" ("Myth Today," 118). Myth tells us who we are.

The situation becomes more complex when, as in the case of Sharpton's title, a single myth operates in multiple settings. The Flight from Egypt, which introduces our meditation on the nature of Black and Jewish identity, is central to African-American and Jewish culture, although the myth plays different roles—I stress the plural here—in each. For Jews the Exodus story is so essential that it is rehearsed at length every year at Passover, as commanded by Jehovah (Exodus 12:1–20).[1] The story is subject to an ever-changing constellation of interpretations, as the myriad *haggadot* (chapbooks detailing the order and meaning of the *seder*) testify. Still, the recounting of Israel's delivery from Egypt, no matter how adapted for contemporary use, has remained through the centuries a fundamental Jewish ritual. "With the exodus of this people," the renowned rabbi Leo Baeck writes, "its national history commences" (28). Israel only came to know itself as a people—a people with a will of its own rather than as an instrument of others' power—when Jehovah brought it out of Egypt. The rehearsal of the Passover narrative, Baeck continues, links Jewish existence from its beginning to the present and thus to the future.

The Exodus story did not remain solely a Jewish myth, and the reason for this can be found in Barthes's observation that "[m]en do not have with myth a relationship based on truth but on use" (133). Although Israel had a distinctly unique link to Jehovah,[2] the epigraph from the prophet Amos shows that "Gentile" nations also had a relationship with the Lord. African-American culture, as it coalesced under slavery, seized upon the Exodus story as a narrative of its own aspirations. Albert Raboteau, preeminent historian of African-American religion, writes:

"The appropriation of the Exodus story was for the slaves a way of articulating their sense of historical identity as a people. That identity was also based, of course, upon their common heritage of enslavement. . . . In identifying with the Exodus story, they created meaning and purpose out of the chaotic and senseless experience of slavery. Exodus functioned as an archetypal event for slaves. The sacred history of God's liberation of his people would be or was being repeated in the American South" (311).

Passages on the hard-heartedness of Pharaoh and the Lord's promise to redeem an enslaved people provided an inspirational text for the early Black preachers. The nineteenth-century African-American poet Paul Laurence Dunbar wittily reconstructed the subversive message of hope and liberation in his dialect poem, "An Ante-Bellum Sermon."

> *But I tell you, fellah christuns,*
>   *Things'll happen mighty strange;*
> *Now, de Lawd done dis fu' Isrul,*
>   *An' his ways don't nevah change,*
> *An' de love he showed to Isrul*
>   *Wasn't all on Isrul spent;*
> *Now don't run an' tell yo' mastahs*
>   *Dat I's preachin' discontent.*

Appropriating the Exodus story, enslaved Blacks routinely related the sufferings of the Hebrews to their own, yearned for the Promised Land of freedom, and referred to the Moses who would liberate them.

Even after emancipation, metaphors of the Promised Land, so familiar from the Black church, were used to envision an America without racism or segregation. In a 1948 essay, James Baldwin wrote, "The more devout Negro considers that he is a Jew, in bondage to a hard taskmaster and waiting for a Moses to lead him out of Egypt" (*Notes of a Native Son*, 67). Continuing in the tradition of African-American religious rhetoric, Martin Luther King Jr. declared in the peroration of a speech delivered the night before his assassination, "I just want to do God's will. And He's allowed me to go up to the mountain. And I've looked over. And I've seen the promised land. I may not get there with you. But I want you to know tonight, that we, as a people will get to the promised land" (286).

The Exodus myth was so ingrained in African-American culture that it could be used for secular writings as well. One of the least religious African-American leaders, Booker T. Washington, preached his gospel of hard work and uplift at the end of the nineteenth century by turning to the myth of Jehovah leading His people from Egypt as a pillar of cloud by day and a pillar of fire by night: "I believe the past and present teach but one lesson—to the Negro's friends and to the Negro himself,—that there is but one way out, that there is but one hope of solution; and that is for the Negro in every part of America to resolve from henceforth that he will throw aside every non-essential and cling only to essential,—that his pillar of fire by night and pillar of cloud by day shall be property, economy, education, and Christian character" (*Future of the American Negro*, 132).

Secular Jews used the Exodus myth in a similarly metaphorical manner. The Jewish historian S. M. Dubnow invoked it in his discussion of Russian Jewish emigration to Palestine and America during the oppressive rule of the late nineteenth-century czars when he spoke of the all-pervasive anti-Semitism as "the new Egyptian oppression" and wrote of Russia as "the land of bondage" (373). But when the end of the nineteenth century gave birth to Zionism as a political movement, the traditional Passover toast for many Jews, "Next year in Jerusalem!" took on an urgent and literal meaning. After World War II, the Jewish settlers of Palestine, trying simultaneously to reopen Palestine for Jewish immigration and to throw off the yoke of British rule, christened one of the ships bringing in new Jewish settlers the *Exodus*. Leon Uris, a postwar Jewish-American novelist, used the name as the title of his fictional recounting of the period. The novel not only hit the best-seller lists in America but was turned into a Hollywood epic, thus bringing the secular use of the Exodus myth into the widest cultural arena.

Even Marxist and leftist political thinkers who express contempt for institutional religion have employed the myth of the Exodus. Richard Wright first came to widespread public notice with "Fire and Cloud," a short story about a Black preacher who leads his congregation on a protest march in alliance with the Communist Party in a small Southern town. The most extended use of the myth in a leftist context is Michael Walzer's *Exodus and Revolution*, a commentary on Exodus as "a paradigm of revolutionary politics" (7).

It is significant that such usages of the Exodus myth in resolutely secular, even anticlerical, contexts should issue from a Black and a Jew respectively. Wright had certainly heard sermons on the Exodus theme while growing up in Mississippi. His grandmother was a zealous Seventh Day Adventist, and, through his mother, he engaged in a brief flirtation with the Methodist church. Walzer's introduction to the myth also transpired in a religious context: the portion of the Torah he had to read as part of his bar mitzvah ceremony was a passage of Exodus known as Ki Tissa (ix). In both cases, the Black and the Jew bring their ethnic heritage in to explicate and amplify their understanding of revolutionary action. For both the Black and the Jew, this shared myth is Exodus, the flight from Egypt.

Exodus is integral to both cultures, yet its interpretation and place within ethnic discourse varies according to religious and political ideology. Black and Jewish culture share histories of oppression and marginality, yet the consequent "subject positions" are far from identical. There are a dizzying number of approaches to the problem of Black and Jewish relatedness, ranging from those that deny all connection to those that deny all difference. Essentialists, those who believe in a "Black soul" or a "Jewish soul," would scarcely admit any commonality between the two identities outside of a generalized human nature. Conversely, cultural theorists such as Abdul JanMohamed and David Lloyd ascribe to minority experience a political unity that tends to elide the distinction between Blacks and Jews. "Cultures designated as minorities," they write, "have certain shared experienced by virtue of their similar antagonistic relationship to the dominant culture, which seeks to marginalize them all" (1).

The Exodus myth resists either extreme: the Flight from Egypt is about movement—escape from an oppressive culture, wandering, and the forging of a group identity that itself changes over time and place. The history of American Jews and Blacks encompasses not only their place in national culture but their memories of and attachment to sites of utopian belonging—Africa, Israel, *shtetl*, and compound. As James Clifford notes, "Transnational connections break the binary relations of 'minority' communities with 'majority' societies—a dependency that structures projects of both assimilation and resistance" (255). The consciousness that creates the modern Black and the modern Jew is, initially, a diasporic one. If, as Clifford wittily phrases it, roots precede routes, the historical metaphors informing the consciousness of Blacks (the Middle Passage) and Jews (exile from Zion) emphasize the experience of travel. "When understood as a practice of dwelling (differently)," Clifford writes, "as an ambivalent refusal or indefinite deferral of return, and as a positive transnationalism, diaspora finds validation in the historical experiences of both displaced Africans and Jews" (269).

With the introduction of diaspora, the scope of inquiry widens well beyond the boundaries of national culture. Ever since their expulsion from Israel under the Romans, Jews have always thought of themselves as a people in exile. Arnold Eisen's *Galut* (1986) explores the history of this self-perception from biblical times through the present day. More recently, Paul Gilroy's influential book, *The Black Atlantic: Modernity and Double Consciousness* (1993), successfully promotes the concept of a diverse Black culture that "transcend[s] both the structures of the nation state and the constraints of ethnicity and national particularity" (207). These diasporic paradigms have yet to be explored in a comparative context. Yet such an approach would finesse the impasse created by the more traditional, nationally-bounded comparison of "minority" communities, which almost always emphasize Black-Jewish tensions. What I propose here is a study not of the interrelations between Blacks and Jews but of the relatedness of Blacks and Jews. Once again, the multilayered myth of the Flight from Egypt points the way, for, as Clifford remarks, "The ongoing entanglement of black and Jewish diaspora visions [is] often rooted in biblical imagery" (268). That imagery itself is the result of the

Christian appropriation of Jewish texts, which were then imposed, with all the psychological and physical violence of domination, upon enslaved and colonized Africans. The entanglement of which Clifford speaks becomes even more knotted in the current debate on the nature and status of relationships between Blacks and Jews in the United States. Clifford and Gilroy point us toward an analysis that should shed light on the common ground occupied by Blacks and Jews in Western culture without either denying difference or rehearsing once again the liberal or Afrocentric narratives of Black-Jewish relations. As Gilroy writes: "[T]he concept of diaspora can itself provide an underutilised device with which to explore the fragmentary relationships between blacks and Jews and the difficult political questions to which it plays host: the status of ethnic identity, the power of cultural nationalism, and the manner in which carefully preserved social histories of ethnocidal suffering can function to supply ethical and political legitimacy" (207).

Black and Jewish encounters with modernity—defined here loosely as the ideology of a global Western hegemony erected upon a superior technology—began well before the founding of the American republic. During the eighteenth century, *philosophes* and enlightened rulers preached and practiced new principles of tolerance. As these ideas gained currency, they created an occasional escape hatch for the exceptional Jew who could provisionally leave the ghetto or the industrious Black who could buy himself out of slavery. As more of these individuals attained recognition in Enlightenment culture, a consciousness grew up between these modernized members of the two groups that can be characterized as diasporic. This consciousness is made manifest in the first "ethnic" writings by Blacks and Jews in the languages of the West, e.g., Moses Mendelssohn's *Jerusalem* (1783), and Ottobah Cugoano's *Thoughts and Sentiments on the Evil and Wicked Traffic of the Slavery and Commerce of the Human Species . . .* (1787). As Clifford writes, "[diasporic cultural forms] are deployed in transnational networks built from multiple attachments, and they encode practices of accommodation with, as well as resistance to, host countries and their norms" (251).

The intellectual premises of the Enlightenment created the first secular, transnational culture that seemed to offer full membership to those who were perceived as different. Paul Berman notes, "Enlightenment liberalism . . . sliced neatly through the knotty problem of being an unloved minority in a majoritarian world" (10). The solution, however, created an intellectual crisis for both Blacks and Jews as they sought to evaluate and come to terms with Enlightenment promise. Summoned to discussion (in European languages and under Enlightenment assumptions), Blacks and Jews were forced to define themselves in opposition to and in conjunction with European ideas about who they were. The "identity" they produced combined categories of European thought, usually stereotypes, with insider knowledge of their own community. Intellectuals of both groups could not help but articulate the "double consciousness" so famously identified by W. E. B. Du Bois, the dual measurement of one's life provided by the ethnic and the Western yardstick. Some discovered elements of their culture and identity that they could not or would not abandon in the call to assimilate. The continued racism of the dominant culture only reinforced these "retrograde" tendencies. As Clifford recognizes, "Peoples whose sense of identity is centrally defined by collective histories of displacement and violent loss cannot be 'cured' by merging into a new national community. This is especially true when they are the victims of ongoing, structural prejudice" (250). As we shall see below, the Enlightenment itself was not sure to what extent it welcomed those still perceived as alien.

The Mendès France case provides a good example of eighteenth-century ideological confusion. In June 1775, Isaac Mendès France, originally from the Bordeaux community of so-called "Portuguese Jews," returned to France after a twelve-year stay in the sugar colony of Saint-Domingue. He brought in his train three slaves: Pampy, born in Saint-Domingue; Cézare, an Arada native; and Julienne, a young woman originally kidnapped from the West Coast of Africa. Seven months after the group had settled in Paris, Pampy and Julienne sued their master for their freedom. Citing natural law as it was understood in the eighteenth century ("All men issuing from the hands of Nature are born free"[3]) as well as cataloguing the master's cruelty, their French lawyer, Maître Dejunquières, availed himself of the prevailing anti-Semitism to argue his case. "Mr. Mendès accuses all Negroes of being crooks and liars. The unfortunates which he pursues could launch the same accusation against the Jewish Nation, and the latter could very well suffer in comparison" (qtd. in Pluchon 28).[4] As Pierre Pluchon points out in his discussion of the case, "One hears a veritable indictment against the inhuman and barbarous Jews, enemies of the true religion; one reads a philosophical discussion on the unnatural condition of servitude, and on the moral rectitude of the Blacks" (17).[5] Mendès France was found guilty and forced to pay damages to his former slaves, who were thenceforth free to go where they wished. Enlightenment convictions about the essential equality of humankind brought freedom to the African slaves, but this noble enterprise was aided by an anti-Semitism that didn't even recognize itself as such.

This is the Janus-faced legacy of the Enlightenment. Eighteenth-century Europe articulated the liberating political philosophies of liberalism (Adam Smith, Locke, and the French *philosophes*) *before* the emancipation of its domestic Jewish communities *while* orchestrating a racialized slave trade and plantation system in its colonies. As Gilroy and others point out, Black oppression is integral to the creation of Western modernity—Gilroy writes of "the internality of blacks to the West" (5). As the Mendès France case demonstrates, the same could be said of the Jews, who functioned as Christian Europe's domestic Other.

Modern conceptions of Black and Jewish identity as well as the modern forms of racism that came to term in the eighteenth century entered American culture intact. Rather than constituting an exception to Enlightenment discourse, the paradox of a slave owner penning the American Declaration of Independence perfectly expressed the dualism of the age.[6] The position of Blacks and Jews in the New World was different, but the logic of proclaiming a democratic republic with legalized forms of oppression drew only perfunctory comment in either Jeffersonian America or Napoleonic France. Still, Enlightenment optimism comes ringing through the Declaration of Independence, the Constitution, and *The Federalist Papers*. For immigrants of the nineteenth century—the Germans, Irish, Scandinavians, and Jews—America represented a new promise, a clean slate, a second chance. The first book-length autobiography published by an American Jew was titled *The Promised Land* (1911), and its author, Mary Antin, consistently secularizes the myth of Exodus. Referring to a Passover celebrated shortly after the wholesale expulsion of Jews from Moscow, she writes: "In the story of Exodus we would have read a chapter of current history, only for us there was no deliverer and no promised land. But what said some of us at the end of the long service? Not 'May we be next year in Jerusalem,' but 'Next year—in America!' So there was our promised land, and many faces were turned towards the West. And if the waters of the Atlantic did not part for them, the wanderers rode its bitter flood by a miracle as great as any the rod of Moses ever wrought" (141).

Unlike Mary Antin, Africans brought to North America did not liken their journey across the water to the Exodus. They came to refer to their transatlantic voyage as the Middle Passage, the second phase of their journey from Africa to their place of servitude. "The hellish conditions of the passage have long made it a byword for horror and a metaphor for human suffering and cruelty," states *The Encyclopedia of African-American Culture* in its article on the slave trade. By the time slaves and their children learned of the Exodus story, they knew that they were living in no land of milk and honey. "I'm on my way to the promised land," they might sing in the spiritual, but they realized that Beulah land didn't exist for them in this lifetime. Yet hope for a secular salvation refused to die. Even after the dream of emancipation vanished with the creation of Jim Crow segregation, Southern Blacks placed new faith in the industrial cities of the north. One of the children of these Black dreamers, Claude Brown, called his fictionalized autobiography *Manchild in the Promised Land* (1965) and wrote in his Foreword about where the name came from. "These migrants were told that unlimited opportunities for prosperity existed in New York and that there was no 'color problem' there. They were told that Negroes lived in houses with bathrooms, electricity, running water, and indoor toilets. To them, this was the 'promised land' that Mammy had been singing about in the cotton fields for many years" (7). The burden of Brown's book was that this secular vision was as illusory as the religious one. New York's Promised Land was a ghetto, one that was soon to be engulfed in crime and drugs. In a prophetic harbinger of the Black-Jewish conflict that was to explode in the ensuing decades, Brown ended his panoptic introduction thus:

> Before the soreness of the cotton fields had left Mama's back, her knees were getting sore from scrubbing "Goldberg's" floor. Nevertheless, she was better off: she had gone from the fire into the frying pan.
> The children of these disillusioned colored pioneers inherited the total lot of their parents—the disappointments, the anger. To add to their misery, they had little hope of deliverance. For where does one run to when he's already in the promised land? (8)

Brown's autobiography marks the end of Enlightenment ideological dominance in America, the period in which ethnic assertion could be held in check by the hegemony of universalistic assumptions. The civil rights movement was already mutating into Black Power, the first widespread legitimization of separation, social difference, and the rejection of melting-pot ideology. The consequence for relations between Blacks and Jews in America was fatal to the so-called Grand Alliance forged between Jewish and African-American intellectuals earlier in the century for the promotion of civic equality. As Clayborne Carson writes,

> The subsequent crisis in black-Jewish relations reflected a generalized decline in popular support for socialism and other forms of radicalism that transcended racial, ethnic, and religious groups. . . . Politics rooted in segregated enclaves based on narrowly conceived notions of racial and cultural identity have challenged and in some places supplanted universalistic egalitarianism. (193)

However, the difference in perspective created by the disparate "promises" of the Promised Land had already resulted in ethnic confrontation during the Harlem riots of 1935, and was articulated in the following decade by such African-American writers as Roi Ottley and James Baldwin. Baldwin's 1948 essay, "The Harlem Ghetto," offered an early extended analysis of Black-Jewish rancor.

> [T]here is a subterranean assumption that the Jew should "know better," that he has suffered enough himself to know what suffering means. An understanding is expected of the Jew such as none but the most naive and visionary Negro has ever expected of the American Gentile. The Jew, by the nature of his own precarious position, has failed to vindicate this faith. Jews, like Negroes, must use every possible weapon in order to be accepted, and must try to cover their vulnerability by a frenzied adoption of the customs of the country; and the nation's treatment of the Negro is unquestionably a custom. The Jew has been taught—and too often, accepts—the legend of Negro inferiority; and the Negro, on the other hand, has found nothing in his experience with Jews to counteract the legend of Semitic greed. Here the American white Gentile has two legends serving him at once: he has divided these minorities and he rules. (*Notes*, 69)

But it was not the "American white Gentile" who created these legends, no matter how much he may have manipulated them to his benefit. They were, and are, a legacy of Europe. The myths of Black inferiority and Jewish greed were not the invention of the Enlightenment, but the eighteenth century gave them their modern form. While the West eventually admitted that Blacks could not mate with orangutans and that Passover matzoh did not require the blood of Christian babies, other theories were propounded to show that Blacks and Jews remained irredeemably alien. It was within this shadow of Enlightenment prejudice that American Jews and Blacks found the common ground of cooperation.

As the writings of Marcus Garvey, Richard Wright, Alfred Kazin, and Norman Podhoretz show, the concept of the Grand Alliance wasn't all-pervasive even during its heyday. Black and Jewish spokespersons have confronted one another again and again in the public arena: the New York teachers' strike of 1968, the demonstrations against "public housing" (code for "poor Black neighbors") in predominantly Jewish neighborhoods, the forced resignation of Andrew Young as U.S. ambassador to the United Nations, the Jewish firestorms of protest against the anti-Semitic slurs of Jesse Jackson and Louis Farrakhan, the anomalous but spectacular Crown Heights riots. It is now commonplace for Jews to charge Blacks with anti-Semitism, just as Blacks routinely accuse Jews of racism. This mutual suspicion, combined with mutual recognition, has given a peculiarly intense quality to the relationship between these two minorities.

When the Jews say to the Blacks, "You are political kin; you are anti-Semites"–are they not right? When the Blacks say to the Jews, "You are political kin; you are oppressors"–are they not right? Yet this tortured and misdirected dialogue takes place in a world that neither Blacks nor Jews created, through identities which neither Jews nor Blacks had control over formulating, and in a language which, though shared by both, has its origins in a culture which devalues each.

The origins of this tension can be traced to Enlightenment attitudes toward non-Western peoples. Eighteenth-century Europe engaged in a discussion about the nature of Black and Jewish identity that set the terms of response by the intellectual representatives of those groups. Drawing from a legacy of classical literature, Christian ideology, and the *realpolitik* of nation-state competition, eighteenth-century discourse coalesced around new theories of race, human nature, and environment that were to remain thematically dominant as long as Enlightenment assumptions defined the political will of the West. For Blacks and Jews, this discussion was more than theoretical; Black and Jewish intellectuals who tried to better the condition of their brethren found that the terms of the debate had already been defined for them. Western attitudes could dictate for both outgroups ostracism or inclusion, slavery or freedom, dialogue or silence. Westernized intellectuals could refute negative stereotypes; they could embrace Enlightenment tolerance and egalitarianism; and they could criticize what the *philosophes* criticized. French, British, and German sympathizers and advocates did the same. What Black and Jewish writers brought to the Western discussion was an insider's perspective, a subjective experience that was as persuasive to its readers as the author's rhetorical skill and mastery of European letters could make it. It was no accident that the same period that saw the publication of the first Black and Jewish "ethnic" writing, the last quarter of the eighteenth century, also saw these two groups, for the first time in Western history, gaining localized emancipation, however briefly and hesitantly.

Because of the historical conditions of the Enlightenment, autobiographies were among the first works these Westernized intellectuals produced. The trickle of ethnic autobiographies produced in the eighteenth century became a veritable torrent in the twentieth, but I will contend that all of the themes, contradictions, and manifestations of double consciousness articulated by the first of these autobiographers were recapitulated a century and a half later by Black and Jewish autobiographers in America who still subscribed to Enlightenment assumptions.

Olaudah Equiano was the first Black to write and publish a book-length autobiography: *The Interesting Narrative of the Life of Olaudah Equiano, or Gustavus Vassa, the African*. His book is regarded as the earliest masterpiece of Black autobiography written in English. Its author did not conceive of himself as a literary man, but his rhetorical skill is evident throughout. As an eighteenth-century document, it embodies the double consciousness and ambivalent engagement with Western discourse that were later to be recognized as a hallmark of Black writing in European languages. As eighteenth-century propaganda, it served as a testament to Black will and intelligence in the centuries following its appearance. Most striking, however, is how its engagement with Black consciousness in the Enlightenment would remain central to discussions of the diasporic experience.

Although Solomon Maimon's *Lebensgeschichte* is currently out of print, is rarely mentioned, and has not seen a new translation into English for more than a century, it plays a similar role in Jewish literature. Its case is not helped by the fact that Maimon was no master rhetorician and that his German style rarely rises above the serviceable. Nonetheless, his autobiography is as revealing as Equiano's as an Enlightenment expression of ethnic identity. We see in it the same themes of divided consciousness, the same desire to harmonize ethnic difference with the promise of Enlightenment acceptance, the same effort to interpret the ultimate meaning of life through the ideology of the dominant culture—in this case Deism rather than Equiano's dissident Protestantism.

In many ways, the terms of debate established during the Enlightenment had not changed by the twentieth century. At least until the 1960s, America offered the same promise of full acceptance in civil society. Although the specific terms differed for each group, the contradictions established a century and a half earlier remained: Blacks still lived under legalized segregation, and Jews still found themselves socially hemmed in by restrictive covenants. Assimilation into a universal culture was still "the price of the ticket," to use James Baldwin's phrase, and ethnic activists who wished to remedy the deficiencies of American liberalism accused the United States of not living up to the ideals of its political culture. Ethnic literature written in English had long been a part of a larger American dialogue, always the product of authors who crossed cultural boundaries. The development of the idea of race, however, had changed the nature of Enlightenment discourse on the subject of group identity. Nineteenth-century conceptions of race as a reified essentialism were just beginning to break up as the social sciences—psychology, sociology, political science—simultaneously emulated and claimed autonomy from the physical sciences. The complexity attending the ethnic autobiographers of the American mid-century was that they were born and raised in a world more structured by essentialist assumptions than the one they wound up writing in. Still, Black and Jewish autobiographers working at the end of Enlightenment hegemony share the same themes as their eighteenth-century counterparts: double consciousness, a striving toward universal culture (variously defined in accordance with the prevailing intellectual climate), and an ambivalent relation to the ethnic community left behind.

Richard Wright's *Black Boy* represents a canonical closure to Enlightenment discourse, the last literary autobiography that accepted, on an ideological level, the universalistic claims of inclusion on the part of the West. Of course, the West had changed with the advent of the Soviet Union as an important power. The Soviets had turned socialism, the dream of the nineteenth century, into Marxism-Leninism, a structure of ideas that seemed to have the same pragmatic drive and will to conquer as liberal capitalism. Wright was a communist when he wrote *Black Boy*, and although he broke with the Communist Party just before its publication, he remained an intellectual fellow traveler for the rest of his life. This is apparent in his views on African-American literature, which he considered (with the exception of his own works) as weak and parochial. His literary models were drawn entirely from European and American writers. Yet paradoxically, his autobiography revived the effective tradition of African-American autobiography that had been dormant since Booker T. Washington's *Up From Slavery*.

In a manner similar to Wright, Kazin wrote his ethnic autobiography while adhering to a latter-day version of Enlightenment inclusionary ideology—in this case, socialism. And, like Wright, Kazin was not interested in reclaiming an American ethnic literary tradition. Yet *Walker in the City* shares themes and perspectives with such other Jewish American writers as Abraham Cahan, Mike Gold, and Delmore Schwartz. The autobiographies of both Wright and Kazin ended up as crucial texts in literary traditions neither writer considered valid.

The autobiographies we shall be examining most closely are what the critic Robert Stepto has labeled "narratives of ascent" (167). As we shall see, ethnic autobiographers had other models from which to choose, most notably the narrative of immersion. Both Blacks and Jews eagerly sought integration into the Enlightenment West; both Blacks and Jews found themselves alienated from Enlightenment ideals when the path to integration was barred by prejudice; both Blacks and Jews turned away in disgust and sought to establish links with the communities they or their parents had left behind. The similarity of these choices demonstrates a shared consciousness of difference: "ethnic," "minority," "racial"— all these labels have been used. This identity—taken to mean sameness as well as describing group subjectivity—shares more than it excludes. Still, it is an identity in motion, sometimes diasporic, sometimes nationalistic, always at odds with the majority culture.

The Light from the West

Eighteenth-Century Perspectives

The Jews were regarded with the same eye as we see
the Negroes, as an inferior species of man.

—Voltaire, *Essaie sur les mœurs*

In the first book-length Black autobiography, *The Interesting Narrative of the Life of Olaudah Equiano, or Gustavus Vassa, the African* (1789), the author offers an ethnographic description of the Ibo people he was kidnapped from while still a young boy. He ends his opening chapter with the first extended comparison between Blacks and Jews in the English language. The analogy, he writes, between the manners and customs of his countrymen and those of the pastoral Jews before they had entered their Promised Land strikes him "very forcibly." Both peoples were ruled by chiefs and elders, both practiced circumcision, both made sacrifices and burnt offerings to their deities, and, on similar occasions, both engaged in washings and purifications. "The law of retaliation prevailed almost universally with us as with them: and even their religion appeared to have shed upon us a ray of its glory, though broken and spent in its passage, or eclipsed by the cloud with which time, tradition, and ignorance might have enveloped it" (23). Equiano concludes from this striking similarity of cultures that "one people had sprung from the other," a conclusion he supports with reference to the writings of various European scriptural "authorities" whose fame has dimmed since their time.

As William Andrews notes, by making Blacks the descendants of biblical Jews,

3

"Equiano removes the African from the status of other and places him in a much more complex relationship to the Euro-Christian scheme of things" (58). If Africans, like their European counterparts, are descended from the Jews, then they cannot be subhuman or the link between man and animal—on par with the orangutan—as some writers had claimed. Equiano makes this strategy explicit when he declaims, "Let the polished and haughty European recollect that his ancestors were once like the Africans, uncivilized and even barbarous. Did Nature make them inferior to their sons? And should they too have been made slaves? Every rational mind answers, 'No'" (24).

The assumption that rationality and a Christian world view are harmonious and benevolent is a very British one in the eighteenth century (the French Encyclopedists put them in opposition), but there are two aspects of Equiano's argument that I wish to bring out. The first is that, in spite of his eloquent depiction of Ibo society as ordered and rational, he does not hesitate to tar the whole of the continent with the brush of European stereotypes concerning African barbarism. Secondly, he picks up on the prevailing environmentalism of eighteenth-century thought to depict Africans as a degenerated species of humanity: the ray of civilized glory broken and spent in its passage. In this he is no pioneer. The French naturalist Georges Louis Leclerc de Buffon provided a lengthy analysis of the origin of the races in the second and third volumes of his *Histoire naturelle* of 1749, integrating the traditional thesis of monogenetic origin with a historical diversification of species under environmental influence. As a scientist, Buffon supported his theory of the unitary origin of man not by appeal to the biblical account of creation but by the empirical criterion of fertile interbreeding. (The best-known example of species interbreeding was the mule, the sterile offspring of the donkey and horse, which gave its name to the "mulatto.") In *Les Époques de la nature* (1788), Buffon developed his evidence for a geographical degeneration of man as he moved from his place of origin into different regions.[1] "The most temperate climate lies between the 40th and 50th degrees of latitude," Buffon wrote, "and it produces the most handsome and beautiful men. It is from this climate that the ideas of the genuine colour of mankind, and of the various degrees of beauty, ought to be derived. The two extremes are equally remote from truth and from beauty" (qtd. in Popkin 251).

Buffon's theories of racial degeneracy cast a long shadow in Western intellectual history. The German anthropologist Johann-Friedrich Blumenbach speculated in 1795 that the original home of these wonderful ancestors was the Caucasus, giving rise to the term "Caucasian" that was to have such appalling success in the subsequent two centuries. In his study of British attitudes toward Blacks during the era of the Atlantic slave trade, Anthony Barker writes:

The barbarism of Africa, in particular, was very often regarded as degeneration, as men compared its contemporary condition with the high civilisation which had once prevailed in

Egypt or Carthage. . . . The vast majority of geographical works remarked on Africa's cultural degeneration briefly and without analysis. For instance, J. R. Forster explained how American Indians and Africans had forgotten or lost most of the "ancient systems" and were "degenerated, debased, and wretched" because they had been unable to replace them "by new principles and ideas" from outside. Much the same message was conveyed to generations of youthful readers by William Guthrie's frequently reprinted *Geographical Grammar*. (96)

The reason for the African's shocking skin color had yet to be resolved. Eighteenth-century authors discussed numerous hypotheses—the curse of Ham, the possibility that Africans were a different species altogether (a religiously heterodox and therefore unpopular argument)—but the one that gained the greatest currency was the environmentalism popularized by the Baron de Montesquieu in the first volume of his *Esprit des lois* (1849). Climate, the Baron learnedly wrote, accounted for the vast differences among people and societies. For physiological reasons, Montesquieu claimed, men are more vigorous in cold climates. "The peoples in hot countries are timid like old men; those in cold countries are courageous like young men" (232). Montesquieu was not the first to speculate about the shaping effects of climate upon the inhabitants of a certain territory (drawing upon classical tradition, Europeans tended to regard savagery as a function of extreme temperatures), but the authority of his scholarship and encyclopedic erudition launched the idea into European thought with impressive and dominant force. Equiano cited with approval British abolitionist Thomas Clarkson's famous *Essay on the Slavery and Commerce of the Human Species* (1786), in which Clarkson advanced the "obvious" explanation that prolonged exposure to the sun had over time turned the Africans black. To support his contention, Clarkson quoted other writings that claimed that the Spaniards and Portuguese who had lived for a long time in "the torrid zone" had become noticeably darker. These instances allowed Equiano to argue that "while they shew how the complexions of the same persons vary in different climates, it is hoped [they] may tend also to remove the prejudice that some conceive against the natives of Africa on account of their color" (23–24).

The same environmentalism allowed the enlightened defenders of contemporary Jews to argue that their manifest inferiority was not innate and ineradicable. "In the eighteenth century," Arthur Hertzberg writes, "Montesquieu's concept of many cultures, which derived their difference from varying origins in nature, was understood as a liberating, egalitarian idea. It is incontrovertible that later in the century Montesquieu was consistently quoted by all those who were on the side of the Jews, either in the past or in the present" (276). Among the first to use Montesquieu in this manner was Isaac de Pinto, a philosopher and economist of Sephardic origin.[2] In *Apologie pour la nation juive* (1762), published in Amsterdam as a response to the hostile description of the Jews in Voltaire's *Dictionnaire philosophique*, Pinto began by quoting Montesquieu to prove that all men, including Jews, are basically the same and that differences among them are the result of climate. Within Jewry itself, Pinto wrote, differing conditions explain the gulf between the wealthy and cultured Sephardim in southern France (known as "Portuguese Jews" due to their relatively recent migration from the Iberian peninsula) and the miserable, uncouth Ashkenazim of eastern France. The Portuguese Jews did not distinguish themselves either in physical appearance or in culture from their European counterparts; they were honest businessmen, not usurers; and they benefited the economies of all countries that allowed them residence. As for those of his coreligionists who were depressed in manners and culture: "Is it surprising that, deprived of all the advantages of society, multiplying in accordance with the laws of nature and religion, despised and humiliated on all sides, often persecuted, always insulted, the degraded and debased nature in them no longer appeared to be concerned with anything but immediate need?" (qtd. in Poliakov, *History of Anti-Semitism*, 5). Hertzberg ably sums up the prevailing themes of Pinto's pamphlet:

> There was a segment of the Jewish community that was worthy of equality because it was already living the highest culture and manners of the majority. The depressed mass of the Ashkenazim were what they were, not by their nature, or even by their faith, but because of persecution and exclusion; more favorable conditions would change them. The attachment of Westernized Jews to their Jewish identity was to religion, but that religion was no longer the orthodox faith, for such men philosophized like other contemporary intellectuals. They persisted in remaining Jews because it was dishonorable to abandon a persecuted community. Mendelssohn quite correctly hailed this pamphlet because much that was going to be said in the next thirty years, mostly by his disciples or people under his influence, was already outlined within it. (182)

The German Jewish philosopher Moses Mendelssohn and his circle had a huge influence in propagating these propositions. When the Jewish community in Alsace found itself under attack for its money-lending role in the local economy, Cerf Berr, a court Jew and a great admirer of Mendelssohn, asked the latter to compose a treatise stating the Jews' claim to fair treatment by the state. Mendelssohn turned this task over to Christian Wilhelm Dohm, a Prussian official and economic physiocrat, who produced an enormously influential volume, *Über die bürgerliche Verbesserung der Juden*, in 1781. Writing from a Prussian perspective, Dohm did not feel compelled to distinguish between the Ashkenazim and the Sephardim. He acceded to the proposition—virtually unquestioned amongst the Christian population—that the majority of Jews were clannish, barbarous, dishonest, retrograde, and economically pernicious. But, Dohm contended, the shortcomings of the Jews were merely the shortcomings of a trading class, common to a people who had been artificially channeled by repressive decrees. Change their circumstances, he said, echoing a major tenet of the Enlightenment, and you will change their natures. Dohm called for "civic betterment" for the Jews (the term "emancipation" had yet to be introduced) because of the contribution a "normalized" Jewish community could make to the state. Using the ideas Adam Smith had developed in his *Wealth of Nations* (1776), Dohm argued that the power of the state increased with the number of its productive citizens and that the best policy would be to transform the Jews from mere consumers to producers.

"Dohm's appeal for reexamination of the Jews' status was a timely call corresponding to the feeling of the times. . . . It became, indeed, the starting point for a prolonged discussion and directed opinions on the subject for more than two decades" (Katz, *Out of the Ghetto*, 71). In Germany, Dohm's work made such an impression that he was flooded with letters from all parts of the country. A French edition prepared by the Comte de Mirabeau served as a guide for advocates of Jewish enlightenment during the French Revolution. Mendelssohn acclaimed the book but found it necessary to defend the Jews against the proposition that they were morally deficient because of their civic disabilities. In his introduction to Marcus Herz's translation of Menasseh ben Israel's apologetic work, *Vindiciæ Judæorum*, published in German as *Die Rettung der Juden* (1782), Mendelssohn outlined the vicious circle in which the Jews found themselves. "They drive us out and remove us from all arts and sciences and other useful callings and occupations of men, bar to us all roads to beneficial improvement, and then make our lack of culture the reason for our further oppression. They tie our hands and reproach us for not using them" (qtd. in Zinberg, *The Berlin Haskalah*, 48–49).

Similar arguments concerning the origin of the Blacks' alleged character flaws were made by both Black and White writers. Hilliard d'Auberteuil claimed categorically in his *Considérations sur l'état présent de Saint-Domingue* (1776) that the Blacks acquired under slavery "an infinity of vices that they did not have in a state of nature" (qtd. in Seeber, *Anti-Slavery Opinion*, 54). Sixteen years later, Equiano echoed this sentiment in a context more reminiscent of Hobbes than of Rousseau.

When you make men slaves, you deprive them of half their virtue, you set them, in your own conduct, an example of fraud, rapine, and cruelty, and compel them to live with you in a state of war; and yet you complain that they are not honest or faithful! You stupefy them with stripes, and think it necessary to keep them in a state of ignorance; and yet you assert that they are incapable of learning; that their minds are such a barren soil or moor that culture would be lost on them; and that they came from a climate, where nature, though prodigal of her bounties in a degree unknown to yourselves, has left man alone scant and unfinished, and incapable of enjoying the treasures she has poured out for him!—An assertion at once impious and absurd. (80–81)

In a masterfully ironic usage of environmentalist thought, Equiano refused to presume that "dealers in slaves are born worse than other men" because the slave trade itself debauches their minds and deadens their morals. "And, had the pursuits of these men been different, they might have been as generous, tender-hearted and just, as they are unfeeling, rapacious and cruel" (80).

Yet the inferiority of the Black race assumed by European discourse, whether couched in terms of environmentalism or religion, was usually assimilated by those Blacks seeking entry to Western society. In an ode composed for a Harvard commencement ceremony, the African-American poet Phillis Wheatley wrote:

> *'Twas not long since I left my native shore*
> *The land of errors, and Egyptian gloom:*
> *Father of mercy, 'twas thy gracious hand*
> *Brought me in safety from those dark abodes.*

Ukasaw Gronniosaw, one of the first former slaves to have his story told in print, narrated his failure to get a book to communicate with him: "I opened it and put my ear close upon it, in great hopes it would say something to me; but was very sorry and greatly disappointed when I found it would not speak; this thought immediately presented itself to me, that every body and every thing despised me because I was black" (*The Black Prince* 9–10).

As Gronniosaw and, less categorically, Equiano were willing to subscribe to Western assumptions of Black inferiority, so enlightened Jews, in their dialogue with the West, made similar concessions. In his autobiography, the Jewish philosopher Solomon Maimon agreed with the members of Mendelssohn's circle that "the evil condition of our people, morally as well as politically, has its source in their religious prejudice, in their want of a rational exposition of the Holy Scriptures, and in the arbitrary exposition to which the rabbis are led by their ignorance of the Hebrew language" (285). Maimon said boldly what the majority of the *maskilim* (Jewish enlighteners), more tied to the Jewish community than the renegade philosopher, expressed with greater circumspection. Yet as Israel Zinberg remarked, Voltaire's motto, "Ecrasez l'infamie" [Crush the infamy (of superstition)], found a particularly sharp resonance in Jewish intellectual circles. "The entire ancient tradition—except for the Bible which was, after all, highly regarded in the Christian world—was declared outmoded and reactionary, and the enlighteners were prepared magnanimously to sacrifice on the altar of 'enlightenment' all the traditions of the Jewish people" (Zinberg, *Berlin Haskalah*, 93).

The enlightened Jews of Eastern France, culturally members of the Ashkenazim, expressed similar sentiments. In a defense of his community published in 1787, Isaiah Berr Bing, the leading *maskil* in Metz, "admitted" that centuries of persecution had not only left the Jews in a cultural backwater but had accounted for "the deplorable materialism and cowardliness of the Jewish character" (qtd. in Hertzberg 331). As Hertzberg writes: "In the course of the six opening months of the Revolution the Jews of eastern France had repeatedly assented to the proposition that in their mass they were inferior to the level of honesty and culture of the majority; that they had to abandon at least some aspects of their religion; and that they needed to become more like all other Frenchmen" (349).

By contrast, the Sephardic Jews of southern France and Holland, much more assimilated than their Ashkenazi coreligionists and already in possession of important trading rights and civic guarantees, were noticeably silent in this eighteenth-century discussion. The firestorm of emotions touched off by Revolutionary debate in the National Assembly over emancipation of the Jews centered on the impoverished and "alien" Ashkenazim of Eastern France. "No one raised the question of the nature of the religion, business practices, or patriotism of the Sephardim. There was more than an implication that a community like theirs was acceptable to the makers of the Revolution, provided that it was decorously inconspicuous" (qtd. in Poliakov, *History of Anti-Semitism*, 218).

The actual course of Jewish emancipation in the French Revolution followed the pattern of these prejudices. The National Assembly moved that the Declaration of the Rights of Man be applied to all French citizens, but Protestants, Jews, and people of color (both mulattos and Blacks) were specifically exempted. These various groups formulated grievances on their own account, with the Alsatian Jews and the Bordeaux "Portuguese" acting independently of one another. As the mood of the National Assembly grew increasingly radical, the religious and "racial" restrictions of the *ancien régime* came under reexamination. The economic thrust of the Revolution moved toward the creation of a modern economy, based on the individual as citizen of the State, and it became impossible to carry over regulations and exclusions from an earlier time. The French Protestants, oppressed by the Catholic Church but least foreign in terms of hegemonically perceived "otherness," acted as a spearhead in the emancipation of the Jews. On December 23, 1789, the total enfranchisement of the Protestants was adopted without difficulty. One month later, on January 28, 1790, the Sephardim obtained equal rights in an eleven-hour session that was the stormiest the Constituent Assembly had ever known. The deputy from Alsace, Jean François Rewbell, reflecting the bitter anti-Semitism of his home province, shouted amidst the uproar, "It is being proposed, Gentlemen, that you declare that the Jews of Bordeaux are no Jews!" (qtd. in Poliakov, *History of Anti-Semitism*, 218).

There the matter rested for the next twenty months. It was only after the fall of the moderate Girondins, under the same spirit that would lead to the execution of Louis XVI and the de-Christianization campaigns, that the question of total Jewish enfranchisement came up again. By then it was an ideological *fait accompli*. On September 27, 1791, the Constituent Assembly voted almost unanimously for total emancipation of the Jews.

Contrary to the inchoate racial ideas taking shape in the European mind through the influence of Maupertius and Buffon, it was the darker "Portuguese" Jews who were considered more civilized and worthier of participation in European culture than the relatively lighter Ashkenazim. Interestingly enough, this difference between the two groups of Jews was cited in a mid-century polemic concerning the origin of the African. The Christian view of history, of course, was that all men were descended from Adam, a theory that entered the history of anthropology under the name of monogenesis. Polygenesis had its advocates—most famously Voltaire—and it gained an added cachet of anticlerical glamor because of its heterodox defiance. As Winthrop Jordan wrote, "The Christian tradition created a rock-hard shelf below which the Negro could not fall" (231), but such a safeguard was removed in the theory that different races had different origins. In 1757 Johann Meckel, surgeon to Frederick the Great and a member of the freethinking côterie that had gathered about the "enlightened" despot, claimed scientific support for the theory of polygenesis when, after dissecting Blacks, he "discovered" that both their brains and their blood were black. This prompted a Dutch physician, Peter Camper, to investigate "the belief of the Christian religion" in a similarly rational manner. To support his thesis, Camper invoked the case of the Jews: the "Portuguese" were dark and the "Teutonics," as he called the Ashkenazim, were light, but everyone knew that their origins were the same. "Having first propounded his conclusions, [Camper] ended his proof by urging Europeans to 'stretch out a fraternal hand to the Negroes and acknowledge them as descendants of the first man, whom we all consider as our common father'" (Poliakov, *History of Anti-Semitism*, 134).

As long as a medieval *Weltanschaaung* prevailed, Blacks, Jews, and religious dissidents were ostracized and persecuted without much need for justification. The foundations of modern thought began to be laid in the seventeenth century with the writings of Locke, Newton, Bayle, Spinoza, and Descartes, but it was the work of the eighteenth century to disseminate their incipient rationalism, to apply it to all fields of human inquiry, and to spread it through the educated classes of Western Europe and America. The Enlightenment expressed itself differently within the various national cultures in formation, and we must be careful not to make the movement of its ideas seem too uniform or too triumphant. The political and social superstructures of France, Germany, Austria, and England ensured that the writings of Voltaire and the Encyclopedists would be differently read and varyingly influential. The "enlightened" despotism of Prussia's Frederick the Great and Austria's Joseph II was a far cry from England's bourgeois parliament. Yet certain broad Enlightenment tenets were widely understood—the desirability of rationalist thought, the shifting of men (the sexism of the term is deliberate) from members of guilds and estates to citizens of a centralized state, the separation of religious and secular thought, the embrace of the idea of progress in the material and moral spheres—and while these can be analyzed in retrospect as the liberal ideology of a rising bourgeoisie, they promoted genuine ferment and fervor within their own time.

The Enlightenment climate of ideas affected Blacks and Jews not only as it penetrated their own thinking but as it brought about change in their social and political status. Their respective starting points—Blacks as colonial slaves and Jews as domestic pariahs—were quite different, but seen from a distance of two hundred years, their first general movement toward a partial integration was similar. As domestic partners in the Western creation of a worldwide capitalist system, Jews were the first to be invited—sometimes forcibly—to the Enlightenment party.

The trend toward change affected the realm of practical politics and that of theoretical conception simultaneously. In 1781, the same year that Dohm published his pamphlet, *Über die bürgerliche Verbesserung der Juden*, the Hapsburg monarch Joseph II promulgated his Edict of Tolerance concerning the Jews of Lower Austria. Eight years later he extended its application to Galacia, that part of Poland that had been annexed by the Austro-Hungarian Empire. The Edict sought to remove Jews from their spheres of economic activity and integrate them into the society at large. Thus, Jewish communities had to establish schools for their children's civic education, or, where this was not feasible, Christian schools were obliged to take in Jewish pupils. Jewish dress could now be discarded, and the rules specified that Jews would be permitted to attend secondary schools and universities. Jews were even free to seek apprenticeships with Christian masters, although guilds retained their rights to exclude them. The body tax was also abolished. However, much of the Edict was coercive. In its effort to change the Jews' traditional source of income, the Edict forbade them to operate inns or to be tax collectors. The Edict also destroyed the political power of the *kehillot*, the governing bodies of Jewish authorities, and limited them to religious activities. Furthermore, Jews had to conduct their business affairs in German rather than Yiddish.

The impetus behind the Edict of Tolerance had its source not from a desire to benefit the Jews but out of the intention of the emperor to transform the state, based on local particularism and class privileges, into a centralized and unified entity. As the historian Jacob Katz points out, however (a prefiguration of later failures of Enlightenment policies promulgated by autocratic rulers and revolutionary decrees), practical implementation fell far short of the theoretical mark. "The Catholic church and the traditionally established estates were too deeply enmeshed in the fabric of state and society to be disentangled by the magic of an edict" (Katz, *Out of the Ghetto*, 163). Thus Jews were still not permitted to settle where they liked. Bohemia and Moravia limited the number of Jewish marriages permitted, and, despite the law, Jews continued to pay special taxes. Even in Vienna, the capital of the empire, every *Schützjude* ("protected Jew") had to pay for his right of residency.

Where Enlightenment ideas did not have to do such strenuous battle with ingrained habits of mind, however, and where the Jewish population was numerically and economically insignificant, full enfranchisement was easily granted. The U.S. Constitution, adopted in 1787, explicitly stated in Article VI that "no religious Test shall ever be required as a qualification to any Office of public Trust under the United States." Among the original thirteen states, restrictions adopted under colonial legislatures still remained—Virginia, for example, withheld from Jews the right to vote in state elections—but Jews and their allies continued to press for changes. New states didn't write restrictions on Jews into their constitutions and generally omitted any religious test for holding office. "By the year 1840, only in five states—New Jersey, North Carolina, New Hampshire, Connecticut, and Rhode Island—did Jews continue to be subject to disabilities. While in twenty-one of the twenty-six states of the Union they generally enjoyed full religious and political equality" (Chyet, 44–45).

In Western Europe, where Jews were clearly marked as the alien "other"—a place firmly occupied in the New World by Blacks—Enlightenment apologists had to vigorously promote the argument for tolerance and "civic betterment." In 1787 the Comte de Mirabeau published a book, *Sur Moses Mendelssohn et la réforme politique des Juifs*, in which he argued that the faults of the Jews were those of their circumstances. Quoting freely from Dohm, he repeated the Prussian's assertion that "the Jew is more of a man than he is a Jew" (qtd. in Hertzberg 296). That same year, the Abbé Grégoire made his public debut with an essay that eventually won first prize in the question propounded by the Metz Academy, "Are there ways of making the Jews happier and more useful in France?" Grégoire's essay was awarded the prize jointly with submissions by Adolphe Thiéry, a lawyer, and Zalkind-Hourwitz, a Polish-Jewish enlightener who figured later in the Revolution as a Jacobin. As Hertzberg says, all three essays, published within a year of their submission, basically agreed that the faults of the Jews stemmed from persecution and that these could be corrected if they were given access to Western education and to the life of the larger society. "It was in the name of this argument that during the Revolution Mirabeau and Grégoire would soon be taking the lead towards achieving the Emancipation of the Jews" (Hertzberg 334).

None of these writers and activists, however, were interested in the emancipation of the Jews as Jews. What they envisioned was the eventual development of enlightened citizens who would forget that their ancestors had once been disfigured by persecution and "superstition." After their regeneration, the Abbé Grégoire dared even hope for their conversion, a phenomenon more noticeable in Prussia before Jewish emancipation than in post-Revolutionary France. Among the advanced thinkers of the time, however, the medieval premise that the Jews ought to be excluded from society was definitively superseded by Enlightenment abstractions about human nature and rights. "We hold these truths to be self-evident," Thomas Jefferson wrote in his famous opening to the Declaration of Independence, "that all men are created equal, that they are endowed by their creator with certain unalienable rights, that among these are life, liberty, and the pursuit of happiness." Slaves were implicitly excluded from the Declaration's pronouncement, but such an ideology was clearly applicable to the regenerated Jew.[3] "It is fortunate that no one can insist on the rights of man without at the same time espousing our own rights," Mendelssohn declared (qtd. in Arendt 88).

The truth of this statement was not immediately apparent to the Constituent Assembly, as we have seen above; but through the lobbying of Jews and the prodding of men like Mirabeau and Grégoire, Enlightenment ideologies *vis-à-vis* the Jews eventually triumphed in France. As Leon Poliakov points out in his monumental *History of Anti-Semitism*, however, Jewish inclusion in the state was relatively easy compared to the issue of "colored" emancipation, which the Constituent Assembly denied in the same month (September 1789) that rights of citizenship were accorded to the Alsatian Jews: "[Slavery] was retained in the colonies, under pressure from the great planters. In this case, prejudice or 'physical repugnance' combined with the operation of powerful interests. Where the Jews were concerned, no organized interest of any great extent was involved, given their small numbers, their heterogeneity and their dispersion. In these circumstances, emancipation could be decreed on the basis of purely ideological considerations, as a statement of principle . . . "(*History of Anti-Semitism*, 220–21).

Since Blacks were seen primarily as a colonial and enslaved population, eighteenth-century discussion never envisioned their enfranchisement and integration into the metropole. When Enlightenment thought turned its attention to the plight of the Black populations in the New World, it focused on the abolition of the slave trade or, more radically, on the abolition of slavery itself, but no one considered for a moment that Blacks could be brought into the public and political life of Western society. Since the battle at hand was the abolition of the trade itself—a battle that was not completely won until the middle of the next century—little thought was given to the eventual fate of those Blacks who might eventually survive their brutal enslavement. The discernible growth of a Black population in London, known as the Black Poor, had triggered the Sierra Leone resettlement scheme, a project that had briefly employed Equiano as Commissary of Stores. The British government gave the resettlement plan its enthusiastic financial backing because it believed the best way of solving the problem of the Black Poor was to send them back to Africa.

Yet for all its patronization and Eurocentrism, there was a genuine element of idealism in the eighteenth-century abolitionist movement. Seymour Drescher writes: "At every major juncture in the history of abolition British policy was undertaken in the teeth of a world economic context which placed a premium on the expansion of slavery" (4). The battle was waged on behalf of the Blacks' recently discovered humanity, an attribute discerned only through the optic of humanitarian thinking.

The growth of humanitarianism, "one of the most profound and least explicable developments of the eighteenth century" (Jordan, 265), was one of the motive forces behind the calls for Jewish emancipation and the abolition of the slave trade. (Here, at least, religion could play a role in a growing intellectual trend.[4]) In both cases the "other" was seen not merely as alien and therefore less than human, but as potentially human, that is to say educable, in the realm of manners and morals and actually human in the realm of the sentiments. Christoph Wieland, a poet, satirist, and critic, published an anonymous article (written most likely by Wieland himself) in a 1775 issue of his widely respected magazine *Der teutsche Merkur*, that opened with the analogous conditions of the two peoples. Reading about the "oppression of the Negro slaves" in Africa had turned the writer's thoughts "to that almost countless mass . . . which lives in the utmost moral wretchedness right among us who are Christians . . . and who first of all should practice genuine compassion" (qtd. in Low 45). "Can we attribute the unity in which [the Jews] live among themselves to anything else but the purity of their customs? Are they less good parents, less good providers, less true spouses than we? I fear lest we lose in this comparison. Can we observe these virtues without being convinced that the germ of all other civil virtues lies hidden in them and merely waits for the opportunity to break out most happily?" (46).

In those areas of eighteenth-century culture where the vogue of sentimentalism held sway, poets and polemicists recognized that the emotions of Blacks and Jews were as strong as those of "more civilized" peoples. A literature sprang up that accorded privileged representatives of the oppressed peoples a positive nobility, viz. Germany's good Jews and Britain's noble Negroes.[5] France read Aphra Benn's *Oroonoko* (Laplace's translation had run to six editions by the beginning of the Revolution) but had also produced its own great-souled Blacks, sentimental Whites, and their horrified descriptions of slavery.[6] Volumes of this antislavery literature still read today are Saint-Lambert's novella, *Ziméo* (1769), and Bernardin de Saint-Pierre's *Voyage à l'île de France* (1773).

But literature per se was distinctly ancillary to the debate over the status of these alien populations. The preferred form of discourse was the essay, the open letter, and the multivolume reference work. Although the time frame for the climax of public discussion on both sets of issues was roughly the same, the 1770s and the 1780s, this new humanitarianism expressed itself differently toward the two populations. In both cases, however, Europeans took upon themselves, or cast upon their offending brethren, the guilt of mistreating an unfortunate people.

For economic and demographic reasons, the earliest considerations of Jewish emancipation took place in the German-speaking world just as the abolitionist movement drew its major impetus from England and its colonies; but France was the intellectual center of the Enlightenment. The pronouncements of the *philosophes* on these subjects, both before and during the Revolution, had an enormous impact on the English and German discourses being conducted about their respective "others." We have already examined some of the French discussion on the Jews. As might be expected, their abolitionist discourse drew from the same intellectual well.

As early as the middle of the century, Montesquieu had declared, "slavery is against that natural Law by which all men are born free and independent" (qtd. in Seeber 61). Following Montesquieu's lead, the Encyclopedists were ardent abolitionists, even if they held a low opinion of the Africans and their cultures. When the Chevalier de Jaucourt wrote his article on slavery for the fifth volume of the *Encyclopédie* (1755), he explicitly presented a condensed version of Montesquieu's opinions. "Next to *L'Esprit des lois*, the *Encyclopédie* was without doubt the most important agent in making antislavery a part of the Enlightenment's overriding concern for the happiness and well-being of mankind" (Davis 415–16). Beginning in 1770, antislavery sentiment moved into the foreground with the Abbé Raynal's *Histoire des deux Indes*, another encyclopedic enterprise. Deleted from the third edition was the line written by Jean de Pechméja, one of Raynal's fiery young collaborators: "Whoever justifies so odious a system deserves scornful silence from the philosopher and a stab with a poniard from the Negro" (qtd. in Davis 418). In 1781, the brilliant mathematician and *philosophe* Antoine-Nicolas de Condorcet published *Réflexions sur l'esclavage des nègres* under the punning nom de plume of Pastor Joachim Schwartz. (Having the book issue from the pen of a Swiss pastor reinforced the idea that Protestant origins conferred outsider status.) Addressing himself to the Blacks, Condorcet's pastor declares, "Nature fashioned you with the same spirit, the same reason and the same virtues as the Whites" (qtd. in Jurt 389).

As in the debate over Jewish emancipation, economic arguments were employed as well.[7] As early as 1755, Benjamin Franklin published his *Observations Concerning the Increase of Mankind*, in which he demonstrated that slave labor was more expensive than "free" labor. In a 1767 visit to Paris, Franklin was lionized by the physiocrats, an association of French free traders who believed that land and agriculture were the only true source of wealth and that population growth was essential to prosperity. Wishing to substitute economic relations for those based on privilege and prescriptive power, the physiocrats disapproved of slavery because it was uneconomical. Humanitarian objections buttressed the economic argument against slavery in Anne-Robert Turgot's classic physiocratic treatise, *Réflexions sur la formation et la distribution des richesses* (1766), in which he declared, "How unprofitable and yet expensive to both masters and humanity is the cultivation performed by slaves" (qtd. in Seeber 109).

The British abolitionists also availed themselves of the economic argument. Adam Smith, the Scottish philosopher, clothed his condemnation of slavery in the language of economic liberalism in *The Wealth of Nations*: "The experience of all ages and nations, I believe, demonstrates that the work done by slaves, though it appears to cost only their maintenance, is in the end the dearest of any. A person who can acquire no property, can have no other interest but to eat as much, and to labour as little as possible. Whatever work he does beyond what is sufficient to purchase his own maintenance can be squeezed out of him by violence only, and not by any interest of his own" (qtd. in Anstey 117).

There was another class in Britain that had no hope of acquiring property, and these men became the allies of those who connected themselves—in theory, at least—to the cause of the Black. Working-class radicalism added a new and powerful element to abolitionist agitation. Although abolitionism as an ideology was initially formulated and promoted by such nonconformist sects as the Quakers and Methodists, abolitionism as a mass movement was the creation of the artisan and working class. In chapter 2 we shall examine the surprising explosion of popular abolitionist petitions to Parliament in 1788, which had begun in Manchester but which had then spread like wildfire throughout the industrialized sectors of British society. "Manchester rather than the Quaker religious network pushed Britain across the psychological threshold into the abolitionist era" (Drescher 71). David Brion Davis sees the radical embrace of the abolitionist cause as both a metaphor for and a displacement of the workingman's fears concerning the vast social dislocations brought about by the Industrial Revolution. "As soon as the rationalizations were stripped away, the African trade and colonial plantation presented heightened analogies to the most disturbing trends in Britain, such as the uprooting of peasants, the separation of families, absentee ownership, and the systematizing of work discipline. The slave system could stand for the insecurity and mobility of labor in a profit-oriented society; and yet the injustice of slavery could be identified with individuals rather than with impersonal forces" (336).[8]

During his travels as a speaker for the abolitionist cause, Equiano stayed in the house of Thomas Hardy, founder of the radical London Corresponding Society, and put him in touch with the abolitionists he had met in the provinces. In Britain, abolitionism became entwined with a general assertion of human rights. The disparity between metropolitan and colonial norms made the wrongs of the slave trade seem more nearly the negation of all rights than any other abuse in the empire.

Abolitionism as a mass movement was nonexistent in France, yet such was the force of the Revolution that, through the odd course of events in Saint-Domingue, Blacks were briefly accorded full citizenship status. In contrast, by the end of the eighteenth century, British abolitionism traversed a fallow period and the trade still had not been abolished. That would come about only in 1808.

Before the Revolution, however, French abolitionists drew inspiration from the activities of Quakers and from the work of the London abolition society. A Sociéte des Amis des Noirs was founded by Brissot de Warville in 1788 after he had voyaged in England and America and had observed the abolitionist movements in those countries. Anthony Benezet, whose writings had so impressed Clarkson and Equiano, had gained prominence among the French enlighteners because of a translation of his *Short Account of the People called Quakers*. In *De la France et des Etats-Unis* (1787) Brissot declared that because of Benezet, those who had not yet been converted to abolition would "blush from their barbarism, and perhaps the day is not far off when all Europeans, ashamed of this scandalous traffic, will abjure it. That is what the example of one lone American will have produced" (qtd. in Seeber 123).

At the time Brissot penned these lines, there was cause to be optimistic about the progress of abolition in North America. Even before the American Revolution, a number of colonial legislatures—Connecticut, Rhode Island, and Pennsylvania— had passed their own anti–slave trade measures. After the Revolution, many states prohibited residents from participating in the trade, and in 1794 the federal government barred the participation of all U.S. citizens. Between 1780 and 1786, six northern states passed manumission acts, and in 1787 Congress added a provision to the Northwest Ordinance that slavery could not exist in those territories. Even in the South, before the invention of the cotton gin and the economic revitalization of forced labor, slavery seemed on its last economic legs. "Slave importation was stopped as much by lack of demand for slaves as by antislavery attack. Between 1774 and 1794 every state acted to ban importation" (Jordan 373).

The success of the abolitionist movements in the English-speaking world had an impact on pre-Revolutionary France. At Brissot's invitation, Clarkson went to Paris to stimulate the formation of the Sociéte des Amis des Noirs, gave it money, and supplied it with British antislavery propaganda. By the beginning of the Revolution, the Société could boast among its adherents names that had played a role in the battle for Jewish emancipation: Count Mirabeau, romantic exponent of liberty, and Abbé Grégoire, who embodied an enlightened and militant Church. Condorcet, Necker, and Pétion, all great names of the early Revolution, also belonged. As even the colonially-inclined historian Gaston Martin admits, however, "few people in the Revolution, even among the reformers, dreamed of linking the status of our equinoctial colonies to the Declaration of the Rights of Man" (Martin 171).

In its sponsorship of citizenship demands made to the National Convention by the mulattos of Saint-Domingue, the Société played a crucial role in the enfranchisement of Blacks under the Revolution. Unlike slavery in the Protestant world, where slave status was a condition of the soul, like election or damnation, and was forever inflicted upon the slave and her progeny (slave status being determined by the condition of the mother), slavery in the Catholic colonies could admit to a relaxed and sensual dimension. A free colored caste of mulattos—*gens de couleur*, as they were called to distinguish them from chattel slaves—had sprung up. The *code noir*, promulgated in 1685, formally defining the status and "rights" of slaves, gave free mulattos and Blacks equal rights with Whites,[9] but as the White population in Saint-Domingue grew larger, numerous civil and social disabilities were imposed. Since there was no restriction on the amount of property these *gens de couleur* could hold, their fortunes as master artisans and proprietors grew with their numbers. The wealthier mulattos sought to imitate the manners and attitudes of the White planters (who despised them) and to repudiate as much as possible their Black ancestry. Some of them sent their children to be educated in France, where there was little color prejudice.

At the time of the Revolution, Saint-Domingue, "the pearl of the French empire," was the richest colony in the world. At the end of the Seven Years' War in 1763, Saint-Domingue's output in cotton, molasses, cocoa, and rum astounded the world in both quantity and quality. As C. L. R. James wrote, "If on no earthly spot was so much misery concentrated as on a slave-ship, then on no portion of the globe did its surface in proportion to its dimensions yield so much wealth" (46). This very wealth, however, put the colonists into conflict with the French government, which, like all metropolitan governments, regarded the colonies as an exclusive source of raw materials and a captive market for heavily taxed goods. The maintenance of this Mercantile System had lost Britain her North American colonies in 1776, but the condition of the Blacks there had not improved appreciably. By contrast, the numerical superiority of Blacks in Saint-Domingue and the internecine warfare among the French and Europeans after the Revolution propelled the colony to declare its independence as the (Black) Republic of Haiti in 1804. Winthrop Jordan ably summarizes the early events that led to Black liberation.

> The revolution in St. Domingo . . . actually began in Paris and was for at least a decade a distorted extension of the French Revolution. The calling of the Estates General in 1788 excited the white planters, some of whom, disregarding the warnings from the more conservative, hustled off a delegation to Paris in hopes of undermining the arbitrary powers of the resident governor-general and intendant. Before the enthusiastic colonial deputies had a chance to do more than air their grievances, events in Paris took an ominous turn. The Bastille fell July 14, 1789, and six weeks later the National Assembly grandly issued its Declaration of the Rights of Man and Citizen, in language strongly reminiscent of the American declaration. Strange talk about equality gave the planter delegates pause, the more so because an obvious corollary was being noisily expounded by Les Amis des Noirs, an abolitionist group with connections in Britain and the United States.
>
> In addition to dividing the forty thousand whites of the colony, revolutionary principles

infected the free colored caste, numbering some twenty-eight thousand, most of whom were mulattos and all of whom suffered galling civil, political, and social disabilities. The National Assembly in Paris, entangled with domestic difficulties, played shuttlecock with the island time bomb by promulgating a vacillating series of decrees which several times granted and withdrew full political equality for the mulattos. The first mulatto revolt was viciously suppressed in 1791. But the example was not lost on the Negroes, and that summer many of the half million slaves seized firebrand and machete and devastated northern parts of the colony. The following years were characterized by bumbling confusion and barbarous atrocities on all sides. Negroes, whites, and mulattos slaughtered each other by turns and the kaleidoscope of alignments whirred ever more rapidly as French troops, Jacobin commissioners, and English and Spanish armies poured in. (376)

In France, the Revolutionary pendulum continued to swing to the left. With the fall of the moderate Girodins in the summer of 1793, Robespierre and the Mountain came to power. In January 1794, while the Terror was really getting under way, Saint-Domingue sent three Deputies to the National Convention: Bellay, a Black slave who had purchased his freedom; Mills, a mulatto; and Dufay, a white man. The presence of the first Black and mulatto deputies to the Assembly excited long and repeated bursts of applause. The day after their admission, Bellay pledged the Blacks to the cause of the Revolution and asked the Convention to declare slavery abolished. In response another delegate suggested that any debate on the matter would simply dishonor the legislative body, and the Convention rose to its feet in acclamation. Thus, swept by emotion, the Assembly passed the decree of 16 pluviôse an II (February 4, 1794), which not only abolished slavery but declared that "all men, without distinction of color, residing in the colonies are French citizens and will enjoy all rights guaranteed by the Constitution" (qtd. in Martin 229).

Robespierre himself had been absent during the vote and did not approve of the step. Many delegates themselves regretted their moment of enthusiasm, but the radicals and Parisian masses hailed the decree as, in Grégoire's words, "a great clearance in the forest of abuses" (qtd. in James 154). As far as the revolution in Saint-Domingue was concerned, however, the impulsive idealism of the Convention proved to be good politics. Toussaint L'Ouverture, an ex-slave and the most capable of the indigenous military men, had been conquering the colony for the Spaniards. Upon hearing the news of the emancipation decree in the summer of 1794, he immediately renewed his allegiance to the French government and eventually ousted the Spaniards and British. "All the French blacks, from the labourers at Port-de-Paix demanding equality, to the officers in the army, were filled with an immense pride at being citizens of the French Republic 'one and indivisible' which had brought liberty and equality into the world" (James 154).

By 1794, the National Convention had formally decreed the full emancipation of both Blacks and Jews. At first blush, it appeared as the inevitable climax of the drum roll of propaganda for tolerance and inclusion sounded during the latter half of the eighteenth century. The tenets of the Enlightenment, expressed most forcefully in the American Declaration of Independence and the French Declaration of the Rights of Man, seemed triumphant. If, at the birth of the National Assembly in May 1789, Jews and *gens de couleur* were denied representation, the Revolution had righted that injustice. But the reaction was soon to set in. The French Revolution changed the tenor and practical strategies of debate for inclusion of Blacks and Jews not only in France but in North America and Europe as well. The Jacobins had gone farthest in promoting the inclusion of these formerly outcast groups into the fabric of the modern state, but these same Jacobins inspired fear and revulsion among the ruling classes of the other European states. This had its effect on the discussion of Black status in England and the Americas as well as on Jewish status in central and eastern Europe. Gains were certainly made, at least in the realm of Jewish emancipation, but the eighteenth century also laid the groundwork for a new style of thinking about Blacks and Jews that would eliminate their potential for accession to full human (White) status, a theorization that would imprison both outgroups in the permanent reification of race.

In the eighteenth century, the concept of a universal culture took off and influenced policy and politics for the first time. Europeans were sublimely unaware that their "universals," human nature and what the French call *culture générale*, were as culturally specific and limited as animism in Africa or Talmudism among the Jews. This was an insight that would not be widely propounded until the late twentieth century. The eighteenth century invented the universal culture that gave Europe the ideological rationale for its ever-increasing domination of the rest of the globe. Paul Hazard points out (in a sexist language that may well have been appropriate to the realities of the age) that "men applied themselves to investigating what united, rather than what separated, man from man; their object was to trace resemblances, not differences" (231). Malebranche, Voltaire, Hume, Jefferson, and Kant all produced philosophical and political writings that defined humanity, implicitly or explicitly, in terms of "universal" mental and psychological characteristics, yet they all contributed to eighteenth-century racism and anti-Semitism.

Such ideologies took both high and low forms. Popular racism and anti-Semitism traded in the familiar intellectual currency of Black and Jewish inferiority, Black barbarism, Jewish iniquity, and the lack of Christianity endemic to both groups. Less intellectually acceptable but viscerally powerful was the physical repulsion both outgroups inspired in northern European populations. Montesquieu satirized these attitudes when he wrote as one of his alleged justifications of slavery, "Those concerned are black from head to toe, and they have such flat noses that it is almost impossible to feel sorry for them" (250). In his refutation of Dohm's treatise,

"Orientalische und exegetische Bibliothek" (1782), German Orientalist Johann Michaelis opined that Jews were worthless as soldiers because of their small stature. The novelist Charles Johnstone gave a middlebrow expression to both types of racism when he wrote in *The Pilgrim* (1775) that if English people mixed with Jews and Blacks "their progeny will not much longer have reason to value themselves on their beauty, wit, or virtue" (qtd. in Fryer 161)—an early warning against the miscegenation that became an obsession with British propagandists against abolition by the 1790s.

Popular prejudice was easily vented against the groups in question. Besides the legal disabilities they had to endure, Jews were constantly in danger of being taunted and stoned as they went about their daily business. In a letter to a friend who was a Benedictine monk, Mendelssohn reported the following dialogue with his children: "'Father,' an innocent child asks, 'what does that fellow have against us? Why do people throw stones after us? What have we done to them?' 'Yes, father dear,' another says, 'they chase after us in the streets and abuse us: Jews! Jews! Is it then such a reproach in people's eyes to be a Jew?'" (qtd. in Poliakov, *History of Anti-Semitism*, 54).

Of course, anti-Jewish sentiment could take much more lethal forms. Portugal, still lost in medieval darkness, burned 139 "heretics," mostly Marranos, between 1721 and 1761. The great 1737 auto-da-fé in Lisbon, in which twelve Marranos perished, excited the disgust of *philosophes* all over Europe. During the first half of the eighteenth century, Cossacks in Poland led repeated attacks on the Jews, a mop-up operation to the pogroms of the previous century in which nearly *half* the country's Jews—one fifth of the world's total—were exterminated.

Blacks suffered an inordinate amount of inhumane and homicidal treatment at the hands of the West. A further rehearsal of the whippings, killings, mutilations, rapes, and tortures Blacks suffered in the New World hardly seems necessary. Anyone who reads Equiano's *Narrative* will have covered some of the territory. Here I quote only one brief passage in which Equiano tries to invoke the counterideology of Christianity against such inhumanity.[10]

One Mr. D———, told me he had sold 41,000 negroes, and he once cut off a negro-man's leg for running away. I asked him if the man had died in the operation, how he, as a christian, could answer, for the horrid act, before God. And he told me, answering was a thing of another world; what he thought and did were policy. I told him that the christian doctrine taught us "to do unto others as we would that others should do unto us." He then said that his scheme had the desired effect—it cured that man and some others of running away. (74–75)

British West Indians exercised a similar division between morality and policy when they argued that the trade in slaves and the produce of the islands enriched the English in all walks of life. However, they also built their ideological edifice on the well-laid foundation of European racism. One widely read British compendium of knowledge, *The Modern Part of Universal History* (1736–65), cited various Greek and Roman authorities to support the view that Africans were "proud, lazy, treacherous, thievish, hot, and addicted to all kinds of lusts, and most ready to promote them in others, as pimps, panders, incestuous, brutish, and savage, cruel and revengeful, devourers of human flesh, and quaffers of human blood, inconstant, base, treacherous, and cowardly; fond of and addicted to all sorts of superstition and witchcraft; and, in a word, to every vice that came in their way, or within their reach" (qtd. in Fryer 153).

The West Indian apologists for slavery had good material with which to advance their theories of Black inferiority, and Equiano first came to public attention refuting the racist pamphlets of James Tobin[11] and Gordon Turnbull.[12] The most famous and influential of what Peter Fryer calls the plantocracy racists was Edward Long, whose three-volume *History of Jamaica* appeared in 1774. Long's views on Blacks were extreme. They had all the vices cited in the *Universal History*: they were bestial, cretinous, and incapable of improvement; they were so alien to the rest of humanity that an impartial observer had to believe they were a different species and, furthermore, probably not much superior to the orangutans with whom they could mate. Blacks were so different from Whites that even their lice were black (and presumably inferior), and, in a shot aimed at Buffon, Long doubted that two mulattos could reproduce. Cloaking these slanders in the mantle of the scientific philosopher, Long's defense of Black slavery came across more plausibly than had any previous statement of the slave owners' case. As David Davis remarks, his opinions "were not only public ideology in Jamaica and South Carolina, but were apparently acceptable to an influential minority in Europe" (459).

Many opinions about Blacks held by the French *philosophes* were hardly more favorable. Though strongly against the slave trade for humanitarian and economic reasons, men like Diderot and d'Alembert differed little from proslavery apologists in promoting the familiar stereotypes of African barbarism and Black degradation, as even a cursory reading of the *Encyclopédie's* articles "Nègres" and "Guinée" would illustrate. The following quote from the latter incorporates the familiar environmentalist argument and even takes a tentative step toward polygenesis before descending into the usual essentialist slanders of eighteenth-century racism.

Not only is their colour different but they are distinct from other men on account of all the features of their faces: the large flat noses, the big lips and the wool instead of hair seem to form a new species of men. If one moves from the Equator to the Antarctic pole, the darkness becomes lighter but the ugliness persists. . . . If one may chance to meet some good people among the Negroes of Guinea (the bulk of them is always vicious) they are for the most part given to lechery, to vengeance, to theft and to lying. (qtd. in Poliakov 352)

Some of the arguments marshaled by the apologists of slavery could also be found in the stock anti-Semitism of the eighteenth century, viz., cannibalism and moral degradation. Following ancient medieval tradition, the Jews continued to be accused of murdering Christian babies to make Passover matzoh. As late as 1779, an Alsatian judge, François Hell, wrote a book taxing Jews with the ritual murder of children,[13] a charge that was repeated by a Polish parson in the course of a plot he had hatched against Solomon Maimon's grandfather. Maimon quotes the parson: "You know that the Jews are a hardened race, and are therefore damned to all eternity. They crucified our Lord Jesus Christ, and even yet they seek Christian blood, if only they can get hold of it for their passover, which is instituted as a sign of their triumph. They use it for their passover-cake" (77).

As for Jewish moral degradation, this was a point upon which everyone—even the maskilim—agreed. The great Enlightenment authority legitimizing this point of view, the one upon whom such lesser lights as Hell and Froissac could draw, was Voltaire, the thinker Hertzberg credits with transforming anti-Semitism into a modern ideology. In Voltaire's *Dictionnaire philosophique* (1769), which prompted Pinto's reply discussed above, Jews are attacked in more than 30 of the 118 articles. The article "Juif" is the longest, and its first part concludes: "you will find them an ignorant and barbarous people, who for a long time have combined the most sordid greed with the most detestable superstition and the most invincible hatred for all the peoples who tolerate them and enrich them" (qtd. in Poliakov, *History of Anti-Semitism* 88). Voltaire's anti-Semitism has come in for much analysis by various historians and literary critics without any appreciable consensus as to its origins or influence (cf. Hertzberg 283–84). What is clear, however, is that Voltaire's ill will toward the Jews was widely understood and imitated in his own time. Such radical enlighteners as the Baron d'Holbach and Denis Diderot could hold and publish virulently anti-Semitic sentiments while advocating tolerance. By attacking the traditional beliefs of the Jews, these *philosophes* were striking yet again at Christianity, the tree whose roots were so visible in the Old Testament; but Voltaire's animus extended very much to the Jews of his day. Eschewing medieval accusations of ritual murder and Christ-killing, Voltaire brought to the fore the peculiarly modern element of anti-Semitism that would have such a profound impact on European thinking in the following two centuries. Many Enlightenment writers, such as Dohm, Mirabeau, and Grégoire, felt the Jews could be regenerated once the state had normalized their economic and political status. Voltaire, for his part, saw the Jews as irretrievably alien. Quoting from such classical authors as Apion, Philostratos, Juvenal, and Cicero, Voltaire characterized the Jews as an alien and oriental influence on the normative Greco-Roman heritage that was truly European. "Christianity is the Jewish religion superimposed on people of a different world, both ethnically and culturally" (Hertzberg 307), and

Voltaire worked mightily for its extirpation. In Hertzberg's summary of Voltaire's attitude:

European men can be freed effectively of Christianity because Christianity is here a long-standing infection; it is not one of the foundations of the European spirit, deriving from its character. The case of the Jews is radically different. Being born a Jew and the obnoxious-ness of the Jewish outlook are indissoluble; it most unlikely that "enlightened" Jews can escape their innate character. The Jews are subversive of the European tradition by their very presence, for they are the radically other, the hopeless alien. Cure them of their religion and their inborn character remains. (307)

We see here the argument of radical alterity applied to both Jews and Blacks that kept them in a subordinate moral and political status vis-à-vis the West. In the case of Blacks, the more extreme statement of this position expressed itself through the theory of polygenesis, which Voltaire also advocated (Poliakov, *The Aryan Myth*, 175–76). The modern version of anti-Semitism that found expression through the writings of Voltaire and Immanuel Kant advanced the inchoate sense that Jews were an insoluble element within the European body politic. Kant's disciple, Johannes Fichte, famously dubbed the Jews a "state within a State" in his first important work, *Beiträge zur Berichtigung der Urteile über die französische Revolution* (1793).

I do not think as I hope to show subsequently that this state is fearful not because it forms a separate and solidly united state but because this state is founded on the hatred of the whole human race. . . . In a state where the absolute monarch cannot take from me my paternal hut and where I can defend my rights against the all-powerful minister, the first Jew who likes can plunder me with impunity. This you see and cannot deny, and you utter sugary words of tolerance and of the rights of man and civil rights, all the time wounding in us the primary rights of man. . . . Does the thought not occur to you that if you give to the Jews who are citizens of a state more solid and more powerful than any of yours, civil rights in your states, they will utterly crush the remainder of your citizens? (qtd. in Poliakov, *History of Anti-Semitism*, 512)

One sees in this Philippic the precursor to the racist myth which was to imprison the European Jew within the otherness of the nineteenth and early twentieth centuries. The disciples of tolerance in the eighteenth century agreed that the Jews had to change before they could become part of the modern state. The question for them was simply "to what degree?" The discourse on the Jews coming out of France and Germany was in accord on this one point. But there were profound differences as well. The Jewish community in Prussia played a pivotal role in relations between Eastern and Western Europe. Because of their relatively strong influence on the German Enlightenment, Prussian Jews had far more influence in shaping the nationalist discourse that defined them for Europe than did the Jews of France. Consequently, before the Revolution, German writing about the Jews had more authority in Enlightenment culture than did their other contributions, where international influence mostly ran from West to East. We have already mentioned Dohm's impact, and Mirabeau, in the 1787 book written after his visit to Berlin, put Mendelssohn on the same pedestal with the framers of the American Constitution and the liberal economist Turgot.

In France the problem of integrating the Jews in the state was more theoretical, with the exception of the remote province of Alsace. (The Jews of Bordeaux had already integrated themselves in that southern opening onto the Atlantic trade.) The Germans were much more bound to their Jews, not only for the economic role they played but for the Jews' influence on the shaping of their *Volksgeist*—an eighteenth-century innovation expounded by Herder. The French were able to play their Jewish card with a lighter touch than could the Germans, and, because of their ideological and military strength, they eventually imposed on Prussia their idea of complete emancipation, which had not been the direction of *Aufklärung* dialogue on the subject. "North German views after 1808 [the date of the first decree of emancipation in the German-speaking world] became a mere variation of the terms stipulated by French legislators" (Schmidt 37).

Much of the success of French ideas in Germany derived from the fact that by 1808 the legacy of the French Revolution was firmly in the hands of Napoleon, and authoritarian Prussians could relate to Napoleonic France. Both societies cloaked their absolutist regimes with a sanitized ideology of *raison d'état*. Napoleon was willing to let the Jews remain "emancipated" as long as it was on his terms. Raphael Mahler writes of this period, "The régime was already so reactionary, both in its aims and achievements, that it could assail the Jews with accusations, abuse and restrictions which reduced the ideals of the frustrated Revolution to absurdity" (60). In 1806 Napoleon convoked an assembly of Jewish Notables chosen by the French Prefects and therefore stacked with plutocrats and assimilationist rabbis. Operating under the veiled threat of withdrawal of enfranchisement,[14] the Assembly successfully and obsequiously abased itself, in the name of the Jewish community, before the power of the state as personified in the new emperor. In their response to twelve questions put to them by Napoleon, the Notables declared that the laws of the state superseded religious laws; that France, not Palestine, was the beloved fatherland of the Jews; that lending money at interest was actually contrary to Jewish law; and, later, when the Twelve Replies were rubber-stamped by a so-called Grand Sanhedrin, they accepted Napoleon's demand that intermarriage with Gentiles should not be punished by excommunication.

This renunciation of all Jewish autonomy was not enough for the emperor. In March 1808 he signed two decrees concerning the Jews. The first established official consistories for the Jewish religion whose primary duty was to maintain rigid supervision of the rabbis. The second, known as *le décret infâme* [the Infamous Decree], forbade Jews from engaging in any form of trade without a prefectoral license, prohibited Jews from moving anywhere in France unless they purchased land and engaged solely in agriculture, and proscribed them from discharging their military service by proxy, the usual resort of the wealthy. As usual, the Jews of Bordeaux were exempted from this decree "since they have caused no complaints and engage in no forbidden practices" (qtd. in Mahler 73).

The Napoleonic reaction to the "excesses" of the Revolution in granting liberty and equality to the Blacks of the French empire was even more extreme. During the first years of the Revolution, royalists and republicans had confronted one another on the island colony of Martinique. When republican victory seemed assured, the royalists asked the British to invade the island, which they did in 1794, thereby maintaining the slave system. France regained Martinique under the provisions of the 1802 Treaty of Amiens, marking a brief lull in the Napoleonic Wars, but never bothered to emancipate the Blacks there. In floréal of year X (May 1802), the councilor of state proposed the reestablishment of slavery in the Iles de France and la Réunion. The First Consul, as Napoleon then styled himself, was still trying to lure Saint-Domingue back into the fold and had already proclaimed that slavery would not be reestablished there. He would have preferred a more decorous piece of legislation that substituted forced labor for slavery, but his advisors were impatient to finish with "this deadly experiment with revolutionary laws which in seeking to render all men in the colonies equal in the eyes of the law succeeded only in rendering them equally unhappy" (qtd. in Martin 246). It was thenceforth decreed that all the colonies would be returned "to the regime under which, since their origins, they have constantly prospered" (246). The reestablishment of slavery effectively scared Saint-Domingue out of the Empire. Toussaint allowed himself to be trapped by promises of conciliation with the French regime, but the rest of the island exploded in revolt at the treachery of *la mère patrie*, and Dessalines, a ferocious inheritor of Toussaint's legacy, ripped the white out of the Revolutionary *tricolore*. By 1804, Haiti had become the second independent country of the New World and was well on its way to purging itself of its European population.

The success of the Haitian slave insurrection had negative repercussions on the abolitionist movements of the English-speaking world. The Revolution, which had ignited the Haitian revolt, had also encouraged the English radicals who so warmly supported abolition. As England split in its response to the Revolution, British abolitionists expressed displeasure about this strange new bedfellow. "It is certainly true and perfectly natural," politician William Wilberforce wrote, "that these Jacobins are all friendly to Abolition; and it is no less true and natural that this operates to the injury of our cause" (qtd. in Anstey 276). News of the instability and violence in Saint-Domingue dealt a powerful blow to the progress of Revolutionary ideology in Britain. The animus of the governing classes was so strong (deepened by a French declaration of war on England, Spain, and Holland in 1793) that abolition as a political movement went into decline and did not regain momentum for more than a decade.

The reaction was even more extreme in the United States. Winthrop Jordan writes, "To trace the spread of Negro rebellion in the New World and to examine American responses to what they saw as a mounting tide of danger is to watch the drastic erosion of the ideology of the American Revolution" (375). Of course the American Revolution, thoroughly European in intellectual origin, had not abolished slavery, which was in the United States a domestic institution. The calculation of the American Black in the Constitution as three fifths of a human being indicated in precise fractions how far the practice of Enlightenment governance fell short of its theory. At the rise of abolitionist sentiment in the 1770s and 1780s practically every Northern state had provided for immediate or gradual emancipation, and only the adamantine resistance of South Carolina and Georgia prevented the Constitutional Convention from placing an outright ban on the slave trade. Once cotton culture had become profitable, however, the advocates of slavery found their case immeasurably strengthened. Empowered by the opening of the southwest to slave culture, in both senses of the term, the Southern states quickly stifled what abolitionist sentiment existed among them, and the North, developing its own form of racism, dropped abolition as a priority.

So this was the score sheet at the end of the century. The majority of Blacks in the West were still enslaved, and French Jews had been emancipated into a society that asked them to cease acting in a Jewish manner. Both groups were taxed with stereotypes, civil disabilities, and obloquy, but the situation of the Blacks was radically injured by their slave status. In the Northern European world, slaves were a caste that could not be integrated into the state under the parameters of Enlightenment thought. However noxious or contemptible the Jews were in European eyes, they were not slaves. "Here, surely, was a crucial factor making for the burial of the Negro at the bottom of mankind. Though other peoples, most notably the Indians, were enslaved by Europeans, slavery was typically a Negro-white relationship" (Jordan 227).

Concerning the status and possible integration of Blacks and Jews into Western society, the eighteenth century set the terms of debate for the next 150 years. The narrow tolerance of the Enlightenment considered all who were capable of civilization and willing to distance themselves from the backwardness or barbarity of their original cultures potential recruits to humanity. The same century that witnessed the growth of humanitarianism on a socially significant scale also saw the greatest volume of Africans torn from their homelands in the Atlantic slave trade. Jews were offered the fraternal hand of emancipation at the price of abandoning their community. For the first time in the history of the slave trade, Blacks were seen as human beings rather than commodities, yet the European mind was serenely convinced that Africans were an inferior—and possibly different—species. The emancipation of science from ecclesiastical tutelage and the abandonment of biblical cosmogony left the way clear for the development of racialist theories. In the 1758 edition of his *System naturae*, Linnaeus, inventor of the term *Homo sapiens*, gave thumbnail sketches of four varieties of the species: Americanus, Europeaus, Asiaticus, and Asser. The character of the African, according to the great classifier, was "crafty, indolent, and negligent" (as opposed to the European, who was "gentle, acute, and inventive"), and he was "governed by caprice," whereas the European was "governed by laws" (qtd. in Popkin 248). Thirty-two years later, Blumenbach, a founder of physical anthropology and the most influential promoter of the pseudoscience of craniology, wrote that "even laymen" had been able to recognize Jewish skulls among his worldwide collection (Blumenbach 10).

The physical kinship of all humankind that nonetheless buttressed the superiority of the European was reproduced on the mental and moral planes. The Enlightenment substituted "human nature" for "soul" in its search for a universal that could dispense with the superstition of revealed religion, but many Enlightenment thinkers, while proclaiming the universality of this human nature, denied that Blacks and Jews had the character for effective and healthy participation in civilized society. (The idea that Jews were a different race, however, had not yet crystallized; only after the mid-nineteenth century did European anti-Semitism take on an overtly racial character.) Hume was "apt to suspect the negroes and in general all the other species of men . . . to be naturally inferior to the whites" (qtd. in Popkin 245), and Voltaire wrote that Jews are "born with a raging fanaticism in their hearts, just as the Bretons and the Germans are born with blond hair" (qtd. in Hertzberg 300).

The ensuing two centuries elaborated the contradictory legacy of the Enlightenment for Blacks and Jews, but the terms of discussion had been set. Ideologies of inclusion had been enunciated, debated, and acted upon, yet slavery, oppression, and intolerance remained social and political norms. A "human nature," common property of the biological species man now recognized himself to be, had been widely postulated, but the concept of "race" had also been introduced and given a similarly scientific basis. The ruthless elimination of communal tradition and a demand for collective adjustment to a newly created national type promoted by the Napoleonic regime had seemingly won the day; yet it was clear from Napoleonic legislation that some citizens were more equal than others. If the eighteenth century had activated the movement that eventually swept away the medieval guilds, estates, and corporations; had loosened the ecclesiastical grip on social and scientific discourse; had discredited among the intelligentsia ancient perspectives of Jews as baby-killers and Blacks as monsters unrelated to humanity; this same century had taken other prejudices of its medieval and Renaissance heritage and clothed them in a modern garb that would be modified but not fundamentally altered in the subsequent 150 years. Privileged spokespersons for the minorities involved responded to the promise of Enlightenment inclusion with contradictory impulses comprising a desire to assimilate attended by an inferiority complex and an intractable ethnic pride. We shall examine four of these autobiographical responses—two at the dawn and two at the twilight of Enlightenment hegemony—in the following chapters.

The
Dawn
Patrol

Should you, my lord, while you peruse my song
Wonder from whence my love of Freedom sprung,
Whence flow these wishes for the common good,
By feeling hearts alone best understood,
I, young in life, by seeming cruel fate
Was snatch'd from Afric's fancy'd happy seat:

—Phillis Wheatley,
   "To the Right Honourable William, Earl of Dartmouth"

TEMPLER: I've nothing against Nathan; 'tis myself
Alone I'm vexed with.
SALADIN: And for what?
TEMPLER: That I
Have dreamt a Jew might once perchance unlearn
To be a Jew, and dreamt it, too, awake.

—Gotthold Lessing, *Nathan the Wise*, IV, iv

James Clifford writes, "As counterdiscourses of modernity, diaspora cultures cannot claim an oppositional or primary purity. Fundamentally ambivalent, they grapple with the entanglement of subversion and the law, of invention and constraint—the complicity of dystopia and utopia" (265). Black and Jewish intellectuals who broke

30

out of the ethnic enclaves—ghetto or slavery—imposed upon them by the West did so with the help of Western individuals and organizations who subscribed to emergent ideologies of enlightenment tolerance and egalitarianism. These pioneers often owed a debt of gratitude to Western allies who championed their cause as individuals or as members of an oppressed people. Nonetheless, the first generation of these emancipated individuals had to contend not only with the memory of ethnic misery but with the consciousness of inferiority ascribed by the West to the ethnic identity they could not escape. Thus the birth of these modern intellectuals was effectuated by twin midwives: gratitude for the opportunities of escape and improvement provided by the Enlightenment, and resentment at the continuing injustice visited upon old ethnic family, friends, and associates.

Jews had always felt they were living in a diaspora, but modern Jews substituted the land of Zion awaited by the rabbis for an earthly exile from the full civic and religious liberty promised by Enlightenment ideologies of inclusion. This created new bonds between the Jewish enlighteners: the maskilim. Modern Blacks, both slaves and freedmen, also quickly recognized their new kinship within the West; it mattered little to them if the oppression was Spanish, Portuguese, British, or French. Likewise an Ibo and a Yoruba whose peoples might war with one another back in Africa had to recognize their commonality of interest in a West that saw them only as Black and usually as chattel. Still, the ideologies of Black opposition borrowed freely, and of necessity, from the West that oppressed them. Gilroy writes of "the articulating principles of the black political countercultures that grew inside modernity in a distinctive relationship of antagonistic indebtedness" (191). This antagonistic indebtedness added an extra layer of complexity to the already complicated condition of double consciousness.

When it comes to the emergence of ethnic expression in Western languages, the stories cannot help but underscore the positive side of the Enlightenment. Equiano's *Narrative* and Maimon's *Geistesgeschichte* would have never seen the light of day without the matrices of British abolition and German philosophical inquiry. Still, these autobiographies reveal a consciousness that is as deeply informed by ethnic particularity as by its participation in a so-called universal culture.

Equiano's sense of that particularity was conditioned by the specific circumstances of British abolitionism. In 1783, a case came before the court of the King's Bench in London concerning a British slave ship, the *Zong*. During a voyage of the Middle Passage, disease ravaged the human cargo, and, since insurance would not pay for unmarketable sick slaves or slaves killed by illness but would pay for drowned slaves, the ship's captain alleged a shortage of water on board and ordered 132 Africans thrown into the ocean. The defendants in this case were not the slavers brought to trial for the murder of 132 souls but the insurers of the cargo, from whom the owners of the *Zong* sought compensation for lost property. Without retiring, the jury gave judgment against the underwriters, and the owners were awarded damages of £30 for each slave. After the trial, Olaudah Equiano, who had been living in London on and off since 1767, called on Granville Sharp to help him "avenge the blood of his murdered countrymen" (Shyllon 437). Sharp, a middle-class idealist and fervent Christian, had been the earliest champion of Black rights in Britain, sponsoring a series of cases defending fugitive slaves that eventually resulted in a 1772 decision by Chief Justice Mansfield forbidding the forcible return of a slave, once on English soil, back to the plantations. Sympathetic to Equiano's appeal, Sharp instructed a lawyer to prosecute the murderers of the Africans, but nothing came of it.

The *Zong* case represented the most extreme consequence of the conviction that African slaves were property and held no rights of their own. This, of course, was the argument of the West Indian interests, whose sugar plantations depended on a steady supply of coerced labor from Africa. As the Mansfield decision of the previous decade showed, however, the British, while benefitting enormously from the Atlantic slave trade, were decidedly ambivalent concerning the institution of slavery within the borders of their own country. A noted judge of Queen Elizabeth's reign had declared that "[t]he air of England is too pure for a slave to breathe" (Adams and Sanders 8–9), but there were legal opinions to the contrary. In 1729 West Indians who brought their slaves back with them were so worried by the law's lack of clarity regarding their property rights that they solicited an opinion from the attorney general, Sir Philip Yorke, and the solicitor general, Charles Talbot, who wrote that neither a presence on English soil nor baptism conferred freedom to the slave and that he or she could be legally compelled to return to the West Indies. The popular view persisted, however, that Black slaves brought to England and baptized were thenceforth entitled to their liberty. The confusion of English opinion in this matter reflected the fact that, as Seymour Drescher so ably argues, "For eighteenth-century Americans slavery was a social and economic fact which had become a racial fact. For eighteenth-century Britons, slavery remained far more a geographically than racially conceived system" (16). The Mansfield decision of 1772 did nothing to alter the status of slavery in the colonies, nor did it actually outlaw slavery in England itself. But the sustained interest the press showed in what became known as the Somerset case (named after the defendant) gave the issue of slavery its first public airing. Many Britons disliked the idea of slavery, but almost all believed it to be a necessary evil in the development of their colonies, an attitude Drescher describes as "the dualism between social distaste and economic fatalism" (19). In building their sugar-producing empire, the British were simply following in the footsteps of the Spanish and the Portuguese. "North-west Europeans who entered the Atlantic slave system in the wake of the Iberians usually approached slavery as part of a world they had not made" (17).

Equiano had an unhappy firsthand experience with this confusion of English thought. Kidnapped from Iboland at the age of eleven, Equiano was eventually sold as the personal slave of a British naval lieutenant, Michael Pascal. He quickly demonstrated an acute intelligence and an amazing capacity for calling forth the affection of the Whites around him. Equiano arrived in England in 1757, approximately a year after his abduction. Two years later, he was fluent in English. Equiano mostly served at sea with Pascal, but at one point he was sent to wait on the lieutenant's cousins, the Guerin sisters, who briefly sent him to school and had him baptized. As a result of Britain's entry into the Seven Years War (1756–63), Equiano served with Pascal in Admiral Boscawen's campaign in the Mediterranean as well as in various sieges and stratagems in the naval war against France. By the war's end, Equiano had become so accustomed to European life and manners that he had absorbed the notion that he was entitled to his freedom. Confused by the preferential treatment shown to him by Captain Pascal and his relatives, Equiano felt further entitled by the fact that he had served in battle during the recently concluded war. "I thought now of nothing but being freed, and working for myself, and thereby getting money to enable me to get a good education" (63). Catching wind of Equiano's aspirations, Captain Pascal forced the eighteen-year-old African into a barge while still in the Thames and searched for some outward bound West Indian vessel to whom he could sell his refractory slave. When Pascal found a Captain Doran willing to make the purchase, Equiano was summoned into the presence of his new master, who declared to him, "You are now my slave."

I told him my master could not sell me to him nor to any one else. "Why," said he, "did not your master buy you?" I confessed that he did. "But I have served him," said I, "many years, and he has taken all my wages and prize-money, for I only got one sixpence during the war. Besides this I have been baptized; and, by the laws of the land, no man has a right to sell me." And I added, that I had heard a lawyer, and others, at different times tell my master so. They both then said, that those people who told me so, were not my friends: but I replied—it was very extraordinary that other people did not know the law as well as they. Upon this Captain Doran said I talked too much English. . . . (65)

This 1763 dialogue preceded the Mansfield decision by nine years. Equiano could be forgiven his erroneous assumption, for his own conviction merely reflected the confusion of popular English opinion. Moreover, Pascal's preemptive action showed that he himself felt insecure about his ability to keep Equiano in slavery once they had returned to English soil. Most telling, however, is Captain Doran's characterization of Equiano's legal knowledge (however unfounded) and his skill at verbal repartee as talking "too much English."

The cold-bloodedness of the *Zong* case notwithstanding, several segments of British society began either to dissociate themselves from the slave trade or to take up the cause of the African. Dissident sects of the Church of England initiated the process out of religious conviction. Many of the abolitionist pioneers on both sides of the Atlantic were Quakers, who, during the third quarter of the eighteenth century, began a slow withdrawal from the slave system. (Equiano's master in the West Indian island of Montserrat, who reluctantly manumitted him, was a Quaker.) In 1783, the same year as the *Zong* trial, Quakers brought the first antislavery petition before Parliament. A year later, Methodists declared slavery contrary to God's law and gave members twelve months to free their slaves. As historian Peter Fryer writes:

It was the Quakers' official printer who published, in 1784, *An Essay on the Treatment and Conversion of African Slaves in the British Sugar Colonies* by James Ramsay, an Anglican clergymen who had spent 19 years on St. Kitts and whose devastating public opposition to slavery, backed by first-hand knowledge, drew down on his head a vitriolic onslaught from the West Indian lobby. . . . When the Society for the Abolition of the Slave Trade was formed in 1787, there were nine Quakers on its committee of twelve. (208)

During the same period, Prime Minister William Pitt encouraged his friend William Wilberforce to raise the matter in Parliament, although his motive sprang not so much from humanitarianism as from a desire to injure the French prosperity of Saint-Domingue, whose planters obtained their Africans from British slave merchants.

As we saw in chapter 1, the increased momentum of the abolitionist movement came not from religious dissenters nor from middle-class humanitarians, but from the emergence of working-class radicalism. Earlier in the eighteenth century, a subculture of apprentices, servants, slaves, laborers and sailors coalescing around common work experiences and a shared cultural life had already participated in the anticolonial demonstrations preceding the American Revolutionary War[1] and in the so-called Gordon Riots of London in 1780. As Peter Linebaugh and Marcus Rediker argue, "The struggle against confinement [waged by this urban portside proletariat] led to a consciousness of freedom which was in turn transformed into the revolutionary discussion of human rights" (244). Thus, without input from the middle-class London Society or the religious Quaker network, Manchester's Society for Constitutional Information, founded to promote Thomas Paine's doctrine of human rights, presented to Parliament in 1787 a petition for the abolition of the slave trade signed by almost two-thirds of the city's eligible male voters. This triggered an explosive response in the rest of the country, and over the following year more than a hundred abolitionist petitions flooded into Parliament.

The abolitionist campaign was the first mass social movement in modern British history. It pioneered petitioning as a political weapon and, in 1791, drew the nonvoting populace into its orbit by initiating a boycott of slave-grown sugar. When in 1788 Josiah Wedgwood created a medallion of a supplicant Negro framed by the question, "Am I not a man and a brother?" as the antislavery movement's symbol, cameos of the design appeared on brooches and snuffboxes—as well as on the frontispiece of the 1814 edition of Equiano's *Narrative*. Inexpensive prints of Thomas Clarkson's plan of a loaded slave ship spoke to the social conscience of countless Britons. "Nothing was more fashionable among ladies of the time than tea-parties or evening gatherings at which the guests were consoled for the scrupulous exclusion of West Indian sugar by the recitation of Cowper's anti-slavery poems, and by thrillingly moving stories of atrocities practised on their black sisters" (Lascelles 78).

The abolition movement provided Equiano with the opportunity to appear as a public figure. As a literate and articulate ex-slave, his opinions on the slave trade and the culture of the West Indies carried considerable weight. In 1788 he published letters in the *Public Advertiser* and the *Morning Herald* that attacked proslavery apologists and urged the suppression of the trade. A short profile of him appeared in a July issue of the *Morning Chronicle* that year stating, "besides having an irreproachable moral character, [he] has frequently distinguished himself by occasional essays in the different papers, which manifest a strong and sound understanding" (qtd. in Shyllon 448). In March 1788 Equiano wrote a long letter, which became the closing pages of his autobiography, to the Privy Council for Trade, urging its president, Lord Hawkesbury, to persuade the government to substitute trade in commodities for trade in humans. A week later, he petitioned Queen Charlotte, wife of George III, to declare herself "in favour of the wretched African" (446).

Equiano wrote his autobiography in the heightened atmosphere of the abolitionist campaign, and it appeared in March 1789 under the title *The Interesting Narrative of the Life of Olaudah Equiano, or Gustavus Vassa, the African*. In his dedication of the book to the members of the two houses of Parliament, Equiano wrote that its chief design was "to excite in your august assemblies a sense of compassion for the miseries which the Slave-Trade has entailed on my unfortunate countrymen" (3). Two months later, Wilberforce, the political champion of the movement who was to achieve suppression of the British slave trade after eighteen years of effort, introduced to Parliament his first bill for the abolition of the slave trade.

Given the *Narrative*'s social midwifery, Equiano is remarkably restrained in his preaching. For the most part, he is content to let the facts of slavery as he witnessed them speak directly to the reader. Only twice does he break into an extended address (38, 80), both times prompted by the recollection of some particular barbarity of the slave condition. Interestingly enough, in both cases he imputes proslavery sentiments to his reader. In the second instance, as he moves into his exhortation, the language of his rhetorical questions partakes of a distinctly biblical color: "Why do you use those instruments of torture? Are they fit to be applied by one rational being to another? And are ye not struck with shame and mortification, to see the partakers of your nature reduced so low? But, above all, are there no dangers attending this mode of treatment? Are you not hourly in dread of an insurrection?" (81). Such outbreaks are exceptional. Through his sober account of the misadventures that befall both him and his enslaved companions, Equiano paints a portrait of slavery that damns itself. In its assessment of Equiano's *Narrative*, *The Monthly Review* for June 1789 commented: "His publication appears very seasonably, at a time when negroe-slavery is the subject of public investigation; and it seems calculated to increase the odium that hath been excited against the West-India planters" (quoted in Costanzo 43).

Both the Narrative and its author were effective agents in advancing the abolitionist campaign. Addressing antislavery meetings around the country, Equiano promoted his book and won new adherents to the cause. As Robert J. Allison writes:

> Equiano's *Narrative* became one crucial link between [religious reformers, intellectuals, blacks, working people, and capitalists]. He knew the great English abolitionists, Sharp, Clarkson, and Ramsay, but he also knew sailors and dockworkers, Black refugees from the West Indies and America, and leaders of London's emerging radical working class. He was recognized by virtually every segment of the antislavery and reform movements, and he could speak of his own experiences in a way to move men and women at every level of society. Among the subscribers to the first edition of his book were members of the English royal family and political radicals who in a few short years would be charged with treason, pacifists and admirals, Anglican bishops and dissenting ministers, Africans living in London, and women and men committed to reform. (15)

When Equiano died in 1797, five years after the *Narrative*'s appearance, his autobiography had run through eight editions in Great Britain, had been published in New York (1791), and translated into Dutch (1790), German (1792), and Russian (1794). Peter Fryer dubbed Equiano's book "the most important single literary contribution to the campaign for abolition" (107). Certainly it was that, but the *Narrative* proved to be far more than an effective piece of propaganda. As the first full-scale representation of an African subjectivity acculturated to the West, Equiano's autobiography revealed itself as the great literary ground-breaker for the Black presence in the literature of the English-speaking world.

In a different country and a different language, the autobiography of a Polish rabbi turned German philosopher introduced an analogous Jewish subjectivity to the world of Enlightenment letters. In 1788, a tattered young rabbi arrived in the city of Königsburg with the ostensible purpose of studying medicine. Born Solomon ben Joshua in a small Lithuanian town, he later assumed the surname Maimon out of reverence for the great medieval Jewish philosopher, Maimonides. Upon his arrival in Königsberg, Solomon Maimon addressed himself to the city's

Jewish physician, begging him for advice and support. The busy doctor referred this newcomer from the countryside to some students lodging in his quarters.

As soon as I showed myself to these young gentlemen, and opened to them my proposal, they burst into loud laughter. And certainly for this they were not to be blamed. Imagine a man from Polish Lithuania of about five and twenty years, with a tolerably stiff beard, in tattered dirty clothes, whose language is a mixture of Hebrew, Jewish German, Polish and Russian, with their several grammatical inaccuracies, who gives out that he understands the German language, and that he has attained some knowledge of the sciences. What were the young gentlemen to think?

They began to poke fun at me, and gave me to read Mendelssohn's *Phaedon*, which by chance lay on the table. I read in the most pitiful style, both on account of the peculiar manner in which I had learned the German language, and on account of my bad pronunciation. Again they burst into loud laughter; but they said, I must explain to them what I had read. This I did in my own fashion; but as they did not understand me, they demanded that I should translate what I had read into Hebrew. This I did on the spot. The students, who understood Hebrew well, fell into no slight astonishment when they saw that I had not only grasped correctly the meaning of this celebrated author, but also expressed it happily in Hebrew. (189)

No choice of text to translate could have been more symbolically appropriate. Moses Mendelssohn (1729–1786) was the first Jew since Spinoza to make a recognized contribution to the European intellectual scene, and his *Phaedon, or Three Dialogues on the Immortality of the Soul* (1767) was the vehicle of his greatest celebrity. This book, an imitation of the Platonic dialogue of the same name, was written in such a splendid style that the Dessau-born Jew was dubbed the German Socrates. According to *The Universal Jewish Encyclopedia*, "Mendelssohn had become a European celebrity. The elite of society and the literary world regarded it as a distinction to meet him. The leading German writers, among them Herder, Wieland, Gleim, Hamann, and Kant, consulted him."

The conditions that had allowed Mendelssohn to participate in European culture were the same that produced the first published Jewish autobiography: the *Aufklärung*, or German Enlightenment. Prior to the eighteenth century, Germany's Jews, numbering 175,000 and making up less than 1 percent of the population, bore numerous civil disabilities. "[T]he Jews of Germany might generally be described as victims of the administrative machinery of hundreds of sovereign entities," writes the historian Raphael Mahler, "bound by decrees that limited their residential and occupational rights, and reduced them to a wretched trade in order to earn a bare livelihood and meet the protection and tax payments exacted from them" (134). Certain Jews who had become rich and influential through trade and banking had escaped the miserable conditions of their coreligionists, but these men, wholly committed to politics and finance, had no opportunity to cultivate European *belles lettres* and were simply tolerated for the services they could provide to the state. Prussia's

Frederick the Great exemplified the utilitarian disdain affected by many of Germany's princes and princelings by granting privileges only to those Jews who could contribute to the country's economic infrastructure and ruthlessly excluding all others. According to an edict issued by Frederick's predecessor, Frederick William I, every *Schutzjude* ("protected Jew") had the right of transmitting his protected status to his three oldest children. Frederick the Great, however, restricted this right of transmission to only the oldest child, noting in so doing that the specific purpose of the Prussian law—namely, to reduce the number of Jewish residents as much as possible—would not otherwise be served. When, after the Seven Years War, the Jews of Berlin submitted a petition requesting that the right of residence be transmitted to at least two of the older children, Frederick was prepared to grant their request only on the condition that the second son obligate himself to establish a new factory.

Thus, as a result of the unique, selective system, the total of wealthy Jews—bankers, factory owners, country-contractors and mint-masters—continued to grow in Berlin. . . . Frederick II with his industrial policy significantly assisted the Prussian Jews, especially those of Berlin, to accumulate large capital and to become a prominent economic force. The Seven Years War, which ruined the country but provided the possibility for many Jews to become rich through supplying the military and through financial enterprises, magnified the social weight of Berlin Jewry, which became the harbinger of the new capitalist-bourgeois era. (Zinberg, *Berlin Haskalah*, 5–6)

Another harbinger of the new era was the penetration of Enlightenment thinking into Germany. Because of its backward economic development, Germany had not produced a middle class comparable to the one that had already achieved its political revolution in England, or the one that was to ignite such worldwide turmoil in France. Enlightened circles comprised mostly state functionaries, plentiful in the hundreds of states and principalities that made up Germany at the time. Enlightenment and modernization were seen as something to be instituted from above, spread through government institutions and their natural allies. Frederick the Great set the supreme example in Europe of the philosopher on the throne, corresponding with Voltaire, refuting the philosophy of Baron d'Holbach, and writing poetry in French. The *Aufklärer*, as they came to be called, were conservative in political outlook and philosophy. They never advanced beyond enlightened despotism, nor did they accept the extremes of French materialism. They did, however, subscribe to the new credo that once men had abandoned the superstition and intolerance of religion and custom, they could meet as equals under the auspices of reason and the natural rights that redounded to all mankind. As Jacob Katz points out in his historical study, *Tradition and Crisis*, a new class emerged that defined itself as a spiritual elite and presumed itself to be above and beyond the medieval estates. "An association formed around the values of the Enlightenment could not restrict membership to the adherents of a single religion. Transcending religious distinctions lay at the heart of the rationalists' creed, and excluding Jews from their group would have struck at the very heart of their principles" (221). Thus the Enlightenment created a social stratum where cultivated and forward-thinking Germans could associate with the small number of physicians, tutors, and scholars serving the Jewish upper class who had acquired a sufficient amount of European culture to be admitted entry. Mendelssohn was the most famous of these early Jewish intellectual immigrants, but not the first. Aaron Gumperz, a wealthy Jew who studied as a physician, gained entry to Berlin's literary and scientific circles through the sponsorship of Frederick II's friend, the Marquis d'Argens. Gumperz in his turn introduced Mendelssohn to the coffeehouse society and discussion clubs where he made the acquaintance of Gotthold Lessing, Friedrich Nicolai, and others. H. I. Bach writes:

> In the Berlin of the seventeen-fifties and sixties small groups such as these were of an importance quite disproportionate to their actual size and even to their combined learning. For unlike London or Paris, Berlin was still a small town. . . . The acceptance of Mendelssohn and his fellow Jews as members of learned societies, while breaking an unwritten taboo that for long centuries had kept Jews as such, except for doctors and sometimes Court Jews, outside polite company, was quite unobtrusive because the very composition of these societies lacked any precedent. Hitherto members of a profession, trade, or craft would have kept to themselves as did members of medieval guilds. Even one generation before, scholars would not have been willing to mingle with businessmen, and army officers would neither have wished to be, nor would have been admitted. (Bach 59–60)

The friendships he formed in these societies carried Mendelssohn to the center of the rebirth of German literature. He and Lessing became allies: Lessing arranged for the publication of Mendelssohn's first books, *Philosophische Gespräche* (1755) and *Briefe über die Empfindungen* (1755), and Mendelssohn contributed important notes on Lessing's draft of *Laocoön*, which was to rocket the German writer to international renown. The eponymous hero of Lessing's *Nathan the Wise*, the most famous Enlightenment plea for tolerance, was supposedly drawn from Mendelssohn's character. With the publisher and bookseller Nicolai, Mendelssohn became the chief adviser and collaborator in the production of periodicals and books that established Berlin as the leading force in German letters.

When Mendelssohn married, his own household became a unique meeting place where the elites of German and Jewish society mingled and conversed. Some time later, Henrietta Herz, wife of the cultivated physician Marcus Herz, founded the first of the Jewish salons on the French model. Although the first generation of Jewish industrialists, wholesalers, and financiers did not have the opportunity or leisure to cultivate the arts and sciences, they came into social contact with the French colony in Prussia as well as with German importers, nobles, and high government officials. They knew of polite society and encouraged their own sons and daughters in the acquisition of the modern languages and graces that would assure them easy intercourse with their German class counterparts. "Wealth and culture helped to throw open the gates of the ghetto," Hannah Arendt wrote, "court Jews on the one hand and Moses Mendelssohn on the other" (86).

When Solomon Maimon appeared in Berlin with his ridiculous appearance and rustic Yiddish, he had no hope of fitting into the bourgeois settings of the *Aufklärung* gatherings. He writes of his first visit to Mendelssohn's house, "When I therefore opened Mendelssohn's door, and saw him and other gentlefolk who were there, as well as the beautiful rooms and elegant furniture, I shrank back, closed the door again, and had a mind not to go in" (215). Once Maimon had established himself in the Berlin community, with Mendelssohn's help, he quickly made an impression on Jewish intellectuals due to his brilliance and terrible manners. When he finally mastered the writing of German sufficiently, he was able to participate in Enlightenment culture. This he did principally through contributions to the various German periodicals of the day. "The learned tomes of the Republic of Letter had been replaced by the journals of the educated classes, journals which were the most important medium of the Enlightenment in Protestant Germany" (Whaley 110). Maimon not only published in Schiller's magazine, *Die Horen*; he was invited by Fichte to become a contributor to his *Allgemeine Literatur-Zeitung*. He even became an editor of the *Magazin zur Erfahrungsseelenkunde* (1783–93), where he first published excerpts of his autobiography.

The *Magazin*, a forerunner to journals of clinical psychology, was the brainchild of the awkward and ambitious German writer Karl Philipp Moritz. Having grown up as a poor son of a Hannovarian regimental musician, Moritz achieved a position in German letters through a prolific output spanning the years 1778 to 1793, the year of his death. In spite of his lower-class background and eccentric behavior, Moritz became an accepted member of *Aufklärer* circles, partially through his friendship with Mendelssohn and as an early member of Henrietta Herz's salon. Moritz was influenced by Mendelssohn's late metaphysical views, expressed in *Morgenstuden* (1785), and Mendelssohn had an impact on Mortiz's psychological thought, manifested most clearly in the programmatic announcements of his project to found the *Magazin*. Marcus Herz was also involved in the preliminary discussion, so that, from its beginnings, the journal proved to be a product of the German-Jewish symbiosis produced by the *Aufklärung*.

Among the many case histories published in the journal, Moritz included excerpts of his autobiographical novel, *Anton Reiser: Ein psychologischen Roman* (1785), his best claim to continued literary interest. When Maimon came to the *Magazin* as an editor during the final years of its publishing life, he printed excerpts of his own autobiography under his Jewish patronymic. Meanwhile, Moritz was made a

"Hofrat" (Aulic Counselor) in April 1791; six months later he was elected to the Berlin Academy of Sciences. He had already, two years previously, secured an appointment as professor in the theory of fine arts at the Berlin Academy of Arts. Wielding considerable influence with the Berlin establishment, Moritz spent the last two years of his life in frenzied activity. One of his projects was the editing of a two-volume book that was to make a splash in Enlightenment Germany: *Salomon Maimons Lebensgeschichte; Von ihm selbst geschreiben und herausgegaben von K. P. Moritz* (1792–93). Though neglected today, the *Lebensgeschichte* is as revealing and important a document in Jewish letters as Equiano's *Narrative* is to the Black world. In the rest of this chapter, I quote extensively from the last English translation, an 1888 version that has long been out of print and is difficult to obtain.[2]

Both Maimon and Equiano engaged in a complicated struggle to master the languages that would allow them to participate in the Enlightenment West. Their subsequent use of these languages to express a new subjectivity had analogs within the Western tradition. As Frederick Karl observes in his magisterial history of Modernism, Chaucer, Dante, and the Provençal troubadours also needed to break with Latin, Europe's intellectual language par excellence, as a way of expressing their present day sensibilities. "We have, then, a constant: the use of language as a way of separating modern from antiquity, as a form of divisiveness and definition. By way of a modern language, rather than antiquity's language, the writer expresses more than equality. He assumes the world has progressed, and a progressive world needs new modes of expression. That shift in languages is connected to slow shifts in modes of perceptions, really cultural earthquakes" (7).

Blacks and Jews experienced these shifts with particular intensity. The pidgin spoken by African slaves cut them off from the aid and sympathy of the *philosophes* as effectively as the "Jewish tongues," Yiddish and Hebrew, restricted the Jews to their ghettoes. Just as the Western allies of Blacks and Jews wrote their sermons, pamphlets, and articles in French, German, and English, so too did Moses Mendelssohn, Solomon Maimon, Ottobah Cugoano, and Olaudah Equiano, for all of them were addressing the same audience: the literate men and women of the West. As Karl indicates, however, this shift in language necessarily entailed a shift in perception. For the Black and Jewish writer, the languages of modernity entered into a dialectical relationship with an inchoate ethnic subjectivity.

Presumably, Equiano's first language was the Ibo tongue of the village he calls Esseke in present-day Nigeria. Although he didn't come into contact with English until his early adolescence, he was a master of its written form by the time he composed his *Narrative* at the age of forty-three. In describing the eighteenth-century kingdom of Benin in his first chapter, Equiano supplemented his recollections of his life there with Anthony Benezet's *Some Historical Account of Guinea* (1771), a sympathetic description of life in West Africa written by a Philadelphia Quaker. However, in describing the social realities with which he was familiar, Equiano had to ressurect a few Ibo words for which there were no English equivalents: *Embrench*, describing the scarification applied to the village leaders; and *Oye-Eboe*, signifying the "red men" who brought European goods to barter at the local market. Catherine Obianju Acholonu suggests that the former term has as its present-day Ibo equivalent *mgburichi*, referring to the men who bear the scars Equiano described, and the latter, *oyibo*, meaning "light-colored person." Acholonu speculates that these may have been the Aro who were involved in the slave trade (10–12, 14, 29–30).

Equiano strove to gainsay the myth of African barbarity in his ethnographic description of the people of Esseke, and to that end he was obliged to call upon the resources of his mother tongue; but in general the Enlightenment evinced little interest in African languages. As these languages possessed no writing—and therefore no literature—they were considered to be the barbaric yawp of a savage populace. The tongues of the kidnapped slaves—Ibo, Fanti, Hausa, and Ashanti—proved useless in the struggle to establish Black humanity in the eyes of the West. Philip Quaque, an African educated in England from 1754 to 1756 who returned to the Gold Coast as a chaplain of the Anglican Society for the Propagation of the Gospel, sent the children of his African wife back to England "in order to secure their tender minds from receiving the bad impression of the country, the vile customs and practices, and above all the losing of their mother's vile jargon" (qtd. in Edwards and Walvin 59). What mattered to the Enlightenment was mastery of the written word, and as no African language could boast of an alphabet (the Islamic transcriptions of Hausa and Swahili were unknown in the West), their mere existence could not be adduced as proof of the Negro's humanity. As Henry Louis Gates Jr. has ably argued:

> What seems clear upon reading the texts created by black writers in English or the critical texts that responded to these black writings is that the production of literature was taken to be the central arena in which persons of African descent could, or could not, establish and redefine their status within the human community. Black people, the evidence suggests, had to represent themselves as "speaking subjects" before they could even begin to destroy their status as objects, as commodities, within Western cultures. (129)

In one celebrated instance, demonstration of Islamic literacy was sufficient to free an African Moslem from bondage in Maryland. Job ben Solomon, the son of a High Priest in the Gambian interior, was captured in 1731 when he traveled with two slaves intended for sale themselves. Purchased as a plantation slave, Job managed to write a letter to his father, appealing for a ransom, and dispatched it by one of the vessels sailing back to the Gambia by way of London. The letter came to the attention of a prominent philanthropist, James Oglethorpe, who had it translated at Oxford. Oglethorpe was so touched by its sentiments that he arranged for Job to be bought out of slavery and brought to London; ben Solomon then spent time in England as a celebrity before returning home as an agent of the Royal African Company.

The difficulty for several of the early texts purporting to convey a Black subjectivity through the written word was the position of the author within Western culture. For the few Africans who had obtained a formal education—Francis Williams, a Jamaican who studied Mathematics at Cambridge; Jacobus Capitein, who studied in Holland from 1726 to 1742; Wilhelm Amo, who matriculated at the University of Halle and taught philosophy at the University of Jena—their respective writings in Latin, Dutch, and German were academic and had little readership outside university circles. Others who offered their narratives to the lay reading public did not possess sufficient literacy to present their stories in an acceptable form. These narratives were mediated by white "amanuenses," who not only wielded a preponderant editorial influence but also dictated, by their use of eighteenth-century literary conventions, the audience and ideological uses. Indeed the first Black biographies (as opposed to first-person narratives) to appear in English were the 1734 memoir of Solomon ben Job and two criminal narratives of 1745 and 1768.[3]

Even when the Black subject communicated in a Western language, oral fluency was insufficient to assure control over the final written product. The narratives of Briton Hammon (1746), Ukawsaw Gronniosaw (1770), and John Marrant (1785) all attest to the wonders of God's providence and have little to say about the evils of slavery. None of these men were adequate enough writers to produce a text that met eighteenth-century standards of literature. Gronniosaw, fluent in both Dutch and English, had mastered Protestant theology well enough that, as he says in his narrative, during a sojourn in Holland "I stood before 48 ministers every Thursday for seven weeks together, and they were all very well satisfied, and persuaded I was what I pretended to be" (27). However, it was Hannah More, a religious author and social reformer, who produced *A Narrative of the Most Remarkable Particulars in the Life of James Albert Ukawsaw Gronniosaw, An African Prince*. In the first edition, the title continues with the phrase "as Related by Himself," and the opening line of the Preface, by the Methodist minister Walter Shirley, reads: "This account of the life and spiritual experience of James Albert, was taken from his own mouth, and committed to paper by the elegant pen of a young Lady of the town of Leominster, for her own private satisfaction and without any intention, at first, that it should be made public" (76). John Marrant had just been ordained as a Methodist minister when he told his story to William Aldridge, another minister, but in spite of Marrant's proven ability to preach the Gospel, his amanuensis wrote in the preface, "I have always preserved Mr. Marrant's ideas, tho' I could not his language" (76).

Black intellectuals could not claim full and effective participation in Enlightenment culture until they could produce for themselves the final text of a narrative, in literate form. That is what partially accounts for the enduring legacy of Phillis Wheatley and Olaudah Equiano, for, as Gates noted, "Literacy, the very literacy of the printed book, stood as the ultimate parameter by which to measure the humanity of authors struggling to define an African self in Western letters" (131). This literate capability of the Black author was still so contested in the eighteenth century that Wheatley's 1773 *Poems on Various Subjects, Religious and Moral* was prefaced by a letter of authenticity signed by the Governor of Massachusetts, seven clergymen, and nine "gentlemen of standing." (Ignatius Sancho, the most learned of the Black autodidacts, acidly noted in a letter of 1778 that while "[t]hese good great folks" had "praised Genius in bondage," none spoke against her servitude, "not one good Samaritan amongst them" [127].) Sixteen years later, a reviewer in the *Monthly Review* speculated about Equiano's *Narrative* "that it is not improbable that some English writer has assisted him in the compilement, or, at least, the correction of his book: for it is sufficiently well-written" (qtd. in Costanzo 43). Even where unassisted authorship was indisputable, Western intellectuals of the first rank could respond with unabashed racism. In a long note appended to a reprinted version of the essay "Of National Characters" (1754), Hume compared Francis Williams, who wrote Latin verse, to "a parrot who speaks a few words plainly" (Chukwudi 31); Jefferson, in his *Notes on the State of Virginia* (1787), spoke of Wheatley's poetry as "below the dignity of criticism" (Chukwudi 100).

White judgment aside, it is significant that the first book of prose aimed at a popular audience to be incontestably written by a Black author was a long antislavery tract of 1787, *Thoughts and Sentiments on the Evil and Wicked Traffic of the Slavery and Commerce of the Human Species, Humbly Submitted to the Inhabitants of Great-Britain, by Ottobah Cugoano, a Native of Africa.* In this work, Cugoano first makes the connection between literacy and protest that is to become an enduring topos of Black literature.

After coming to England, and seeing others write and read, I had a strong desire to learn, and getting what assistance I could, I applied myself to learn reading and writing, which soon became my recreation, pleasure, and delight; and when my master perceived that I could write some, he sent me to a proper school for that purpose to learn. Since, I have endeavoured to improve my mind in reading, and have sought to get all the intelligence I could, in my situation in life, towards the state of my brethren and countrymen in complexion, and of the miserable situation of those who are barbarously sold into captivity, and unlawfully held in slavery. (Edwards and Dabydeen 44–45)

We see here the expression of a diasporic consciousness, one that recognizes the newly created kinship of "countrymen in complexion" where no kinship existed before. The "Fanti" Cugoano and the "Ibo" Equiano forge their commonality and new identity as Negroes, ex-slaves, and champions of abolition. Even Sancho, the most Anglicized of the autodidacts, responded warmly to the distress of enslaved Blacks, introducing himself in a letter to Lawrence Sterne with the command, "think in me you behold the uplifted hands of thousands of my brother Moors" (214). Both Cugoano and Equiano belonged to the Sons of Africa, a London-based group that authored petitions and organized letter-writing campaigns to politicians and public figures in an effort to secure basic human rights for other Blacks. Several scholars believe, in fact, that Equiano assisted Cugoano in the composition or editing of *Thoughts and Sentiments*, as there is such a disparity between the language of his book and that of a surviving letter.[4] The probable circumstance of one Black author offering silent editorial support to another (as opposed to the well-publicized interventions of White writers and editors) adds a layer of irony to the history of the transition of the Black narrative from oral to written. That the silent partner of Cugoano's groundbreaking work was Equiano himself makes the irony more pungent, for Equiano was the first author to use literary techniques successfully in the portrayal of Black subjectivity.

"[W]e cannot honestly conclude that slave literature was meant to exemplify either polite or humane learning or the presence in the author of literary culture," Gates writes (128), but Equiano proves the exception to what otherwise holds true. In his dedication of the book to the members of Parliament, Equiano is quick to disclaim any high-culture pretensions, but the language with which he does so shows such elegance and rhetorical skill that the contentions therein are immediately belied. "I am sensible I ought to entreat your pardon for addressing to you a work so wholly devoid of literary merit; but, as the product of an unlettered African, who is actuated by the hope of becoming an instrument towards the relief of his suffering countrymen, I trust that *such a man*, pleading in *such a cause*, will be acquitted of boldness and presumption" (3). Having said that, Equiano proceeds to quote from Pope's translation of *The Iliad*, Milton's *Paradise Lost*, and Thomas Day's now-forgotten poem "The Dying Negro"; he also includes verses from several Methodist hymns and makes reference to writings by abolitionists Anthony Benezet and Thomas Clarkson. His use of the Bible, through allusion and direct quotation, is varied indeed. Through intertextuality alone, Equiano's *Narrative* swims in literary culture.[5]

Yet the literary language of the eighteenth century was ill equipped to express the reality of bondage or the subjectivity of the slave. In spite of this, slavery had been given literary treatment since the 1688 publication of Aphra Behn's *Oroonoko*, initiating in English literature the tradition of the noble Negro. In 1696, Thomas Southerne dramatized Behn's novella, and from then to the beginning of the nineteenth century *Oroonoko*, in one version or another (John Hawkesworth removing the "Restoration indecency" in 1759), was produced at least once a season. "Hawkesworth revised in no anti-slavery mood; but the audiences of the later years of the century undoubtedly found a humane doctrine in his version" (Sypher 116). In the last half of the eighteenth century, enlightened and humanitarian thinking among Britain's writers brought about a development of antislavery themes even before the upsurge of abolitionist agitation in the late 1780s. The Somerset case of 1772 prompted "The Dying Negro" (1773), and antislavery sentiments could be gleaned from such classics as Sterne's *Tristram Shandy* (1760–67) and Thomas Day's *Sandford and Merton* (1783–89) as well as numerous novels, plays, and works of fiction since consigned to obscurity. In his survey of such antislavery literature, Wylie Sypher concludes, "The novels and more especially the poems extolling the Negro are a singular illustration of the extreme pseudo-classicism whereby what is observed is cast into a highly artificial 'literary' form" (5).

The best example of this, and one that illustrates the inadequacy of European belletristic conventions for the purposes of portraying a Black subjectivity, is Day's "Dying Negro," quoted with approbation in Equiano's *Narrative* as "elegant and pathetic." The poem itself was occasioned by a news item summarized by Day in the following manner: "Tuesday last a Black, who a few days ago run [*sic*] away from his master, and got himself christened, with intent to marry his fellow-servant, a white woman, being taken, and sent on board the Captain's ship, in the Thames, took an opportunity of shooting himself through the head" (vi). The form of the poem is a "poetical epistle" in pentameter couplets and triplets, from the narrator to his intended wife. Before donning the persona of the dying Negro, however, Day prefaces his poem with the following verse from Shenstone:

> Yet the muse listen'd to the plaints he made,
>   Such moving plaints as nature could inspire;
> To me the muse his tender plea convey'd,
>   But smooth'd, and suited to the sounding lyre.

Here we have the first instance of a phenomenon we will encounter again in our study of ethnic autobiography: literary convention claiming redemption and proper expression for subliterary experience. Let us look to a passage of Day's poem that describes a territory, both geographical and emotional, also covered by Equiano.

> My tortur'd bosom, sad remembrance spare!
> Why dost thou plant thy keenest daggers there?
> And shew me what I was, and aggravate despair?
> Ye streams of Gambia, and thou sacred shade!
> Where in my youth's first dawn I joyful stray'd,
> Oft have I rouz'd, amid your caverns dim,
> The howling tyger, and the lion grim,
> In vain they gloried in their headlong force,
> My javelin pierc'd them in their headlong course.

But little did my boding mind bewray,
The victor and his hopes were doom'd a prey
To human breasts more fell, more cruel far than they.

Day's Negro pines for Africa in a way Equiano, Phillis Wheatley, Ukawsaw Gronniosaw, and Ottobah Cugoano do not. (In their reminiscences of Africa, Equiano, Gronniosaw, and Cugoano mention family much more than animals—and certainly not tigers, foreign to the continent.) Unlike the Black narrators of the eighteenth century, Day's Negro, while accepting Christianity, does not embrace its spirit, gladly exchanging salvation for a visitation of vengeance from God.

Now let us consider an analogous passage from Equiano's *Narrative*, similar not for its description of Africa but for the relation of the speaker vis-à-vis a creature seen at that time as more unfortunate than he.

I have often seen slaves, particularly those who were meager, in different islands, put into scales and weighted; and then sold from three-pence to six-pence or nine-pence a pound. My master, however, whose humanity was shocked at this mode, used to sell such by the lump. And at or after a sale, even those negroes born in the islands it is not uncommon to see taken from their wives, wives from their husbands, and children from their parents, and sent off to other islands, and wherever else their merciless lords choose; and, probably, never more, during life, see each other! Oftentimes my heart has bled at these partings; when the friends of the departed have been at the water-side, and, with sighs and tears, have kept their eyes fixed on the vessel till it went out of sight.

A poor Creole negro I know well, who, after having been often thus transported from island to island, at last resided in Montserrat. This used to tell me many melancholy tales of himself. Generally, after he had done working for his master, he used to employ his few leisure moments to go a fishing. When he had caught any fish, his master would frequently take them from him without paying him; and at other times some other white people would serve him in the same manner. One day he said to me very movingly, "Sometimes when a white man take away my fish I go to my maser, and he get me my right; and when my maser, by strength, take away my fishes, what me must do? I can't go to any body to be righted; then," said the poor man, looking up above, "I must look up to God Mighty in the top for right." This artless tale moved me much, and I could not help feeling the just cause Moses had in redressing his brother against the Egyptian. I exhorted the man to look up still to the God in the top, since there was no redress below. Though I little thought then that I myself should more than once experience such imposition, and need the same exhortation hereafter, in my own transactions in the islands; and that even this poor man and I should some time after, suffer together in the same manner. . . . (79–80)

These two paragraphs reveal a tonal and linguistic complexity absent in the white antislavery writers. The biting sarcasm of Equiano's evocation of his master's "humanity" is as subdued as his description of the Blacks' distress at seeing their loved ones disappear forever. Not being a reader of sentimental novels, Equiano has little vocabulary with which to describe intensely subjective states (except, of course, for religious exaltation), but his very realism and understatement allow him to avoid the clichés of other antislavery writers: the Africa of the imagination, the noble Negro, the heartless West Indian, the gratuitous horrors and overplayed pathos of plantation scenes. Most amazingly, Equiano reports an "artless tale" more or less in the manner in which it was related—one of the first instances of Black English being used for literary purposes. Instinctively Equiano feels that the Creole's dialect will move the reader without being smoothed to the strains of a "sounding lyre." Nobody is going to sing the ordinary theft of a poor slave's labor—his lot by definition—while strumming an instrument under the shades of Arcadia. Although Equiano reverts to an educated English in commenting upon the story, he does so with what will become a standard Anglo-African and African-American rhetorical strategy—by comparing himself to an Old Testament figure. He even linguistically prefigures his ultimate identity with his fellow Black in bondage (though he is more privileged in educational attainments and type of servitude) by partially modeling his "standard" English on the Creole's "artless" dialect: "I exhorted the man to look up still to the God in the top."

Within the space of fifty years, Black expression made the transition from African to Western languages, from oral transmission mediated by Whites to a full-blown Black authorship that included composition, editing, and the literary use of Black English.[6] Wheatley's poems, Cugoano's antislavery tract, Equiano's autobiography, and Ignatius Sancho's letters signaled the arrival of the Black author on the Enlightenment scene. Yet the conditions of this achievement were precarious at best. As long as colonial slavery persisted (as it did until 1838), the Black community would never rest easy with whatever partial freedom it had attained. Free Blacks were viewed through the inherited perceptions of a literary and oral tradition that had cast them in the role of inferior beings even before interracial relations were so fatally structured by chattel slavery. It was hard to imagine the Blacks as free and equal when colonial practice and domestic usage, sanctioned by law, consigned them to a lifetime of servitude. It was the achievement of these pioneer writers that their products—however mediated, composed, and otherwise contested—helped persuade the British public that the Black was indeed "a man and a brother."

For the Jewish maskilim, German books would perform a similar function. Solomon Maimon grew up speaking a Polish form of Yiddish, which at the time was considered an inferior language. Maimon himself subscribed to this prejudice and expressed the disdain that all Jewish intellectuals held for the people's vernacular until the middle of the nineteenth century. Mendelssohn described the Yiddish used in translations of the Pentateuch as "a tongue of buffoons, very inadequate and corrupt; a reader capable of elegant speech must recoil from it in disgust" (Mahler 161).[7] According to Maimon, this "Jewish German" (the word "Yiddish" is derived from the German *Jüdische Deutsch*) hindered his study of Hebrew and, in consequence, of the Torah as well. "For the Hebrew [of the Bible] must be explained by means of the mother tongue. But the mother tongue of the Polish Jews is itself full of defects and grammatical inaccuracies; and as a matter of course therefore also the Hebrew language, which is learned by its means, must be of the same stamp. The pupil thus acquires just as little knowledge of the language, as of the contents of the Bible" (34).

Even if Hebrew could only be mastered by translation into an "imperfect tongue," it had nonetheless to be done, for a knowledge of Hebrew was the *sine qua non* of the rabbi. That was only the first step, however. As Maimon's father told him in his earliest years, "He who understands the Talmud understands everything" (26). Mastery of the Talmud presented even greater difficulty than that of the Torah, for the Talmud consists of two distinct parts: the Mishnah and its commentary, the Gemara. The language of the Mishnah is Neo-Hebrew, which is Aramaic in both morphology and syntax. The Gemara of the Babylonian Talmud was composed in Eastern Aramaic, into which Hebrew passages had been interwoven. Under the circumstances, an understanding of even the literal meaning of the Talmud could not be acquired through Hebrew. Its language had to be learned just as arduously—and under the same unfavorable conditions.

The study of the Talmud is carried on just as irregularly as that of the Bible. The language of the Talmud is composed of various Oriental languages and dialects; there is even many a word in it from Greek and Latin. There is no dictionary, in which you can turn up the expression and phrases met with in the Talmud; and, what is still worse, as the Talmud is not pointed [has no vowel dots], you cannot even tell how such words, that are not pure Hebrew, are to be read. The language of the Talmud, therefore, like that of the Bible, is learned only through frequent translation. . . . (45)

In spite of the accepted wisdom that *talmud torah* was the be-all and end-all of learning, Maimon's intellect thirsted for more. Through Hebrew books he came upon by chance, he gained "some disconnected knowledge in history, astronomy, and other mathematical sciences" (89). But the linguistic paths to science and secular knowledge were not open to one who had at his disposal "only" Yiddish and the languages of *talmud torah*.

In order to gratify my desire of scientific knowledge, there were no means available but that of learning foreign languages. But how was I to begin? To learn Polish or Latin with a Catholic teacher was for me impossible, on the one hand because the prejudices of my own people prohibited to me all languages but Hebrew, and all sciences but the Talmud and the vast array of its commentary, on the other hand because the prejudices of Catholics would not allow them to give instruction in these matters to a Jew. (89–90)

So in the midst of medieval darkness, Maimon began to teach himself German in perhaps the most singular manner imaginable. Noticing that the signatures for the binding of folio pages in the printing of "stout Hebrew volumes" (90) consisted of several lettering systems, Maimon studied these to gain mastery of the Latin and German alphabets. Because of the similarity of Yiddish and German, Maimon was able to guess at many of the sounds represented by the German alphabet, and thus began combining various German letters into words. When he finally came across some pages of a German book, Maimon found, to his joy and surprise, that he could comprehend what he was reading.

Unable to obtain more volumes in German, Maimon turned to other sources of intellectual nourishment and delved into the Cabbalah, the Jewish tradition of oc-cult teachings. This he found ultimately unsatisfying, however, and upon learning that the chief rabbi of a neighboring town possessed a library of German books, Maimon made a pilgrimage there and was able to borrow "an old work on Optics and Sturm's Physics" (107). "After I had studied these books thoroughly, my eyes were all at once opened. I believed that I had found a key to all the secrets of nature, as I now knew the origin of storms, of dew, of rain, and such phenomena. I looked down with pride on all others, who did not yet know these things, laughed at their prejudices and superstitions, and proposed to clear up their ideas on these subjects and enlighten their understanding" (107–8).

Thus, after his first encounter with Western science through the conduit of the German tongue, Maimon fell naturally into the role of the maskil, the enlightened Jew. He would teach his benighted brethren the truths of the modern world. At first, this led to some misunderstandings.

> On another occasion I went to take a walk with some of my friends. It chanced that a goat lay in the way. I gave the goat some blows with my stick, and my friends blamed me for my cruelty. "What is the cruelty?" I replied. "Do you believe that the goat feels a pain, when I beat it? You are greatly mistaken; the goat is a mere machine." This was the doc-trine of Sturm as a disciple of Descartes.
> My friends laughed heartily at this, and said, "But don't you hear that the goat cries, when you beat it?" "Yes," I replied, "of course it cries; but if you beat a drum, it cries too." They were amazed at my answer, and in a short time it went abroad over the whole town that I had become mad, as I held that *a goat is a drum*. (108–9)

Surrounded by such ignorance and pressed in constantly by the misery and want of his circumstances, Maimon's impatience and desire to escape grew over the years. A flirtation with the Chassidic sect did nothing to retard this growth. He had tasted the waters of Enlightenment, and he finally resolved to go to its sources. "I deter-mined to betake myself to Germany, there to study medicine and, as opportunity offered, other sciences also" (187). Königsberg was his first stop, and it was there that he amused the cosmopolitan Jewish students with his rustic appearance and his strange mixture of Hebrew, Yiddish, Polish, and Russian. When they had him read Mendelssohn's *Phaedon* to prove his knowledge of German, they had chosen the most famous writing by a Jew since Spinoza's *Tractatus theologicus-politicus*. "The sense of pride and achievement with which Mendelssohn inspired his contemporaries in the *haskalah* movement came principally from the eminence which he achieved in non-Jewish Enlightenment circles—an eminence that was evanescent and short lived" (Mahler 155).

Like Spinoza, Mendelssohn made his contribution to European culture in non-Jewish spheres of intellectual endeavor—and in a non-Jewish tongue. During his apprenticeship to European learning, undertaken with Jews and Germans alike, he studied both classical and modern European languages. He read Locke and Hume in English, Virgil in Latin, Rousseau in French. Upon the appearance of Frederick the Great's *Poèsies diverses* (1760), the Berlin Jew wrote a review in which he chided his king for having neglected the German tongue. (As Maimon noted, however, French "was then regarded as the highest point of enlightenment" [236].) Mendelssohn's *Phaedon* was an elegant elaboration of the Leibnitzian philosophy as popularized by Baron Christian von Wolff. All of this work had been produced in German. The first time Mendelssohn wrote publicly as a Jew (also in German), he took on the task with reluctance, and then only under the pressure of a public challenge made by a Swiss theologian, Lavatar, that he either refute Christianity or embrace it. Unlike Spinoza, Mendelssohn remained a Jew—a practicing Jew—and this, combined with his recognition in the field of European culture, created the special character of his achievement. "More than anyone before him, Mendelssohn deserves credit for bringing the Jew out of the ghetto and into the mainstream of modern culture. . . . What Luther did for the Jews vis-à-vis the Roman Catholic Church, Mendelssohn did for the Jews vis-à-vis Talmudism" (Beiser 92).

Within the Jewish community, Mendelssohn did all he could to promote scientific knowledge and a greater mastery of German, the tongue by which modern thought could be acquired and the one that was indispensable for eventual emancipation. Through his initiative the first Jewish model school, "Hinnuch Nearim" (*Jüdische Freyschule*), was founded in 1778. There not only Talmud and the Bible, but German, French, and general subjects were studied. In the same year Mendelssohn began his translation of the Torah into German. This posed a radical challenge to rabbinical culture, which considered the Talmud more important than the Torah and which had adopted the system of instruction developed in Poland based on casuistic reasoning (*pilpul*) and exposition. As Israel Zinberg comments, Mendelssohn in his translation set himself the triple task of facilitating the acquisition of German as a literary language; of turning Jewish youth "away from tortuous *pilpul* and arid scholasticism," returning them to the Bible and biblical style; and of supplanting the Old-Yiddish Bible translations of Yekutiel Blit (Zinberg, *Berlin Haskalah*, 39-40).

Though Mendelssohn was later seen as a standard-bearer of the haskalah, he was far less radical in his views than other friends and younger disciples, such as Herz

Homberg and David Friedländer, who formed his circle and claimed to carry on his work. Mendelssohn was drawn to German letters and European culture out of intellectual sympathy. Contempt for the rabbinical culture of his coreligionists had nothing to do with his embracing the modern world. "When Mendelssohn was already renowned as a brilliant aesthetic critic in the German literary world, he remained in the Jewish milieu, the traditional *talmid hacham*, or sage, who strictly observed all the commandments of the Torah, had an attitude of profound reverence for the rabbis of his time, and even requested the greatest of them to bestow on him the honorary title *haver*" (*Berlin Haskalah*, 17).

In fact, according to a letter he addressed to Naftali Herz Wessely, Mendelssohn originally intended to compose his affirmation of the immortality of the soul in Hebrew. However, he wrote: "Numerous weighty factors did not permit me to carry this through and compelled me to write my projected work in a language of the nations of the world, as many greater and more important men than I did in their day when they composed their works in Arabic" (qtd. in *Berlin Haskalah*, 17–18). This last statement could easily allude to Maimon's eponymous idol, Maimonides, who wrote his *Guide for the Perplexed* in "the language of Ishmael," as he called it, because he wanted to give circulation to his ideas and teachings amongst the widest possible audience (Minkin, 84).

As an extension of Leibnitz-Wolffian optimism, the *Phaedon* was neither Jewish nor Hebrew in its form or content. Mendelssohn himself held the opinion, expressed in a letter to the mathematician Raphael Levi, that "Phaedon does not allow itself to be translated; at least in Hebrew it would cease to be understandable" (qtd. in Zinberg, *Berlin Haskalah*, 30).[8]

Yet a third reason for composing the *Phaedon* in German lay in the nature of its audience. With their intellectual origins in Plato and Western philosophy, Mendelssohn's dialogues addressed themselves to Western intellectuals, few of whom could read Hebrew. Composing the work in the language of the Jews would have condemned it to a hostile reception, for rabbinical authority, which had a stranglehold on intellectual discourse conducted in Hebrew, stood unalterably opposed to the dissemination of Enlightenment ideas in the Jewish community. These, they correctly perceived, would undermine their preeminence and bring about their downfall. Solomon Maimon ran into this problem when, at the behest of his haskalah friends who wished to see him gainfully employed, he wrote a Hebrew textbook on mathematics and failed to get it published.

My friends . . . began, though too late to see that their ill-considered project must of necessity collapse, because they had no assurance of a market for such voluminous and expensive works. From the religious, moral and political condition of the Jews up to this time it was easy to foresee that the few enlightened men among them would certainly give themselves no trouble to study the sciences in the Hebrew language, which is very ill-adapted for the exposition of such subjects; they will prefer to seek science in its original sources. The unenlightened, on the other hand,—and these form the majority,—are so swayed by rabbinical prejudices, that they regard the study of the sciences, even in Hebrew, as forbidden fruit, and persistently occupy themselves only with the Talmud and the enormous number of its commentaries. (269)

As Maimon indicates, the only roads to enlightenment during the eighteenth century were those of the Western European languages. But though Maimon himself had mastered the reading of German through his own initiative, it was a long time before he learned to speak or write it properly, and this was to be the source of much trouble for him.

Once Maimon had succeeded in gaining entry to Berlin, the major lighthouse of the *Aufklärung*, he brought himself to Mendelssohn's attention by means of dissertations written in Hebrew discussing philosophical points in Baron Wolff's *Metaphysics*. Impressed by the Polish rabbi's acuity, Mendelssohn introduced Maimon to others of the Berlin maskilim; but, owing to his imperfect grasp of German, these did not take him seriously at first. Maimon writes of the physician and philosopher Marcus Herz that he "regarded me as a speaking animal, and entertained himself with me as one is apt to do with a dog or a starling that has been taught to speak a few words" (216). However, he continues, "By degrees the fun was turned to earnest."

As brilliant as Maimon proved himself to be, his refusal to master the proper expression of German betokened an indiscipline that was to hound and mentally cripple him for most of his life. He refused to acquire a trade, and though he applied himself to studying the sciences, he did so out of inclination with no plan or end in mind. This intellectual fecklessness combined with the growing perception that he was dissolute and a heretic (championing Spinoza even to Mendelssohn) served to alienate his friends and made his position in Berlin untenable. After receiving a dressing down from Mendelssohn himself, Maimon decided to leave Berlin and traveled via Hamburg to the Hague. Finding no employment or intellectual stimulation in Holland, he traveled back to Hamburg.

[H]ere I fell into circumstances of the deepest distress. I lodged in a miserable house, had nothing to eat, and did not know what to do. I had received too much education to return to Poland, to spend my life in misery without rational occupation or society, and to sink back into the darkness of superstition and ignorance, from which I had hardly delivered myself with so much labour. On the other hand, to succeed in Germany was a result on which I could not calculate, owing to my ignorance of the language, as well as of the manners and customs of the people to which I had never yet been able to adapt myself properly. I had learnt no particular profession, I had not distinguished myself in any special science, I was not even master of any language in which I could make myself perfectly intelligible. It occurred to me, therefore, that for me there was no alternative left, but to embrace the Christian religion, and get myself baptised in Hamburg. (253–54)

Maimon still ran into the problem of communication, however. Unable to present his circumstances through oral discourse with a German clergyman, "I put my thoughts into writing in German with Hebrew characters, went to a schoolmaster, and got him to copy it in German characters" (254). After failing the most rudimentary test of Christian belief, discussed below, Maimon was forced to fall back again on the Jewish community for succor and support. Good fortune lead him to "Herr W—," who diagnosed his problem correctly.

He said that in his opinion the unfortunate position of my affairs arose from the fact that I had devoted myself with zeal merely to the acquisition of scientific knowledge, but had neglected the study of language, and therefore I was unable to communicate my knowledge to others, or make any use of it. Meanwhile, he thought, nothing had been lost by delay; and if I was still willing to accommodate myself to the circumstances, I could attain my object in the gymnasium at Altona, where his son was studying, while he would provide for my support. (257–58)

For the next two years, Maimon presented himself as an irregular student at the Altona institute for secular secondary education, during which time he acquired a firmer foundation in German. Upon his return to Berlin, he felt capable of undertaking an intellectual project and entered into the ill-fated translation referred to above.

Maimon finally broke into the publishing world with a German manuscript, a commentary, written in a style derived from *pilpul*, on Kant's *Critique of Pure Reason*. When Marcus Herz, a former pupil of Kant, sent him Maimon's commentary in 1789, the philosopher delivered the following verdict on the manuscript: "a glance soon enabled me to recognize its merits and to see not only that none of my opponents had understood me so well, but that very few could claim so much penetration and subtlety of mind in profound inquiries of this sort" (qtd. in Beiser 285). With this recommendation, Maimon was able to find a publisher for his work, and it appeared the following year under the title *Versuch über die Transcendentalphilosophie*. Then in 1791 Maimon published a *Philosophisches Worterbuch* [Philosophical Dictionary]. During the following two years, Maimon saw the publication of his *Lebensgeschichte*, and although he later published three more volumes of philosophical analysis, his autobiography outstripped his other writings in popularity. Goethe and Schiller read it with admiration and spoke of Maimon in their correspondence to one another. "Goethe was so fascinated by Maimon's heroic struggle that he invited him to Weimar. Maimon's life was regarded as an illustration of the struggle of the human will, of the freedom and sovereignty of the mind, of the capacity of the human spirit to overcome all obstacles to the attainment of intellectual preeminence" (Atlas 12).

But the Jewish community did not celebrate the appearance of the *Leben-*

sgeschichte. The "obstacles" overcome by Maimon's "human spirit" were the pillars and foundation of Jewish culture. Maimon wrote his autobiography in German for the same reason that any work of the Enlightenment had to appear in French, German, or English—even if its author were a Jew writing about Jews. Mendelssohn had already set that linguistic precedent in his *Jerusalem* (1783). As for his autobiography, Maimon "realized quite well that such a work in Hebrew would be like a voice crying in the wilderness; it would have no readers. Indeed more than a hundred years passed before his masterpiece was translated into Hebrew" (Zinberg, *Berlin Haskalah*, 30).

Yet, as testament to the tenacious hold of the ethnic intellectual's double allegiance, Maimon never stopped writing in Hebrew, even though most of his Hebrew works remained unpublished. Besides the mathematical work mentioned above, he also wrote a *Torat Ha-Teva*, expounding Newtonian science, a translation of Jacques Basnage's *Histoire des Juifs*,[9] and a translation of Mendelssohn's final book, *Morgenstuden*. In this regard, Maimon's double consciousness was representative of the maskil's desire to enlighten his fellow Jews in a language that was available to them. A younger generation of maskilim established an association in Kônigsberg called *Hevreat Doreshei Leshon Ever* [Society of Exponents of the Hebrew Language] for the purpose of producing a Hebrew monthly on the model of the popular *Berliner Montasschrift*. In September 1783 the first number of *Ha-Meassef* [The Collector] appeared, a journal which had an enormous influence in Germany and on the Galician Jewry of the nineteenth century.

> The literary value of *Ha-Meassef* for the three years that it appeared in Koenigsberg is . . . rather slight. Nevertheless it forms a whole epoch in neo-Hebrew literature. The very fact that there had appeared in the Jewish quarter a periodical of secular content in which are treated not questions of ritual cleanness and uncleanness, but in which the sun and the spring are celebrated, worldly issues are discussed, and newly published books are reviewed—this alone was a great event that stirred up the congealed way of life and brought a bit of fresh air into the stifling environment. (Zinberg, *Berlin Haskalah*, 86)

Although Maimon was skeptical that anything written in Hebrew would penetrate the rabbinical darkness he attributed to the Jewry outside of enlightened circles, he contributed a number of articles to the enterprise. One of these, "an exposition of an obscure passage in the commentary of Maimonides on the Mishnah, which I interpreted by the Kantian philosophy" (287), was put into German and inserted in the *Berlinsiche Monatsschrift*—the first piece of modern Hebrew writing to be translated for a European readership. As a result of this publication, the society responsible for the publication of *Ha-Meassef* invited Maimon to write a commentary on Maimonides' *More Nebhochim* [Guide for the Perplexed]. He accepted the task and produced the outstanding commentary *Giv'at Ha-More*, coming full circle to the book that had awakened his philosophical spirit and affirmed his rationalist bent. "Belatedly," Mendelssohn's biographer wrote, "Maimon had become a member of the group that formed the vanguard of Haskalah" (Altmann 364).

Out of the Babel of languages with which Maimon came into contact—Yiddish, Polish, Russian, Dutch, and French—he mastered only Hebrew and German in his writings. That he unwillingly became a German author late in life is a reflection of the linguistic shift that took place within the German haskalah itself. *Ha-Meassef* enjoyed a lifespan, from its founding in 1783, of less than ten years. When in 1794 an attempt was made to revive *Ha-Meassef*, one of its former editors, Isaac Euchel, an ardent lover of the holy tongue, refused to share the task because he was certain that there was no Hebrew-reading public left among the nonrabbinical German Jews. As he wrote in a letter to the maskil proposing the reestablishment of the magazine:

I have also tasted the cup of poison that has been poured out on the Jewish people and on its enlightened. Gone are the precious days, departed are the days of my covenant with the sons of Israel when the shoots of wisdom appeared and the Hebrew language bloomed in glory and splendor. Now they have fled and are no more. Woe, they will no longer return! Since they have decided in their hearts to say, "The whole earth is filled with science and knowledge," the language of their ancestors has become despicable to them and they have rejected it. (qtd. in Zinberg, *Berlin Haskalah*, 139)

Predictably, the successor to *Ha-Meassef* was a Jewish periodical in German that appeared in Leipzig in 1806. Though certain of the old *Meassef* group saw which way the wind was blowing, fully half a century passed before it was widely acknowledged that the ideology of the Berlin haskalah led not only to a wider participation in European culture, but to apostasy and assimilation. The new subjectivities expressed by the maskil's German and the ex-slave's English not only described their "premodern" worlds with ethnographic detachment, they adumbrated an initial, seemingly wholehearted acceptance of Enlightenment ideology that turned out to be, in the course of history, something of an illusion.

As with language, Black and Jewish intellectuals had to adopt some form of Western religion if they were to gain an audience among the eighteenth-century intelligentsia. However, these people came from societies with highly elaborate belief systems; they were not *tabula rasa* upon whom the West could write its various beliefs. In some cases, as with the West African religions, the old ways were either abandoned in favor of Christian forms of enthusiasm, or transformed into complex syncretic beliefs featuring Christian names and African spirits. (The former "solution" predominated in the literary expression of the first writers of the Black Atlantic, even though syncretism became the norm for most slaves who sought to bring religion into their lives.) In others, as with Judaism, the traditional belief system could be sufficiently wrenched to fit into an ecumenical Enlightenment mode.

The Jews of Germany formed an intermediate link between the traditional culture of eastern European Jewry, comprising half of Europe's Jews, and the cultures of the West. In 1770, Poland hosted the greatest number of Jews—800,000, or 9 percent of the country's inhabitants. Modernization had not yet touched Poland; the kingdom tottered under an antiquated feudal system. As Raphael Mahler writes: "The deterioration in the economic situation in Poland during the eighteenth century was bound up with its social system. The absolute subjugation of the peasants and the unbridled rule of the *szlachta* [the nobility] over the townsmen and the Jews were the main causes of the sharp economic, political and cultural decline. The closed manorial economy prevailing in western Europe at the beginning of the Middle Ages was a characteristic feature of Polish feudalism in the eighteenth century" (280). Under these circumstances, the struggle for physical survival dominated the lives of most Jews, yet the cultural ideal for the Jewish male was a life devoted to scholarship and study. It was a religious duty to educate one's son, as all Jewish males had to read a section of the Torah in the synagogue on the Sabbath. The link between the synagogue and the *chedar*—the Jewish "primary" school—took precedence over any desire to establish a pedagogically logical course of study or one that covered the practical matters of daily living. But even the *chedar,* an institution supposedly designed to serve the general public, was elitist in orientation. As Jacob Katz notes, "Familiarity with the Bible and training in Mishna were seen not as accomplishments in themselves but only as preparatory to the ultimate educational goal: creating a talmid hakham who had extensive knowledge of the Talmud and halakhic codes" (Katz, *Tradition and Crisis*, 163).

"[E]very Polish Jew is destined from his birth to be a rabbi," Maimon wrote, not without irony, "and only the greatest incapacity can exclude him from the office" (154). Following his prescribed destiny, Maimon did indeed become a rabbi, a Talmudic prodigy at the age of eleven, yet he died thirty-five years later as the charge of a Christian nobleman and was mockingly given an apostate's burial behind the fence of Glogau's Jewish cemetery. Though Maimon was seen in his lifetime and by later commentators as an extremist, hostile to orthodox Judaism, the views expressed in his autobiography reveal a much more complex attitude.

When Maimon displayed a love of drawing in his earliest years, his father rebuked him with these words: "You want to become a painter? You are to study the Talmud and become a rabbi. He who understands the Talmud understands everything" (26).

The Talmud, the authoritative code of rabbinic Jewish law since the Torah and its commentary, was the alpha and omega of Jewish daily life from its completion in the sixth century A.D. to its overthrow in segments of the Jewish community by the Reform Movement in the nineteenth. Interpreting the exigencies of daily life and bringing them into line with the precepts and spirit of the Talmud was the

highest occupation to which a man could devote himself, and all honor was be-
stowed upon those who chose it. As Maimon himself writes in an ethnographic
gloss on the society from which he came:

> The study of the Talmud is the chief object of a learned education among our people.
> Riches, bodily advantages, and talents of every kind have indeed in their eyes a certain
> worth, and are esteemed in proportion; but nothing stands among them above the dignity
> of a good Talmudist. He has the first claim upon all offices and positions of honour in the
> community. If he enters an assembly,—he may be of any age or rank,—every one rises be-
> fore him most respectfully, and the most honourable place is assigned to him. He is the
> director of the conscience, lawgiver and judge of the common man. He, who does not meet
> such a scholar with sufficient respect, is, according to the judgment of the Talmudists,
> damned to all eternity. The common man dare not enter upon the most trivial undertaking
> if, in the judgment of the scholar, it is not according to law. Religious usages, allowed and
> forbidden meats, marriage and divorce are determined not only by the rabbinical laws
> which have already accumulated to an enormous mass, but also by special rabbinical judg-
> ments which profess to deduce all special cases from general laws. A wealthy merchant,
> farmer or professional man, who has a daughter, does everything in his power to get a good
> Talmudist for his son-in-law. As far as other matters are concerned, the scholar may be as
> deformed, diseased, and ignorant as possible, he will still have the advantage over others.
> (43–44)

One can see from the tenor of his comments that Maimon had distanced himself
considerably from the common view expressed by his father that "He who understands the Talmud understands everything." But this was no sour-grapes mentality
on Maimon's part. As a child Talmudic prodigy he was viewed as such a desirable
matrimonial prospect that, through a complicated set of circumstances related in the
autobiography, he was simultaneously betrothed to two women and was kidnapped
one night by a prospective father-in-law. But, as Maimon writes, even though he had
attained an enviable position at an early age, "My life in Poland from my marriage to
my emigration, which period embraces the springtime of my existence, was a want of
all means for the promotion of culture, and necessarily connected with that, an aimless application of my powers, the description of which makes the pen drop from my
hands along with the painful memories I strive to stifle" (80).

What Maimon means by "culture," so sorely lacking, is philosophy, both natural
(as science was then called) and speculative. For religious illumination Maimon had
no feeling at all. There is no breath of mysticism in his autobiography, nor even an
indication that God is a part of his world. Insofar as the post of rabbi was an intellectual one, Maimon could excel, but as far as spiritual enlightenment was concerned, Maimon was as dull in this area as he claimed his coreligionists to be in
logic. Specialists in the field of Jewish studies will recognize that Heinrich Graetz is
parti pris, but in his famous *History of the Jews*, he writes as if this lack of religious
feeling was endemic to the whole tradition in which Maimon had been raised.

Rabbinical Judaism, as known in Poland, offered no sort of religious comfort. Its representatives placed the highest value upon the dialectic, an artificial exposition of the Talmud and its commentaries. Actual necessity had besides caused that portion of the Talmud which treated of civil law to be closely studied, as the rabbis exercised civil jurisdiction over their flocks. Fine-spun decisions of new, complicated legal points occupied the doctors of the Talmud day and night. Moreover, this hair-splitting was considered the sublimest piety and superseded everything else. If any one solved an intricate Talmudic question, or discovered something new, called Torah, he felt self-satisfied, and assured of his felicity hereafter. All other objects, the impulse to devotion, prayer, and emotion, or interest in the moral condition of the community, were secondary matters, to which scarcely any attention was paid. The mental exercise of making logical deductions from the Talmud, or more correctly from the laws of Mine and Thine, choked all other intellectual pursuits in Poland. Religious ceremonies had degenerated, both amongst the Talmudists and the unlearned, into meaningless usages, and prayer into mere lip-service. (5:385)

Both worlds—of the Cabbalah and of the Chassidim—to which Maimon's intellectual curiosity led him proved unsatisfactory: the Cabbalists could not abide the intrusion of reason, and the Chassidim fell short of the piety they claimed for themselves.

Given his upbringing, however, Maimon could hardly escape religious influence; and in one instance at least this provided a tiller to his aimlessly wandering bark. Although Maimon became a skeptic, this did not happen overnight. As he himself declared, "In my youth I was of a somewhat strong religious disposition" (132). Nor did his occasional contacts with science immediately rid him of superstition. During his flirtation with the Cabbalah, he believed that his master in the subject could teach him the trick of invisibility. When he twice failed in this, he was told by his master that he was "unfit for being thus divested" (102). "This disappointed hope was followed by a new delusion. In the preface to the Book of Raphael, which the angel of that name is said to have delivered to our first father Adam at his banishment from paradise, I found that promise, that whoever keeps the book in his house is thereby insured against fire. It was not long, however, before a conflagration broke out in the neighborhood, when the fire seized my house too, and the angel Raphael himself had to go up into heaven in this chariot of fire" (103).

Yet even at this early stage, a judgment passed upon the actions themselves, viewed for themselves and not for the ends they presumably served, gave Maimon a critical perspective his peers seemed to lack. "It is remarkable, that at the time when I still observed the rabbinical regulations with the utmost strictness, I yet would not observe certain ceremonies which have something comical about them" (135). As with Spinoza and Mendelssohn, Maimon's intellect sought out logic and philosophy in his environment; and like his two predecessor philosophers, he found Maimonides' *Guide for the Perplexed* to be the first great signpost at the beginning of that road. The twelfth-century thinker composed his *Guide* in an attempt to reconcile faith and logic, Judaism and philosophy. "The design of the work," he wrote in his introduction, "is rather to promote understanding of the real spirit of the Law, to guide those religious persons who, adhering to the Torah, have studied philosophy and are embarrassed by the contradictions between the teachings of philosophy and the literal sense of the Torah" (qtd. in Minkin 116).

Curiously enough, Maimon does not mention his first encounter with this great work, though its influence on him was profound enough to last his lifetime. Not only did he compose Hebrew articles and commentaries on the writings of Maimonides, as we saw above, but the first ten chapters of the *Lebensgeschichte*'s second volume are wholly occupied with a commentary on the *Guide*—a huge chunk of discursive flotsam in the narrative stream. Most significantly, Solomon Maimon substituted his given patronymic, ben Joshua, for that of his intellectual idol, also called Moses ben Maimon. As the disciple himself writes:

> My reverence for this great teacher went so far, that I regarded him as the ideal of a perfect man, and looked upon his teachings as if they had been inspired with Divine Wisdom itself. This went so far, that, when my passions began to grow, and I had sometimes to fear lest they might seduce me to some action inconsistent with those teachings, I used to employ, as a proven antidote, the abjuration, "I swear, by the reverence which I owe my great teacher, Rabbi Moses ben Maimon, not to do this act." And this vow, so far as I can remember, was always sufficient to restrain me. (xiv, note)

In fact, it was partially his enthusiasm for the *Guide* that brought about Maimon's initial failure to gain entry to Berlin. For its own protection, Berlin's Jewish community took it upon itself to turn away beggars and other Jewish "undesirables." After an arduous journey of two months, Maimon arrived at the Rosenthaler gate carrying a commentary on the *Guide* that he had composed in Poland. Entering into a conversation with a rabbi he met at the gate, Maimon naively told him about his life in Poland, revealed to him his reasons for coming to Berlin, and showed him his commentary on the *Guide*. Alas, he had chosen the wrong man.

> The rabbi, of whom I spoke, was a zealot in his orthodoxy. Accordingly when he had discovered my sentiments and purposes, he went into town, and informed the elders about my heretical mode of thinking. He told them I was going to issue a new edition of the *Moreh Nebhochim* with a commentary, and that my intention was not so much to study medicine, but mainly to devote myself to the sciences in general, and to extend my knowledge. This the orthodox Jews look upon as something dangerous to religion and good morals. (194)

When the elders came that evening to question the Jewish newcomers about their motives for entering Berlin, Maimon was refused permission point blank. Then followed one of the most remarkable periods of a remarkable life: for nearly half a year Maimon allied himself with a Jewish beggar and lived as a wandering vagrant. "I was an educated rabbi; he was an idiot" (97). As an educated man, Maimon had alternatives. Polish rabbis were held in high esteem by the German Jewish communities. The Polish rabbinical method of study had long dominated the Talmudic schools of Germany and Italy through the abundant literature produced by Polish authors. Disseminated by the fugitives from the Cossack massacres of the seventeenth century, this method had established its supremacy amongst the orthodox. Even with his linguistic deficiencies, Maimon could have obtained a position as a scholar or family tutor. Yet he chose to plunge himself into the deepest degradation. The reasons for this can only be speculated on; as is typical of his narrative, Maimon doesn't reveal much of his psychological motivation.

Eventually he does deliver himself from the self-imposed mortification, religious feeling, in this one instance, acting as a positive influence.

> When we arrived in Posen we took up our quarters in the Jewish poorhouse, the master of which was a poor jobbing tailor. Here I formed the resolve, at whatever cost, to bring my wandering to a close. It was harvest-time, and already began to be pretty cool. I was almost naked and barefoot. By this vagrant life, in which I never got any regular meals, for the most part had to content myself with bits of moldy bread and water, and at night was obliged to lie on old straw, sometimes even on the bare earth, my health had seriously suffered. Besides, the sacred seasons and fast-days in the Jewish calendar were coming on; and as at that time I was of a somewhat strong religious disposition, I could not endure the thought of passing in complete idleness this period which others employed for the welfare of their souls. (198–99)

During the next two years, Maimon not only obtained a place of honor as a tutor in a wealthy house, he was recognized by the Posen scholars as a man of unusual learning and ability.

> This period was undoubtedly the happiest and most honourable in my life. The young scholars of the town passed a resolution at their meeting to make up for me a salary, for which I was to deliver lectures to them on the celebrated and profound work of Maimonides, *Moreh Nebhochim*. This proposal, however, was never carried out, because the parents of these young people were anxious lest their children should be thereby led astray, and by independent thinking on religion be made to waver in their faith. They acknowledged indeed that, with all my fondness for religious speculation, I was still a pious man and an orthodox rabbi. But they could not rely upon their children having sufficient judgment, to be able to enter upon this course without passing from one extreme to the other, from superstition to unbelief, and therein perhaps they were right. (205)

Certainly this road, from superstition to unbelief, was one on which the rabbi was making his journey. The credulity of the Jewish populace excited his contempt, and he openly mocked the story of a talking carp circulating about town.

> Having by this time emancipated myself pretty thoroughly from superstitions of this sort by diligent study of the *Moreh Nebhochim*, I laughed heartily over the story, and said,

that, if instead of burying the carp, they had sent it to me, I should have tried how such an inspired carp would taste.

This *bon mot* became known. The learned men fell into a passion about it, denounced me as a heretic, and sought to persecute me in every way. But the respect entertained for me in the house where I was tutor, made all their efforts fruitless. As I found myself in this way safe, and the spirit of fanaticism, instead of deterring me, rather spurred me on to further reflection, I began to push matters a little farther, frequently slept through the time of prayer, went seldom to synagogue, and so on. (208)

The apostate's turn results from the conflict between the inner compulsion to pursue rationalism and the outer one dictating conformity to the prevailing beliefs of the community. As orthodox pressure is brought to bear in greater measure, so Maimon's desire for enlightenment grows, to the point where he abandons his position in Posen for an uncertain future. "This fanaticism stirred up in me the desire to go to Berlin, and destroy by enlightenment the remnant of superstition which still clung to me" (209).

The Berlin of the 1780s that Maimon entered (successfully this time, due to having arrived by coach) was by now the center of a growing conflict between the promoters of the haskalah and the rabbinate. When the mild and credulous but otherwise orthodox Naftali Wesseley published a Hebrew letter in 1782 urging that all Jewish youths be taught history, geography, the natural sciences, and philosophy, the synagogues echoed with imprecations against him, and in Lissa his letter was publicly burned. Many maskilim tried to avoid conflict by breaking, often privately, with the orthodox tradition. Nonetheless they were still Jews—Prussian society certainly viewed them as such—and they had to forge a new identity within that context. As Eisenstein-Barzilay writes in his lucid essay, their views on religion in general and on Judaism in particular were shaped by three major influences: the Enlightenment, Moses Mendelssohn, and the emancipationist aspirations of the post-Mendelssohn generation (49).

"Enlightenment is man's exodus from his self-incurred tutelage," Kant wrote in a popular essay published in 1784. "Tutelage is the inability to use one's understanding without the guidance of another person. This tutelage is self-incurred if its cause lies not in any weakness of the understanding, but in indecision and lack of courage to use the mind without the guidance of another. *Sapere aude!* Have the courage to use your own understanding; this is the motto of the Enlightenment" (qtd. in Cassirer 163).

Given this self-definition, religious orthodoxy, which depended on tradition and authority to maintain its position, was understandably hostile to the spirit of the Enlightenment—and the feeling was mutual. Following the seventeenth-century lead of Bayle and Spinoza, the *philosophes* placed the Scriptures themselves against the yardstick of rationalism, morality, and historical accuracy and found them wanting. They abhorred dogma as tutelage to an insufficient authority. These men and women were not unbelievers but believers in a "natural religion" whose principles were accessible to all who employed reason. It was the exercise of reason that emancipated the eighteenth-century intellectuals from the dogma of the ruling class and the superstition of the masses. The *philosophes* considered philosophy and natural religion to be sisters, if not one and the same. In his chapter on Mendelssohn, Maimon "assents" to the former's assertion that "a Jew cannot, by simply passing over to the Christian religion, free himself from the laws of his own religion, because Jesus of Nazareth observed these laws himself and commanded his followers to observe them. But how, if a Jew wishes to be no longer a member of this theocratic state, and goes over to the heathen religion, or to the philosophical, which is nothing more than pure natural religion?" (230). This was clearly the road Maimon had traveled. Once in Berlin, he discovered speculative philosophy, and revealed religion fell from him like a tattered garment that has lost its last button.

In Western Europe the Enlightenment widened the cleavage between the official bodies of priests and ministers and the loose assembly of lay thinkers intent on establishing the authority of reason. These latter represented the ideas of the rising middle class, and they frequently occupied positions outside the aristocracy. By the same token, the writers of the Berlin haskalah also came from elements that would soon wrest control of Judaism from the rabbinate: physicians like Aaron Gumperz and Marcus Herz; merchants and businessmen like Moses Mendelssohn, Naftali Wesseley, and David Friedländer; pedagogues and school inspectors like Herz Homberg and Aaron Wolfson-Halle; even rabbis "infected with heresy," such as Solomon Maimon and Saul Berlin.

If tolerance was a shared principle among the *philosophes*, it did not arise so much out of the spirit of live-and-let-live as from the suspicion that all revealed religions were equally false—or equally true, if one remembers Lessing's parable of the rings in *Nathan the Wise*. Tolerance among the enlightened allowed Jews access to their company and approbation well before emancipation came about. And of all the intellectual activities of the eighteenth century, philosophy was not only the most revered and widely admired, but also the one most congenial to the training received by Jewish boys with their eyes upon the rabbinate. For all his varied literary activity, Mendelssohn achieved his greatest renown with a book of philosophical dialogues. However, not all nations philosophized in the same manner. Mendelssohn passed his own judgment upon their differences when he wrote that "the French philosophize with wit, the English with sentiment, and the Germans alone are sufficiently sober to philosophize with the intellect" (qtd. in Altmann 31). What one of Mendelssohn's later biographers wrote of him held equally true for Solomon Maimon and Marcus Herz, Kant's chosen "respondent" at the defense of his Inaugural Dissertation in 1770. "It seems that his thorough training in Talmud had so disciplined his mind that only a philosophy of the German type, a philosophy involving subtle distinctions and penetrating to the core of a problem, was able to satisfy him" (Altmann 31). Thus arose one of the many ironies of German Jewish history: that nation which in its civic treatment of the Jews proved one of the most intractable and anti-Semitic in Western Europe created in its intellectual life the first stage on which Jews could play to the rest of the world. Mendelssohn's *Phaedon* and Maimon's *Lebensgeschichte* were widely recognized as products of Enlightenment culture.

Mendelssohn, of course, bestrode both the *Aufklärung* and the haskalah. "From Moses to Moses there is none like Moses," the maskilim said of their leader, echoing a phrase that had originally been applied to Maimonides. Mendelssohn was unquestionably the central figure of the Berlin haskalah—Maimon devotes a whole chapter to him—but there was a fatal cleavage between his orthodox religious practice and his enlightened religious thought. "Instead of a synthesis," writes Raphael Mahler, "Mendelssohn merely produced a delineation of Judaism and humanity as two apparently separate provinces" (155). The consequences of this dichotomy, a characteristic product of double consciousness, could be measured by the suspicion he occasionally aroused in orthodox circles and by the indifference of his younger disciples to maintaining religious practices.

In spite of the fact that Mendelssohn brought honor to the Jews as a critic, philosopher, and defender of his people, he barely escaped condemnation from the more conservative element of the rabbinate. When he published a prospectus and sample translation of the Pentateuch in 1778, several rabbis regarded this new bridge to German culture with alarm. The fanatical Raphael Cohen of Hamburg even proposed placing the translation under a ban until Mendelssohn managed to have the king of Denmark, who then had sovereignty over Hamburg, sign up as a subscriber. The biblical scholar and Hebrew philologist Solomon Dubno originally collaborated with Mendelssohn in the enterprise, writing for his edition of the Pentateuchal text a commentary (*Biur*). However, after being reproached by the teacher of his youth, rabbi Naftali Herz, for "working with men whose entire thought is to uproot the Oral Torah," Dubno broke with Mendelssohn's circle and left Berlin (Zinberg, *Berlin Haskalah*, 44).

Mendelssohn's attitude concerning violations of the Law by some of his close friends and disciples was nonchalant. Two of the latter, Herz Homberg and David Friedländer, excited great antipathy among the orthodox. Mendelssohn appointed Homberg tutor to his son Joseph until 1782, when Homberg left Berlin for Vienna. Joseph II of Austria had just published his Edict of Toleration, and Homberg returned to his native land in the expectation of obtaining a government post, now open to Jews. As inspector of Austria's Jewish normal schools, he revealed himself a bitter enemy of rabbinical Judaism. "Taking the position that traditional Judaism consists only of 'prejudices' and that the government is the radiant bearer of progress, Homberg considered it necessary to carry through 'enlightenment' among Jews by coercive methods" (*Berlin Haskalah*, 109).

Friedländer, a year older than Homberg and formerly a student of Kant, came to Berlin in 1771, when he was twenty-one and Mendelssohn forty-two.

> Friedländer continued to cultivate his friendly relationship with Kant but it was Mendelssohn whose devotee, disciple, and friend he became. Among Mendelssohn's many admirers none was so deeply and unreservedly attached to him as David Friedländer, and Mendelssohn responded with equal warmth. It was to Friedländer that Mendelssohn would reminisce about his early childhood, and it would not have been surprising if he had appointed Friedländer his literary executor, had he appointed anyone. (Zinberg, *Berlin Haskalah*, 44)

Yet thirteen years after Mendelssohn's death, Friedländer authored the Teller Letter, in which he and his association of like-minded maskilim offered to assume the Christian faith—on condition that they be permitted not to recognize the divine birth of Christ.

Maimon was one of the first to discern the contradiction between Mendelssohn's religious practice and thought. "As far as is known," he wrote, "Mendelssohn lived in accordance with the laws of his religion" (230). Concerning Mendelssohn's real sentiments, Maimon candidly confesses his ignorance. "Mendelssohn was unable to hold any conversation with me on the subject," lest Maimon accuse the famous philosopher of hypocrisy (229). "For at that time, as an incipient freethinker, I explained all revealed religion as in itself false, and its use, so far as the writings of Mendelssohn had enabled me to understand it, as merely temporary" (228).

The element in Mendelssohn's religious writings that allowed his interpreters comfortably to pass over to freethinking and conversion from Judaism was Deism, the great religious dogma of the *Aufklärung*. Deistic thinking—the belief in a rational God and in a religious practice founded on natural reason rather than on supernatural revelation—had been most prominent in the England of the late seventeenth and early eighteenth centuries. There it approached the status of a movement through the writings of Lord Herbert of Cherbury, John Toland, and Matthew Tindal. What had been radical for England in the early eighteenth century was far less so for Germany fifty years later, familiar now with the atheistic tendencies of French materialism. With the exception of a handful of self-proclaimed "Spinozists," who misread the philosopher's pantheism as atheism, the *Aufklärer* were satisfied with the moderate heresy of Deism. Not only Mendelssohn but Lessing and Kant were prominent believers in a Supreme Being apprehendable by any rational mind. The limits of *Aufklärer* acceptance of religion also defined the parameters of haskalah. "It is true that I recognize no eternal verities except those which can not only be comprehended by the human intellect but also be demonstrated and verified by man's reason" (Zinberg, *Berlin Haskalah*, 44). Mendelssohn wrote in *Jerusalem* (1783) of his advocacy for tolerance and rationality in religious matters. When Maimon spoke his final piece to the Lutheran pastor whom he would have made his instrument of Christian conversion, his words could have issued from Mendelssohn's mouth. "I must confess, Herr Pastor, that I am not qualified for Christianity. Whatever light I may receive, I shall always make it luminous with the light of reason. I shall never believe that I have fallen upon new truths, if it is impossible to see their connection with the truths already known to me. I must therefore remain what I am,—a stiffnecked Jew. My religion enjoins me to *believe* nothing, but to *think* the truth and to *practise* goodness" (256–57).

Mendelssohn would have added one other crucial element: Moses had revealed to the Jews "in a miraculous and supernatural way" the laws and commandments they were to follow, but this "divine legislation" was not to be construed as or confused with "dogmas, propositions concerning salvation, or self-evident principles of reason" (Mendelssohn 61). These latter were the property of all men. In fact, insofar as, according to the Deistic version, Judaism had no dogmas, only law, it was truer to the spirit of humanity than Christianity was. How can I believe, Mendelssohn slyly asked the hereditary prince of Braunschweig-Wolfenbuttel, in a threefold deity who imposes suffering and death on the Son for the satisfaction and gratification of the Father (123)?

For all his pride in maintaining his Judaism, however ("Love for the religion of our fathers is stronger than death and misery," he wrote to the Swiss scholar Charles Bonnet[10]), Mendelssohn had to suffer the same indignities and civil disabilities as his more obscure coreligionists. "The laws of Saxony place in the same category the educated Jews of Berlin and Polish oxen," he remarked in 1776 after having paid a head tax to the city of Dresden in order to gain entry (qtd. in Waxman 3:59). Even after the resounding success of his *Phaedon*, when Mendelssohn was proposed for the Berlin Academy of Sciences, King Frederick struck his name from the list. Throughout the myriad states and principalities that made up Germany, the Jews groaned under a burden of imposed social and civic inferiority. They could not buy real estate; they could not engage in agriculture; their movements were restricted; they lived within ghetto walls; they bore the imposition of special taxes; many could not marry without the permission of German authorities. They were in every respect second-class citizens and victims of social opprobrium. Escape from Judaism was not only a flight from legal discrimination but a movement toward social acceptability.

The contrast between the legal status of the Jewish masses, who had no rights at all, and the position that the Jewish bourgeoisie occupied in the economy of the state and its social and cultural life was more striking in Prussia than anywhere else. As the gap widened, the bourgeoisie endeavored to withdraw further and further away from their miserable and despised lower middle class co-religionists and to strengthen their foothold in the culture and way of life of the German ruling classes. (Mahler 207)

Enlightened Catholics and Protestants welcomed Jews to their new religion. Caught, as they perceived it, between an ossified rabbinism and an enlightened Christianity, scores of rich and cultivated Jews shed the religion of their fathers with little regret. ("A baptismal certificate is the ticket of admission to European culture," Heinrich Heine wrote in the nineteenth century.) The rush to assimilation ravaged Mendelssohn's own family after his death. Dorothea Mendelssohn, his oldest daughter and wife of the Jewish industrialist David Veit, eloped with Friedrich Schlegel, consented to baptism as a Protestant in order to marry him, then converted with him four years later to Catholicism. She also succeeded in converting her two sons from her previous marriage, even though their father begged her to desist. Henriette Mendelssohn was also proselytized by her older sister, and she too joined the ranks of the faithful, vying with Dorothea in her devotion to Catholicism. Mendelssohn's second son, Abraham, raised his children as Christians, because, as he wrote to his famous son Felix, "while truth is one and eternal, its forms are many and transient." "Naturally when you consider what scant value I placed on any form in particular, I felt no urge to choose Judaism, that most antiquated, distorted, and self-defeating form of all. Therefore I reared you as Christians, Christianity being the more purified form and the one most accepted by the majority of civilized people" (qtd. in Wener 37).

Like Abraham, many abandoned Judaism not because they were spiritually drawn to Christianity but out of intellectual conviction, convinced that the Jewish Deism espoused by Mendelssohn and other maskilim allowed them to accept any enlightened form of religion. In 1799 David Friedländer applied to the head of the Consistory of Berlin for admission to the Christian faith, since the position of his associates—outside of believing in the divinity of Jesus—conformed to the position of the Church. "There is one God, there is one soul, and men were created to become happy" (Zinberg, *Berlin Haskalah*, 116). Pastor Teller, however, balked at accepting "converts" who craved a Christianity without Christ, and rejected the proposal. Friedländer remained a Jew, but his children pressed forward to be baptized without conditions.

Friedländer might have spared himself the ignominy of the Teller Letter with which, in Jewish history, his name is indissolubly linked had he read Maimon's *Lebensgeschichte*, which had appeared six years earlier. Exiled from Berlin, the closest thing he would know of an earthly paradise, and caught in the linguistic trap described above, Solomon Maimon despaired. Ill-housed, hungry, and aimless, the philosopher resolved to convert to Christianity. He then composed one of the haughtiest "confessions of faith" of all time. He was guilty as a Jew, he wrote, of loving knowledge for its own sake.

> But as our nation is unable to use, not only such planless studies, but even those conducted on the most perfect plan, it cannot be blamed for becoming tired of them, and pronouncing their encouragement to be useless. I have therefore resolved in order to secure temporal as well as eternal happiness, which depends on the attainment of perfection, and in order to become useful to myself as well as others, to embrace the Christian religion. The Jewish religion, it is true, comes, in its articles of faith, nearer to reason than Christianity. But in practical use the latter has an advantage over the former. . . . (254–55)

The "prominent clergyman" to whom this letter was given immediately divined its purpose.

"So," he said, "I see your intention is to embrace the Christian religion, merely in order to improve your temporal circumstances" (256).

Not exactly, Maimon explained. "[M]y object is the attainment of perfection."

"But," asked the pastor, "do you not feel any inclination of the soul to the Christian religion without reference to any external motives?"

"I should be telling a lie," replied truth-loving Maimon, "if I were to give you an affirmative answer."

"You are too much of a philosopher," said the pastor, "to be able to become a Christian."

Solomon Maimon, David Friedländer, and, in her own tormented way, Rahel Varnhagen remained Jews out of an inability to embrace Christianity—an unwillingness, on some unarticulated level, to relinquish their Jewish identity.

During his first stay in Berlin, the rabbi Solomon lost the remainder of his religiosity. Speculative philosophy eclipsed Jewish religion completely. Wolff led to Mendelssohn, who gave way to Spinoza, who yielded to Kant. By the time he wrote his autobiography, Maimon was an Enlightenment philosopher and, by extension, a deist. And, as it happened, the Jewish patriarchs, when properly understood, held the same beliefs as he. "Moses, as well as the prophets who followed him sought constantly to inculcate that the end of religion is not external ceremonies, but the knowledge of the true God as the sole incomprehensible cause of all things, and the practice of virtue in accordance with the prescriptions of reason" (184).

As Israel Zinberg and Isaac Eisenstein-Barzilay have noted, Maimon was more balanced in his estimate of Judaism than many other proponents of the Berlin haskalah. In his autobiography he not only praises rabbinical morals but justifies Jewish theology and even defends the rabbinical deduction of the laws (123–31). In this he displays a historical sense and cultural relativism—a legacy of Maimonides—that puts him in stark contrast to other maskilim. Yet he can be devastatingly critical in his analysis of Jewish society.

For since the nation is divided into such unequal classes as the common people and the learned, and since the former, owing to the unfortunate political condition of the nation, are profoundly ignorant, not only of all useful arts and sciences, but even of the laws of their religion on which their eternal welfare is supposed to depend, it follows that the exposition of Scripture, the deduction of religious laws from it, and the application of these to particular cases, must be surrendered wholly to the learned class which the other undertakes the cost of maintaining. The learned class seek to make up for their want of linguistic science and rational exegetics by their own ingenuity, wit, and acuteness. (286)

Solomon Maimon opted out of the Jewish nation. He no longer subscribed to its belief system nor observed its laws. It was, in his eyes, a theocratic state he could choose to abandon. "The fundamental laws of the Jewish religion are at the same time the fundamental laws of the Jewish state. They must therefore be obeyed by all who acknowledge themselves to be members of this state, and who wish to enjoy the rights granted to them under condition of their obedience. But, on the other hand, any man who separates himself from this state, who desires to be considered no longer a member of it, and to renounce all his rights as such, whether he enters another state or betakes himself to solitude, is also in his conscience no longer bound to obey those laws" (229).

Yet Maimon could not abandon his identification with the Jews. He dedicated his first published work, *Versuch über die Transcendental-Philosophie*, to the King of Poland with the sentiment that he would deem himself fortunate if, through his authorship, he could help "give the noble Poles a good opinion of my nation, namely the Jews who live under your protection" (qtd. in Daiches 161). Not surprisingly, the *Lebensgeschichte* is shot through with ambivalence concerning a self-perceived Jewish identity: Maimonides remains a culture hero, and his follower and namesake Maimon consistently refers to the Jewish people as *meine Nation* or *unsere Nation*. Such ambivalence was to echo throughout the tortured career of Judeo-German literature. Small wonder that this same culture produced such great artists and theorists of alienation as Kafka, Freud, and Marx. In his own half-conscious way, Solomon Maimon was their forefather.

Coming to the West not from the inside, as with the Jews, but from the outside, Africans experienced Western religions much more as an assault on their belief systems. Christianity had, after all, accepted the Jewish Pentateuch as a valid (if now superseded) Old Testament. If Mendelssohn was challenged, as an enlightened intellectual, to explain why he didn't embrace Christianity, he had an answer that could satisfy the more liberal *Aufklärer*. African religions, by contrast, had no validity at all; they were only fit for the dustbin. Nonetheless, in spite of the West's ignorance, Africans venerated their own deities, practiced their own forms of worship, narrated their own etiologies. Some African gods—Yoruba's Ogun, for example—traveled across the Atlantic and survived in the slave religions of the Caribbean and

Latin America. Equiano, at pains to disabuse his reader of the notion that African religion consisted of childish superstition, describes the beliefs of his people in his opening chapter.

> As to religion, the natives believe that there is one Creator of all things, and that he lives in the sun, and is girted round with a belt; that he may never eat or drink, but, according to some, he smokes a pipe, which is our own favorite luxury. They believe he governs events, especially our deaths or captivity; but, as for the doctrine of eternity, I do not remember to have ever heard of it; some, however, believe in the transmigration of souls in a certain degree. Those spirits which were not transmigrated, such as their dear friends or relations, they believe always attend them, and guard them from the bad spirits or their foes. For this reason they always, before eating, as I have observed, put some small portion of the meat, and pour some of their drink, on the ground for them; and they often make oblations of the blood of beasts or fowls at their graves. (19)

Equiano goes on to delineate various ceremonies, offerings, and purifications, as well as the place and powers of the Esseke priests and magicians, portraying a belief system that was, in its sophistication, far from the stupid idolatry often ascribed to African religions by the arrogant West. Much of his description would be recognizable to present-day Africans. Indeed Equiano himself relates how the supernatural method of discovering a murderer was "still used by the Negroes in the West Indies" (21).

The Africans transported to Britain's North American colonies could not maintain their connection to their homeland. Cut off from fellow Africans who possessed a common language and culture, slaves were forced to acquire the language and culture of the new environment as quickly as possible. The transformation of African elements in slave culture insured that Black culture in North America would metamorphose into something new—with residual African features, to be sure, but a culture growing out of and suited to the different American colonies. During the seventeenth and eighteenth centuries, American slavery could still be a kind of continuous indentured service, with the master required to provide proper food and care for his slaves. Over time, slavery as an institution degenerated to the familiar nineteenth-century plantation system, where the owner was complete master and the slave was bound for life with few legal rights and protections. During the colonial period, however, in the cities both North and South, the slaves worked as household servants (e.g., Briton Hammon, Phillis Wheatley, and Ukawsaw Gronniosaw), farm hands, and laborers in commerce and industry. To the south of Maryland the slaves were plantation hands, and their lot was much harder. Still, except for the plantation areas, slavery was milder than it later became as far as restrictions and punishments were concerned. Slaves who worked in close communion with their White masters, particularly in the North, often adopted their religions. Apart from these urban slaves, however, few Blacks converted to Christianity prior to the American revolution. The established congregations, mostly of the Church of England, were not evangelically minded, nor were they much concerned for the spiritual welfare of Blacks and Indians. Furthermore, the difficulties of travel made it hard for the few ministers to serve their own members, let alone to seek out new converts. And, among the recent "immigrants" from Africa, few had a sufficient grasp of English to understand the sermons, even had they the opportunity to attend. In most cases, the masters were indifferent or hostile to exposing their slaves to Christianity.

The picture changed, however, with the coming of the Methodists, Baptists, and Presbyterians. These groups, aspiring to preach the Gospel to every creature, actively sought salvation for the slave's soul, often leading to a concern for his or her earthly welfare as well. Most active among the evangelical bodies that proselytized during the colonial period were the Methodists.

Methodism, founded in the eighteenth century by John Wesley, was a drive for a renewed holiness within the Church of England. John Wesley and his brother Charles lived and died as priests of the Anglican Church, even though the growing popularity of their movement brought criticism and ostracism from other Anglicans. Through such radical techniques as open-air preaching and strenuous evangelism among the poor, Methodism, once founded, gained an impressive number of converts in England and the Americas. Even though, as David Hempton asserts, Wesley "became one of the most eclectic churchmen in history," his religious crisis of 1738 turned into the foundational model of early Methodism (116). Harry Richardson, historian of the Black church in America, describes it thus:

It included, first, a conviction of sin and a sense of guilt; secondly, faith in the possibility of divine forgiveness through the merits and death of Jesus Christ, who died that men might be saved; and thirdly, a feeling of justification or divine pardon for previous sins and failings. The feeling of forgiveness always came in a joyous, releasing, transporting experience that confirmed to the repentant sinner that he was forgiven, and therefore was an heir to life eternal.

This was the "experimental" or experiential form of faith characteristic of Methodism. It was simple, personal, and direct. It required no mediation on the part of priests, and very little liturgical or sacramental accompaniment. It was well suited to the unlettered and rough masses of the colonies, and it was especially suited to the illiterate and oppressed slaves. (39)

Methodism was also well suited to British who were suffering the adverse effects of the industrial revolution: the neglected masses of the declining rural areas and the nascent proletariat of the new towns and mining areas. As Elie Halévy points out in his influential essay, "The Birth of Methodism in England," Wesley adopted his most successful evangelistic technique, open-air preaching, from two Welsh evangelizers, Griffith Jones and Howell Harris, who worked the mining areas of

South Wales. It was George Whitefield, another founder of Methodism, who began open-air preaching near Bristol among the miners of Kingswood.

Whitefield played a prominent role in both Great Britain and the North American colonies. His career illustrates the importance of a "white Atlantic" that exists alongside Gilroy's Black Atlantic. Whitefield became the most powerful and popular preacher in America, participating in the colonial religious revival known as the Great Awakening. A gifted orator, Whitefield traveled up and down the colonies sermonizing to masses numbering at times in the tens of thousands. He often preached to Blacks, and many were converted under his influence. Equiano remembers hearing Whitefield preach, "sweating as much as ever I did while in slavery on Montserrat-beach," in Philadelphia in early 1766,[11] commenting dryly further on: "I had never seen divines exert themselves in this manner before; and was no longer at a loss to account for the thin congregations they preached to" (97).

Indeed, Whitefield became a topos of early Black writing. Gronniosaw professed to have known Whitefield both as a preacher and as friend to his master, Theodorus Frelinghuysen, another seminal figure in the Great Awakening. Marrant claimed his spectacular conversion resulted directly from the preaching of Whitefield, whom he had gone to see in the spirit of derision. The poem that first brought Phillis Wheatley to public attention was an elegy, "On the Death of the Reverend George Whitefield. 1770." Casting his speech into heroic couplets, Wheatley has the Reverend Whitefield urge the acceptance of Christ on sinners, preachers, Americans in general, and lastly, the Blacks, for whom such acceptance confers dignity and status.

> *"Take him, ye Africans, he longs for you,*
> *"Impartial Saviour is his title due:*
> *"Wash'd in the fountain of redeeming blood,*
> *"You shall be sons, and kings, and priests to God."*

The dissident sects of the eighteenth century offered Black men and women an alternative scale of values, one in which what counted was the state of one's soul, not education, birthright, material wealth, or place of origin. Methodists, like other Protestant sects of the time, believed in the common depravity of all humanity. In a "Letter to the Inhabitants of Virginia and Maryland . . ." (1740), Whitefield wrote: "Think you that your children are any better by nature than the poor Negroes? No, in no wise. Blacks are just as much and no more, conceived and born in sin, as White Men are" (qtd. in Sandiford 53). Although some Whites feared that the spiritual enfranchisement of Blacks might translate into expectations of political emancipation, Whitefield approved of slavery and was instrumental in getting the institution introduced into Georgia for the benefit of his orphanage there. To quote again from Richardson: "[Whitefield] felt that slavery was good for the African. It gave the African . . . a chance for a much higher life than he could have had in his native, 'savage,' state. Some slaves were able to get educations. But above all, the African, though a slave, got the chance to hear the Gospel and to be saved, and thus to attain eternal life. This great good, eternal life and blessedness, transcended all earthly conditions and sufferings in Whitefield's view" (9).

The earliest Black writers in English—Briton Hammon, Jupiter Hammon, Ukawsaw Gronniosaw, and Phillis Wheatley—concur with these views. There is nothing in their writings that condemns slavery but everything that points to gratitude for God's providence. One of Wheatley's most famous poems expresses this sentiment precisely.

On Being Brought from Africa to America

'Twas mercy brought me from my Pagan land,
Taught my benighted soul to understand
That there's a God, that there's a Saviour too:
Once I redemption neither sought nor knew.
Some view our sable race with scornful eye,
"Their colour is a diabolic die."
Remember, Christians, Negroes, *black as Cain,*
May be refin'd, and join th' angelic train.

Wesleyan Methodism offered an alternative to Whitefield's proslavery views. Wesley fought against slavery all his life. In 1772, after reading Anthony Benezet's work on the Africans of Guinea, Wesley wrote the celebrated pamphlet *Thoughts Upon Slavery*, in which he declared that there could never be any justification for the brutality of the slave trade. Though the Methodism in the slave-holding colonies followed a different trajectory, Methodists in England and the free labor colonies moved toward a more uncompromising position. "In Britain they became identified as abolitionists par excellence through each phase of their movement" (Drescher 188). Equiano's *Narrative* was the last secular book Wesley read before his death in 1791.

The fact that the Black writers mentioned above embraced Whitefield over Wesley indicates that their concern in the matter sprang from spiritual rather than political interests. Whitefield appealed to these writers not only because of his hortatory skills but because of his Calvinist convictions concerning the predestined salvation or damnation of the individual's soul. Gronniosaw, Marrant, Cugoano, and Equiano all subscribed to the Calvinist world view. Equiano's *Narrative* makes it clear that this equality of sin rather than of deeds was difficult to swallow. To a man as driven and accomplished as Equiano, this submission to an ideology that placed

election beyond human endeavor was an enormous struggle. Sometime after his vision of redemption, he wrote a poem "During my first Convictions of the Necessity
of believing the Truth, and of experiencing the inestimable Benefits of Christianity"
(145) with the following verses:

> *I, ign'rant of his righteousness,*
> *Set up my labours in its place;*
> *'Forgot for why his blood was shed,*
> *And pray'd and fasted in his stead.'*
>
> *He died for sinners—I am one;*
> *Might not his blood for me atone?*
> *Though I am nothing else but sin,*
> *Yet surely he can make me clean!*
> *Thus light came in, and I believ'd;*
> *Myself forgot, and help receiv'd!*
> *My Saviour then, I know, I found*
> *For, eas'd from guilt, no more I groan'd.*
> *. . . .*
>
> *Bless'd be thy name; for now I know*
> *I and my works can nothing do;*
> *"The Lord alone can ransom man—*
> *For this the spotless Lamb was slain." (148)*

Yet this was another difference between Whitefield and Wesley. Wesley
preached Arminianism, a belief in the free and universal grace of God, which not
only put him at odds with the Calvinist doctrine of predestination espoused by the
Church of England but caused a doctrinal rift within Methodism itself.[12] The first
noblewoman to convert to Methodism, Selina Hastings, Countess of Huntingdon,
sided with Whitefield over the issue. She made Whitefield her chaplain in 1748 and
from then until his death supported his work in England and North America. In
1768 she established a college at Trevecca in South Wales for the education of ministers for what came to be known as "The Connexion," an association of chapels,
congregations, and itinerant preachers who subscribed to the Countess's brand of
Calvinist Methodism.

The Countess and her Connexion assumed a central importance in the publishing history of early Black literature. Phillis Wheatley dedicated her book of poems
to her. John Marrant was ordained a minister in the Connexion in 1785, and it was
around the time of his ordination that William Aldridge, another Connexion minister, wrote down his life story and published it as Marrant's *Narrative*. Gronniosaw

also dedicated his *Narrative* to the Countess, and the Reverend Walter Shirley, Selina's first cousin, provided a preface. Shirley offered Gronniosaw's life as an example of the Calvinist elect—a man who, "though born under every outward disadvantage, and in the regions of the grossest darkness and ignorance," comes, through the "most wonderfully appointed providence," to "full possession and enjoyment of the inestimable blessings of [God's] gospel" (Shirley 27). If Methodism provided an ideology that afforded Blacks an unquestioned humanity, it encouraged, produced, and published their poems and autobiographies as examples of God's providence.

The Methodist view also surfaced in those Black writings produced as political documents. Such uncompromising antislavery writers as Cugoano and Equiano viewed their bondage as, in some measure, a blessing in disguise. Cugoano compared his case to that of Joseph, who was also sold into slavery in accordance with a greater plan. In recalling his emotions upon experiencing his Wesleyan vision of salvation, Equiano writes: "Now every leading providential circumstance that happened to me, from the day I was taken from my parents to that hour, was then in my view, as if it had but just then occurred. I was sensible of the invisible hand of God, which guided and protected me, when in truth I knew it not" (143).

Equiano's diasporic consciousness resides most comfortably in an ideology that allows for both salvation and abolition. The illustration of this identity can be found in the frontispiece of the *Narrative*, depicting Equiano in European dress holding an open book in his right hand. At first glance the engraving clearly conveys the elements of the narrator's double identity: a black body sheathed in a frilly-collared shirt and frock coat. It is the book Equiano is holding that provides the mediating factor for these seemingly disparate elements: an English Bible open to Acts 4:12. The quotation from Peter explains in a trial before the Sanhedrin how he brought about the healing of a cripple: "Neither is there salvation in any other: for there is none other name under heaven given among men whereby we must be saved, but only Jesus Christ." This passage precipitated Equiano's conversion scene, in which he is finally convinced that he is among the elect.

In the evening of the same day, as I was reading and meditating on the fourth chapter of the Acts, twelfth verse, under the solemn apprehensions of eternity, and reflecting on my past actions, I began to think I had lived a moral life, and that I had a proper ground to believe I had an interest in the divine favour; but still meditating on the subject, not knowing whether salvation was to be had partly for our own good deeds, or solely as the sovereign gift of God. In this deep consternation the Lord was pleased to break in upon my soul with his bright beams of heavenly light; and in an instant, as it were removing the veil, and letting light into a dark place (Isa. XXV. 7). I saw clearly, with the eye of faith, the crucified Saviour bleeding on the cross on Mount Calvary: the Scriptures became an unsealed book; I saw myself a condemned criminal under the law, which came with its full force to my conscience, and when 'the commandment came, sin revived, and I died.' I saw the Lord Jesus Christ in his humiliation, loaded, and bearing my reproach, sin and shame.

. . . .

Now the Ethiopian was willing to be saved by Jesus Christ, the sinner's only surety, and also to rely on none other person or thing for salvation. Self was obnoxious, and good works I had none; for it is God that worketh in us both to will and to do. Oh! the amazing things of that hour can never be told! It was joy in the Holy Ghost! (142–43)

It may seem paradoxical to assert that this complete acceptance of Christian ideology represents a diasporic mentality, but Equiano's first thought after experiencing the ecstasy of knowing that he is saved is for other Africans. "I felt a deep concern for my mother and friends, which occasioned me to pray with fresh ardour; and in the abyss of thought, I viewed the unconverted people of the world in a very awful state, being without God and without hope" (143).

Equiano spends too much time and energy on his spiritual crisis for the reader to dismiss it as irrelevant (though Paul Edwards, in his widely disseminated abridgment of the *Narrative*, makes just such an editorial judgment[13]). Although Equiano knows moments of deep despair during his West Indian servitude, forcing him to the recourse of quoting from Milton's *Paradise Lost*, only his later uncertainty as to the state of his soul, well after he has obtained his freedom, drives him to thoughts of suicide. "I often wished for death, though at the same time convinced that I was altogether unprepared for that awful summons" (135). During his depression of 1774, he looked for solace in several religious systems, including the Society of Friends, the Church of England, Catholicism, and even Judaism, "which availed me nothing, as the fear of eternity daily harassed my mind" (133). (Judaism does not believe in an afterlife until the return of the Messiah.) Equiano finally settled on the Protestantism of the Evangelical Revival as the religion that came closest to the truth as he understood it from his own reading of the scriptures, but as this required that each communicant be vouchsafed the certainty of his or her salvation through a personal vision, he continued to live in uncertainty until he was at last visited by the mandatory revelation.

In spite of its abolitionist context, Equiano's autobiography is a conversion narrative, a genre that was familiar to his original readers. The author of the June 1789 article on the *Narrative* in *The Monthly Review* wrote with enlightened condescension: "He is a Methodist; and has filled many pages, toward the end of this work, with accounts of his dreams, visions, and divine impulses; but all this, supposing him to have been under any delusive influence, only serves to convince us that he is guided by principle; and that he is not one of those poor converts who, having undergone the ceremony of baptism, have remained content with that portion, only, of the Christian Religion . . . "(qtd in Costanzo 44). In point of fact, Equiano was admitted to communion in the Congregational church of Westminister, London, but many people who were reached by the Methodist preaching found their way into Congregational churches. Whitefield had close relations with Congregationalism, and many of the churches founded by the Countess of Huntingdon long retained a connection with Congregationalism.

As a Franklinesque figure, Equiano could certainly take pride in his accomplishments. He perfectly mastered English language and culture, bought himself honorably out of slavery through capitalist acquisition, performed heroically in several life-threatening situations, became a recognized spokesperson for his fellow Blacks, consorted easily with middle-class abolitionists and gentry, and addressed the Queen herself. For a White man, this might have been sufficient; however, Equiano, remarkable as he was, could not be satisfied with these achievements. He had to find a venue for the expression of his diasporic identity, and in eighteenth-century Britain, to one of his station, that opportunity could only be found in one of the evangelical sects.

Yet Equiano's embrace of Protestantism, and by extension, that of his peers who made it into print, brings up a capital question. How does an ideology founded on faith rather than reason jibe with the reigning assumptions of Enlightenment thought? Deism was clearly closer to the beliefs of the *philosophes* than Methodism, and the Calvinist brand embraced by the "literary" Blacks of the eighteenth century stood in even sharper relief to liberalism's political beliefs that all men were created equal. But this was the point. Blacks knew in a way that bourgeois and noble *philosophes* could overlook that divisions in humanity were *not* accidental, not subject to eventual disappearance in an enlightened State. Nothing could erase the difference of being Black in the British (and British colonial) world. Ignatius Sancho, the most assimilated of Britain's Blacks, clearly revealed how frustrated he was by the stereotyping: "[F]rom Othello to Sancho the big—we are foolish—or mulish—all—all without a single exception" (72). Yet like the Jewish Deists of the Berlin haskalah, Black Methodists could form associations, influence events, and rise to leadership in spheres of belief and endeavor recognized by the West. All this was based upon a private, individual experience of salvation that no authority—master, minister, or mayor—could gainsay or deny. The Methodists had, in their way, affirmed a human attribute that was as universal as Deism deemed reason to be.

As the pioneering generations were followed by ever-greater numbers of Blacks and Jews, diasporic consciousness grew stronger within the new religions. Jewish Deism soon gave way to the founding of Reform Judaism. Isaac Jacobson held Reform services in Berlin in 1815, and from there the movement spread to the rest of Europe. In the United States, one year later, Black Methodist congregations from around the country banded together as the African Methodist Episcopal Church. In spite of their ethnic coloration, these religions of the nineteenth century were extensions of the Western ideologies that had served as chrysalis in the eighteenth. The reactions to Western hegemony–modern Jewish orthodoxy, Zionism, Pan-Africanism and Garveyism–had not yet set in.

American Assents

Oh Lawd, I'm on my way
I'm on my way to a Heav'nly Land
Oh Lawd, it's a long, long way
But you'll be there to take my han'

DuBose Heyward, *Porgy and Bess*

Mid-
Century
Perspectives

The formal abolition of the ghetto and the granting of
the rights of citizenship did for the Jews about what
the emancipation proclamation did for the American
Negro.

—Louis Wirth, *The Ghetto*

The intellectual and social history of America in the first half of the twentieth century vis-à-vis its minorities offers numerous parallels with that of eighteenth-century Europe. The terms of Enlightenment emancipation had not yet changed—assimilation into a universal culture was still "the price of the ticket," to use James Baldwin's phrase. Blacks and Jews held to their strategies of capitulation, resistance, and dialogue. Capitulation found public expression in humor (Bert Williams on the minstrel stage; Potash and Perlmutter in print and on Broadway); resistance rhetoric was mostly intraethnic (the Nation of Islam; orthodox Jews). Ethnic literature—that written in English—was always part of a larger American dialogue, always the product of authors who crossed cultural boundaries.

Race, however, had changed the nature of Enlightenment discourse on the subject of group identity. Nineteenth-century conceptions of race as a reified essentialism were just beginning to break up as the social sciences—psychology, sociology, political science—simultaneously emulated and claimed autonomy from the physical sciences. One complexity attending the ethnic autobiographers of the American

81

mid-century was that they were born and raised in a world more structured by essentialist assumptions than the one they wound up writing in.

W. E. B. Du Bois established a framework for negotiating the changing terrain. The principal challenge of the new century, Du Bois predicted, would be "the color line." The racial ideologies so elaborately worked out by the nineteenth-century scientific disciplines of anthropology and biology were firmly established in both Europe and America. These ideologies, still available to the American folk idiom a hundred years later, posited a tight correlation between racial origin, innate abilities, and social character. Although the principal movement in American intellectual discourse was away from these nineteenth-century shibboleths to an eventual rejection of race as a significant biological factor, mainstream academic pronouncements on the immutability of the races persisted into the 1920s. Lothrop Stoddard, a Harvard Ph.D., published a widely read book in 1920 entitled *The Rising Tide of Color against White World-Supremacy*, in which he relied upon nineteenth-century clichés of race to rail against the impossibility of the American melting pot.

Each race-type, formed ages ago, and "set" by millenniums of isolation and inbreeding, is a stubbornly persistent entity. Each type possesses a special set of characters: not merely the physical characters visible to the naked eye, but moral, intellectual, and spiritual characters as well. All these characters are transmitted substantially unchanged from generation to generation. . . . Where the parent stocks are very diverse, as in matings between whites, negroes, and Amerindians, the offspring is a mongrel—a walking chaos, so consumed by his jarring heredities that he is quite worthless. (165–66)

The nineteenth-century titans of scientific and social thought—Charles Darwin, Alfred Wallace, Thomas Huxley, Ernst Haeckel, Herbert Spencer—regarded racial difference as essential to the understanding of human behavior. All adhered to the simplistic equation of graded physical types (quantified by caliper-wielding anthropometrists) with graded cultural types. Twentieth-century publicists of racism such as Lothrop Stoddard and Madison Grant could make their assertions about the innate inferiority of the Negroes, the ineradicable alienness of the Jews, and the advanced energies of the Anglo-Saxons based upon the incipient environmentalism of the eighteenth century refined and linked to the scientific racism of the nineteenth. "The impulse that inaugurated the development of mankind seems to have had its basic cause in the stress of changing climatic conditions in central Asia at the close of the Pliocene, and the human inhabitants of Eurasia have ever since exhibited in a superlative degree the energy developed at that time. This energy, however, has not been equally shared by the various species of man . . . " (Grant xii). This sentence, taken from Madison Grant's introduction to Stoddard's *chef-d'œuvre*, is little more than an update on the theory proposed by Montesquieu in his *Esprit des Lois*.

Yet within the American academic communities and scientific circles, these certainties were coming under harsher attack and being abandoned by increasing numbers of intellectuals. Franz Boas, a major force in the academic and professional development of anthropology in the United States, turned the discipline away from the dominant geographical determinism of the nineteenth century. (Boas, a German citizen of nonpracticing Jewish parents, emigrated to America at the age of twenty-nine because he could not stomach the requirement of Bismarck's Germany that all appointees to academic positions had to declare a religious affiliation.) Before Boas, race, language, and culture were understood as expressions of the same essence and were treated as interrelated. Boas transformed anthropology by establishing the relative autonomy of physical anthropology, linguistics, and ethnology. Rejecting geographical determinism as the root cause of racial difference, Boas argued that human cultures were not simply adaptations to the natural environment, but rather that they interacted with preexisting cultures that had themselves risen out of historical circumstance. As early as 1904 he wrote that the difference in types of thought and feeling between different peoples were not expressions of organic or biological differences but the product of the diversity of cultures. Though Boas accepted in his early work the dominant view that "anatomical characteristics of the present races" have been permanent since Neolithic times, his anthropometric study of the New York immigrant populations, "Changes in Bodily Form of Descendants of Immigrants" (1912), in which some 17,000 Eastern Europeans, Jews, and Italians were measured, forced him to change his views and eventually ended anthropologists' obsessive reliance upon the cephalic index as a key to genetic history. Though Boas himself never discarded the idea of race as a meaningful category of species classification, his work and influence gave powerful impetus to the rising notion that social conditions were as powerful a factor as biology in human development.

The challenge of social conditioning to the dominance of racial thinking could be seen as early as the 1911 monograph *The Jews: A Study of Race and Environment*, by Maurice Fishberg, a member of several American anthropological associations. European investigation of the Jews in the first half of the twentieth century was skewed by the power of modern anti-Semitism donning the academic guise of Aryan and Nordic discourses; but America, much less invested in "the Jewish Question," was able to undertake a scientific study with fewer ideological filters. If somatic similarity was the *sine qua non* of racial classification (whether it be skin color or shape of the body or some part of it), it was perfectly obvious to even the casual investigator that no visible trait could be applied to the Ashkenazi, Sephardic, Asian and African peoples who called themselves and were regarded as Jews. Fishberg diligently catalogued the various physical characteristics of the Jews and came to the conclusion that the "Jewish type" so easily discernible to the European eye was, in fact, drawn from observations of Jews in or recently emerged from the ghetto. Thus a race was created where none in fact existed. "Though scattered in various countries, among diverse races and peoples of different culture, language, traditions, and religion, the Jews, owing to the homogeneity of their own Ghetto environment, presented a uniform social type. Basing their assertions on superficial observation, writers have confounded this uniformity of the social type of the Jew with homogeneity of the physical or anthropological type" (504). In his introduction, Fishberg expressed optimism that all distinctions between Jews and Christians in Europe and America would ultimately be obliterated because "the differences . . . are not everywhere racial, due to anatomical or physiological peculiarities, but are solely the result of the social and political environment" (vii).[1]

The idea of social environment as the determining factor in human development received powerful support from the young discipline of sociology being pioneered in America by Robert B. Park. Park had been a journalist for ten years; he then undertook graduate studies in philosophy and sociology at Harvard and in Germany. Invited to become secretary of the Congo Reform Association after completing his degree, Park in 1906 published an exposé of the atrocities in the Belgian Congo that brought him to the attention of Booker T. Washington. Washington invited him to study the situation of the American Black at Tuskegee. As Park wrote in an autobiographical note, "I think I probably learned more about human nature and society, in the South under Booker Washington, than I had learned elsewhere in all my previous studies" (vii). Only after collaborating on Washington's book, *The Man Farthest Down* (1912), did Park turn finally to an academic career, joining the University of Chicago's fledgling department of sociology in 1914 at the age of fifty. Working there until his retirement in 1929, Park developed the hugely influential Chicago School of urban sociology, publishing a seminal textbook in 1921 with Earnest W. Burgess and training other prominent sociologists who were to carry on the spirit of his work: Louis Wirth, E. Franklin Frazier (to be discussed below), and W. O. Brown, who became an early authority on African nationalism. After World War I, Park published two books on the immigrant populations of America, adding a second expertise to that already acquired in the area of race relations. "More than anyone else, [Park] tried to understand both Negroes and immigrants in the United States in the context of a global process that also affected European nationalities and Asian races in varying but related ways" (Higham 217).

One of Park's principal achievements was to break the hold that social Darwinism had over sociological discourse by focusing attention on race relations rather than on the "races" themselves. Analyzing racial hostility as the product of the norms of social distance and prejudice individuals learned as they were socialized into their communities, Park underscored the constructed nature of social categories. "[A] mind is the instrument with which men think," he wrote, "and, according to the sociologists of knowledge, this instrument is very largely, if not wholly, a social and socialized product" (305). Park created a conceptual scheme that brought both Blacks and immigrants into the same framework of analysis, a radically extended melting pot that would eventually assimilate all comers. In a 1926 essay, Park posited that this would happen to the Jews before it happened to other peoples with marked racial characteristics, since race prejudice is a function of visibility. Citing Fishberg's belief that Jews acquired a "characteristic, psychic type" because of their centuries of ghettoization, Park wrote that when the Jew finally emerges from his ghetto, "he loses his characteristic type, his cast of countenance, and sometimes even his soul. In the vast tide of cosmopolitan life the Jewish racial type does not so much disappear as become invisible. When he is no longer seen, anti-Semitism declines" (247).[2]

Louis Wirth, a German Jew who emigrated to the United States at the age of fourteen, carried on Park's work first as a student and then as a professor at the University of Chicago.[3] In his comparative study of German and American Jewish communities, *The Ghetto* (1928), Wirth elaborated on Fishberg's contention that strict isolation and the consequent inbreeding, which had its foundation in religious tenets, had developed a ghetto type; but, he wrote, "The Jew is a much more clearly defined social type than physical type" (72). Wirth's task, as he saw it, was to explain why Jews in America had voluntarily recreated the ghetto when the American body politic, at least in its legal expression, never required it of them. As an exponent of the Chicago School of sociology, he could only reply that it was because of their social conditioning. Their historical experience of persecution and enforced confinement left profound effects not only upon their bodies but upon their minds. Following, perhaps, the comparative example of his teacher, Wirth briefly extended this insight to the African-American community.

The abolition of Negro slavery did not make the Negro free and equal. In fact, race prejudice against the Negro seemed to arise only as the Negro became emancipated. Slavery was more than a mere legal relationship between master and slave. The ghetto was more than just a legal measure. It had become an institution, and, as such, had come to exist not only in statutes and decrees but in the habits and attitudes of individuals and in the culture of groups. Though the physical walls of the ghetto have been torn down, an invisible wall of isolation still maintains the distance between the Jew and his neighbors. (118)

E. Franklin Frazier, an African-American student who received his Ph.D. from the University of Chicago in 1931 and who joined the program of research on the urban community and on race relations directed by Park, based his sociological writings on the tenet that the determinant force shaping the Black American community was its historical experience. In *The Negro Family in the United States* (1939), Frazier advanced the view that the structure of values in the African-American family (matriarchy, social status accorded to skin color, the high incidence of illegitimate births and common-law relationships) resulted from the impact of slavery, emancipation, and urbanization. Frazier was fiercely antiessentialist in his thinking, not only ignoring any racial determinism but even denying the possible historical links with the traditions and beliefs of West Africa. Like the other Chicago sociologists, he also believed in the inevitability of the melting pot.

[T]he Negro, stripped of a relatively simple preliterate culture in which he was nurtured, has created a folk culture and has gradually taken over the more sophisticated American culture. Although only three-quarters of a century has elapsed since the arrival of the last representative of preliterate African races, the type of culture from which he came was as unlike the culture of the civilized American Negro today as the culture of the Germans of Tacitus' day was unlike the culture of German-Americans. (Frazier 359)

These beliefs involved Frazier in a brief polemic with the anthropologist Melville Herskovits, a (Jewish) student of Boas who was just then publishing *The Myth of the Negro Past* (1940), which asserted that New World Blacks revealed their West African heritage in their motor habits, codes of behavior, social institutions, family organization, religion, language, and art. Herskovits did not conceive of African-American social behavior as the expression of a Black essence; he saw it rather as a culture of historical survivals.[4] The argument between Frazier and Herskovits was about the historical determinants of the African-American experience; neither subscribed to theories of racial expression.

Around the same time another student of Boas, Ruth Benedict, published *Race: Science and Politics* (1940), in which she sought to discredit theories of racial difference that had been contradicted by research demonstrating the mental equivalence of different racial and ethnic groups. By the time of America's entry into World War II, nineteenth-century tenets about race and heredity were so undermined in the scientific community that a liberal New York organization, The Public Affairs Committee, asked the American Association of Scientific Workers to prepare a pamphlet exploding these beliefs for the general public. Ruth Benedict and Gene Weltfish's *Races of Mankind* included such section headings as, "One Human Race," "Customs Not Racial," "Character Not Inborn," and "Civilization Not Caused by Race." Much of this was an explicit, if simplified, refutation of Nazi ideology. The pamphlet stated plainly that Hitler's use of the term "Aryan" "has no meaning, racial, linguistic, or otherwise," and that Jews "are of all races, even Negro and Mongolian" (Benedict and Weltfish, 17)

Yet the racial myths and typologies of the nineteenth century died hard, particularly in American popular culture. Up until the revelation of the Holocaust, after which any use of Nazi categories was strictly *verboten* in public discourse, the press and radio regularly referred to Jews as a race—as did many Jews themselves. In 1933, for example, Congressman Samuel Dickstein of the U.S. House of Representatives earned the displeasure of *Time* magazine for being too avid in "spreading the record of the plight of members of his own race in Germany" (qtd. in Feingold 224). Nor was the U.S. government as advanced in its thinking as the Public Affairs Committee. The USO prohibited distribution of *The Races of Mankind* in its clubs, a ban that prompted an outcry from the NAACP. The Red Cross, in spite of a section entitled "Blood the Same," segregated Black and White donations made to the banks established for the relief of wounded soldiers. The irony here, of course, was that the very technology of blood transfusion was made possible by the work of African-American scientist Charles Drew.

The beliefs and practices of the nineteenth century showed tremendous staying power in the intellectual community. Anthropology and biology, older and more established disciplines than sociology, had a more difficult time divesting themselves of the racial thinking they had been so instrumental in setting up. As late as 1942, Carleton Stevens Coon, a Harvard professor of anthropology, could write an article asserting that the Sephardic Jews "preserve with reasonable fidelity the racial character of their Palestinian ancestors" (31) and that the product of Ashkenazi "blending" with the European Nordic and Alpine races produced "features which are popularly labeled as Jewish. These are the combination of a relatively wide head and narrow face, with a slanting axis to the ears; a narrow lower jaw; a narrow interocular distance; and a considerable nose length, with convexity of profile and tip depression" (33). Coon supported his contention that Jews have more in common with each other anthropometrically than with their Gentile neighbors by the time-honored means of a cephalic index table.

Refuting Coon's article, Melville Jacobs, another anthropology professor, questioned the validity of anthropometric data and scoffed at the notion that anyone could measure or identify ancient Palestinian heritage in a modern-day population. Though Jacobs did not identify himself as Jewish, his surprising and out-of-context reprimand to the Jews for believing in a causal connection between race and culture indicated a familiarity and concern with Jewish views that would have come naturally from an insider's perspective. "There is no evidence for the existence of a distinctive Jewish blood or 'race,' nor has there ever been a group of family lines of Jews that could be called a 'race.' The Jewish leader who speaks about 'our race' is talking unadulterated nonsense. When he or she accedes to such a notion, or uses such words, there is an admission in effect that the racial nonsense uttered by the bitterest enemies of the Jewish people is likewise biologic truth" (53).

In his last sentence, Jacobs points to the unholy kinship between racists and those among their victims who accept their categories. Both Blacks and Jews were able to find comfort in the racial assertions of the nineteenth-century West. Confronting the unbridgeable chasm between those who believed that race was an inalienable essence and those who viewed it as a social construction, ethnic minorities never knew whether their salvation lay with assimilationists, who were generally condescending to the deeper aspects of their communal experience, or with the racialists, who accorded each ethnicity its spirit but usually did so in ways that preserved a disadvantageous status quo. Many minorities cast their lot with the racialists, contesting not their structural assumptions but their unjust treatment of others.

"Race consciousness is the natural and inevitable reaction to race prejudice," Robert Park wrote (294), and African Americans, having been subjected to social reenslavement as the end of Reconstruction in the South brought about a new architecture of repression based on race rather than chattel slavery, were the first to come up with a minority version of Western racism. In an 1897 address, "On the Conservation of Races," to the newly formed American Negro Academy, W. E. B. Du Bois (who later moved away from his early essentialism) proclaimed that it was the duty of the race to preserve its physical powers, its intellectual endowments and spiritual ideals; that African Americans would reach their broader humanity through racial organization, solidarity, and unity. "For this reason, the advance guard of the Negro people—the 8,000,000 people of Negro blood in the United States of America—must soon come to realize that if they are to take their place in the van of Pan-Negroism, then their destiny is not absorption by the white Americans" (256).

This was the corollary to race consciousness: the various "races" in America were not destined to melt together in the assimilationist ideal. White racists, of course, felt that the melting pot was dangerous and wrong-headed—and they found themselves in agreement with minority racialists. Horace Kallen, an American philosopher of Jewish descent, published a famous article in a 1915 issue of *The Nation*, "Democracy versus the Melting-Pot," in which he argued that democracy had encouraged the development of a cultural consciousness and a sense of social autonomy among immigrant ethnics, a development he celebrated. Freed from poverty, the Jew becomes more Jewish. That was inevitable, Kallen reasoned, because whatever else the immigrant changed in America, he could not change his grandfather. Though he specifically excluded the African American from his discussion of American ethnic groups, Kallen's description of human nature accorded well with the ideas put forth by Du Bois eighteen years earlier.

At his core, no human being, even in a "state of nature" is a mere mathematical unit of action like the "economic man." Behind him in time and tremendously in him in quality, are his ancestors; around him in space are his relatives and kin, carrying in common with him the inherited organic set from a remoter common ancestry. In all these he lives and moves and has his being. They constitute his, literally, *natio*, the inwardness of his nativity. . . .
(*Culture and Democracy*, 39)

Kallen did not go so far as to call the Jews a race, but he certainly conceived of them as a nation in the Romantic Herderian way that so fed the fires of European race pride. In a 1910 essay, he coined the term "Hebraism" to describe that spirit of Jewishness that manifests itself in the accomplishments of the Jews in all areas of human endeavor. "Hebraism . . . is the life of the Jews, their unique achievement,—not as isolated individuals, but as a well-defined ethnic group—in government, in industry and commerce, in social economy, in the arts, in religion, in philosophy" (*Judaism at Bay*, 39). Though the term did not catch fire, the idea it expressed has been a perennial theme in the consideration of Jewish identity outside of Judaism.

Ludwig Lewisohn shares the essentialist stasis common to such a conception of identity. Jews are almost as changeless in their character as "the olives and the pines and cypresses upon the Pincian hill," he wrote in his autobiography, *Mid-Channel* (*A Jew Speaks*, 34). Staking a middle ground between religious adherence and assimilation, Lewisohn agreed with Kallen that Jews do not need to believe in Judaism any more than the Greeks had to believe in their pantheon, because religion is an expression of national character, "our essentially eternal traits" (*A Jew Speaks*, 7). "Assimilation is bankrupt," he baldly declared in a 1934 polemic, pointing toward Germany (55). Having been shocked back into Jewish identity by his own experience of anti-Semitism in America, Lewisohn not only celebrated an immutable Jewish essence that could never be lost, but—the inevitable obverse of the essentialist coin—he castigated assimilationist ideology as hypocritical and undesirable. Though the assimilated Jew may never think a Jewish thought or read a Jewish book, Lewisohn declared, "in the essential character of all his passions as well as of all his actions he remains a Jew" (53).

Similar assertions of racial sentiment were to be found in the writings of African Americans, weirdly echoing the stereotypes of Western culture. In the same year that Kallen penned his panegyric to ethnicity, Benjamin Brawley, a professor at Morehouse College, wrote an article on "The Negro Genius," in which he declared, "the faculties intellect, feeling, and will, are respectively the Anglo-Saxon, the Negro, and the Jewish" (327). He went on to predict that the Negro would reach his greatest heights as an artist. In the following decade, the achievements of the Harlem Renaissance seemed to fulfill his prophecy, bringing to literary expression a racial pride that had been previously rare in the belletristic tradition of African-American literature. As Lewisohn had written that the books of the Old Testament were the expression of Jewish national character—"these are our Iliads and Nibelungen Lays"—so African-American artists and intellectuals of the 1920s viewed the spirituals, folklore, and rhetorical inventiveness of Black Christianity that were the legacy of slavery and still to be found in the life of the Black masses.

"[Spirituals] are to negro culture what the works of the great poets are to English culture," Paul Robeson wrote in 1934, "they are the soul of the race made manifest" ("Culture of the Negro," 331). Robeson, an internationally famous singer and actor, was as skeptical of cultural assimilation for the Blacks as Lewisohn was for the Jews. "[The Negro] is too radically different from the white man in his mental and emotional structure ever to be more than a spurious and uneasy imitation of him" (333).

Racial essentialism, with its ahistoricity and its negation of the melting pot, was anathema to the Chicago sociologists. Park's reading of African-American literature in the 1920s was as sensitive and intelligent as any White of the time could have produced, but he stated flatly that, because of their themes of surrender and resignation, spirituals had no message for the present day. Park saw in the poetry of what was then called the Negro renaissance not an expression of Black soul but "the natural expression of the Negro temperament under all the conditions of modern life" (294). African-American poetry was a manifestation of African-American historical conditions. Declaring that nationalist movements have always been literary as well, Park drew an analogy between the literature of the Harlem Renaissance and that of the European "nationalities" that had been agitating for independence since the nineteenth century. "Nationalist movements, whether they occur in Ireland or Slovakia, whether they are called Zionism among the Jews, Irredentism among the Italians, or socialism among the Finns, all have the same natural history" (298). As early as 1913 Park had written that African Americans had had their race consciousness forced upon them by their exclusion from White society. Thirty years later his views had not changed: "The whole history of the United States, North and South, has forced upon the Negroes in slavery and in freedom a race consciousness that has slowly created out of individual men and women without history and without traditions a people conscious of common destiny" (310).

Gunnar Myrdal's magisterial volume, *An American Dilemma* (1944), made explicit the links between Enlightenment thought, assimilationist beliefs, and the sociology of identity as social construction. In 1937 the Carnegie Corporation of New York decided to sponsor a comprehensive "scientific" study of the American Black. Since it was felt that no American could conduct such research without bias, the Swedish social economist Myrdal was invited to head a research team, and the resulting 1,400-page volume was published under his name. The "dilemma," as Myrdal analyzed it, was America's failure to live up to the political ideals stated explicitly in the Declaration of Independence, the Preamble to the Constitution, and the Bill of Rights—a political inheritance he terms the "American Creed." Enlightenment liberalism minimized the differences between individuals and peoples as to inborn capacities and aptitudes, but because chattel slavery was also part of the American system, the doctrine of biological racial inequality allowed the nation to maintain simultaneously institutions of complete dehumanization and of

Enlightenment equality. After emancipation, the caste system set in place through Jim Crow laws inherited slavery's ideological justification. "The need for race prejudice is, from this point of view, a need for defense on the part of the Americans against their own national Creed, against their own most cherished ideals" (89). In Myrdal's view, there is nothing lacking in the political ideals of the eighteenth century, nothing that might justify a reassessment of its conception of human nature and human society. Race exists only as a condition embraced by Whites as an ideological justification and forced on Blacks as their caste definition. "The definition of the 'Negro race' is . . . a social and conventional, not a biological concept" (115). While Myrdal recognized the existence of Black pride, he saw it as a defense against the ideology of White superiority. Anticipating the sentiments that Richard Wright would express in *Black Boy*, Myrdal stated that African-American culture was "a distorted development, or a pathological condition, of the general American culture" (928). The cure, of course, was assimilation. Justified not in terms of White ethnocentrism but from a pragmatic point of view, Myrdal declared in italics, "*we assume that it is to the advantage of American Negroes as individuals and as a group to become assimilated into American culture, to acquire the traits held in esteem by the dominant white Americans*" (929).

Myrdal's magnum opus represented the pinnacle of pre–World War II liberal scholarship, but the sociological tradition brought to such impressive fruition in this great synthesis denied the African American community any possibility of positive self-definition. In the eyes of Park, Myrdal, and Frazier, African Americans were victims, and their culture "pathological." This sociological tradition produced one more significant book, Oliver Cox's *Caste, Class, & Race* (1948), before the widespread reawakening of ethnic assertion in the 1960s permanently changed the terms of the assimilationist debate. Cox brought a Marxist epistemology and a detailed knowledge of Indian culture to his discussion of class and caste, but his analysis of race added nothing new to what had already been said. He believed of the African-American community that "its social drive is toward assimilation," an American cultural trait, and that Black solidarity would endure only so long as the White ruling class successfully blocked assimilation (545–46). "The destiny of Negroes is cultural and biological integration and fusion with the larger American society," he wrote (572).

His discussion of anti-Semitism is another feature that makes Cox so representative of the new Enlightenment discourse that, for a few brief decades, enjoyed widespread intellectual support. "Anti-Semitism is an attitude directed against the Jews because they are Jews, while race prejudice is an attitude directed against Negroes because they want to be something other than Negroes. The Jew, to the intolerant, is an enemy within the society; but the Negro, to the race-prejudiced, is a friend in his place" (393). One sees in this statement not only a complete negation of Black pride (with none of the experiential ambivalence attributable to Wright in similar pronouncements) but also an unusually explicit reiteration of the ideological bone of Jewish identity in the throat of the Christian West: "The Jews are a people who refuse to assimilate" (394).

Who were these Negroes who wished to be White and these Jews who refused to assimilate? Such assumptions were insulting to W. E. B. Du Bois, Jackie Robinson, and Ralph Ellison; potentially threatening to Felix Frankfurter, Irving Berlin, and Walter Winchell. Yet light skin color *was* considered socially desirable within the African-American community, and assimilated, nonobservant Jews *still* considered themselves Jewish. By the end of the 1940s, essentialist thinking about race had been largely discredited in mainstream intellectual discourse and was not to find influential expression in the Black and Jewish communities for another decade and a half. Social construction had won the day; still ethnic writers continued to wrestle with an internalized essentialist sentiment. Richard Wright, even in his French exile, was obsessed with blackness, and Kazin, for all his expertise on American and European literature, kept returning to his life as a Jew. The defeat of Nazism had seemingly dealt racial ideologies a fatal blow, and both superpowers used condemnations of American racism and Russian anti-Semitism to score ideological points. In America, intolerance as a nationally sanctioned passion seemed to have turned away from race and toward Communism. (Of course, Jews were still somewhat tainted by their notorious history of left-wing activism, but knowledge of the Holocaust had now rendered taboo any official reference to Jewish collective identity except in an ecumenical, nonsectarian context.) Enlightenment principles had once again triumphed, at least on the level of national political and intellectual discourse, and yet this same time period—the 1950s and early 1960s—witnessed the flowering of Jewish-American writing and a "renationalizing" of African-American political thought. Within the quiet womb of this seemingly conformist era, the repressed was preparing to return with a vengeance. At mid-century, America felt itself once again bathed in the illumination of the Enlightenment, putting its racial house in order, forbidding public expression of anti-Semitism. But the shadow side of Black and Jewish identity, the race pride and the refusal to assimilate—these seeds of dissent barely discernible in the writings of Wright and Kazin lay silently germinating in the humus of Western history.

The disturbing undercurrents exploded into public view in 1913 when a thirteen-year-old female worker was found brutally murdered in the basement of an Atlanta pencil factory managed by a Northern Jew, Leo Frank. Frank was arrested, and Tom Watson, a former Populist senator from Georgia, founded an organization called the Knights of Mary Phagan as part of a campaign to convict Frank of her murder. "Frank belonged to the Jewish aristocracy," he proclaimed, "and it was determined by the rich Jews that no aristocrat of their race should die for the death of a working-class Gentile" (qtd. in Lipset and Raab 98). During the trial, a Black factory employee testified that he had helped dispose of the body. Convicted amid a frenzy of indignation, Frank was spared by the governor of Georgia, who commuted his death sentence to life imprisonment. Watson then extolled the role of lynch law and vigilante committees. On August 16, 1915, a mob snatched Frank from prison and hanged him in the woods. Three months later, on a mountain top outside Atlanta, thirty-three members of the Knights of Mary Phagan gathered under the leadership of Colonel William Simmons, an Atlanta preacher, who began that Thanksgiving night to implement his dream of reviving the Ku Klux Klan. The purpose of the Klan, said Simmons, was to "maintain Anglo-Saxon civilization on the American continent from submergence due to the encroachment and invasion of alien people of whatever clime or color" (qtd. in Gossett 340).

The tangle of racist sentiments depicted in this set of incidents was representative of the lower depths of American culture in the early part of the twentieth century, but these crudities of thought and action had their upper-class counterparts. What was unusual about the Frank case was the level of violence visited upon the Jew. Lynching had been an accepted part of Southern culture since the 1880s, and Blacks increasingly found themselves at the wrong end of a rope or a torch or with a knife at their genitals. From 1893 to 1904 an average of more than a hundred African Americans were lynched each year, as compared to an average of twenty-nine whites. Jews were relatively rare in the South, and they did not elicit a uniform animosity. The lynching of Leo Frank was something of an anomaly.

America entered the twentieth century as one of the most profoundly racist countries in the history of civilization. Bolstered by European theories of race propagated in the nineteenth century, American racism was directed most virulently against Blacks. In spite of the guarantees in the Fourteenth and Fifteenth Amendments to the Constitution, the Southern states had legally segregated African Americans in schools, restaurants, theaters, public spaces, residential areas, vehicles of public transportation; had proscribed them from marrying across the color line; and had deprived them of their right to vote. Until the formal abolition of Jim Crow laws in the 1950s, many writers spoke of African Americans as a separate caste, bringing attention to the impermeable legal and social dividing line between Black and White America. I shall adopt this convention while discussing this historical period, for, unlike the eighteenth century, where the term "slave" and "Jew" encompassed an explicit legal status, the forms of social ostracism practiced against the Jews in America rarely reached legal expression and even the Jim Crow laws were not uniform. Nonetheless, as Myrdal dryly observed, the difference between the South and the North was only one of hypocrisy. "We can, in the North, witness the legislators' obedience to the American Creed when they solemnly pass laws and regulations to condemn and punish such acts of discrimination which, as a matter of routine, are committed daily by the great majority of the white citizens and by the legislators themselves" (67). Thus, although African Americans were not always subjected to *de jure* discrimination and disenfranchisement, their *de facto* status was sufficiently similar within the national culture to make the caste analogy meaningful.

Up until the advent of the New Deal, African Americans found their efforts to break out of their subordinate status blocked by every branch of local, state, and federal government. During his successful campaign for the governorship of Mississippi in 1900, James Vardaman declared that the Black was a "lazy, lying, lustful animal which no conceivable amount of training can transform into a tolerable citizen." The U.S. Senate hosted such colorful characters as Ben Tillman of South Carolina, who declared in 1913 that "forty to a hundred Southern maidens were annually offered as a sacrifice to the African Minotaur, and no Theseus had arisen to rid the land of this terror" (qtd. in Gossett 271). Twenty-five years later, Senator Theodore Bilbo of Mississippi denounced a federal antilynching bill, advocated the resettlement of American Blacks in Africa, and attacked a Washington, D.C. law permitting racial intermarriage, claiming that the offspring of such a union would be a "motley melee of miscegenated mongrels."

The executive branch offered no greater refuge. William Taft began his administration in 1909 by assuring the South that he would appoint no federal officials in their region who would be "offensive to local sensibilities." Democrats were worse than Republicans. Under Woodrow Wilson, and with his express approval, federal workers were segregated in employment, with separate eating and toilet facilities. As president, Warren G. Harding praised Stoddard's *Rising Tide of Color*, which repeated the old slanders that Africans had "vegetated in savage obscurity" (88), had contributed "virtually nothing" to civilization (91), warred constantly among themselves, and were "widely addicted to cannibalism" (90).

The courts were more decorous in expression but scarcely any friendlier. The *Plessy vs. Ferguson* decision of 1896 gave legal sanction to the doctrine of "separate but equal," meaning, in practice, that the Southern states could do with their Black populations anything they pleased without fear of federal interference. In 1907, when Kentucky passed a law forbidding Berea College to educate African Americans along with its White students, the Supreme Court refused to pass judgment on the constitutionality of the issue, thus sanctioning laws against integration even in private institutions. In 1921 Justice McReynolds declared that a state primary was not part of a federal election and was therefore not subject to regulation by the U.S. government. The Southern states took the hint and instituted various versions of White-only primaries. In summing up the era, Thomas Gossett writes,

"American thought of the period 1880–1920 generally lacks any perception of the Negro as a human being with potentialities for improvement" (286).

The Jews in America labored under fewer and milder disabilities, but this same period also witnessed a dramatic growth in anti-Semitism. Prior to the wave of immigration from Eastern Europe, the small population of German Jews who had arrived earlier in the nineteenth century had quietly assimilated, bringing with them a religious ideology—Reform Judaism—that allowed them to break with halakhic law and to switch their national allegiance from Israel to the host country: "Americans of the Mosaic persuasion," as they called themselves. The Eastern European Jews were a much more gregarious lot: boisterous, contentious, steeped in a vivid and visibly Jewish culture that had developed its own style of modernity, comprising a higher percentage of skilled laborers, intellectuals, and socialists than other immigrant groups of the period. Most of all these new Jews were urban, numerous, and easily visible because of their settlement and employment patterns. The Jewish population of New York grew from 80,000 in 1880 to 1,225,000 in 1910. With visibility came opprobrium. In 1908, the city's police commissioner, General Bingham, made a statement that Jews made up 50 percent of New York's criminal population. (He later recanted.)

At the beginning of this transformation, public perception often distinguished between the German Jews and the newer arrivals, but soon all Jews got tarred with the same ethnic brush. Discrimination at summer resorts, country clubs, and private schools increased during the years before World War I. In 1913 the *Chicago Tribune* published its first resort advertisements specifying a "Christian" or "Gentile" clientele. American nativists saw Jews as part of the great wave of non–Anglo-Saxon immigrants who threatened to overrun and mongrelize the "old stock." In the fifteen years before the outbreak of the First World War, which reduced the movement of European populations to a trickle, the United States received 13 million immigrants, almost 75 percent of whom originated from southern and eastern Europe. In the 1880s, the United States had welcomed these new peoples as the North's Industrial Revolution fed on a steady diet of cheap labor, but eventually the inhabitants of the cities of the Eastern seaboard grew frightened at their numbers. During this period the debate grew loud about what kind of people could assimilate, and the lines were drawn between the "100 percent Americans"— self-styled Nordics or Anglo-Saxons who subscribed to the theory of ineradicable racial difference—and those who believed that the immigrants would eventually Americanize. The celebrated metaphor of the melting pot came into currency from a 1908 Broadway production of a play of that name and theme by the Anglo-Jewish writer Israel Zangwill. "[T]he melting-pot may mix but does not melt," Lothrop Stoddard declared (165), and the rising call for the American government to shut the door on unrestricted "non-Nordic" immigration (the first Chinese Exclusion Act dated from 1882) indicated that a growing number of people agreed with him. In 1921 the goal was partially achieved through an act restricting immigration from each country to 3 percent of the number of foreign-born residents in the United States in 1910. Even that still allowed for too many undesirables. Three years later Congress decreed that the quota should be reduced to 2 percent, and pushed the determining date back to 1890. In signing the Immigration Act of 1924, President Coolidge stated, "America must be kept American" (qtd. in Gossett 407).

What caused this crescendo of xenophobia and racism? At the dawn of the twentieth century, the United States was undergoing profound changes. Unregulated industrial capitalism had transformed the countryside, which was losing its population to the urban areas. The cities, where ordinary citizens had to work as alienated labor, worried about a rising crime rate and contended with a cultural drift toward sexual and social permissiveness. The immense heterogeneous immigration combined with these social dislocations to feed an upsurge of nativism in an insecure middle class. As the South slowly came into the orbit of the new economic order, the mass of African-American serfs glimpsed the possibility of escape, and the first wave of the Great Migration broke upon the Northern cities. The American war effort had drained the Northern workforce, and between 1910 and 1920, 300,000 African Americans moved North, stimulated by the temporary lowering of the color bar in industrial employment. During the next decade, 1.3 million of their brethren followed. Faced with economic competition from Blacks and immigrants, the American working class descended into an ugly and sometimes violent ethnocentrism. "Protestant moralism and fundamentalism . . . became the currency of the backlash of the 1920s because it happened to be the prime cultural property of those being displaced" (Lipset and Raab 118).

The end of the Great War ushered in a period of extreme racial violence in the United States. The newly assertive attitudes of returning Black veterans clashed with a general desire to return to pre-war "normalcy" in which segregation was rarely questioned. The violence exploded during the "Red Summer" of 1919; in twenty-five race riots, Whites rampaged through Black communities. After a period of steady decline from a peak in 1904, lynchings once again increased: more than sixty in 1918, and seventy-six the following year. The Ku Klux Klan, which had grown slowly during the war, made a spectacular entry into the life of the nation. Within ten months after the armistice it sponsored more than 200 rallies in twenty-seven states, adding hundreds of thousands of recruits in the Midwest and the North. At the peak of its influence, around 1923, the Klan claimed to have 4.5 million members, and Klan candidates won local elections in Ohio, Michigan, Indiana, and Wisconsin. The Klan was equitable in its dissemination of hatred to all who were not Protestant and White. One popular formulation for its roster of enemies was Koons, Kikes, and Katholics.

The anti-Semitism visited upon the Jews in this heightened nativist atmosphere was much less spectacular than the psychic and physical violence against Blacks that served as the usual vehicle of national catharsis, but social ostracism of the rising Jews increased as well. When the United States opened its doors to unrestricted European immigration in the 1880s, few Americans imagined that immigrant children would be knocking at the gates of academia within a generation; but the rapidly expanding industrial economy provided opportunities for class mobility, and, given their advantages as skilled workers, Jews were the first to assail the battlements of WASP society. By 1906 enough had entered Harvard to form the Menorah Society, and fifteen years later, universities of the industrial East had a "Jewish problem." As a campus song of the 1920s put it:

> *Oh, Harvard's run by millionaires,*
>   *And Yale is run by booze,*
> *Cornell is run by farmers' sons,*
>   *Columbia's run by Jews.*

Columbia reduced its 40 percent Jewish enrollment by instituting covert quotas, a stratagem adopted by other schools. Only Harvard president Abbott Lowell got caught out in this policy because he was naive enough to advertise it as a way to reduce anti-Semitism. "The anti-Semitic feeling among the students is increasing," he wrote in a letter to the *New York Times* in 1922, "and it grows in proportion to the increase in the number of Jews. If their number should become 40 percent of the student body, the race feeling would become intense" (qtd. in Steinberg 241).

With the victory of Bolshevism in Russia in 1917, the European myth of the Jew as political agitator and participant in an international Jewish conspiracy found fertile soil in which to take root. Between 1920 and 1927, Henry Ford hammered away at these themes in his paper, the *Dearborn Independent*, with such articles as "Jewish Gamblers Corrupt American Baseball," "Jewish Jazz Becomes Our National Music," and "The Jewish Associates of Benedict Arnold" (Lipset and Raab 136). The hate campaign reached its zenith with the paper's serialization of the *Protocols of the Elders of Zion*, a text allegedly dealing with plans for world conquest dating from the time of King Solomon.[5]

Within the context of this inflamed provincialism, even the notorious blood libel of the Middle Ages could return from the ideological dead. In Messina, New York, state troopers illegally entered the home of the town rabbi during the High Holy Days in September when city authorities grew alarmed over the disappearance of a four-year-old girl. The mayor and police brought the rabbi downtown for questioning because they had heard rumors that Jews required the blood of Christian children to perform religious rituals. Robert and Helen Lynd, in their famous sociological study of the eponymous Middletown [Akron, Ohio], report other quaint folk beliefs of the period: "Negroes have a powder which they put on their arms which turns their bodies white, and . . . Jews have all the money, but when the Klan gets into power, it will make a new kind of money, so that the Jews' money will be no good."

"We are charged with being against the Jew," thundered a lawyer from the state capital at a Klan rally. "We are against no man. Jesus Christ is the leader of the Ku Klux Klan, and we are for Him. The Jew is not for Him, and therefore the Jew has shut himself out of the Klan. We are not against the Negro. Rome fell because she mixed her blood. God Almighty has commanded us, 'Thou shalt not mix thy blood.' . . . We must protect American womanhood." (483)

Black and Jewish responses to this climate of bigotry differed in predictable ways. African Americans subscribed to their own mass movement of racial solidarity—Garveyism—and the Jews discreetly defended themselves. Marcus Garvey, a Jamaican citizen, arrived in the United States to further his Universal Negro Improvement Association, a nationalist organization promoting pan-Africanism and the establishment of an African republic that would accept the wholesale migration of African Americans. Stating outright that Whites would always be racist, Garvey was the one man who reached the frustrated masses in the urban ghettoes. During its heyday in the early 1920s, his movement not only claimed millions of adherents but collected more money than any Black organization had ever done before. In 1921, Garvey announced the establishment of a Black republic with himself as president and purchased two steamships for his Black Star Line, which was supposed to provide passage for the back-to-Africa emigrants. "The widespread interest in Garvey's program was more a protest against the anti-Negro reaction of the postwar period than an approbation of the fantastic schemes of the Negro leader," John Hope Franklin wrote in his influential history of African Americans (322). Garvey brought race pride to the Black masses, extolling the African past and teaching that God and Christ were Black. Roi Ottley, an African-American journalist who was a close observer of the Harlem scene, pointed out that Garvey's racial doctrine brought him the open support of the Ku Klux Klan and the Anglo-Saxon clubs; he sometimes shared a platform with White supremacist leaders. "It is the duty of the virtuous and morally pure of both the white and black races," Garvey declared, "to thoughtfully and actively protect the future of the two peoples, by vigorously opposing the destructive propaganda and vile efforts of the miscegenationists of the white race, and their associates, the hybrids of the Negro race" (qtd. in Ottley 73).

In 1923, the federal government jailed Garvey on a charge of mail fraud in raising money for his steamship line; four years later he was deported as an undesirable alien and the movement was eviscerated.

Nationalism among the Jews was a more pragmatic affair. With the British acquisition of Palestine as a League of Nations mandate and the advent of the Balfour Declaration expressing official British approval for the creation of a Jewish homeland, the Zionist dream no longer seemed quite so utopian. American Jews weren't interested in emigrating to Palestine, but they were aware of the rising tide of anti-Semitism in Europe. Hamstrung by their own desire not to make waves and thereby call attention to themselves, American Jews split over the Zionist question. Reform Jews had always advocated assimilation and strenuously objected to any sort of Jewish nationalism that could bring their allegiance to America into doubt. The new movement of Conservative Judaism, created as a middle ground between the assimilationist extremes of Reform Judaism and the rigidity of Orthodoxy, recognized that Zionism offered the greatest opportunity for American Jews to bridge the gulf between the ethnic and the religious components of Jewish identity. Conservative rabbis became the staunchest proponents of cultural Zionism and among the earliest to advocate political Zionism. But discussions of Jewish nationalism were very much a family affair, conducted within specialized publications, Jewish parlors, and synagogues. Gentile America wasn't interested, and Jews weren't eager for public attention.

Yiddishism, the other form of Jewish nationalism that wanted to see the survival of a distinctly secular Jewish culture within the matrix of the language, was strictly confined to the ghetto and made no impact on the national discourse. In his 1915 brief for cultural pluralism, Kallen described the Jewish quarter in New York, "a city within a city," as filled with vibrant institutions: "It has had its sectaries, its radicals, its artists, its literati; its press, its literature, its theater, its Yiddish and its Hebrew, its Talmudical Colleges and its Hebrew Schools, its charities and its vanities, and its coordinating organization, the Kehilla, all more or less reduplicated wherever Jews congregate in mass" (*Culture and Democracy*, 113). With the closing of America's doors to new Jewish immigration in the 1920s, however, the hope of maintaining a language and way of life based on Eastern European culture died with the last of the immigrant generations. Yiddishists grew so alarmed at the waning of their cultural base that in 1943 the leading pedagogue of the Jewish People's Fraternal Order declared that "the melting pot has a scorched bottom" (qtd. in Buhle 191).

By the end of the 1920s the prolonged orgy of racism and xenophobia seemed to be somewhat on the wane, not because the mood of the country had shifted to one of greater tolerance but because the issues of concern to the Klan and the evangelical Protestants seemed to have been settled in their favor. Jews continued to rise within the economic structure, but they accepted social ostracism without public protest; Blacks likewise seemed resigned to their second-class citizenship, although there were movements of protest and amelioration, as we shall see below. The onset of the Great Depression had a dampening effect on the boosterism that had fueled so much of the support for the nativist doctrine. America, with its soup kitchens and bread lines, no longer seemed a model of successful capitalism. More and more people gave heed to the rising voice of the American Left. The Klan's membership declined to 30,000, and it would never again find itself so near the center of American politics. With the Hoover Administration's hollow optimism in the face of economic disaster, the laissez faire philosophy of the Republican Party sustained a serious blow, and Roosevelt, elected in 1932, would transform the relationship of the federal government to its citizens.

Within most American communities, however, racial and ethnic relations continued along the lines already laid down during the previous thirty years. No effective attack was made on the Jim Crow laws of the South; African Americans suffered from caste disabilities in a way that was unique to America's checkered relations with its minorities. "The boundary between Negro and white is not simply a class line which can be successfully crossed by education, integration into the national culture, and individual economic advancement," Myrdal wrote in *An American Dilemma*. "The boundary is fixed. It is a not a temporary expedience during an apprenticeship in the national culture. It is a bar erected with the intention of permanency" (58). At mid-century, well after African Americans had proved their patriotism and courage by fighting in both World Wars, there were laws on the books of twenty-nine states—more than half—forbidding marriage between Blacks and Whites. During World War II, 3 million African Americans served in segregated armed forces. The Navy didn't allow Blacks to enter the service other than in menial capacities; the Air Force trained Black fighter pilots but sent them on no missions. Incidents of race-baiting and harassment were legion, the court martial of Jackie Robinson being only the most notorious example. "The nation cannot expect colored people to feel that the United States is worth defending if the Negro continues to be treated as he is now," Eleanor Roosevelt declared early in the war (qtd. in Franklin 405), but Blacks served all the same. White attitudes remained largely unchanged. Myrdal described the racial stereotypes that were current during wartime and which still find a *sub rosa* affirmation in contemporary America: "that they are criminal and of disgustingly, but somewhat enticingly, loose sexual morals; that they are religious and have a gift for dancing and singing; and that they are the happy-go-lucky children of nature who get a kick out of life which white people are too civilized to get" (48).

During the 1930s and 1940s Jews continued to find themselves excluded from the professions and white-collar jobs in the private sector. The relatively high visibility of Jews in the American Left and in the Roosevelt Administration fed the fantasies of those who shared Henry Ford's vision of the international Jew bent upon world power through revolutionary conspiracy. Conservatives latched onto the term "Judeobolshevism" during the interwar period, and the less refined among them taxed Roosevelt's program with the epithet "Jew Deal." In 1933 Congressman Louis McFadden rose on the floor of the House of Representatives to allege the existence of an international Jewish conspiracy. When the American Jewish Committee requested that the statement be retracted, McFadden responded with accusations that Louis Brandeis and Felix Frankfurter, both Supreme Court Justices, were "communist henchmen." Not all shared Congressman McFadden's beliefs to the same degree, but polls commissioned during the Second World War showed that 60 to 65 percent of the American public believed that Jews had too much power.

The spectacular rise of fascism in Europe bolstered anti-Semitism in American society and spawned protofascist fringe groups as well. The Defenders of the Christian Faith attacked Roosevelt as an agent of the Jews and Communists, while the Silver Shirts, a West Coast organization, blamed Communism, the Depression, and the spread of immorality on the Jews. The most influential voice in American anti-Semitism during the 1930s belonged to Father Charles Coughlin, a Catholic priest who orated about politics on a national radio program. Moving steadily to the right during the course of the decade, he formed the National Union for Social Justice as a political arm and issued a weekly magazine, *Social Justice*, which reprinted *The Protocols of the Elders of Zion* in 1938. Increasingly willing to advocate profascist positions, the magazine defended the persecution of the Jews in Europe, linking them to a communist threat and holding them responsible for the outbreak of World War II.

As the condition of their European brethren worsened, American Jews became aware of the urgency of finding a place of emigration, but in a nation still stagnating under the Depression, public opinion adamantly opposed reopening America's gates. The resulting refugee crises of the 1930s and early 1940s finally won American Jews over to Zionism; by 1943 most affiliated Jews had become Zionists of one sort or another. But the movement itself was hopelessly divided between those who wanted to concentrate their energies on a rescue effort and those who felt that the establishment of a Jewish commonwealth in Palestine superseded all other goals. The American Jewish community was insufficiently powerful to persuade the government to change its restrictive immigration policy, and the worldwide Zionist movement could not get Great Britain to renounce its White Paper of 1939 forbidding further Jewish immigration to Palestine.

The decade between 1935 and 1945 was the worst in world Jewry's long history. "At home, open antisemitic advocacy was growing common, structural discrimination had spread, government concern was minimal, and extreme right-wing groups operated freely" (Weinberg 223). The mood of American Jews at the beginning of the European conflict was one of fear and pessimism. In August 1942 Rabbi Stephen Wise received a copy of the Riegner telegram (at first suppressed by the U.S. government) confirming the details of the "final solution." Leadership of world Jewry had passed by default to the American Jews, but there was no single movement or leader who could speak for this vanished entity. "Despite the desperate need," the historian Henry Feingold writes, "every attempt to achieve unity failed, and American Jews faced the Holocaust as a riven, fearful people" (265). Jewish leaders suggested the bombing of the gas chambers and the rail lines leading to them, but the military rejected these plans on the grounds that they required an unacceptable reordering of war priorities.

By the conflict's end, one out of every three Jews worldwide had been exterminated while America and other governments had refused refuge. In 1941 Congress turned down a proposal to admit 20,000 German Jewish children; the following year the State Department rejected Sweden's proposal for a joint rescue of 20,000 Jewish children from Germany. After the Holocaust and the butchery of the Second World War, the 5 million Jews of America found that they now constituted half of the world's Jewish population . (A century earlier, the U.S. Jewish population of 50,000 accounted for 1 percent.) The irony was that since the close of the First World War, the fragmentation of American Jews had proceeded at such a pace that one could no longer describe them as a community. The religious bond no longer unified, and the ethnic bond based on a Yiddish-speaking culture was on the wane. Horribly enough, the new touchstone of Jewish identity—once the shock had worn off—would be the Holocaust itself.

The prolonged and massive butcheries of the two world wars had begun to unseat Enlightenment certainties for large segments of the population. World War I had shaken the faith of European intellectuals in European civilization, and into that breach had rushed the German expressionists, the French surrealists, the British Bloomsbury crowd, the Italian futurists, the American expatriates—all of the Western avant gardes. For most citizens, however, the reaction to this glimpse into the abyss was to hold on yet more tightly to the exploded shibboleths of God, race, and country, preparing the ground for the rise of fascism. Blacks and Jews both found themselves on the wrong side of the racial equation, but the *zeitgeist* that encouraged caste restriction and social segregation in the United States sprouted much more poisonous weeds in Nazi Germany. When the final solution was put into operation, the first Germans to be taken away were those who had been fathered by Black GIs during World War I. The Holocaust was not uniquely directed against the Jews, and they had no monopoly on its horror. In his preface to Elie Wiesel's *Night*, a searing memoir of Auschwitz, French Catholic writer François Mauriac spoke of the sorrow he felt in witnessing the boxcars of children headed for the death camps. "The dream which Western man conceived in the eighteenth century, whose dawn he thought he saw in 1789, and which, until August 2, 1914, had grown stronger with the progress of enlightenment and the discoveries of science— this dream vanished finally for me before those trainloads of little children" (Mauriac, xi)

In the United States, however, even during the most difficult moments, Blacks and Jews were able to draw on a political culture that offered more hope. In one of his early panegyrics to the American Creed, Myrdal claimed that all of the "Old Americans"—his term—adhered to the ideals of liberty and equality for all as the faith of their ancestors. "The others—the Negroes, the new immigrants, the Jews, and other disadvantaged and unpopular groups—could not possibly have invented a system of political ideals which better corresponded to their interests" (13). The irony, as Myrdal was well aware, was that the American Dilemma of separate caste status for African Americans was as firmly in place at the time of his writing as it had been fifty years earlier. That same half century had witnessed enormous psychological, demographic, and economic changes in the Black American community, but its legal status had not been significantly ameliorated. Jews, as many students of American ethnic relations had pointed out, did not labor under the disabilities of caste status. Although they suffered social ostracism and some form of economic discrimination, there was no legal bar to their rising to higher and higher economic levels. This they did—and in spectacular fashion. By mid-century, Jews had progressed so dramatically in economic achievement, the attainment of high educational levels, and the acquisition of mainstream culture that their entry into American institutions as full-fledged citizens seemed already well under way. Yet the price of the ticket, as Robert Park observed as early as 1913, was the loss of ethnic soul. This was a dilemma that would not confront African Americans until well after their caste status had been declared unconstitutional.

As Stephen Steinberg has written, the rapidity of the Jewish rise in America was a matter of historical timing: "there was a fortuitous match between the experience and skills of the Jewish immigrants, on the one hand, and the manpower needs and opportunity structures, on the other" (103). The Eastern European Jews had come to America with a rich cultural heritage, certainly; but had they not also possessed the industrial and entrepreneurial skills already developed in the modernizing economies of Russia, Poland, and the Ukraine, the high literacy rate (in Hebrew) and the perceived predilection toward study (confined to a minority of religious men) that casual observers often cite as the reason for Jewish success in America would have counted for little. Steinberg underscores the point that Jewish immigrants were not peasants emerging from semifeudal conditions but an urban working class, already possessed of the skills, including secular literacy, that gave them a head start in climbing the economic ladder. When Jewish immigrants first filled the ghettoes of the Lower East Side and later Brownsville, conditions there were as bad as in any other poor and overcrowded neighborhood; but as soon as their economic circumstances permitted, they got out. The proportion of Jews on the Lower East Side declined from 75 percent in 1892 to 23 percent in 1916. Although they encountered social ostracism when they moved to better neighborhoods and suburbs, they established their own country clubs, frequented their own hotels, formed their own voluntary associations.

They also defended themselves in the face of egregious anti-Semitism. In the Messina blood libel incident mentioned earlier, Louis Marshall, head of the American Jewish Committee, extracted a public apology from the mayor by threatening to take the case before the appellate division of the Supreme Court of New York. Using the courts in a complicated libel case brought against Henry Ford by a secular Jew, Aaron Shapiro, Marshall was able to wrest from the tycoon a skillfully worded public apology that professed ignorance of the seven years of vilification that had been a staple of the *Dearborn Independent*. Marshall, a lawyer of German Jewish background, preferred to work quietly within the system to achieve his results. There were certainly more boisterous and provocative elements of the Jewish populace, most notably the Jewish socialists, but these were marginal to American society, and their effect, other than dismaying their more assimilated kin, was minimal. The quiet persuasion and pressure employed first by the German Jews and later by their Eastern European successors produced better—though less publicized—results than the mass pressure favored by the radicals.

Such a strategy could not move African Americans out of their caste status. Booker T. Washington had been able to accumulate immense personal power by turning White paternalism and patronage to his advantage, but he had done nothing to reduce the dimensions of the color line that split the United States into two nations. "In all things that are purely social we can be as separate as the five fingers," he declared in his famous Cotton Exposition speech of 1895, "yet one as the hand in all things essential to human progress" (*Up From Slavery*, 148). Only a sustained campaign of public protest, legal challenge, and political agitation could move the nation to a reexamination of its caste system, but Washington's power at the beginning of the century was so great and his opposition to such a strategy so unremitting that he successfully stymied the attempt by W. E. B. Du Bois to form a Black protest organization, the Niagara Movement, in 1905. He could not control the Whites as effectively, however, and in 1908 when a race riot in Abraham Lincoln's home town of Springfield, Illinois, resulted in the deaths of eight African Americans and a mass exodus of Blacks, a White journalist reporting the incident issued an appeal for the revival of the abolitionist spirit. The resulting interracial organization, which in 1910 changed its name to the National Association for the

Advancement of Colored People (NAACP), included among its founding members Du Bois, who resigned his position as a professor at Atlanta University to assume the post of executive secretary. (Washington refused to have any association with the organization unless he was given a guarantee that Du Bois would not formulate its policies.) Four years later, the NAACP had 6,000 members in fifty branches and a circulation of more than 31,000 for its magazine, *The Crisis*, edited by Du Bois. From its inception, the NAACP put its emphasis on effecting change by lobbying for corrective legislation, educating public opinion, and securing favorable court decisions. In the latter enterprise, Jewish lawyers such as Arthur Spingarn, Milton Konvitz, and Jack Greenberg helped found the Legal Defense Fund, which split off from the NAACP in 1939.

Although advocating greater militancy in the securing of civil rights and social justice, the NAACP was never a force for Black nationalism. Its Black leaders were drawn from the African American elite, the section of the population that Du Bois had termed the Talented Tenth. It was the duty of these leaders, Du Bois argued, to show their less fortunate brethren the modes of social and economic behavior that would demonstrate the worthiness of the race as a whole for the status of full citizenship. In order to further this cause, another interracial organization, the National Urban League, was founded in 1910 to help the pilgrims of the Great Migration adjust to life in the cities. As David Levering Lewis points out, Black and Jewish assimilationist leaders of both ethnic groups shared the same agenda. "Just as Schiff [a Jewish leader of Germanic descent] had pleaded with Lower East Side leaders to urge immigrant parents not to speak Yiddish to their children, National Urban League workers delivered lectures on proper English, boisterousness, proper dress, and soap and toothbrushes" (22). In this shared task of "civilizing" the greenhorns and transplanted sharecroppers—and combating the rising tide of Anglo-Saxon ideology—the Black and Jewish elites formed the beginning of an interethnic coalition. Louis Marshall and his son were behind an unsuccessful effort to pass an antilynching law in New York state. The philanthropist Julius Rosenwald disbursed millions of dollars to build schools for Southern Blacks and allocated moneys toward the endowment and construction of Black colleges and universities. Joel Spingarn, one of the founders of the NAACP, provided money for the Spingarn Medal, awarded annually to an exemplar of Black achievement.

Significantly, the great majority of Jews closely associated with the NAACP and the NUL, including Franz Boas and Melville J. Herskovits, opposed Zionism. Likewise the Talented Tenth found Garvey's Black nationalism discomfiting, but given its explosive grassroots appeal they were hesitant to oppose it publicly. The alliance between the Black and Jewish elites of the early twentieth century, Lewis argues, was a defensive one, based on a shared aversion to White supremacy and ethnic nationalism. The assumptions guiding both elites were Enlightenment ones.

"By assisting in the crusade to prove that Afro-Americans could be decent, conformist, cultured human beings, the civil rights Jews were, in a sense, spared some
of the necessity of directly rebutting anti-Semitic stereotypes; for if blacks could
make good citizens, clearly, most white Americans believe, all other groups could
make better ones" (31).

For African Americans, racial amelioration on a national level was impossible
given the obdurate opposition to it in the South. When the NAACP won its first
significant legal victory in 1915 with the Supreme Court banning of the "grandfather clause," which stipulated that no male who was not the descendent of a pre-
Emancipation Proclamation voter could participate in the election process, the
Southern states instituted the "White primary," throwing up a barrier to Black vot-
ing rights that remained in place until the *Smith vs. Allwright* decision of 1944.

For a certain sector of the sophisticated urban population, however, Black music,
theater, and (to a lesser extent) writing came into vogue with the Harlem Renaissance of the 1920s. Although sustained by White patronage and occurring, as Lewis
cleverly points out, in "rented space"—that is, in a Harlem they did not own—the
Renaissance made a simultaneous and ambiguous contribution to Black assimilation by presenting talented artists and performers for public consumption and to
Black nationalism by promoting racial difference (usually under the cover of exoti-
cism), Black pride, and a new appreciation of Black folk culture. Americanizing
Jews of the same period, by contrast, were less concerned with preserving traditional culture than with creating a space for an acceptable, modified Jewishness that
would easily fit into the mainstream. During the 1920s, Rabbi Mordecai Kaplan
elaborated a notion of Jewishness that deemphasized the intransigent religious elements in favor of a collective culture and ethos—language, folkways, patterns of social organization—that could adapt comfortably to its home in America.[6]
Reconstructionism, as Kaplan's movement came to be known, celebrated Jewish
civilization and denied the basic tenet of religious Judaism, i.e., that Jews had a
special relationship with God. Reform Judaism handled the problem somewhat differently, converting the specifically Judaic notion of election to a vaguer, less millennial sense of mission. Even the Zionism of the period was relatively discreet. The
motto of Louis Brandeis, leader of the Zionist Organization of America, was "Silence in America; service in Palestine" (Lewis 24).

The career of Brandeis illustrated perfectly the peculiar predicament of
American Zionists, for Brandeis was the first Jew to serve on the United States
Supreme Court. Appointed by President Wilson in 1916, Brandeis refused to
emerge from behind the scenes in his leadership of a stormy and fratricidal movement. The paradox of a "discreet" Zionist who was also a Supreme Court justice
could hardly be reproduced in the African American sphere. Garveyites were anathema to the mainstream; the federal government eventually found a way to put the

Black nationalist leader out of action. Less political figures who promoted any kind of cultural nationalism—Langston Hughes, Paul Robeson, Claude McKay—moved leftward into another kind of marginality. White America had no interest in coopting Judaism either as a religion or as a civilization (that work had been accomplished centuries before by the early Christians), and it was this very indifference that gave American Jews a protected space for internal dialogue. The reverse side of the coin was that although it was out of the question for an African American to gain influence in national culture outside of a racial context, American Jews could do so only at the price of ethnic invisibility. As Feingold writes, "Social mobility was . . . accompanied by a dilution of ethnic identity as part of the trade-off for gaining access and acceptance" (145–46).

Blacks and Jews who came to prominence as a result of their association with New Deal policies perfectly illustrated the shaping influence of mainstream attitudes. The Roosevelt administration marked a turning point in the history of both groups: never before had there been such representation of minority issues and personnel within the executive branch. Although Roosevelt's advocacy of minority interests fell far short of the expectations he raised among the Black and Jewish populace, his activist presidency, revolutionizing the role of government in the lives of all Americans, seemed to promise the creation of a new sphere of opportunity that would hew more closely to the American Creed. As Myrdal wrote in the early 1940s, "The New Deal has actually changed the whole configuration of the Negro problem" (74). Jews too had a well-known and well-documented love affair with FDR. Yet the Jews who were close to the President—Henry Morgenthau Jr., Secretary of the Treasury; Felix Frankfurter, Supreme Court appointee of 1939; Samuel Rosenmann, political manager and speech writer—never advocated Jewish causes or presented themselves as Jewish spokespersons.

By contrast, the African Americans who occupied high positions in the Roosevelt administration were always hired as Negro specialists and advisors in various governmental departments: Robert Vann, special assistant to the attorney general; William Hastie, who entered government service as assistant solicitor in the Department of Interior; Mary McLeod Bethune, the first Black woman to receive a major federal appointment as the director of Negro Affairs in the National Youth Administration. For the first time in American history, the U.S. government opened up to professional Blacks, and African Americans were employed as architects, lawyers, engineers, economists, and librarians. The number of African American employees on the federal payroll quadrupled from 50,000 in 1933 to approximately 200,000 by 1946. By far the most influential New Deal voice speaking on behalf of the nation's Black population was that of Eleanor Roosevelt, "the New Deal's conscience." She included Black and integrated organizations on her itineraries, welcomed such groups to the White House, and spoke out for racial equality. In a famous 1939 incident, when the Black classical singer Marian Anderson was refused permission by the Daughters of the American Revolution to perform in Constitution Hall, Mrs. Roosevelt secured permission to use the Lincoln Memorial for a concert attended by 75,000.

Hit hardest by the prolonged Great Depression, the Black communities bene-fited in varying degrees—although not nearly enough to alleviate the stress of eco-nomic hardship—from such New Deal programs as the Federal Employment Relief Administration, the National Recovery Administration, and the Works Projects Administration. The NAACP also began making headway in dismantling Jim Crow legislation through a series of court decisions requiring southern universities to provide "separate but equal" institutions for Blacks' graduate education, thus making segregation ruinously expensive. On four separate occasions between 1938 and 1950, an African American sought admittance to a white graduate school on the grounds that there were no equivalent Black institutions, and the Supreme Court ordered the admission each time.

The 1930s also saw gifted African Americans contribute to national life in un-usual and symbolic ways. In 1936 Jesse Owens won four gold medals at the Olympics hosted by Nazi Berlin, a harbinger of the role America would find itself thrust into as the most powerful opponent of fascism in later years. The following year when the boxer Joe Louis defeated Max Schmelling for the heavyweight cham-pionship, the whole African American community greeted the news in a delirium of justificatory celebration. Paul Robeson began his extraordinary career as a singer and actor, and Richard Wright became the first bestselling Black author with the 1940 publication of *Native Son*.

Following the pattern outlined above, Jews who were making contributions to national culture at this time did so from a peculiar angle. The humor of the Marx Brothers, for example, was certainly not mainstream WASP, but it was a humor in which Jewishness never spoke its name. The same could be said for the plays of Clifford Odets in spite of their Yiddishized English. Irving Berlin's songs and an-thems came close to being entirely deethnicized, and other prominent Jews in the cultural scene—George Gershwin, Benny Goodman, Samuel Goldwyn, Edna Ferber—created equally "American" products. There was little in their music, their moviemaking, or their writing that pointed to an ethnic solidarity with other Jews. (Hank Greenberg, the baseball player who was twice elected the American League's Most Valuable Player, represented a partial exception to the rule; he refused to play a game in 1934 scheduled on Yom Kippur.) With the massive alteration of the Jewish occupational profile that began in the 1920s, ever greater numbers of Jews moved away from their immigrant origins while the Yiddish-speaking culture of the ghetto underwent a visible decline. The atrophy of immigrant culture and lan-guage shocked its members, but this was inevitable given the stanching of new biological and cultural infusions from Eastern Europe. A 1940 survey showed that native-born Jews did not acquire Yiddish, even though it was the language of their parents. "Unlike the Jews of eastern Europe, American Jewry would not sustain a separate secular culture with its own language that could break the fall of those abandoning Judaism" (Feingold, 88). Their communal ties weakened by assimilation, American Jews on the eve of the Holocaust found they no longer shared a common culture and could not speak with a single voice to the plight of European Jewry.

As we have already seen with the growth of a Zionist consensus among American Jews, international events leading to World War II produced nationalist reactions in both groups—Haile Selassie, the Ethiopian emperor, became a hero to Black Americans after Italy invaded his country in 1935—but the more significant thrust of the conflict was toward greater integration of Blacks and Jews into the American mainstream. The increasing acceptance of liberal thought and policy that had been inaugurated by the popularity of FDR and the New Deal gained added impetus from the ideological opposition of fascism that was part of the war effort. This greater atmosphere of liberalism, although certainly not uniform (the South continued to resist all forms of integration), provided greater toleration for the Jews and a space for African Americans to press more vigorously for economic and social parity. As the defense industries geared up in the late thirties and early forties, it became apparent that, as in World War I, Black job applicants were again experiencing discrimination. A. Philip Randolph, a Black labor organizer, threatened FDR in 1941 with a march on Washington, and the president responded to the pressure by issuing Executive Order 8802 banning discrimination in war industries and government work. For Black America, the Executive Order was a landmark. "This was the first presidential executive order on race relations since the Emancipation Proclamation and it changed the climate of the civil rights struggle" (Bennet 367). The following year saw the founding of the Congress of Racial Equality (CORE), which staged its first sit-in at a restaurant in Chicago's Loop. World War II brought about several "firsts" for Black military men. FDR appointed B. O. Davis Sr. as a Black general in the regular Army; Bernard W. Robinson, a Harvard medical student, became the first African American to win a commission in the Navy; and in 1941 the Army dedicated a flying school for Black cadets at Tuskegee. Black soldiers fought for the first time in the Marines and the Air Corps. For the Jews, as Edward Shapiro writes, World War II represented the great watershed in the creation of an integrated national identity. "Military service broadened the cultural perspective of Jewish servicemen, and American Jewry emerged from the struggle convinced that they were no longer an exotic ethnic and religious minority but an integral part of American culture" (Shapiro 15).

Contrasting sharply with the national mood after the armistice of 1919, American culture saw dramatic gains in tolerance and liberalism after the end of

World War II. Jews had fully participated in the war effort, and of course most citizens were now aware that the Allied victory had halted—though tragically late—the complete extermination of European Jewry. In the postwar conflict and controversy surrounding the 1948 establishment of Israel, the vast majority of Americans favored the Jewish cause and supported the creation of a Jewish state. (Furthermore, a Jewish homeland relieved the United States of any responsibility for absorbing Europe's displaced Jews.) Anti-Semitism was no longer acceptable in public discourse, and a series of polls testified to a real decline in its expression even as Jews moved quickly into the social, cultural, and economic mainstream. "After the Holocaust, anti-Semitism meant not merely the exclusion of Jews from clubs, exclusive neighborhoods, and elite colleges. It also involved mass murder" (Shapiro 16). In 1945 Bess Myerson of the Bronx was elected the first Jewish Miss America. Twentieth Century Fox's movie about anti-Semitism, *Gentlemen's Agreement*, not only won the Academy Award for best film in 1947 but also proved to be the studio's most profitable venture that year.

The times offered increased possibilities for African Americans as well. Black leaders had educated the nation to the necessity for change during the interwar years; military demands and labor shortages during wartime had opened up new employment opportunities; and the position of the United States as leader of the Free World made its support of legal segregation—a social injustice fully exploited by Communist propaganda—an international embarrassment. The Truman Administration proved to be a surprisingly vigorous champion of Black civil rights. In September 1946, after NAACP Executive Secretary Walter White led a delegation to the White House to plead for executive action on behalf of African Americans, Truman established a Presidential Committee that produced a 1947 document, *To Secure These Rights*, expressing the following sentiments:

> The pervasive gap between our aims and what we actually do is creating a kind of moral dry rot which eats away at the emotional and rational bases of democratic beliefs. There are times when the difference between what we preach about civil rights and what we practice is shockingly illustrated by individual outrages. There are times when the whole structure of our ideology is made ridiculous by continuing, quiet, omnipresent practices which do irreparable damage to our beliefs. (Committee on Civil Rights, "Program of Action," 376)

The report contained an impressive range of recommendations for remedial actions, but the proposals were rejected by a Congress still in thrall to "the solid South." Congressional recalcitrance did not reflect the mood of the nation, however. Truman won the 1948 election in spite of a walkout by the so-called Dixiecrats protesting a strong civil rights plank. In July of that same year he issued Executive Order 9981 establishing a Committee on Equality of Treatment and Opportunity in the Armed Services, which marked the beginning of the end for a segregated military.

Breaches appeared in the wall of segregation in other areas as well. Most famously, Jackie Robinson began playing for the Brooklyn Dodgers in 1947, and that same year saw a Black sociologist, Dr. Ira Reid, appointed to the faculty of New York University. In 1949 William Hastie became the first African American judge to sit on the U.S. Circuit Court of Appeals. Ralph Bunche, who mediated the Palestine crisis for the United Nations, received a Nobel Prize in 1950.

Liberal scholarship flourished, and its practitioners made optimistic pronouncements about the changing status of America's most visible minority. In a wartime essay, Robert Park declared that Northern Blacks were no longer a caste but rather a racial and cultural minority "like the Jews, the Japanese, and perhaps, the Indian and Mexican" (311). Five years later, Oliver Cox wrote, "Negroes are moving away from a condition of extreme white domination and subjection to one of normal citizenship" (498). Even Richard Wright pronounced from his European exile that America was attempting to put its racial house in order. Such books as W. J. Cash's *Mind of the South* (1941) and Myrdal's *American Dilemma,* describing American race relations with a pitiless accuracy, made a significant impact in academic circles.

America at mid-century was a much different country than what it had been fifty years earlier. Sustained postwar prosperity would make a place for Blacks and Jews in the fabric of national life. The Jews were on the threshold of their visible impact on national culture, and of course that same decade would witness for African Americans the Supreme Court death knell of legal segregation in the *Brown vs. Topeka Board of Education* decision of 1954 as well as the beginning of the civil rights movement. Myrdal, in his Enlightenment envoi at the end of *American Dilemma,* expressed the hopes of liberal society, hopes that seemed to have a chance of finding their expression in a not too distant future.

Behind all outward dissimilarities, behind their contradictory valuations, rationalizations, vested interests, group allegiances and animosities, behind fears and defense constructions, behind the role they play in life and the mask they wear, people are all much alike on a fundamental level. And they are all good people. They want to be rational and just. They all plead to their conscience that they meant well even when things went wrong. (1023)

The irony was that the very liberalism that allowed for this final resurgence of Enlightenment optimism gave birth shortly thereafter to an African American identity that would never again subscribe to an implicitly White set of assumptions about assimilation and the supremacy of mainstream culture. Richard Wright's *Black Boy* and Alfred Kazin's *A Walker in the City* were both expressions of their time, both movements from an oppressed ethnic and racial space to one more liberated and "universal," but the declarations of difference that lurk just underneath the surface of these life stories were to become the principal structuring devices of the Black and Jewish autobiographers of an America that by the 1970s had lost its Enlightenment innocence.

The
Sunset
Generation

. . . when I tried to talk to [my father] I realized that,
though ties of blood made us kin, though I could see a
shadow of my face in his face, though there was an echo
of my voice in his voice, we were forever strangers,
speaking a different language, living on vastly distant
planes of reality.

—Richard Wright, *Black Boy*

Secretly, I thought the synagogue a mean place, and went
only because I was expected to. . . . Whether I agreed
with its belief or not, I belonged; whether I assented to
its rights over me or not, I belonged; whatever I thought
of them, no matter how far I might drift from that place,
I belonged. This was understood in the very nature of
things; I was a Jew. It did not matter how little I knew
or understood of the faith, or that I was always reading
alien books; I belonged, I had been expected, I was now
to take my place in the great tradition.

—Alfred Kazin, *A Walker in the City*

Richard Wright and Alfred Kazin belonged to the last generation of American
writers who adhered, on a conscious level, to the ideology of ethnic transcendence

that had come down from the eighteenth century. The liberal American mainstream continued to pay lip service to the proposition that all citizens should receive equal treatment under the law, but the general acceptance of blatant inequalities based on class, race, and gender drove many men and women of conscience into radical critiques of Enlightenment liberalism. Although socialism and communism never had a major impact on American electoral politics, their ideologies made significant headway among activists and intellectuals during the 1930s and prewar 1940s. Kazin and Wright emerged in the public arena at a time when the radical Left exerted its greatest influence, both culturally and politically, upon the American mainstream. Yet the militant optimism of the Left was merely another expression of Enlightenment ideals. "I grew up as a Socialist," Kazin declared, "that is, as a believer in the Enlightenment" ("Interview," 208).

The term "socialism" made its debut around 1830 in relation to the writings of Fourier and the Saint-Simonians in France, and to those of Robert Owen in Britain. From the beginning, the intellectual debt owed by socialism to the Enlightenment and, above all, to the French Revolution was apparent. The Enlightenment had enshrined an absolute confidence in a Lockean reality of the senses and engendered a religion of Reason that transformed intellectual activity in all domains. One of the avowed goals of the *Encyclopédie*, the quintessential compendium of Enlightenment views, was to gather all of human knowledge together in a demonstration that human happiness was within humanity's reach once it had rid itself of beliefs and mental habits that had shackled its progress. Both the conviction of humanity's limitless power and the optimistic desire to bring about the greatest good for the greatest number became basic tenets of socialist thought. Although the *philosophes* sought to destroy religious prejudice rather than to revolutionize the foundations of civil society, there were "radicals" among them—Jean-Jacques Rousseau, the Curé Meslier, Morelly, and the Abbé Bonnot de Mably—whose work clearly anticipated the critique of private property, the belief in the fundamental goodness of human character, and the utopianism that became hallmarks of socialism and its progeny.

The Revolution itself, especially at its culmination, deepened these socialistic currents of thought. The *philosophes* had never wearied of denouncing the evils of luxury or of proclaiming the virtues of the life of simple sufficiency, and the leaders of the Revolution were deeply imbued with the moral fervor of these intellectual reformers. Furthermore, the Revolution envisioned a general redistribution of wealth and put it into practice through the burning of title deeds, the sack of the country manors, and the ouster of the nobility. The Revolution even spawned what Marx termed the first active communist party in the so-called Conspiracy of Equality directed by Gracchus Babeuf against the Directory in 1797. Babeuf's conspiracy became a landmark in the theory and practice of revolution because he advanced both a technique for the seizure of power and a belief that an era of universal equality could be inaugurated by a final revolution in which all private property would be destroyed by a popular dictatorship. "Communism," Jean Juarès wrote in his *Histoire socialiste de la révolution française*, "was like the tip of the republican flame and the high revolutionary temperature in France ripened the European proletariat before its time" (562)[1]

Almost a century and a half later, on another continent and within the belly of a stumbling capitalism, leftist radicalism would nourish, for a brief period, the Black and Jewish inheritors of the Enlightenment legacy. Nonetheless, for Wright and Kazin the restatement of Enlightenment ideals within the leftist context neither acknowledges nor frees them from the contradictions of double consciousness.

At the nadir of the Great Depression, Wright, then twenty-seven and the sole support of his mother, aunt, and younger brother, reluctantly joined the bread lines at the Cook County Bureau of Public Welfare in Chicago. He had lied and schemed his way out of the South, had succeeded in bringing his family to the promised land of the North, but, like half the male population of Chicago, Wright found himself without work. His intelligence and determination availed him nothing; the promise of the American dream—that hard work and application would be rewarded—had been given the lie, and he found himself with the destitute and the homeless. "The day I begged bread from the city officials was the day that showed me I was not alone in my loneliness," he wrote in his autobiography, "society had cast millions of others with me. But how could I be with them?" (*American Hunger*, 44).

The answer came in the form of an invitation from a fellow worker, Abraham Aaron, whom Wright knew from a previous job at the post office, to check out the Chicago branch of the John Reed Club. These Communist-sponsored organizations, named after the American journalist who celebrated the Soviet Revolution in *Ten Days that Shook the World*, mixed Marxist discussion with the encouragement of young artists and writers. As opposed to the premier Communist literary journal, *New Masses*, which only accepted the writings of established authors, the John Reed organs—Chicago's *Left Front* and New York's *Partisan Review*—catered to beginners. The Communist Party sponsored The John Reed Clubs, which operated openly as recruiting bodies for artists and writers. Anybody could belong, and many disaffected young writers found the Clubs to be their introduction to left-wing politics.

In autumn 1933, Wright went to the dingy headquarters of the John Reed Club filled with skepticism and curiosity. Treated courteously and without condescension by the White, middle-class membership, Wright returned home "probing the sincerity of the strange white people [he] had met" with an armful of Communist literature. Reading these magazines revealed a world which promised united action for the wretched of the earth. "The revolutionary words leaped from the printed page and struck me with tremendous force."

[I]t seemed to me that here at last in the realm of revolutionary expression was where Negro experience could find a home, a functioning value and role. Out of the magazines I read came a passionate call for the experience of the disinherited, and there were none of the same lispings of the missionary in it. It did not say: "Be like us and we will like you, maybe." It said: "If you possess enough courage to speak out what you are, you will find that you are not alone." It urged life to believe in life. (*American Hunger*, 63–64)

Wright heard in the call of the Communist Party a place "where the Negro experience could find a home." What the Abolition movement had been to Equiano and Douglass, Marxism would be to Wright. Wright was far to the left on the intellectual spectrum of Black America, but his belief in integration was as genuine as that held by Black activists of the National Association for the Advancement of Colored People and the National Urban League. As Mark Naison writes, the high point of the Communist Party's influence in Black America coincided with Wright's emergence as a public figure.

Between 1936 and 1939, the Communist Party emerged as an important focal point of political and cultural activity by Harlem intellectuals. "My memory and knowledge," Party organizer Howard Johnson recalls, "is that 75% of black cultural figures had Party membership or maintained regular meaningful contact with the Party." Harlem critics of the Party spoke bitterly of Party dominance of the black intelligentsia and feared they would use this to "capture the entire Negro group." "Most of the Negro intellectuals," Claude McKay wrote, "were directly or indirectly hypnotized by the propaganda of the Popular Front." (Naison 193)

If Wright had much in common with other African American intellectuals, he also shared certain attitudes with White intellectuals who found themselves drawn to the radical Left. Despair, stemming from the apparent breakdown of capitalism, combined with a genuine idealism to bring many prominent writers and artists into the Party orbit. During the 1932 presidential campaign, John Dos Passos, Sherwood Anderson, Theodore Dreiser, Lincoln Steffens, and Kenneth Burke publicly endorsed the Communist Party ticket of William Foster and James Ford. Michael Gold, author of *Jews Without Money* (1930) and clearly the Party's most influential literary critic, promoted the idea of proletarian literature, which brought to the fore such younger writers as James Farrell, Erskine Caldwell, and Jack Conroy.

It was the Depression rather than the Party itself that drew most intellectuals to the Communists. If anything, the Party remained suspicious of these potential converts. Intellectuals usually came from the wrong class, and they were notoriously reluctant to submit to the discipline the Party demanded of its members. The American Communist Party was subordinate to Communist International, or Comintern, whose publicly announced aim was to bring about the overthrow of the international bourgeoisie and institute a worldwide Soviet republic as a transitional stage to the complete abolition of the State. According to historian Harvey Klehr, "It was abroad, in Moscow, that the decisive formulations were made which the Americans labored to apply to American conditions. Communist policies and language are incomprehensible unless one recognizes that they were largely responses to Comintern directions" (11).

At the time Wright was recruited, the Party was operating under the tactics of the so-called Third Period, an era of capitalist decay and revolutionary ferment proclaimed by the Comintern in 1928.[2] In the belief that it was acting in accordance with the science of history, the Party favored an uncompromising militancy that isolated it within American politics and cost it allies on the Left. Yet the militant stance could also be an asset. During the 1930s, the Communists led a large number of strikes; focused national attention on the plight of the coal miners in Harlan County; organized rent strikes, fights against evictions, and hunger marches. The social breakdown of the Great Depression seemed to validate the Comintern's characterization of the Third Period millennium, and the Communists embraced a multitude of tactics that brought them notoriety, respect, and rage. Left-leaning intellectuals were both fascinated by the Party's willingness to fight for the disinherited and dismayed by its immoderate rhetoric and allegiance to the Soviet Union. Socialism as an American phenomenon had peaked in influence before World War I and the anti-Stalinist Left had yet to be born. "Despite its inhospitable behavior [toward intellectuals]," Klehr writes, "the Communist party was very nearly the only game in town" (79).

The other element that made the Communist Party unique in American politics, and solidified its appeal for Wright, was its commitment to Black participation and civil equality. In 1929 the Comintern ordered the American Party to support a Black Belt separatism based on Stalin's work advocating self-determination for the minorities of the Tsarist empire. This idea was so far out of mainstream American thinking (and was particular anathema to the NAACP, the largest and most influential civil rights organization) that the Party never found it useful in recruiting new members or inspiring successful actions. Yet Communists did focus on discrimination within their own ranks and staged several highly successful show trials against "white chauvinism." James Ford, the Party's vice presidential candidate in 1932, was an African American, a fact that galvanized the attention of Blacks all over the country. The Party also reaped great public relations benefits from its defense of the Scottsboro Boys, nine Black youngsters charged with raping two white women on a freight train near Scottsboro, Alabama, in 1931. That same year, a Black Communist organizer, Angelo Herndon, was arrested in Atlanta, charged with "inciting to insurrection," and sentenced to twenty years on a Georgia chain gang.

Both these cases established the Party's image as a force for racial justice in Black communities. Prominent Black artists such as Langston Hughes, Countee Cullen,

Claude McKay, and Paul Robeson were either Party members or fellow travelers at some time in their careers. Whenever possible, the Party sent promising Black members to the Soviet Union for training as high-ranking cadres, an invitation Wright refused in order to pursue his writing. As Mark Naison notes:

> Communist sponsorship of black arts also took place within its own organizations. In 1938, the Harlem section of the International Workers Order opened the "Harlem Suitcase Theatre," a repertory company organized by Langston Hughes and Louise Thompson. Its first production, Hughes' *Don't You Want to be Free?*, was an agitprop drama which, in the words of one critic, "plunges the Negro, fresh from the sweet barbaric freedom of Africa, into the degrading slavery of America, depicts his glorious fight in throwing off the shackles of slavery to the tune of 'Go Down Moses' and gives hope for a bright new day in the unity of black and white workers." (209)

Nonetheless, Communists had a difficult time recruiting and maintaining a significant Black membership. Their slogans and activities rarely reflected the central elements of African-American culture, many of which drew directly on religious imagery. The symbols of Communism—the red flag, the personality cults of Lenin and Stalin, the Third Internationale—were alien to the vast majority of Black experience.[3] As columnist Murray Kempton observed in his book on the thirties, Black nationalism always struck a deeper chord in the Black masses than any leftist utopia.

> The reasons why Garvey, disgraced and dead, would always deserve a chapter in the history of the American Negro were the reasons why Communists could never be more than a footnote in that history. They labored very long to bring the negro into the army of revolution; at no time have there been more than 5,000 American Negro Communists and they have always been strangers to their brothers. For the Communists, whatever their affirmations, were white men offering a potion, and most Negroes expected them after a while to exact a white man's fee. (245)

When the Comintern deemphasized racial issues to focus on the plight of a besieged Soviet Union at the beginning of World War II, few Blacks were surprised. After the war, Wright and Ralph Ellison would write of the Communist's fee with exceptional acerbity.

Still, the Black intelligentsia of the prewar period did respond positively to the Communist Party's vision. At the Second Convention of the Popular Front's National Negro Congress in 1937 young emerging writers such as Sterling Brown and even Harlem Renaissance stalwart Alain Locke advocated a class vision over the racial one. "This is the only nationalism that, in the long run will be effective," Adam Clayton Powell Jr. wrote of the congress, "a nationalism that aims toward solidifying our race into a militant oneness and to cooperate with other groups in the fight for social justice" (qtd. in Naison 202).

Although the Party had recruited Wright as a Negro and hoped to advance him into the cadres, his own interests in the Left were inseparable from his literary ambitions. From 1934 to 1937, Wright published a number of poems in *Left Front, The Anvil, New Masses,* and *International Literature.* When he attended the second and third national congresses of the John Reed Clubs in 1935 and 1936, he was known as a revolutionary poet rather than as a fiction writer. This period coincided with the Comintern transition from the take-no-prisoners radicalism of the Third Period to the alliance-building activities of the Popular Front. With the alarming rise of Nazism in Europe, the Soviet Union decided that fascism rather than the capitalist bourgeoisie of the Western democracies represented the principal threat to Communism. At the Comintern's Seventh World Congress in the summer of 1935, the main speaker, Georgi Dimitroff of Bulgaria, unceremoniously laid the Third Period to rest by proclaiming that the Communists were ready "to arrange joint actions between the proletariat and the other toiling classes interested in the fight against fascism" (qtd. in Klehr 170). For the American Communist Party, this eventually led to an embracing of President Roosevelt, formerly branded a "social-fascist" under Third Period rhetoric.

The Popular Front strategy brought about two other significant Party reversals, both of which exerted a significant impact on Black intellectual life. The Party quietly dropped its support for Black Belt self-determination, "an albatross isolating the Party from virtually every Negro organization" (Klehr 343), and the John Reed Clubs were replaced by an American Writers' Congress limited to already established authors. Wright had nothing public to say about the Communist about-face on Black separatism (though *American Hunger* describes the show trial of another Black Communist, David Poindexter, who was arraigned for his refusal to abandon the now obsolete policy), but he vainly protested the dissolution of the Clubs.

I was informed that the People's Front policy was now the correct vision of life and that the clubs could no longer exist. I asked what was to become of the young writers who were ineligible for the new group, and there was no answer. This thing is cold! I exclaimed to myself. To effect a swift change in policy, the Communist party was dumping one organization, scattering its members, then organizing a new scheme with entirely new people! (*American Hunger,* 91)

Wright, however, reluctantly made the transition to the new Popular Front auxiliary. He attended the April 1935 meeting of the American Writer's Congress in New York, which resulted in the founding of the League of American Writers. As Communist management of the League receded discreetly into the background, more prominent writers allowed themselves to be associated with the organization. In addition to those who had given support to the Communist presidential ticket in 1932, Thomas Mann, John Steinbeck, Archibald MacLeish, Lewis Mumford, Van

Wyck Brooks, Lillian Hellman, William Carlos Williams, and Nathanael West all participated in League affairs over the next few years. The most conspicuous participant of the Second American Writer's Congress of 1937 was Ernest Hemingway, back from Spain where he had cheered the heroism of the Popular Front resistance to fascism. "So respectable had the League of American Writers become that when Van Wyck Brooks offered President Roosevelt honorary membership inasmuch as 'your writings constitute a unique contribution to the body of American letters,' Roosevelt responded with 'hearty appreciation' in accepting the invitation" (Klehr 356).

Moving in these broader left-wing circles, Wright served an apprenticeship that brought him to the notice of non-Communist literati. "Big Boy Leaves Home" was chosen for inclusion in a mainstream short story anthology, *The New Caravan* (1936). When "Fire and Cloud" won first place in the 1937 *Story Magazine* contest, major publishing houses opened to his work. In 1938, Harper & Row brought out *Uncle Tom's Children*, four novellas of Black resistance to Jim Crow conditions in the South. The *Story Magazine* prize winner, "Fire and Cloud," depicted the heroic struggle of a Black preacher who eventually leads an interracial protest march supported by the Communists.

The evident literary merits of *Uncle Tom's Children* transformed Wright into one of the Party's greatest assets. As Fabre writes in his biography of Wright:

> Under the Party's aegis, Wright received countless honors, which often meant suffering numerous ordeals. . . . [E]very few days of the spring and fall he would be attending a meeting, reception, ball, theater or lecture, or himself be giving a speech for some benefit. Despite his simple tastes and his horror of social functions, he was leading almost a "public" life, never refusing for that period, along with his political activities, to play the role which the Party expected of him as one of its best-known writers. (*Unfinished Quest*, 164–65)

Wright's success had been nurtured within the Communist Party, but from the beginning he had had to fight for his creative autonomy. Party demands for political organization cut into his writing time, and, as he records in *American Hunger*, he met with nothing but contempt and suspicion for his intellectual aspirations, both from the higher cadres of the Chicago Party and from the members of his South Side cell. "The word 'writer' was enough to make a black Chicago Communist feel that the man to whom the word applied had gone wrong" (*American Hunger*, 77). When the African American Harry Haywood, a former member of the Politburo, was assigned to Chicago in 1934 as South Side regional organizer, he summoned Wright to an interview recreated in *American Hunger*. Haywood told Wright that the Party wanted to make him a mass leader and that he was to organize a committee against the high cost of living. Wright protested that his time would be better spent writing, to which Haywood responded, "the trouble with you is that you've been around with those white artists on the North Side too much. . . . You even talk like 'em. You've got to know your own people" (106).

There was some small truth to this accusation. During Wright's Chicago years with the Communists, the friends most influential in guiding him toward literary models were White. Joyce and Ed Gourfain, non-Communist progressives, encouraged Wright in his reading of Henry James, e. e. cummings, Gertrude Stein, Joyce, Eliot, and Faulkner. The African-American poet Margaret Walker, who became friends with Wright around that time, wrote, "If there were two literary books that were Wright's bible they were Henry James' *Collected Prefaces on the Art of the Novel* and Joseph Warren Beach's *Twentieth Century Novel*" (qtd. in Gayle 77). This was a far cry from *proletkult*.

Although Party leaders had difficulty understanding Wright's ambitions as an artist, the Party remained the only venue where a young Black man with an eighth-grade education could connect with the larger society. "As anyone with common sense could easily guess," he wrote to his editor Edward Aswell in 1955, "I was a Communist because I was Negro. Indeed the Communist Party had been the only road out of the Black Belt for me" (qtd. in Fabre, *Unfinished Quest*, 230). In spite of his disheartening experiences with the Communist Party in Chicago, thoroughly chronicled in *American Hunger*, Wright had not given up on Communism when he moved to New York in 1937. Once there, he was given charge of the Harlem bureau of the *Daily Worker*. Between June and December he wrote more than two hundred articles for the paper, all composed strictly from the Party perspective.

In the meantime, Wright made his way in the New York literary establishment. At the beginning of 1939 he received second prize in the O. Henry Memorial Award competition for "Fire and Cloud." In April of that year, the Guggenheim Foundation granted him a fellowship along with John Steinbeck and Robert Penn Warren. With this literary pedigree, Wright had no trouble publishing his novel of poisoned race relations, *Native Son*, in 1940. The story of Bigger Thomas's accidental murder of his white employer's daughter was even chosen as a Book-of-the-Month Club selection, insuring it a readership outside the intelligentsia. When *Native Son* became the first African-American novel to turn into a best seller, Wright's place in the literary firmament was assured.

Using techniques of naturalism and modernism he had garnered from European and American literature, Wright presented his brief against the exclusion of Blacks from Western culture. The novel is filled with racist Whites and their institutions (i.e., the press and the courts). Liberal Whites in *Native Son* are so blind to the desperation of the Black masses and to their own complicity in a racist society that they are portrayed as virtually ineffectual. Only the Communists are presented as genuine, if humanly flawed, proponents of a Western ideology of inclusion. Mary's Communist boyfriend, Jan, begins to acknowledge the limits of his understanding vis-à-vis the Black masses once confronted with Bigger's act. Max, the Jewish lawyer retained for Bigger by the Communist Party, is usually seen as a spokesperson for Wright's Marxist analysis of American racism.[4] Although the novel implicitly presents Communism as the best means for Black liberation, the Communist Party would have preferred a novel that had not stressed so powerfully (and ambiguously) the autonomy of a Black perspective. Max recoils at Bigger's final realization that "What I killed for, I am!" Black Communists like Benjamin Davis Jr. and James Ford took Wright to task for what they called "the nationalist racial spirit" of the novel. After a long silence in the Communist press, Mike Gold finally came to the defense of the novel in his *Daily Worker* column, which constituted the official Party verdict, but Wright was hurt both by Gold's delay and by some of the more doctrinaire reactions.

Nor was Wright the only intellectual unhappy with the Communist Party. On August 23, 1939, Germany and the USSR signed a nonagression pact, clearing the way for the mutual partition of Poland. Shortly afterward, the Soviet Union occupied the Baltic States and invaded Finland. The new Soviet strategy dictated another 180° turn in Communist policy: no longer was fascism the number one enemy. As long as the Soviet Union had needed the United States as a potential ally in a system of collective security to contain Nazi aggression, American Communists had received permission to embrace the New Deal. Now that it was in the best interests of the Soviet Union to remain out of the war Germany had precipitated by its invasion of Poland, the American Communist Party was enjoined to break with its former allies in the Popular Front and to return to Third Period militancy. Revolted by such obvious manipulation from abroad, many intellectuals left the Communist Party and its numerous auxiliary organizations. Among the hardest hit was the League of American Writers. Most of the prominent names associated with the league—Thomas Mann, Van Wyck Brooks, Malcolm Cowley—summarily departed.

Wright himself was not much fazed by the Party's about-face. The Comintern's pacifist stand to keep America out of the "capitalist" war coincided with his own conviction that African Americans had nothing to gain by fighting in a segregated army for a country that persecuted Black soldiers upon their demobilization. In July 1940 he was elected a vice president of the League of American Writers and was also elected to the board of the American Peace Mobilization. "On June 22, 1941, the day after the American Peace Mobilization had organized a National Peace Week, Hitler invaded Soviet Russia. The A.P.M., shamelessly renamed overnight the American People's Mobilization, immediately organized an aid program for Great Britain" (Klehr 225).

Wright found this turnabout harder to stomach. He had been a staunch pacifist, but the Party required him to toe the new line. When he accepted the Spingarn

Medal of 1941, the highest literary award for African Americans, Party leaders forced him to change his speech into an appeal for Blacks to volunteer to defend democracy. According to Wright's biographer, Michel Fabre, "this episode marked the beginning of . . . his ultimate split with the Communists" (*Unfinished Quest*, 226).

With the United States' entry into the war, official Soviet policy no longer labeled the American government a crypto-fascist organization, and the American Communists did all they could to promote a "democratic" victory, even to the extent of opposing a march on Washington organized by A. Philip Randolph to protest against discrimination in armament factories and the armed services. Not only was Wright refused permission to participate in the event, but the African American cadre leaders, James Ford and Benjamin Davis, suggested that he go back to his novels and leave politics to the Party.

Increasingly alienated, Wright distanced himself from Party activities. However, when he received a Party directive to apply for work in the Office of War Information, Davis helped him fill out the application. Rebuffed by the Office (FBI supervision of Wright, which was to continue for the rest of his life, began in December 1942), Wright discovered to his astonishment that Davis denied that Wright had received any Party directive or that he, Davis, had participated in Wright's application process. Personal insult had been added to the injury of the Party's abandonment of racial justice. It was clear that the Party would not hesitate to sacrifice either him as an individual or African Americans as a whole to the "higher" ends of Soviet policy. "On October 14, 1942," an informer told the FBI, "Richard Wright . . . had split with the Party because of his dissatisfaction with the way the Party handled the Negro question" (qtd. in Gayle 146).

Wright's autobiography, originally titled "American Hunger," was part of his painful separation from the organization that had nurtured his coming of age as a writer and national figure. Written in 1943, the original manuscript described Wright's life up to his departure from Chicago in 1937. The second part, titled "The Horror and the Glory," covered his years in Chicago, and described his disillusionment with the Party, its ignorance of the lives of the Black working class, its authoritarianism and ruthless suppression of individual expression. Unable to deal with his New York experiences, Wright telescoped all his hurt and dismay into his Chicago years, making it appear as if his break with the Party occurred as a result of his persecution there. In an episode that echoes Wright's feelings for the Party at the time of writing, he depicts himself as lying on his bed after walking out of the horrible spectacle of his fellow Black Communist's "trial" as a recalcitrant nationalist. "I'll be for them, even though they are not for me," he thinks (125). The Communists, despite their theoretical commitment to justice and equality, were all too flawed.

Although Wright's autobiography (especially as edited) is best known as a portrait of his Southern childhood and adolescence, Addison Gayle brings out the unity
of theme underlying Wright's depiction of himself as a Negro in the South and as a
Communist in Chicago.

> The ethics of communism were as grounded in authoritarianism as those of Jim Crow.
> Appeals to arbitrary decision were useless. Codes of conduct were already prescribed, codi-
> fied. They were carried out by insensitive men and women, enforced by party discipline,
> and handed down without consultation with those who were most affected by them, as were
> the rules and ethics formulated by the aristocracies of the South. (151)

The practices of the Communist Party were ultimately inimical to the Enlightenment ideals the Party claimed to promote.

In August and September 1944, the chapters concerning the Chicago Party,
which had been excised in the published version of *Black Boy*, appeared as a two-
part article in *The Atlantic Monthly*, "I Tried to Be a Communist." Wright's piece
on the Communist Party was notable for its moderation. He did not condemn the
ideals of Communism, nor did he rail against the authority of the Soviet Union.
Wright criticized (under pseudonyms) individual leaders and aired his grievances
against the Black comrades in his South Side cell; he exposed the authoritarianism and mind control of the Party apparatus; but he never recanted his belief in
the solidarity of progressive forces. His farewell to the Party in the final pages of
American Hunger is tinged with nostalgia and regret, the sorrow of a parent taking
leave of a wayward child. He acknowledges the role Communism played in his
literary life, "the stories in which I had assigned a role of honor and glory to the
Communist party," and his leave-taking of this inspiring idealism betrays a bitter
pathos. "I knew in my heart that I would never be able to write that way again,
would never be able to feel with that simple sharpness about life, would never
again express such passionate hope, would never again make so total commitment
of faith" (133).

The authoritarianism of Soviet-style Communism engendered a reaction among
those who considered themselves radicals. Like Wright, many left the Party disillusioned by its leadership but still believers in the vision of a classless society. Others
adhered to different ideologies: Trotskyism, socialism, anarchism. Socialism in particular had been successfully transplanted from Europe, antedating Soviet Marxism
by several decades. Brought over in large part by the immigrants at the end of the
nineteenth century, socialism was far more central to the Eastern European Jewish
milieu than was communism in the lives of African Americans. "You might say I
was born into two Jewish orthodoxies," Kazin remarked in a 1982 interview. "My
mother was an Orthodox Jew, and my father was an orthodox Socialist" ("Interview," 194). In the opening pages of *New York Jew*, the third volume of his auto-

biography, Kazin describes how his father "lovingly enlarged . . . our working-class solidarity, father and son, as he described great labor struggles and the struggle for Socialism—in my childhood the only Jewish religion that could take him out of himself. I saw him break down when Eugene V. Debs died, when Robert M. La Follette lost the Presidency, when Sacco and Vanzetti went to the chair" (15). As this litany reveals, socialism had its own history of radicalism in America. Between 1880 and 1921 when xenophobic sentiment shut the door to immigration, three million Jews came to the United States seeking economic advancement and escape from anti-Semitism. Many of these Jews had encountered modern currents of thought in the Old World: socialism, Zionism, Marxism, anarchism. The majority of these new immigrants settled in the ghettoes of New York, sunk at the bottom layer of an expanding industrial society. Many who had not subscribed to radical ideas before immigration were receptive to these visions as they found themselves brutally exploited in the garment industry.

When American socialism crested in the years immediately preceding the outbreak of World War I, this Jewish proletariat formed the backbone of the Socialist Party; Socialist strength centered in the garment trade of the Lower East Side. In 1914, 1916, and 1920, the Jewish Ninth District sent Meyer London to be the sole Socialist Representative in the United States Congress. Another Jewish immigrant, Morris Hillquit, served as the main intellectual guide of American Socialism during this period. Although harsh internal splits, a repressive national atmosphere in the early twenties, and an improvement in economic conditions for Jewish immigrants contributed to a weakening of socialism as a political force, it remained a part of the immigrant world, one of several secular millennial visions—along with anarchism, Zionism, and Communism—that had its Jewish followers and avatars. The children of these immigrants, the second generation, inherited radical politics as part of a family legacy. When the economic dislocations of the thirties brought a resurgence of radical politics, these second-generation Jews were already familiar with the ideologies and rhetorical styles of the Left and thus could meet the newly radicalized sons and daughters of the American middle class as equals. In the opening of his second autobiographical volume, Kazin describes how all-pervasive this socialist milieu was.

"Socialism" was a way of life, since everyone else I knew in New York was a Socialist, more or less; but I was remarkably detached from it intellectually, and spent my days reading Blake and Lawrence and Whitman. I felt moral compulsions to be a Socialist, since the society in which sixteen million people were jobless that summer and a million on strike did not seem to admit saving except by a Socialist government. But my socialism, though I felt it deeply, did not require any conscious personal assent or decision on my part; I was a Socialist as so many Americans were "Christians"; I had always lived in a Socialist atmosphere. (*Starting Out*, 3–4)

The Socialists benefitted less than the Communists from the social dislocations of the Great Depression. The actual membership of the Party in 1932, when Socialist presidential candidate Norman Thomas received 900,000 votes, was only 17,000. Although the Communist candidate, William Z. Foster, received only 100,000 ballots in the nadir of the Depression, the Party dominated the radical scene with an optimistic militancy and vitality that pulled prominent men and women into its orbit. As Murray Kempton observed, although the Communists failed with ordinary Americans, they succeeded for a time with some extraordinary ones (*Part of Our Time*, 117). Kazin noted that even the controversy sparked by the Moscow Trials of 1936—the open announcement of Stalinism on the worldwide scene—did not diminish the Party's luster. "[B]ecause the Fascist assault on Spain and the ever-growing strength of Hitler had made the United Front necessary, I found myself more sympathetic to the Communists. They had, they had just had, they still seemed to have, Silone, Malraux, Hemingway, Gide, Rolland, Gorky, Aragon, Picasso, Eluard, Auden, Spender, Barbusse, Dreiser, Farrell, while the Socialists seemed to have only their own virtue" (*Starting Out*, 85).

During its militant Third Period, however, the Communist Party had no qualms about alienating its potential allies on the Left. Even when it adopted a conciliatory policy of alliance building, bad blood remained from its previous tactics. Kazin recalls one infamous incident in February 1934 when the Communist Party violently disrupted a Socialist rally in Manhattan. "I had watched Communists break up Socialist meetings and in February I had seen them throwing chairs from the balconies of Madison Square Garden down on the decent trade unionists who had met to honor the Socialists of Vienna hanged by [the Austrian chancellor] Dolfuss," Kazin, then nineteen, wrote in his memoir of the period (*Starting Out*, 3). Among the signers of the open letter of protest immediately following the incident were writers and critics who were to contribute to New York's postwar intellectual preeminence: Elliot Cohen, past editor of *The Menorah Journal* and future editor of *Commentary*; Lionel Trilling, the first Jewish-American literary critic since Ludwig Lewisohn to win a national reputation; Edmund Wilson, already famous for *Axel's Castle* (1931), a study of literary modernism; and John Chamberlain, a literary journalist for *The New York Times*. It was the latter who gave Kazin his entree as a book reviewer for *The New Republic* while he was still an undergraduate in history at City College of New York.

The Communists hit their high-water mark of influence upon American radicalism during the Popular Front period between 1935 and 1939, but this was also a time when many radicals, often ex-Communists, appalled by the tactics and increasing totalitarianism of Soviet-style Communism, formed a loose constellation of parties and alliances now referred to as the anti-Stalinist Left. Within this crucible of radical ideologies (Marxism, Socialism, radicalized pragmatism) and volatile factions

(Trotskyites, Musteites, Cannonites, Lovestoneites), the group of writers and critics now known as the New York Intellectuals first formed the political and cultural views that would bring them together under a recognizable ideological umbrella after World War II. "In any view of the American cultural situation," Trilling wrote in 1966, "the importance of the radical movement of the Thirties cannot be overestimated. It may be said to have created the American intellectual class as we now know it in its great size and influence" (qtd. in Bloom 46).

In the same way that Enlightenment philosophy and literary pursuits allowed exceptional Jews of the Berlin haskalah to participate in the intellectual life of their host country, radical politics offered second-generation American Jews a similar opportunity. These children of the ghetto did not have to deny their Jewish background in order to participate in the work of the various leftist organizations; their ethnic origin simply had no affective value in their view of themselves as agents of change. The Jewishness of the ghetto was one bound in culture and family, one in which religious tradition, political radicalism, and a fierce desire to Americanize could coexist in varying proportions. Kazin grew up in a Yiddish-speaking household celebrating the rituals and holidays of Judaism. Yet outside the ghetto, the connection between Jewishness and radical politics could not be comfortably discussed or examined. Within the utopian visions of Marxism and socialism, such atavistic identities would disappear. "The cosmopolitan philosophy of radical causes offered the hope of a world where being Jewish would not make any difference," Bloom notes in his book on the New York Intellectuals (31). The public discussion of radical politics could never point to the Jewish background of an activist or comrade, yet all were aware during the first Stalinist controversies that Leon Trotsky was a Jew. Kazin wrote of the gap between the radical WASPs—Dwight MacDonald, John Chamberlain, and Malcolm Cowley—and himself, who returned each evening from Manhattan to the immigrant poverty of his Yiddish-speaking family.

For Kazin, George Goetz, a Baltimore Jew of German descent who founded the *Modern Monthly* under the name V. F. Calverton, was "the first literary person in New York who at that time most clearly brought my two worlds together" (*Starting Out*, 63).

It was Calverton's personal resistance to the cult of Stalin that I most admired about him; he had been shocked by the cultural authoritarianism of the Communists, and by the time of the first big Moscow Trial, August, 1936, was sickened and outraged by Stalin's frame-up of his old rivals and opponents in the Party. At a time when the literary editor of the *New Republic* [Malcolm Cowley] was urging intellectuals to accept the official verdict in the Moscow Trials, the *Modern Monthly* rallied every shade of independent opinion on the left against such submission. (66)

Calverton's significance for the young Kazin was not bound up in any public identification he made of himself as a Jew—one could hardly come up with a more Anglophile *nom de plume*—but simply as a radical man of letters, "a premature anti-Stalinist" of Jewish descent.

Neither of Kazin's two "orthodoxies" brought him into the limelight; that would be accomplished by literature. Books and authors flash through the surface of Kazin's memoir of his growing-up years: Sir Thomas Browne, Chekov's *Cherry Orchard*, D. H. Lawrence, T. S. Eliot, William Blake, Somerset Maugham, *The Education of Henry Adams*, Turgenev's *Fathers and Sons*, Galsworthy's *Forstye Saga*. "I read as if books would fill my every gap, legitimize my strange quest for the American past, let me into the great world that was anything just out of Brownsville" (*A Walker in the City*, 172). Kazin gladly assumed his place in the tradition of Jews who won their place in the tolerant world promised by the Enlightenment. Lionel Trilling, Clifton Fadiman, and William Phillips, co-founder with Philip Rahv of the famous *Partisan Review*, were Jews who had preceded Kazin through this literary gate into the cosmopolitan City; he would be followed by such younger critics and editors as Irving Howe, Leslie Fiedler, and Norman Podhoretz.

Kazin graduated from City College of New York in 1935. By then he had discovered his vocation and enrolled in the graduate program in English at Columbia University, receiving an M.A. in 1938. At the suggestion of Columbia professor Carl Van Doren, Kazin began work on a study of modern American prose. For the next five years, aided by a Guggenheim grant in 1940, Kazin researched and drafted the book that interpreted American literary history as a Hegelian march toward cultural and political liberation. When *On Native Grounds* appeared, its twenty-seven-year-old author turned overnight into an authoritative voice in American criticism. "One dreamlike week in 1942," he begins his third volume of autobiography, "I published my first book, *On Native Grounds*, became an editor of *The New Republic*, and with my wife, Natasha, moved into a little apartment on Twenty-fourth Street and Lexington" (*New York Jew*, 3).

Kazin had made it. His background had put the fire in his belly to succeed on American and cosmopolitan terms, but there was no Jewish content in the nature of his achievement. The triple juxtaposition of his first sentence was symptomatic: Kazin had established his credentials as an authority on American culture, assumed literary editorship of a once-influential Progressive magazine, and finally made the move from the periphery (Brooklyn) to the center (Manhattan). Quickly disillusioned by the patriotic liberalism of *The New Republic* (and its untroubled acceptance of "Uncle Joe" as an American ally), Kazin found himself drawn to "a procession of young Village poets and philosophers—Delmore Schwartz, William

Barrett, Isaac Rosenfeld, Weldon Kees—for whom the only real magazine was *Partisan Review*" (*New York Jew*, 23).

By 1942, *Partisan Review* had established itself as the premier cultural organ of the anti-Stalinist Left. Under the editorship of William Phillips and Philip Rahv, the magazine carved for itself a precise location on the cultural and political landscape, one that drew into its circle a brilliant and contentious group of writers. Phillips and Rahv had become editors of *Partisan Review* when it was still the organ of the New York John Reed Club. Although initially subscribing to the Communist line that a proletarian literature accessible to the masses was the highest end to which the writer could devote himself, Phillips had come from an academic background where he had been an early disciple of modernism. Rahv, an exceptional Jewish autodidact from Russia who acquired English at the age of fourteen, also came to an appreciation of modernism. In the Communist *Partisan Review*, according to Alan Wald, Phillips and Rahv pursued three objectives: "a desire that proletarian fiction and criticism should incorporate certain aspects of the literary achievement of the 1920s; an opposition to schematic, sectarian, and reductive applications of Marxism; and a concern with developing a full Marxist aesthetic that acknowledged the special needs of radical intellectuals" (*The New York Intellectuals*, 78).

These special needs eventually brought about a split between the young editors and the Communist Party. When they relaunched *Partisan Review* in 1937 as an independent organ, they were able to call upon the talents of ex-Communist writers and disaffected fellow travelers. "The characteristic stance of *Partisan Review* and its circle in the late 1930s came from the persistent effort to combine radical politics with critical support for an advanced literature and art" (Cooney 146). By 1942 *Partisan Review* had attracted to its circle an impressive array of young and established talent: Delmore Schwartz, who burst upon the literary scene with an electric short story in the premier issue; Lionel Trilling and Irving Howe, both of whom were to make their reputations as literary and cultural critics; Edmund Wilson, already a famous man of letters; Mary McCarthy, who came into the magazine as Rahv's companion; James T. Farrell, author of the celebrated Studs Lonigan trilogy; Saul Bellow, whose first published story appeared in the *Partisan Review*. As can be seen from this partial list, Gentiles played a prominent role in the *Partisan Review* crowd (neither of the other two writing editors, Dwight Macdonald and F. W. Dupee, was Jewish), but second-generation Jews made up an imposing element. In his retrospective essay, "The New York Intellectuals," Howe applies the label almost exclusively to the Jewish writers of the anti-Stalinist Left,[5] but explains "precisely at the point in the thirties when the New York intellectuals began to form themselves into a loose cultural-political tendency, Jewishness as idea and sentiment played no significant role in their expectations" (*Margin of Hope*, 252). It is understandable that Kazin, who had come into prominence on his own, should feel a kinship with this circle and find an occasional home in its pages. "[T]hese people saw themselves as loyal to a great cultural tradition," he wrote. "It was my tradition. We shared a fundamental realism about our society and obstinate hopes for mankind that were to be conspicuously missing from the intellectual scene as America went to war again" (*Starting Out*, 161).

Kazin shared another important value with the *Partisan Review* crowd: a sophisticated version of the Enlightenment belief that full participation in modern society was evidently richer and more valuable than immersion in any parochial culture. Marxism held this as an article of faith, and the radicals of the anti-Stalinist Left considered themselves to be truer to the revolutionary ideal than the communists who had replaced their original vision with a Soviet personality cult. Speaking for the Jewish New York Intellectuals of the time in his "intellectual autobiography," Howe wrote, "We refused to acknowledge ourselves as part of an American Jewish community encompassing all classes and opinions, since we claimed that inner divisions of social interest and political opinion among the Jews remained decisive. . . . We had made another choice of comrades, the straggling phalanx of the international anti-Stalinist Left" (*Margin of Hope*, 252).

As in the Berlin haskalah, double consciousness was to manifest itself. Some Jews went from this radical belief in universal culture to a recognition and even a celebration of their ethnic background. World War II ushered the New York Intellectuals into a new era. As the Allies fought the Axis powers, the Intellectuals' distaste for the leadership of the Soviet Union was compromised by the evident necessity of overcoming fascism. For the Jews in the group, the slaughter of their coreligionists in Europe gave the international conflict extra personal urgency. Kazin was among the first to bring attention to the Holocaust in a 1943 piece in which he accused an indifferent world of "dump[ing] three million Jews into the furnace" (qtd. in *New York Jew*, 30). Not until several years after the war had ended would the full horror of the Holocaust impress itself upon the consciousness of the West. The great irony of the postwar situation was that although this was when the New York Intellectuals moved into the cultural mainstream, exerting considerable influence upon the acceptance of avant-garde notions in academia, culture, and intellectual discourse, the Jews among them had to deal with the fact that they were living witnesses to a phenomenal evil that had been directed most particularly against their people. "To recognize that we were living after one of the greatest and least explicable catastrophes of human history," Howe wrote, "one for which we could not claim to have adequately prepared ourselves either as intellectuals or as human beings, brought a new rush of feelings, mostly unarticulated and hidden behind the scrim of consciousness" ("The New York Intellectuals," 244-45 in *The Decline of the New*, 211-265). Struggling to deal with the fact of the Holocaust, some of the New York

Intellectuals began to talk about themselves publicly as Jews, something they had rarely done before.

This revival of ethnic identity among the Jews of the anti-Stalinist Left was by no means universal, but it was more widespread among the "second generation" of New York Intellectuals, the generation to which Kazin belonged. Among these Jewish critics who came to postwar prominence were Irving Howe, a publishing industry of his own and an important promoter of Yiddish literature; Clement Greenberg, an art critic who helped champion New York's Abstract Expressionist School to international renown; Irving Kristol, a journalist who became a neoconservative ideologue during the Reagan years; Nathan Glazer and Daniel Bell, both of whom achieved fame through their sociological writings; and Leslie Fiedler, the bad boy of literary criticism during the fifties and sixties. For some, the rediscovery of Jewishness coincided nicely with an increasing deradicalization; others, such as Kazin himself, struggled to integrate this renewed sense of ethnic identity with the Enlightenment ideal of a just society.

The Jewish side of double consciousness, which had been repressed through emotional responses of Jewish self-hatred and intellectual ideologies of cosmopolitanism, came to new life under the shock of the Holocaust and the increasing disintegration of the radical Left. In 1982, Kazin still confessed to "an enormous fascination with Jewish culture and a great dislike of certain features of it." "That didn't mean conflict. I was simply part of two civilizations. I lived in both at the same time and there were two pulls. Then, because of the Holocaust, and some wreckage in my personal life during the war, I became much more consciously Jewish" ("Interview," 196).

The revival of Jewish feeling among the New York Intellectuals manifested itself in the 1945 founding of *Commentary*, a journal published by the American Jewish Committee. Under the leadership of Elliot Cohen, reemerging as the managing editor of a Jewish intellectual magazine after an absence of fifteen years, *Commentary* drew from the same pool of talent as did *Partisan Review*. "The main difference between the two," Kazin reports Cohen remarking, "is that we admit to being a Jewish magazine and they don't" (qtd. in *New York Jew*, 30). Bloom identified another crucial difference, one he attributed to the different eras in which the two magazines were born. He characterized *Partisan Review* as "a bastion of high-culture radicals defending standards against Stalinists and philistines." In the forties some of the Jewish writers of that group "believed that their role should combine their Jewishness and their intellectualism" (163).

The New York Intellectuals moved into the mainstream at a remarkable juncture of historic conditions. For a few postwar years New York was the intellectual and artistic center of the West, and Jews played a significant role in New York culture, a role augmented by the influx of high-profile Jewish refugees from Nazi

Europe. Knowledge of the Holocaust and the high drama attendant upon the establishment of the state of Israel also generated sympathy for the Jews. For the first time in American history, Jews found themselves at the center of literary culture. Jewish intellectuals could speak as experts in alienation to a nation still traumatized by a decade of depression and struggling to assimilate the experience of the war. Kafka was championed as the ultimate visionary of this experience. The Jewish intellectual could now see himself as a representative man; he had something of importance to communicate, learned from his experience on the margins, from the journey he had made out of the ghetto, from his questionable status in Christian America. For the first time, double consciousness was attributed a kind of authority within the mainstream. As Terry Cooney writes, "Those among the New York Intellectuals who were Jews took their bearings from the sense that they stood outside two cultures. It was Jewishness that allowed them to claim, with some accuracy, that their plight was a heightened form of the typical plight of intellectuals. It was Jewishness that made possible the assertion of a double exile that promised exceptional insight" (242).

Several Jewish writers within or connected to the New York circle began to produce imaginative works featuring Jewish protagonists. *Partisan Review* published short stories of this description by Delmore Schwartz, Lionel Trilling, and Saul Bellow. Bellow's career as a novelist, which would culminate in both a Pulitzer and a Nobel Prize, began in the 1940s with *Dangling Man* (1944) and *The Victim* (1948), both existentialist parables with Jewish reverberations. Isaac Rosenfeld, "revered by the New York Intellectuals but largely unknown" (Bloom 291),[6] published his novel of second-generation angst, *Passage from Home*, in 1949. Floundering in the "personal wreckage" of American success, two failed marriages, and a definitive estrangement from the ghetto, Kazin in the late 1940s also began working on a book of Jewish content. "Brownsville was a foreign country now, a forbidden country to the prospering Jews who had once lived there. It was a poison spot on the New York map even to the hundreds and thousands of blacks from the South wearily making it into the ghetto vacated by Jews. Walking back into the country of my birth, I felt separated from everything except my youth" (*New York Jew*, 236).

Kazin's autobiography would prove to be simultaneously an homage to and a repudiation of his Jewish upbringing, the best effort to encompass in literary form the tremendous ambivalence that attended the postwar reawakening of double consciousness. Symptomatic of the place Jewish intellectuals had made for themselves in the wider American world, Kazin first unveiled extracts of his autobiography in *Commentary* and *The New Yorker*. In 1951, *A Walker in the City* appeared to a chorus of positive reviews. *Partisan Review* anointed it with a literary reading— more discussion of Joyce than of Jewishness—by Leslie Fiedler ("The City and the Writer"). The Gentile world also accorded it value. "It is a small book," Brendan Gill wrote in *The New Yorker*, "but an immense achievement" (180). Only David Daiches, reviewing for *Commentary*, demurred with one small but significant caveat, noting that "There is American Yiddish chatter and 'folkways,' but no Hebrew culture and no contact whatever with a living religious tradition" (605). As we shall see, this lack of a diasporic consciousness was endemic not only to the New York Intellectuals but to the Black intellectuals of the period as well.

Although the promises of Enlightenment inclusion had not changed since they were first articulated, nineteenth-century nationalism transformed the nature of the political entities into which Blacks and Jews were attempting to assimilate. Nations were no longer defined primarily in terms of a (heterogeneous) people who shared an allegiance to a temporal sovereign. Increasingly the idea of the nation was expressed in relation to volatile conceptions of race and territory. Thus assumptions of national allegiance were made for Wright and Kazin that simply would not have applied to Equiano and Maimon.[7] The unquestioned Americanness of Wright and Kazin entailed a minority status within the nation as a component of their ethnic consciousness. This minority status stood in binary relation to a majoritarian norm that Americans understood as WASP, White, or Euro-American. It became second nature in American discourse to speak of ethnic groups—especially groups whose somatic differences from the majoritarian norm were presumed to be instantly visible—as minorities. Minority consciousness was born within and effectively bolstered the ideology of nineteenth-century nationalism that still holds sway.[8]

As James Clifford makes clear, diasporic consciousness violates the structure nationalism imposes on ethnic difference. "Transnational connections break the binary relation of 'minority' communities with 'majority' societies—a dependency that structures projects of both assimilation and resistance" (255). Even when ethnic difference in America is naturally channeled into minority categories, diasporic consciousness does not disappear. Rather, it adds yet another layer of complexity to double consciousness. As Daniel and Jonathan Boyarin argue, diasporic identity, which they characterize as "a disaggregated identity," is an integral part of Jewish consciousness. "Jewishness disrupts the very categories of identity because it is not national, not genealogical, not religious, but all of these in dialectical tension with one another" (721). As we shall see below, Jewish discourse possessed a model of diasporic consciousness, dating from the Roman Empire, that informs the discussion of Jewish identity down to the present day.

There have been, in Jewish thought, two enduring attitudes toward separation from the land of Israel. The first, described by the term "diaspora," refers to voluntary exile. Even before the destruction of the Second Temple in A.D. 70, diaspora Jews in the Roman Empire far outnumbered the Jews in Palestine. After the forced dispersion of the Palestinian community, however, all exile came to be referred to as *galut*, a Hebrew word expressing the concept of a Jewish nation uprooted from its homeland and subject to alien rule. *Galut* would end when the Messiah returned to establish a Jewish state in Palestine and bring about an ingathering of the exiles. The concept of diaspora as voluntary exile regained currency as a result of the Enlightenment promise of Jewish integration into the host state. Voluntary exile now substituted the literal longing for a return to Zion for the vision of a secular Promised Land where Jews could live and worship freely. As Arnold Eisen writes, Mendelssohn was the first to alter the traditional conception of *galut* by spiritualizing the notion of return to a goal that could be achieved without the intervention of the Messiah. "In *Jerusalem* the real city of Jerusalem, in the Land of Israel, loses its reality as a place in which, and for which, Jews might actually live. The center of Jewish concern, religious as well as political, the locale of Jewish aspirations, shifts to exile" (64). Until the creation of the state of Israel in 1948, all exile was technically galut, but, as the *Encyclopaedia Judaica* notes in its article on the subject, "The feeling of exile does not always necessarily accompany the condition of exile."

In the American context, Reform Jews officially sanctioned the denial of *galut* in the Pittsburgh Platform of 1885, which declared that Jews should no longer look forward to a return to Israel. From then until the rise of Nazism on the world scene, Reform Jews were hostile to Zionism. In 1937, however, the Central Conference of American Rabbis officially abrogated this anti-Zionist plank. With the establishment of Israel, *galut* was again transformed to diaspora, since the scattered Jewish communities once again had a political-ethnic center to which they could return. It is now customary to refer to the Jewish communities in the world as *tefuzot*, the Hebrew word for diasporic communities. The term *galut*, though technically incorrect, continues to be used for polemical purposes. Zionists have traditionally argued that Jewish life outside of Israel is doomed to annihilation, extinction, or assimilation into something no longer Jewish. Non-Israeli Jews, responding to the Zionist challenge, usually try to establish the importance of the diaspora community's Jewish credentials.

Questions of *galut* and diaspora held no interest for the young Jewish radicals of the Depression. As the philosopher Sidney Hook said in an interview, "we took ourselves for granted as Jews and were concerned with the Jewish question primarily as a political one" (qtd. in Wald, *New York Intellectuals*, 28). Still, as Howe noted, even then an incipient double consciousness manifested itself by the contempt some of these secular Jews reserved for Jewish intellectuals and academics who tried to pass for something else.

We too had a tradition of sorts behind us, the tradition of the estranged Jew, which had grown increasingly strong in the life of the Jewish people these past two centuries. It is a tradition that goes back at least to the moment in the late eighteenth century when Solomon Maimon, an "alienated" Jew if ever there was one, wandered away from his Lithuanian *shtetl* to become a junior colleague of German Enlightenment philosophers. In our own century this type has been embodied in such leaders of European radicalism as Julian Martov, Rosa Luxemburg, and Leon Trotsky—those who, in Isaac Deutscher's coinage, were "non-Jewish Jews." Unsatisfactory as this cosmopolitan style would show itself to be, it was nevertheless a familiar Jewish choice, a part of Jewish history. (*Margin of Hope*, 252)

Any identification with Jewish history, however, was strictly *sub rosa*. It did not enter into the writings of the *Partisan Review* before the war. Remarkably, this public disinclination of the New York Intellectuals to write about themselves as Jews persisted during their period of ascendancy in the 1940s and 1950s. Old habits die hard, and even such earth-shaking events as revelation of the Holocaust and the establishment of Israel did not bring about much public reexamination of Jewish identity. "Among writers and critics usually quick to analyze and philosophize," Alexander Bloom writes, "there developed a curious tongue-tiedness on the question of the Nazis and the destruction of the European Jews" (141). After having consciously and aggressively moved out of the world of their childhood, Jewish intellectuals had no easy way of coming back. They were intellectually unfit for religion; they had no interest in Zionism; and, with the exception of Howe, they did not seek to make contact with the dying world of Yiddish culture.

Still, there was something residual, something that refused to go away. As Howe wrote of his generation, "This 'Jewishness' might have no fixed religious or national content, it might be helpless before the assault of believers. But there it was, that was what we had—and had to live with" (*Margin of Hope*, 251). Occasionally intellectual debates and polemics would erupt around certain works analyzing "the Jewish Question" or some aspect of the Holocaust: Sartre's *Anti-Semite and Jew* (1948) or Hannah Arendt's *Eichmann in Jerusalem* (1963). What was notable about these affairs, however, was that the works in question arose out of a European context, written by European intellectuals. The Jewish American community contributed nothing major to the body of literature accreting around the Holocaust, the persistence of anti-Semitism, or the establishment of Israel. Nonetheless, some individuals among the New York Intellectuals made an effort to reconnect with their Jewishness. In 1949, Irving Kristol, Daniel Bell, and Nathan Glazer formed a study group with Milton Himmelfarb, director of information and research for the American Jewish Committee, to read Maimonides' *Misneh Torah*. Irving Howe embarked upon a project of editing and translating books of Yiddish poetry. Rabbis and Jewish leaders invited the New York Intellectuals to return to an affiliated fold, but the ex-radicals were still contemptuous of the middle-class, materialistic values they perceived to be dominant among the suburbanizing Jewish communities. In his dismissive review of Milton Steinberg's influential book, *Basic Judaism* (1947), Kristol characterized contemporary Judaism as the refuge of Babbitry. "What we have left are political lectures, fund-raising, Zionism, interfaith activities, public relations, social work, and so on" (Kristol 34).

The philistinism of the American Jews, however, could not diminish the horror of the Holocaust. There had been no comparable event in modern experience. For Jews and Gentiles alike, no rationality could explain it. As much as the "betrayal" of Stalinism, the Holocaust dealt a death blow to the Enlightenment optimism that undergirded socialism in its various guises. After such knowledge, who could put their faith in the coming of a society that granted its bounty to all out of idealism alone? Still, for Howe, "One's first response—not the sole response, but the first— had to be a cry of Jewish grief" (*Margin of Hope*, 251). Kazin describes his emotional reaction to his first encounter with the Holocaust as a reporter in London.

Late one Friday afternoon near the end of the war, I was waiting out the rain in the entrance to a music store. A radio was playing into the street and, standing there, I heard the first Sabbath service from Belsen. In April a British detachment had stumbled on Belsen by accident, had come upon forty thousand sick, starving, and dying prisoners. Over ten thousand corpses were stacked in piles. Belsen was the first Nazi camp to be exposed to the world, and the *London Times* correspondent began his dispatch: "It is my duty to describe something beyond the imagination of mankind." Now I heard the liberated Jewish prisoners in Belsen say the *Shema*—"Hear O Israel the Lord our God the Lord is One." Weeping in the rain, I said it with them. For a moment I was home. (214)

The juxtaposition of Holocaust and home is significant. What Kazin means by "home," as he makes clear in *A Walker in the City*, is the tenement in Brownsville where he grew up.[9]

Walker is Kazin's attempt to reconnect to his Jewishness. It was his literal and metaphorical return to the scenes of his childhood—"home" even after he had been accepted into the American mainstream. For Kazin, being transported back "home" was not a return to Judaism, an embrace of Zionism, or even an unproblematic acceptance of a secular Jewish identity. "Home" was not Zion but America—a Jewish ghetto in America, to be sure, but America nonetheless. What one perceives, upon reading certain passages of *Walker*, is how powerful diasporic consciousness remains, even at the lower end of Jewish society. Kazin describes the Sabbath evenings during the 1920s in his parents' apartment with his sophisticated Russian cousin and her friends.

They had great flavor for me, those three women; they were the positive center of that togetherness that always meant so much to me in our dining room on Friday evenings. It was a quality that . . . found its unexpectedly tender voice in the Yiddish folksongs and Socialist hymns they taught me—"Let's Now Forgive Each Other"; "Tsuzamen, Tsuzamen, All Together, Brothers!" I was suddenly glad to be a Jew, as these women were Jews—simply and naturally glad of those Jewish dressmakers who spoke with enthusiastic familiarity of Sholem Aleichem and Peretz, Gorky and Tolstoy, who glowed at every reminiscence of Nijinsky, of Nazimova in *The Cherry Orchard*, of Pavlova in "The Swan."

Often, those Friday evenings, they spoke of *der heym*, "Home," and then it was hard for me. *Heym* was a terrible word. I saw millions of Jews lying dead under the Polish eagle with knives in their throats. I was afraid with my mother's fears, thought I should weep when she wept, lived again through every pogrom whose terrors she chanted. I associated that old European life only with pain, mud, and hopelessness, but I was of it still, through her. (58–59)

Kazin depicts both the positive and the negative side of diasporic consciousness: the comfort and sentimentality of group identification, the helpless attachment to group oppression even when that oppression takes place in another lifetime, on another continent. "When Jews are murdered in a Polish pogrom," Howe wrote in a 1948 essay on his cohort of what he described as lost young intellectuals, "he feels a sense of communal martyrdom . . . because in a very real and bitter sense it is he too against whom the pogrom has been committed; it is his blood that stains the streets of Kielce" ("Lost Young Intellectual," 362).[10]

When the New York Intellectuals turned to Jewish topics or championed Jewish writers, the European orientation of their diasporic consciousness manifested itself in their discussions of Franz Kafka, Martin Buber, Sholem Aleichem, even the Hassids and rabbis of the Talmud. The Hebrew modernist writer S. Y. Agnon, who lived in Israel and won the Nobel Prize for Literature in 1966, barely entered their purview.[11] Their European focus was a ramification of their literary and political orientation before the war. Socialism and modernism had been primarily European phenomena. Palestine was not on the cultural map, and Zionism, although it had its socialist variant, was part of the Jewish world the young radicals had left behind.

By the same token, American culture and politics also played only a secondary role in the *Partisan Review* articles before the war. Kazin's passion for American literature was exceptional among the New York Intellectuals of the prewar years. Unable to feel at home in America because of their ethnicity and immigrant backgrounds, young Jewish radicals made a place for themselves in the internationalist—and unavoidably Eurocentric—movements of politics (socialism and Marxism) and culture (modernism and proletarian literature). After the war, however, radicalism fell into ruins, attacked by the cold war politicians and undercut by the increasing acceptance some of the radicals found in the mainstream. "The ex-radical intellectuals were in fact total *arrivistes*," Kazin wrote reprovingly, "and accommodating in their thinking" (*New York Jew*, 292).

Quite against their expectations, the New York Intellectuals had found a home—but not as American Jews. Rather, they were accepted as intellectuals whose Jewishness gave them special insight into postwar society. "In this apocalyptic period of atomization and uprooting," Leslie Fiedler wrote in a 1949 article about anti-

Semitism in British literature, "of a catholic terror and a universal alienation, the image of the Jew tends to become the image of everyone; and we are perhaps approaching the day when the Jew will come to seem the central symbol, the essential myth of the whole Western world" ("What Can We Do about Fagin?" 418). The emergence and popularity of Jewish-American literature in the following decade only seemed to corroborate the point—the Jew was, to use Alexander Bloom's phrase, "a specialist in alienation."

It was an odd place to find a home, but one that was most congenial to the temperament of these new cultural arbiters: insiders and outsiders, Americans and Jews. It was double consciousness played to the greatest possible effect. "I was born in galut," Daniel Bell proclaimed grandly in a 1961 *Commentary* essay, "and I accept— now gladly, though once in pain—the double burden and the double pleasure of my self-consciousness, the outward life of an American and the inward secret of the Jew. I walk with this sign as frontlet between my eyes, and it is as visible to some secret others as their sign is to me" (475).

For the Black American, the "secret" sign of double consciousness was all too visible. It insured an institutionalized oppression that had barely begun to be dismantled when the Jews came into their version of American acceptance. Yet this greater, more visible oppression produced a mentality quite different from the Jew who was still only a generation or two removed from the genocidal Old World.

Black identity, while created within a diaspora forced on Africans and their descendants, had no centralizing theory of unity that all subscribed to. Diasporic consciousness might be *felt* when Blacks from different nations met up with one another, but these emotions didn't always translate into an articulated ideology. Early attempts to theorize the Black diaspora, such as those of Equiano (22-23) and Edward Wilmont Blyden (120), modeled themselves on Jewish history. "The precise genealogy of the diaspora concept in black cultural history remains obscure," Gilroy writes (211), and such modeling further added to the ideological cross-fertilization between the two groups. Even after the articulation of diasporic ideologies, however, many Blacks declined to subscribe to them. In the generation under discussion—the last Americans for whom the Enlightenment assumptions remained hegemonic and effectively unchallenged—ethnic histories, both national and diasporic, created an identity in which the mix of minority to diasporic awareness differed considerably.

Discourses concerning the African diaspora entered the West in several guises. Some involved the curious nexus of abolitionism and White supremacist beliefs that the races could never coexist. The Back-to-Africa movements supported by Whites in Britain and America, for example, resulted in the founding of Sierra Leone and Liberia. More influential in the twentieth century was the strain that Wilson Jeremiah Moses chronicles in *The Golden Age of Black Nationalism* that culminated in Marcus Garvey's United Negro Improvement Association. While Garvey's movement created no national entity, it triggered a sea change in the mentality of the African-American masses, affecting writers and intellectuals as well as large numbers of working people grappling with their own versions of double consciousness. Pan-Africanism as an ideology saw its first theoretical elaboration in the nineteenth-century writings of the Caribbean scholar who made his home and career in Liberia, Edward W. Blyden. As Gilroy points out, Blyden had studied Jewish history, religion, language, and culture, all of which had an impact on his formulation of Black identity (208–12). Henry Sylvester-Williams of Trinidad, who practiced at the English Bar, convened a pan-African conference in London in 1900 as a forum of protest against the aggression of European colonizers and, at the same time, an appeal to the missionary and abolitionist traditions of the British people to protect Africans from the depredations of the empire builders. Pan-Africanism played a less central role in Black thought until it was revived by W. E. B. Du Bois after World War I. Between 1919 and 1945, Du Bois, who viewed Garveyism as a sideshow lacking intellectual rigor and real political goals, was largely responsible for the organization of five international congresses. In terms of African-American intellectual life, Du Bois stands as the most influential figure largely because he understood the intricate connections between Enlightenment ideals, double consciousness, and the diaspora. As historian and advocate of Pan-Africanism George Padmore wrote, "For more than thirty years, Dr. Du Bois watched over the gradual growth of the Pan-African Congress with the loving affection of a father until such time as his child had found a home on African soil" (96). During the years following World War II, Pan-Africanism was taken up by such leaders in the movement for decolonization in the Anglophone world as Padmore himself and Kwame Nkrumah, the first Prime Minister of Ghana. Curiously, even though Pan-Africanism was nurtured by Caribbean and American intellectuals, it occasioned little discussion among American Blacks, who showed but small enthusiasm for involving themselves directly in the struggle for African independence. It must be remembered, however, that the efforts of African Americans during this period were bent toward making a place for themselves in American society. Particularly after World War II it seemed as if the mainstream might eventually open to Blacks the way it was visibly opening to Jews.[12]

Consequently, Richard Wright encountered serious diasporic thought only when he went into exile in Paris. In the Francophone world, theories of a Black or "Negro-African" essence surfaced in the poetry and essays of Black writers in Paris during the 1930s and 1940s, mostly notably the Senegalese poet Léopold Senghor and Aimé Césaire from Martinique. This *négritude* movement came to dominate the Black Francophone literary scene during and immediately after the era of decolonization. Among its many achievements was the launching of the literary and intellectual journal *Présence africaine*, in 1946. Wright attended the first board meeting and contributed Boris Vian's translation of "Bright and Morning Star" to its first issue. Even though the *négritude* writers acknowledged an intellectual and artistic debt to the Harlem Renaissance, African-American writers who came into contact with *négritude* ideas during the 1940s and 1950s did not share its belief in a racial essence that manifested itself in all art and culture throughout the diaspora. Because of the Black expatriate community in France, encompassing such major writers and musicians as James Baldwin, Chester Himes, Sydney Bechet, and Bud Powell, there was far more engagement with the ideas of *négritude* than with those of Pan-Africanism.

Wright participated peripherally in both movements. In his introduction to Padmore's *Pan-Africanism or Communism?*, on the occasion of his prefatory remarks to George Lamming's autobiography, and in his participation in *négritude* conferences, he consistently prophesied the inevitable integration of Blacks into the Enlightenment West. At the historic 1956 Conference of Black African Writers and Artists organized by *Présence africaine*, Wright offended the sensibilities of those inclined to celebrate traditional African culture by consigning it to the dustbin of history.

[T]he spirit of the Enlightenment, of the Reformation, which made Europe great, now has a chance to be extended to all mankind! A part of the non-West is now akin to a part of the West. East and West have become compounded. The partial overcoming of the forces of tradition and oppressive religions in Europe resulted in a roundabout manner, in a partial overcoming of tradition and religion in decisive parts of Asia and Africa. The unspoken assumption in this has been: WHAT IS GOOD FOR EUROPE IS GOOD FOR ALL MANKIND! I say: So be it. ("Tradition and Industrialization," 64)

Profoundly committed to Enlightenment ideas, Wright (as we shall see below) passed a similar judgment on the ultimate expendability of African-American culture.

Wright's take on Black identity was fiercely and uncompromisingly anti-essentialist. In this he remained true to his Marxist intellectual foundation. In a 1960 interview for the newspaper *L'Express*, he stated flatly, "I am opposed to any racial definition of man. I write about racial problems precisely to bring an end to racial definitions. And I do not wish anybody in the world in which we live to look at it from a racial perspective, whether he is white, black, or yellow" ("Interview," 201). He accorded a political reality to race, but no metaphysical one. When he christened the 1954 description of his trip to a Gold Coast preparing for independence *Black Power*, the phrase did not have the connotations of militant ethnicity that Stokely Carmichael gave it in the following decade. In a letter to his German translator, Wright stated, "The title: *Black Power* means political and state power. I did not have in mind any racial meaning" (qtd. in Fabre 607). Wright was, in fact, one of the few African-American writers or intellectuals of the period to seek firsthand contact with African culture, but, as he writes in a disturbed refrain on the discomfort he felt in the Gold Coast, "I was black and they were black, and my blackness did not help me."

Nevertheless, Senghor continued to use Wright's writings to illustrate his thesis that the heritage of the American Negro was an African one. Baldwin, who reported on the Conference of Black African Writers and Artists, wrote about Senghor's assertion that Wright's early poem, "Black Hands," was "involved with African tensions and symbols, even though Wright himself had not been aware of this" ("Princes," 153). Discussing Senghor's claim that *Black Boy* too would reveal its African characteristics under proper analysis, Baldwin pointed to a gaping hole in *négritude* ideology. How could the American Negro writer make claims to an African heritage with which s/he had had no living contact for generations? Unlike the Greco-Roman world, whose heritage had been preserved in writing, African civilizations were oral.

Granted that there was something African in *Black Boy*, as there was undoubtedly something African in all American Negroes, the great question of what this was, and how it had survived, remained wide open. Moreover, *Black Boy* had been written in the English language which Americans had inherited from England, that is, if you like, from Greece and Rome; its form, psychology, moral attitude, preoccupations, in short its cultural validity, were all due to forces which had nothing to do with Africa. ("Princes," 154)

Baldwin's understanding of historical linguistics may have been off the mark, but his larger point—that *Black Boy* was essentially a work of Western literature— echoed the fundamental argument of African-American writers and intellectuals of the period. *Négritude* understood Black identity to be essentially African, something shared by all those of African ancestry. Negroes considered themselves Americans first, Westerners second, and Africans not at all. America treated the Negro shamefully, and that was America's problem. Such treatment, however, only strengthened the Negro's claim to national identity. "I am the darker brother," Langston Hughes wrote in his poem "I Too." The sentiment remained valid for Baldwin, Ellison, and Wright. This was the difference, Baldwin wrote, between Negroes and the Blacks from Africa and the Caribbean—that the struggle for American Blacks was not to throw off the yoke of imperialism but to force the United States to live up to its Enlightenment ideals. "We had been dealing with, had been made and mangled by another machinery altogether. It had never been in our interest to overthrow it. It had been necessary to make the machinery work for our benefit and the possibility of its doing so had been, so to speak, built in" ("Princes," 148). Wright expressed similar sentiments in his interview with *L'Express*.[13]

So great was the consensus among African-American intellectuals that they were a unique subset of Black humanity that the challenge of a diasporic consciousness was rarely posed on American soil. The Black literary critic Saunders Redding could present a paper to the First Conference of Negro Writers in 1959 entitled "The Negro Writer and His Relationships to His Roots" without once mentioning Africa or the Caribbean. When asked about "Negro culture" by a French interviewer who was clearly formulating his questions out of *négritude* assumptions, Ralph Ellison issued an unusually bald statement:

[T]he American Negro people is North American in origin and has evolved under specifically American conditions: climatic, nutritional, historical, political and social. It takes its character from the experience of American slavery and the struggle for, and the achievement of, emancipation; from the dynamics of American race and caste discrimination, and from living in a highly industrialized and highly mobile society possessing a relatively high standard of living and an explicitly stated egalitarian concept of freedom. Its spiritual outlook is basically Protestant, its system of kinship is Western, its time and historical sense are American (United States), and its secular values are those professed, ideally at least, by all of the people of the United States. (*Shadow and Act*, 262–63)

Ellison knew better, as his portrait of the Garveyesque Jamaican rabble rouser Ras the Exhorter in *Invisible Man* testifies, but his "minority" vision was typical of the times. In spite of the enormous impact Marcus Garvey had had on African American culture, there was little discussion before the 1960s of the fact that Caribbean immigrants such as Hubert Harrison, C. L. R. James, Claudia Jones, and George Padmore held roles of leadership in the various movements of Black radicalism. Claude McKay, one of the principal figures of the Harlem Renaissance, was from Jamaica and had first published there. In fact, tension between different diasporic communities was very much a part of African American life. During the 1920s, 25 percent of Harlem consisted of foreign-born blacks, the majority of whom were from the Caribbean. In New York, there had always been friction between the Caribbean immigrants and African Americans as the two groups competed for the same jobs and viewed each other through the lens of their differing cultural backgrounds. Novelist Paule Marshall and actor Sidney Poitier, both of whom participated in Harlem's cultural life in the 1950s, had significant Caribbean connections. In 1959, Marshall published *Brown Girl, Brownstones*, her stunning debut novel about the Barbadian community in New York, to limited critical praise but to commercial failure. The eyes of the Negro, like those of Marshall's protagonist, were trained firmly on the United States.

This seems all the more surprising given the training so many Black intellectuals had had under the tutelage of the radical Left. As Harold Cruse makes evident in *The Crisis of the Negro Intellectual*, the writers and artists of postwar Harlem remained in thrall to the Communist Party long after the New York Intellectuals had rejected it. In the late 1940s, the Committee for the Negro in the Arts, organized as the cultural arm of the Harlem left wing, included White Communists, White left-wing sympathizers, and such Black artists as Sidney Poitier, Alice Childress, Ossie Davis, and Ruby Dee. "At the time of the CNA's founding these aspiring novelists, dramatists, poets, actors and performers could not afford to be attacking the downtown whites—radical or liberal—with whom they were in league" (212), Cruse observed, emphasizing their dependence on White patronage. Little had changed since the Harlem Renaissance. There were thus political reasons in the embattled left wing to maintain an ideology of interracial unity.

The traditional liberal camp—always a proponent of integration—benefited enormously from wartime propaganda against Nazi racial theories. NAACP membership rose from 50,000 in 1940 to 350,000 in 1945. Enlightenment thought had always placed its highest hopes on the proper education of the good citizen, and the court victories won by the NAACP during the 1940s and 1950s battered the legal structure that kept Blacks from receiving the same education as Whites. The term "integration," understood in its social sense, entered public discourse during the 1940s. As Albert Murray noted:

In point of historical fact, it is the wartime generation that is most responsible for the accelerated activism that has come to be known as the Civil Rights Movement or the Negro Revolution. Nevertheless, that generation whose leaders by and large were derived directly from the same intellectual environment that had produced Richard Wright, placed little emphasis on black consciousness and black culture. (*Omni-Americans*, 176)

Whether it was the promotion of left-wing cosmopolitanism or liberal integration, the times seemed inauspicious for the development of a diasporic perspective. Cruse, an early and ferocious advocate of Black consciousness, purposely conflated the two tendencies in his intellectual history.[14] Several pronouncements he cites from prominent Black writers as late as 1964 corroborate his claim that there was essentially no difference.

The very premise of racial integration negates the idea of Negro ethnic identity. It means the shedding of the race tag. It means, insofar as ideological creativity is concerned, that a James Baldwin will constantly demur against being classified as a Negro writer, that a Lorraine Hansberry will deny her play was a Negro play. . . . If there is no such thing as a Negro writer or a body of Negro literature, then, it follows, there is or can be no such thing as a Negro psychology or a distinctly Negro sociology, or a Negro political theory or a particular kind of Negro cultural theory that has relevance to American society as regards the Negro situation in America. (247–48)[15]

Cruse's polemics make the central point forcefully: Enlightenment thought still had no way to validate ethnic difference. With the 1954 Supreme Court decision to dismantle legalized segregation and the 1964 passage of the Civil Rights Act, the creative Black intelligentsia found itself swept up in a triumphant liberalism. What need was there of a diasporic consciousness? Indeed, if America continued to live up to its Enlightenment ideals, what need would there be for any form of minority consciousness? Wright suggested such a possibility in the conclusion of a lecture, "The Literature of the Negro in the United States," he delivered frequently during his European exile.

If . . . our expression broadens, assumes the common themes and burdens of literary expression which are the heritage of all men, then by that token you will know that a humane attitude prevails in America towards us. And a gain in humaneness in America is a gain in humaneness for us all. When that day comes, there will exist one more proof of the oneness of man, of the basic unity of human life on this earth. ("Literature of the Negro," 149–50)

As yet, however, that blessed day had not arrived. Minority consciousness, whether a curse, as Wright believed, or a mixed blessing, as Baldwin and Ellison contended, still characterized the Negro. But, using the same strategies as those of the New York Intellectuals, Black writers could turn the sociological negative of ethnic identity into a cultural plus. The Negro became America's metaphor—not of alienation, as was the Jew, but of man's inhumanity to man. Turn again to Wright's lecture: "The history of the Negro in America is the history of America written in vivid and bloody terms; it is the history of Western Man writ small. It is the history of men who tried to adjust themselves to a world whose laws, customs, and instruments of force were leveled against them. The Negro is America's metaphor"(74). Ellison universalized the condition in *Invisible Man*. "Who knows," says his nameless narrator in the final line, "but that, on the lower frequencies, I speak for you?" (439). Once again, as with the Jew, extraordinary suffering conferred special insight.

Paradoxically, however, these ethnic sensibilities could not produce a valid literature—at least such was the contention of Kazin and Wright. For both Blacks and Jews, the literary culture produced by ethnic consciousness could assume quite different forms. Both minority and diasporic consciousness could be seen in the American Jewish community. Yiddish literature was diasporic by definition, as the writings of American-based writers such as Sholem Asch and Isaac Bashevis Singer testified. In their flight from their immigrant backgrounds, however, Jewish intellectuals writing in English usually threw out the cultural baby with the religious bath water. Literature written in English by American Jews—that which was recognizably ethnic—was not seen as constituting any sort of tradition. Most of these works dealt primarily with the immigrant experience that dominated so much of the Jewish-American world: Abraham Cahan's *Rise of David Levinsky*, Anzia Yezierska's *Hungry Hearts*, Michael Gold's *Jews Without Money*, Daniel Fuchs's Williamsburg trilogy. These works received little comment from the New York Intellectuals, primarily because they were viewed as uninteresting. As a student of

American literature, Kazin was familiar with some of these precursors to the brilliant renaissance of Jewish American writing of the 1950s, but didn't think much of them.

In African-American letters, the relation between diasporic and minority consciousness was murky at best. Despite the Ethiopianism of nineteenth-century Black nationalists and the primitivist vogue of the Harlem Renaissance, no useful diaporic consciousness was available to Wright when he embarked on his literary career. In fact, Wright was even more unsparing of his literary predecessors than was Kazin. For both Wright and Kazin these negative judgments were formulated within the ideological structure of the Enlightenment. What mattered to them both was a Western tradition that had already been defined as central.

Paul Gilroy astutely points out that Wright's importance to Black literature lies precisely in the intensity he brought to the divided mind of the minority writer. "Wright is fascinating above all because, in his life and work, the tension between the claims of racial particularity on one side and the appeal of those modern universals that appear to transcend race on the other arises in the sharpest possible form" (147). But though Wright bears the double consciousness common to all minority writers in the West, in his discursive pronouncements on African-American writing he was remarkably consistent and, in keeping with his Marxist training, thoroughly hostile to an essentialist philosophy. "Negro writers," he declared in a 1937 essay, "must accept the nationalist implications of their lives, not in order to encourage them, but in order to change and transcend them" ("Blueprint," 338). Wright made this first foray into the subject, entitled "Blueprint for Negro Writing," when he was still surprisingly unaware of the previous achievements of African-American writers. As several famous passages in *Black Boy* make painfully explicit, Wright felt thoroughly alienated from African-American culture.

Whenever I thought of the essential bleakness of black life in America, I knew that Negroes had never been allowed to catch the full spirit of Western civilization, that they lived somehow in it but not of it. And when I brooded upon the cultural barrenness of black life, I wondered if clean, positive tenderness, love, honor, loyalty, and the capacity to remember were native to man. I asked myself if these human qualities were not fostered, won, struggled and suffered for, preserved in ritual from one generation to another. (*Black Boy*)

Those who celebrate African-American culture as manifested in spirituals, the blues, Black English, and the folktales have often felt pained by such lines, especially the one about the cultural barrenness of Black life.[16] But Wright was not blind to the strengths of African-American culture. In "Blueprint for Negro Writing" he identifies them as pathways to the potential radicalization of the Black community. "There is, however, a culture of the Negro which is his and has been addressed to him; a culture which has, for good or ill, helped to clarify his conscious-ness and create emotional attitudes which are conducive to action. This culture has stemmed mainly from two sources: 1) the Negro church; and 2) the folklore of the Negro people" (335). The phrase "for good or ill" separates Wright from Langston Hughes or Zora Neale Hurston. No celebrant of Afro-American culture would dream of diminishing the value of what Wright calls the African-American's "most indigenous and complete expression" (336). But, as Ralph Ellison points out, this is the very culture Wright had to escape in order to achieve his identity as a writer and human being. "Wright learned that it is not enough merely to reject that part of the South which lay within. As a rebel he formulated that rejection negatively, because it was the negative face of the Negro community upon which he looked most often as a child" (*Shadow and Act*, 92–93).[17] For Wright, African-American culture is embedded within American culture, and both are sick unto death. There is, he rec-ognizes, "a Negro way of life in America," a way steeped in enforced double con-sciousness.

> The Negro people did not ask for this, and deep down, though they express themselves through their institutions and adhere to this special way of life, they do not want it now. This special existence was forced upon them from without by lynch rope, bayonet and mob rule. They accepted these negative conditions with the inevitability of a tree which must live or perish in whatever soil its finds itself. ("Blueprint," 337–38)

Wright projects his own negative (though still ambivalent) feelings about the culture in which he grew up onto African Americans as a whole. Marxism provided the intellectual framework for the articulation of this anti-essentialist perspective, but the development of the attitudes behind this perspective are traced in *Black Boy*. As Michel Fabre points out, Wright wrote not out of racial pride nor even racial vindication, but out of rebellion. "In this broader circle [of the Communist Party], his rebellion was not directed only against the subservience inculcated by racial oppression but against the American capitalist system" ("Introduction," xi). As early as 1942, when he wrote "The Man Who Lived Underground," Wright's re-bellion went beyond racial protest and Marxism, taking a decidedly existential turn. This experientially based existentialism, later nourished by Sartre and de Beauvoir, lay at the base of *Black Boy*'s message that rebellion is the only human choice. Like Wright's version of "Negro culture," his existentialism was something forced upon him.

This complex of attitudes makes for a curious assessment of African-American culture. Wright recognizes the strength of the culture in its oral forms—"Negro folklore contains in a measure that puts to shame more deliberate forms of Negro expression, the collective sense of Negro life" ("Blueprint," 337)—but discards these as fruits in the poisoned garden of racist ideology. Wright also considers African-

American writing, and finds it wanting. Assimilating the Marxist insight that culture is an expression of class consciousness, Wright points out that African-American written expression distanced itself, to its detriment, from the bulk of its people.

> One would have thought that Negro writers in the last century of striving at expression would have continued and deepened this folk tradition, would have tried to create a more intimate and yet a more profoundly social system of artistic communication between them and their people. But the illusion that they could escape through individual achievement the harsh lot of their race swung Negro writers away from any such path. Two separate cultures sprang up: one for the Negro masses, unwritten and unrecognized; and the other for the sons and daughters of a rising Negro bourgeoisie, parasitic and mannered. (336)

Such a statement ignores the achievements of Charles Chesnutt, Langston Hughes, Jean Toomer, Sterling Brown, and Zora Neale Hurston, but Wright didn't discuss specific cases in his essay. His intention was polemical, and his remarks did apply to the bulk—if not the best—of African-American writing. It is a classic illustration of Henry Louis Gates's observation that "in general, black authors do not admit to a line of literary descent within their own literary tradition" (120).

The main problem for African-American literature, according to Wright, stemmed from the fact that it addressed itself to "a small white audience rather than to a Negro one" ("Blueprint," 318). Wright dismissed the literature of the Harlem Renaissance as "the fruits of that foul soil which was the result of a liaison between inferiority-complexed Negro 'geniuses' and burnt-out white Bohemians with money" (333). Though Wright considered African-American culture to be unhealthy and undesirable, Black writers had to work with it for both personal and social salvation. (Folk culture at least had the merit of not being bourgeois.) "Negro writers who seek to mould or influence the consciousness of the Negro people must address their messages to them through the ideologies and attitudes fostered in this warping way of life" (338).

But African-American writers, while using the tradition, must have an enlightened understanding of it that transcends its limited perspective. Wright urges Black authors to make modernist and socialist writers their literary ancestors. "Eliot, Stein, Joyce, Proust, Hemingway, and Anderson; Gorky, Barbusse, Nexo, and Jack London no less than the folklore of the Negro himself should form the heritage of the Negro writer" (340–41). Marxism, of course, could also provide a "transcendent" vantage point: "Hence, it is through a Marxist conception of reality and society that the maximum degree of freedom in thought and feeling can be gained for the Negro writer" (340).[18] "Blueprint" was very much a clarion call for a new kind of writing, the kind of writing Wright was developing, which would come to such astonishing fruition in *Native Son* and *Black Boy*.

Twenty years later, during his European exile, Wright returned to the subject of Black writing in his lecture, "The Literature of the Negro in the United States," later published in *White Man, Listen!* His own fame as a Black writer long established, Wright was widely regarded as a spokesperson for his people—a paradoxical position for one with his beliefs. Now he looked at African-American literature with a more benign eye and a greater knowledge of its history, but his perspective remained conditioned by the Marxist framework of racial transcendence. One of the principal assertions of his lecture was that "the word Negro in America means something not racial or biological, but something purely social, something made in the United States" ("Literature of the Negro," 83). Wright quotes from Dumas and Pushkin, both of whom would have been classified as Negroes by American racial codes, and remarks that there is nothing "Negroid" about their writing. Even America, before being psychologically debased by the racial assumptions upon which slavery was predicated, could produce a Phillis Wheatley, whose poetry "showed almost no traces of her being a Negro or having been born in Africa" (78).

With the calcification of thought under the institution of slavery, however, the Negro was created as an oppressed social entity, and his literary expression took on a distinctive coloration. Wright says of the slave poet George Moses Horton:

Horton's writing does not stem from racial feeling, but from a social situation; and Horton's cry for freedom was destined to become the tradition of Negro literature in the United States. . . . This tradition of bitterness was to become so complex, was to assume such a tight, organic form, that most white people would think upon examining it, that all Negroes had embedded in their flesh and bones some peculiar propensity toward lamenting and complaining. (81)

This, according to Wright, represents the Negro literary tradition down to the advent of Marxism on the American scene. "Alien ideologies gripped men's minds and the most receptive minds in our land were those of the rejected Negroes. Color consciousness lost some of its edge and was replaced in a large measure by class consciousness; with the rise of an integral working-class movement, a new sense of identification came to the American Negro" (102). Such thinking, Wright claimed, marked a watershed in the Negro literary tradition. For the first time since Phillis Wheatley, the American Negro could write out of the shared hopes and aspirations of a grouping larger than the racial minority.

Wright ends his lecture by noting that America's then-current position of world leadership exposed it to international scrutiny and criticism, forcing the country to make an attempt at putting its racial house in order. Still operating within a vision of a raceless society, Wright predicts a possible end to Negro literature. "As the Negro merges into the main stream of American life, there might result actually a disappearance of Negro literature as such. If that happens, it will mean that those conditions of life that formerly defined what was 'Negro' have ceased to exist, and implies that Negroes are Negroes because they are treated as Negroes" (108). Here we see Wright replay the environmental arguments of Montesquieu, Equiano, and Pinto in the eighteenth century; Park and the Chicago School of sociology in the twentieth. Marxism as an aesthetic philosophy could never countenance an essentialist approach to literary production. "Expression springs out of an environment, and events modify what is written by moulding consciousness," he stated in "Blueprint" (322).

Wright was no innovator in the field of literary criticism, and his analysis of African-American literature is both derivative and based on incomplete information. He was, as the FBI documents characterized him, a "philosophical communist" even after he broke with the Party. Yet the racial particularism so successfully repressed in his discursive writing galvanizes his imaginative and autobiographical work. Before turning to *Black Boy*, however, it is instructive to compare Wright's rejection with Kazin's analogous response to Jewish-American literature.

When he burst upon the critical scene with *On Native Grounds*, Kazin succeeded in capturing the mind of America during the half century between 1890 and 1940. This magnum opus traced the rise and eventual triumph of literary realism from its beginnings in William Dean Howell's promotion of the American naturalists to the recent writings of John Steinbeck. It was an exemplar of the school of criticism championed by the New York Intellectuals, avoiding the aestheticism of the New Criticism and the mechanical rhetoric of a Party-approved Marxism. In *On Native Grounds*, the young Jew from Brownsville wrote of American literature, its writers and its critics, with, as Norman Podhoretz put it, "the aggressive conviction that this literature was his" (123). Yet Kazin's portrait shows little evidence of a Jewish presence. Absent from the history are Abraham Cahan, Anzia Yezierska, Daniel Fuchs, Meyer Levin, and Henry Roth. The only Jewish writers mentioned even in passing (with no reference to their Jewishness) are Budd Schulberg (*What Makes Sammy Run?*) and Michael Gold (*Jews Without Money*), brought up within the context of "the failure of so many . . . left-wing naturalists" of the 1930s to do more than shock and indoctrinate their audience (301–2). Kazin does consider Ludwig Lewisohn, a German-Jewish critic of drama and American literature, seeing Lewisohn's tenacious hold on his "Hebraism"—along with his European education—as a factor alienating him from the American twenties. But Lewisohn's alienation did the critic a disservice, Kazin writes. "By one of those summary psychic equations and emotional transferences that contribute so much to imaginative art but can corrupt the necessary poise of criticism, Lewisohn solemnly reasoned out his critical position to a point where he could evaluate literature in America solely in terms of his own character, his own sense of race, his own vicissitudes, and his own private aspirations as citizen, lover, and artist" (207–8). This was not a mistake that

Kazin would repeat. In his own case he felt his "Hebraism" had no bearing on his work as a literary historian and critic.

Two years later, Kazin made this explicit when asked in a symposium conducted by the *Contemporary Jewish Record* to comment on the relation that Jewish heritage had to his writings. Kazin stated flatly, "I learned long ago to accept the fact that I was Jewish without being a part of any meaningful Jewish life or culture" ("Under Forty," 11). Yet unlike Wright, Kazin recognized the greatness in the culture from which he felt himself estranged. The first part of his answer cites leading writers (Scholem Aleichem and I. L. Peretz), artists (Marc Chagall and Ernest Bloch), and political figures (Nello Roselli and Rosa Luxemburg) "for whom the word [Jew] meant and means something" (9). It wasn't Jewish culture that was lacking in art and vision. "But I have never seen much of what I admire in American Jewish culture, or among Jewish writers in America generally" (10).

Kazin's autobiographies reveal a more complex evaluation of Jewish American culture. In the second volume of his autobiography, *Starting Out in the Thirties*, he writes of his excitement at seeing the production of Clifford Odets's *Awake and Sing* in 1936.

In Odets' play there was a lyric uplifting of blunt Jewish speech, boiling over and explosive, that did more to arouse the audience than the political catchwords that brought the curtain down. Everybody on that stage was furious, kicking, alive—the words, always read but never flat, brilliantly authentic like no other theater speech on Broadway, aroused the audience to such delight that one could feel it bounding back and uniting itself with the mind of the writer. (8)

So taken was Kazin with this Jewish-American play that he quoted it as an epigraph to *Starting Out in the Thirties*. Yet central as Odets's achievement was to Kazin's conception of himself as a writer (a theme we shall take up later), no hint of this comes through in his early criticism. Kazin's consciousness bifurcated itself neatly into separate compartments: Kazin the autobiographer was, as he titled the third volume of his autobiography, a *New York Jew*, but Kazin the critic was "a prisoner of the Anglo-Saxon bias that prevailed in American literary history until the post–World War II period" (Harap 65).

The adherence to cosmopolitan values assumed by radical intellectuals made it difficult for Kazin to acknowledge anything positive in a "parochial" Jewishness. Terry Cooney summarizes the Enlightenment-style values of the anti-Stalinist Left:

[W]hen the evidence of Jewish consciousness is put in its rightful context, it appears as an integral part of a logical and consistent position on the place of ethnicity. At the core of *Partisan Review*'s position stood an adherence to cosmopolitan values. Those values . . . assumed the desirability of a broad and inclusive culture. No individual or group was to be scorned or excluded on the basis of heritage; instead, social and cultural differences were to be esteemed for what they could bring to the general perspective and a more comprehensive understanding of experience. . . . What the *Partisan Review* intellectuals rejected in the name of cosmopolitan values was, as they saw it, the cultural blight of parochialism, narrowness, and prejudice. (233)

Like the other New York Intellectuals, Kazin accepted the modernists' definition of literature expounded most famously by T. S. Eliot in "Tradition and the Individual Talent." There Eliot spoke of the historical sense, acquired with great labor, by the writer who would continue to be a poet beyond the first flush of youth. "[T]he historical sense compels a man to write not merely with his own generation in his bones, but with a feeling that the whole of the literature of Europe from Homer and within it the whole of the literature of his own country has a simultaneous existence and composes a simultaneous order" (49). This Great Tradition, to appropriate the title of a work by the Communist critic Granville Hicks, clearly valued the "aesthetic" and the "universal" over the "tendentious" and "ethnic." But, as Eliot made clear both in his essay and in his own poetry, the Great Tradition expressed "the mind of Europe," and the Jew occupied a peculiar and unfortunate place in that mind. Champions of modernism, the New York Intellectuals promoted the writings of Eliot, Pound, Henry James, and Dostoevsky in spite of their anti-Semitism. "How we love them, though they love us not!" Kazin exclaimed in his reflections in a *Commentary* symposium on "The Jewish Writer and the English Literary Tradition" (367). More important than the anti-Semitism of those whom Kazin called "our literary dictators," however, was their artistry, their modernism, their commitment to Literature as the highest end in life. Concentrating on the alienation of the artist from society, documenting the fragmentation of all community and spiritual values, the high modernist view of Literature could not perceive the value of an ethnic expression. It was seen as provincial.

This is how Kazin views the Jewish novels that appeared before the Jewish Renaissance of the 1950s. "Even in the best of them," he wrote in 1971, "like Daniel Fuch's *Low Company, Summer in Williamsburg, Homage to Blenholt*, one had been aware that 'Jewish' equals 'ghetto'" (*Bright Book of Life*, 130). If Jewish-American writing was to recommend itself to the attention of the critics, it had to pass the pearly gates of the Great Tradition; it had to be brilliant, modernist, universal, and, most importantly, perceived as such by the Gentiles.

This, of course, is exactly what happened. Within the space of seven years, three Jewish-American novelists won the prestigious National Book Award: Saul Bellow for *The Adventures of Augie March* (1953), Bernard Malamud for *The Magic Barrel* (1958), and Philip Roth for *Good-bye Columbus* (1959). Beneath these peaks of recognized achievement, the decade also saw fine Jewish-American writing by Harold Brodkey (*First Love and Other Sorrows*), Grace Paley (*The Little Disturbances of Man*), and, somewhat later, Edward Lewis Wallant (*The Pawnbroker*). Though far more

than simply a Jewish-American writer, Isaac Bashevis Singer also attracted the notice of the general public with his first collection, *Gimpel the Fool and Other Stories*
(1957). During the 1970s, an international imprimatur was given to the achievements of the Jewish Renaissance when two of its foremost authors were awarded the
Nobel Prize, Bellow in 1976 and Singer in 1978.

Finally the New York Intellectuals—themselves part of the Renaissance and ex-
ercising ever greater influence as they entered the mainstream of publishing and
academia—could write of Jewish-American authors as authentic inheritors of the
Great Tradition. The Jew, to paraphrase the title of a *Commentary* article written by
Kazin in 1966, had become a Modern Writer.

[I]t was a fact that there were new Jewish novelists who, as writers, had mastered the complex resources of the modern novel, who wrote English lovingly, possessively, masterfully,
for whom the language and the form, the intelligence of art, had become as natural a way of
living as the Law had been to their grandfathers. Literature had indeed become their spiritual world, their essential personal salvation. . . . ("The Jew as Modern Writer," 41)

What more explicit statement could there be of the transfer of allegiance the
Jewish-American critics had effected within their generation?

Kazin's major meditation on Jewish-American writing is a chapter of a 1971 volume, *Bright Book of Life*, titled "The Earthly City of the Jews: Bellow to Singer." In
contrast to the approach of *On Native Grounds*, Kazin makes no attempt to place the
Jewish Renaissance in a historical perspective, nor does he try to understand the relationship between the writings of its major authors and the intellectual debates of
the time. His chapter is rather a compendium of Kazin's insights into the minds of
Bellow, Malamud, Roth, Mailer, and Singer via their fiction. He correctly observes
that Malamud's Jewishness is different from Bellow's and that "[t]he 'Jewish' identity of Norman Mailer lay precisely in the fact, as he said in *The Armies of the Night*,
that to be a nice Jewish boy was the one role unacceptable to him" (149). But Kazin
provides few clues as to what underlying unity there might be, if any, to these various versions of Jewishness. One gets the sense—*mutatis mutandis*—that Jewishness
is the provincial origin that all these minds have transcended.

Jewishness as the novelist's material (which can be quite different from the individual
material of Jews writing fiction) is constructed folklore. It is usually comic, or at least hu-
morous; the characters are always ready to tell a joke on themselves. With their bizarre
names, their accents, *their* language, they are jokes on themselves. And so they become
"Jewish" material, which expresses not the predicament of the individual who knows himself to be an exception, but a piece of the folk, of "Jewishness" as a style of life and a point
of view. (138)

Such a perspective is, of course, inimical to the transcendent universalism of the
Great Tradition. And so the "depiction of life as incessant mental struggle, of

heaven and hell in the same Jewish head . . . made Bellow's readers recognize a world the reverse of provincial" (131); Malamud archly transposed Jewishness into "serious literature" (139); and Singer's "extraordinary intelligence and detached point of view turned the heart of the [Jewish] tradition—acceptance of God's law, God's will, even God's slaughter of His own—into story, legend, fantasy" (159). Again and again we see in Kazin that "Jewishness" can only be redeemed by (modernist) Literature.

Kazin attempts just such a redemption in *A Walker in the City*. Brownsville could never have been perceived as beautiful if the writer hadn't made the move to Manhattan. By the 1950s, in an America that was at the apogee of its international and economic power, the promise of the second generation had been fulfilled: the New York Intellectuals had made it, Jewish-American writing had entered the mainstream. Why, then, were they not happy? Kazin provided part of the answer in his essay, "The Jew as Modern Writer," but it is only a pointer, in its Eliotic reverberations, to the double consciousness that makes *A Walker in the City* so much more revealing in its engagement with Jewishness than in the blinkered judgments of Kazin's literary criticism.

The real drama behind most Jewish novels and plays even when they are topical and revolutionary in feeling, is the contrast between the hysterical tenderness of the Oedipal relation and the "world"; in the beginning there was the Jewish mother and her son, but the son grew up, he went out into the world, he became a writer. That was the beginning of his career, and usually the end of the novel. Jews don't believe in original sin, but they certainly believe in the original love that they once knew in the *shtetl*, in the kitchen, in the Jewish household— and after that knowledge, what forgiveness? ("The Jew as Modern Writer," 39–40)

Despite their rejection of Black and Jewish liteary tradition, Wright and Kazin made a major contribution to those literatures through their autobiographical writings. In both personal narratives ethnic assertion, in some measure at odds with the writer's expressed beliefs, finds ways of sneaking through the ideological censor of Enlightenment values. Both writers trace an intellectual itinerary from the oppressed margins toward a more cosmopolitan center, yet these marginal communities—Wright's South and Kazin's Brownsville—are vividly peopled and conveyed to the reader in a way that resists inclusion in a larger discourse. Wright may err on the side of harshness, as Kazin does with sentimentality, but both deliver revealing studies of the conflicting demands of double consciousness. "[I]n leaving," Wright concludes in *Black Boy*, "I was taking a part of the South to transplant in alien soil, to see if it could grow differently, if it could drink of new and cool rains, bend in strange winds, respond to the warmth of other suns, and, perhaps, to bloom" (284). Like *Black Boy*, Kazin's memoir is also a bloom in alien soil. These are the tales of outsiders who have forced their way in, looking back—with cold anger in Wright's case, ambivalent nostalgia in Kazin's—to ethnic communities that would eventually reclaim not them but their narratives of ascent. *Black Boy* and *Walker* represent the final moments of the unquestioned Enlightenment hegemony that laid down the central themes of Black and Jewish autobiography since the time of Maimon and Equiano.

The place of Wright's autobiography in African-American letters was prefigured by doubly conscious Black writers such as Charles W. Chesnutt. In his novel *The Marrow of Tradition* (1901), Charles Chesnutt describes a race riot fomented against the Blacks in the Southern town of Wellington. In the chapters preceding the riot episode, the writer had created two exemplary figures with diametrically opposed reactions to the intimidation and killing. The first of these, close to Chesnutt in both background and education, was Dr. Miller, a talented surgeon of aristocratic bearing. The second was a laborer, Josh Green, who defended his dignity as a man out of a natural sense of justice. When the riot breaks out, Josh gathers together a band of like- minded men to defend themselves and the institutions that serve the Black population. On two occasions they run into Dr. Miller, who is frantically trying to locate his wife and child. Josh urges Dr. Miller to join them, but the professional man refuses for what appears to be the soundest of reasons.

"Josh—men—you are throwing your lives away. It is a fever; it will wear off to-morrow, or to-night. They'll not burn the schoolhouses, nor the hospital—they are not such fools, for they benefit the community; and they'll only kill the colored people who resist them. Every one of you with a gun or a pistol carries his death warrant in his own hand. I'd rather see the hospital burn than have one of you lose his life. Resistance only makes the matter worse,—the odds against you are too long."

"Things can't be any wuss, ductuh," replied one of the crowd sturdily. "A gun is mo' dange'ous ter de man in front of it dan ter de man behin' it. Dey're gwine ter kill us anyhow; an' we're tired,—we read de newspapers,—an' we're tired er bein' shot down like dogs, widout jedge er jury. We'd ruther die fightin' dan be stuck like pigs in a pen!" (295)

As in *Black Boy*—and indeed everywhere in African-American literature—difference in English indicates a difference in class. The sentiments expressed by the unnamed character, however, are certainly no less noble than Dr. Miller's high-minded activities. Dr. Miller assumes—erroneously, as it turns out—that the White and Black communities of Wellington are too dependent on one another to allow the race war to escalate into an event that touches his personal well-being. It is no accident of literary invention that Dr. Miller can cross the town in daylight with relative impunity, for, as a member of the middle class, he owns a horse and buggy and he is so light-skinned that if he sits back in the shadow of the carriage he won't be immediately recognized as a Black man. Because of his class position, Dr. Miller is too compromised by the status quo to offer effective resistance even in the face of rank and violent injustice. Josh Green and his men operate under no such constraints. As Donald Gibson points out, this makes the laborer a prototype for the characters of *Uncle Tom's Children*: "Because of his socioeconomic class, Josh may act directly to exert influence on the world; Dr. Miller, because of his, may not. Josh therefore has a certain power not available to Dr. Miller" (86).

By the same token, *Black Boy* wins for itself a centrality in the African-American literary tradition that is denied to the autobiographers of the middle class. Between the publication of Booker T. Washington's *Up From Slavery* in 1901 and the appearance of *Black Boy* in 1945, James Weldon Johnson (*Along This Way*, 1933), Langston Hughes (*The Big Sea*, 1940), W. E. B. Du Bois (*Dusk of Dawn*, 1940), and Zora Neale Hurston (*Dust Tracks on the Road*, 1942) all published autobiographies. Although Johnson, Hughes, Du Bois, and Hurston were literary figures in a way that Washington was not, their autobiographies could not match his in importance because their life stories did not reflect the movement and yearning of the majority of the Black population. In *Black Boy*, Ellison avows, "thousands of Negroes will for the first time see their destiny in public print" (*Shadow and Act*, 94). Wright describes this gulf separating the classes when he mulls over the future course of his life towards the end of his autobiography. "I had no hope whatever of being a professional man. Not only had I been so conditioned that I did not desire it, but the fulfillment of such an ambition was beyond my capabilities. Well-to-do Negroes lived in a world that was almost as alien to me as the world inhabited by whites" (*Black Boy*, 277).

Yet it is the White world that ultimately provides the tools for self-expression, not that of the African American. In *Black Boy* Wright singles out H. L. Mencken, Theodore Dreiser, Stephen Crane, Dostoevsky, and Gertrude Stein as influences. As he says of his reading in Memphis, "It would have been impossible for me to have told anyone what I derived from these novels, for it was nothing less than a sense of life itself. All my life had shaped me for the realism, the naturalism of the modern novel, and I could not read enough of them" (274). No mention is made of Jean Toomer, Langston Hughes, or any slave narrative. "The Literature of the Negro in the United States" makes one feel as if the African-American literary tradition were one long cry of outrage, frustration, and pain, that no positive expression of love or humanity had ever appeared in Black writing. "My habitual kind of thinking," he wrote in *Black Power*, "had no race in it, a kind of thinking that was conditioned by the reaction of human beings to a concrete social environment" (qtd. in Gayle 238).

African-American readers and critics have noted Wright's refusal to identify himself with Black culture and have taken him to task for it. An early reviewer of *Black Boy*, Beatrice Murphy, accused Wright of using his pen "as a sword to stab his own race in the back" (32). In his famous essay, "Many Thousands Gone," James Baldwin criticized *Native Son* for cutting away a necessary dimension of experience, "this dimension being the relationship that Negroes bear to one another, that depth of involvement and unspoken recognition of shared experience which creates a way of life" (35). More contemporary African-American critics, most notably Robert Stepto and Henry Louis Gates Jr., have made similar criticisms. Carla Cappetti summarizes these views in *Writing Chicago*, which examines the influence of the Chicago School of sociology on the naturalist novelists of the 1930s (187–97). Capetti finds that Gates and company are reacting against Wright's embrace of the Enlightenment. "The terms Wright uses to characterize African-American culture—'formless,' lacking in 'individuality,' 'elemental,' 'impulsive'—and that are so jarring to Gates and to our postsixties sensibilities define a point of view Wright shared with sociologists and modernist artists of the first half of this century" (191).

It is the curious mixture of modernity and class position that makes *Black Boy* such a striking achievement of double consciousness. Wright makes clear that he is an early rebel against everything in his environment, but it is an environment that he knows to the marrow. As Wright himself said in an interview given upon the publication of *Black Boy*, "I wanted to give, to lend my tongue to the voiceless Negro boys" (qtd. in Fabre, *Unfinished Quest*, 251–52). Of course these boys are not literally voiceless; Wright himself reproduces "the talk of black boys who met at the crossroads." Unable to merely record the bantering and signifying that goes on in the vernacular, Wright frames the dialogue with stage directions and commentary in standard English.

"Hey." Timidly.
"You eat yet?" Uneasily trying to make conversation.
"Yeah, man. I done really fed my face." Casually.
"I had cabbage and potatoes." Confidently.
"I had buttermilk and black-eyed peas." Meekly informational.
"Hell, I ain't gonna stand near you, nigger!" Pronouncement.
"How come?" Feigned innocence.
"'Cause you gonna smell up this air in a minute!" A shouted accusation.
Laughter runs through the crowd.
"Nigger, your mind's in a ditch." Amusingly moralistic.
"Ditch, nothing! Nigger, you going to break wind any minute now!" Triumphant pronouncement creating suspense.
"Yeah, when them black-eyed peas tell that buttermilk to move over, that buttermilk ain't gonna wanna move, and there's gonna be war in your guts and your stomach's gonna swell up and bust!" Climax. (88–89)

The linguistic alienation of this passage is symptomatic of Wright's position in African-American letters as a whole. No one can deny him his hard-won authenticity, yet he clearly turns his back on a community—and mode of expression—he knows from the bottom up. When Wright speaks in the first person singular, as the articulate hero of his own autobiographical writings, he neither avails himself of the verbal resources of Black English nor celebrates the culture of the people from which he springs.

> After I had outlived the shocks of childhood, after the habit of reflection had been born in me, I used to mull over the strange absence of real kindness in Negroes, how unstable was our tenderness, how lacking in genuine passion we were, how void of great hope, how timid our joy, how bare our traditions, how hollow our memories, how lacking we were in those intangible sentiments that bind man to man, and how shallow was even our despair. After I had learned other ways of life I used to brood upon the unconscious irony of those who felt that Negroes led so passional an existence! I saw that what had been taken for our emotional strength was our negative confusions, our flights, our fears, our frenzy under pressure. (*Black Boy*, 45)

Over and over *Black Boy* portrays Wright's inability to become a part of the Black community. The tyrannical narrowness of his grandmother's household keeps him from any kind of normal social intercourse. The traditional modes of communal interrelationship—family, church, school—are closed to him. His own attitude is often one of superiority, stemming not only from an awareness of his own intelligence and sensitivity but from a bitter pride at the depths of misery he has already survived. His judgments on his mother's coreligionists at a "black Protestant church" where he briefly attends Sunday school are typical: " . . . snobbery, clannishness, gossip, intrigue, petty class rivalry, and conspicuous displays of cheap clothing . . . I liked it and I did not like it; I longed to be among them, yet when with them I looked at them as if I were a million miles away. I had been kept out of their world too long ever to be to become a real part of it" (*Black Boy*, 166–67).

The wistfulness of this final line—a wistfulness stemming from Wright's own awareness of his alienation from the African-American community—is an element his harsher critics overlook. It is the emotional ambivalence of his rejection that lends such power to his best writing, that continues to make *Black Boy* central to African-American literature in spite of its overt rejection of African-American culture. Even as it flees Black culture for the Promised Land of Enlightenment equality, it cannot help being Black. That is why Ellison characterized *Black Boy* as a blues. "The blues is an impulse to keep the painful details and episodes of a brutal experience alive in one's aching consciousness, to finger its jagged grain, and to transcend it, not by the consolation of philosophy but by squeezing from it a near-tragic, near-comic lyricism. As a form, the blues is an autobiographical chronicle of personal catastrophe expressed lyrically" (*Shadow and Act*, 78). Like Wright, Ellison believed in the Enlightenment ideal of a universal, Western culture. Unlike Wright, he believed you could attain that culture through Black expression. Nevertheless, Wright retraces in *Black Boy* the classic African-American patterns found elsewhere in the tradition: the struggle for literacy, the longing to go North, the agonizingly slow and incremental steps toward freedom, the all-pervasive enmity of the Whites. Other elements of the African-American tradition—the celebration of kin, of religion, of folk culture—are certainly lacking, but enough of the classic content is present to assure *Black Boy* a firm and central position in the African-American canon. Inadvertently it revived the perspective of the slave narrative by witnessing simultaneously social injustice and the triumph of the Black spirit in autobiographical form. It became the spiritual progenitor of later autobiographies tracing a similar itinerary: Claude Brown's *Manchild in the Promised Land* (1965), Maya Angelou's *I Know Why the Caged Bird Sings* (1969), and *The Autobiography of Malcolm X* (1964). Turning its back on Black culture, it sparkles as one of the bright diamonds in that culture's crown. Because of its place in the African-American tradition, because that place makes explicit the structural equivalence between the color caste of chattel slavery and the class system of twentieth-century America, *Black Boy* turned out to be much Blacker and more celebratory than perhaps it knew itself to be.

Kazin was not the first to depict his generation's alienation from its Jewish origins. In Delmore Schwartz's gemlike story "America! America!" a young man sits in the kitchen listening to his mother relate the history of some family friends, the Baumanns. The young man, Shenandoah Fish, represents the second-generation intellectual, a promising young artist—self-conscious and self-absorbed—enduring a period of unemployment during the Depression. His mother relates the Baumann saga, speaking of "human beings who, being of her own generation, did not really interest Shenandoah in themselves" (11). In her self-conscious, oddly stilted English—itself filtered through the style of the omniscient narrator—Mrs. Fish details the frustrations of the immigrants in their failure to understand their children.

The generation gap between the Baumanns and their children is echoed in the relationship between Shenandoah and his mother. As he listens to her narrative, he is assailed by contradictory thoughts and emotions.

He reflected upon his separation from these people, and he felt that in every sense he was removed from them by thousands of miles, or by a generation, or by the Atlantic Ocean. What he cared about, only a few other human beings, separated from each other too, also cared about; and whatever he wrote as an author did not enter into the lives of the people, who should have been his genuine relatives and friends, for he had been surrounded by their lives since the day of his birth, and in an important sense, even before then. (19–20)

As Howe notes, Shenandoah Fish is a portrait of the New York Intellectual as a young man. Educated in a language and tradition alien to their parents, the young men and women of the second generation took pride in rejecting the world of their fathers. "The lower middle-class of the generation of Shenandoah's parents had engendered perversions of its own nature, children full of contempt for every thing important to their parents" (20). Because of its commerce with the art and culture of America, the great world beyond the Jewishness of their parents' lives, the second generation felt it had a better understanding of life in America, of life in general. Yet it is Mrs. Fish who grasps the moral of the Baumanns' story and who concludes it with the observation "that it was a peculiar but an assured fact that some human beings seemed to be ruined by their best qualities" (32). The characteristics that would have made the Baumanns ideal parents in the European Jewish community are precisely those that ruin and estrange their American children. Already alienated in his own manner, Shenandoah listens to the Baumanns' story "from such a distance that what he saw was an outline, a caricature, and an abstraction. How different it might seem, if he had been able to see these lives from the inside, looking out" (32). Then comes the revelation:

And now he felt for the first time how closely bound he was to these people. His separation was actual enough, but there existed also an unbreakable unity. As the air was full of the radio's unseen voices, so the life he breathed in was full of these lives and the age in which they had acted and suffered. Shenandoah went to his room and began to dress for the day. He felt the contemptuous mood which had governed him as he listened was really self-contempt and ignorance. He thought that his own life invited the same irony. (32)

Realizing that he too will be an object of ridicule to the next generation, Shenandoah asks, "What will I seem to my children? What is it that I do not see now in myself?" (33) And the story ends on this dismaying realization of the American predicament—the repeated rejection of the parents by their children—that links the generations in the midst of their conflict.

Written before World War II, "America! America!" brilliantly captured the ambivalence of the second-generation intellectuals casting uneasy backward glances in their rush toward acculturation. It was an ambivalence that Kazin shared. In *A Walker in the City*, he describes Brownsville as "notoriously a place that measured all success by our skill in getting away from it" (12), a tag that could apply to Williamsburg, the Lower East Side, or any of the immigrant ghettos. There was a difference in class between the Baumanns and the working poor, which made it easier for their sons and daughters to desire an escape from the squalor and oppression of their parents' lives; but for all the grown-up children of the second generation, real life was elsewhere, the real work ascending to full participation in Western culture. Part of the brilliance of Schwartz's story was the knowledge—divined even before the shock of the Holocaust—that the achievement of the second generation sprang from its contradictory relation to the Jewishness of its parents: the estrangement and belonging, the contempt and the tenderness, the anger and the love.

Shenandoah had thought of this gulf and perversion before, and he had shrugged away his unease by assuring himself that this separation had nothing to do with the important thing, which was the work itself. But now as he listened, as he felt uneasy and sought to dismiss his emotion, he began to feel that he was wrong to suppose that the separation, the contempt, and the gulf had nothing to do with his work; perhaps, on the contrary, it was the center; or perhaps it was the starting-point and compelled the innermost motion of the work to be flight, or criticism, or denial, or rejection. (20)

Such are the conditions that brought about the creation of *A Walker in the City*, a lyrical remembrance of Brownsville childhood. Deeply ambivalent about its origins, *Walker* is both an homage to and a negation of the past—simultaneously a loving memoir and a flight, a criticism, a denial, a rejection. Howe wrote of this "ambiguous compound of rejection and nostalgia" ("Lost Young Intellectual," 152), describing in generic terms the situation of the second-generation Jew alienated from his parents' world but not yet accepted into America. Kazin's autobiography illustrates this "ambiguous compound" as profoundly as the fiction of Delmore Schwartz and Isaac Rosenfeld or the essays of Howe and Daniel Bell. "The youthful experiences described by Alfred Kazin in his autobiography are, apart from his distinctive outcroppings of temperament, more or less typical of many New York intellectuals" (Howe, "New York Intellectuals," 216). Kazin is so imbued with the overriding ambivalence of his generation that it infuses every line of his memoir. These two dominant themes—rejection and nostalgia—are sounded in the opening paragraph:

Every time I go back to Brownsville it is as if I had never been away. From the moment I step off the train at Rockaway Avenue and smell the leak out of the men's room, then the pickles from the stand just below the subway steps, an instant rage comes over me, mixed with dread and some unexpected tenderness. It is over ten years since I left to live in "the city"—everything just out of Brownsville was always "the city." Actually I did not go very far; it was enough that I could leave Brownsville. Yet as I walk those familiarly choked streets at dusk and see the old women sitting in front of the tenements, past and present become each other's faces; I am back where I began. (5–6)

As Proust so definitively established, the senses of smell and taste could bring the past washing over us, and Kazin's case is no different. First the smell of squalor, then the smell of food, the usual synecdoche for secular Jewish culture in America, the mixture of these (rejection and nostalgia) invoking an instant rage, provocatively unexplained. Rage that his childhood culture should have been so poverty-stricken? Rage that he had to leave? Rage that he has to return? The dread is explained in the next paragraph: "I sense again the old foreboding that all my life would be like this" (6). And the "unexpected" tenderness is one of the mainsprings of the book, the other side of second-generation estrangement.

Published seven years after Kazin had gone on record saying that he had never seen much to admire in Jewish-American culture, *A Walker in the City* has been crit-icized by some as an indulgent exercise in nostalgia or, less flatteringly, a hypocrisy.[19] The point here, however, is that Kazin chose his literary ancestors from the American canon: Emerson, Thoreau, and Whitman—not Michael Gold, Ludwig Lewisohn, or Henry Roth.[20] Alvin Rosenfeld overstates the case when he writes that in spite of "the rich sociological representations of *Yiddishkeit*," *A Walker in the City* is "a book fundamentally lacking in Jewish interest," but he is right when he observes that "its pieties are those of the Romantic tradition, as these were localized in America by Emerson and Whitman" (142).

Rosenfeld makes the point that *A Walker in the City* was conceived of as American literature, not Jewish-American literature. As we saw above, Kazin rec-ognized nothing in Jewish-American writing that he wanted to claim as his own. His desire was to represent the world of his childhood in terms that were acceptable to an aesthetic dictated by the Great Tradition, to do for Brownsville what Joyce had done for Dublin. He eschewed Yiddishisms, stereotypes, and vaudeville rou-tines—anything that smacked of ethnicity and provincialism. The local color of an American ghetto was to be conveyed in an American style worthy of Literature. As Rosenfeld writes, "An impassioned attachment to history and later to literature, but emphatically not to Jewish history and literature, was his ticket out of Brownsville and into the promised land beyond" (141).

Yet both the literary history, *On Native Grounds*, and the literary memoir sprang out of that Jewish background. In the first work, the gesture of denial is so complete that Kazin himself must uncover its hidden ontogeny. When asked in a 1962 inter-view how he came to write *On Native Grounds*, Kazin replied:

I think the most important single influence on me was the fact that I was a Jew who grew up in the immigrant world of Brooklyn, the son of very poor Russian Jewish working peo-ple—my mother worked as a dressmaker, my father as a house painter. Now that was an extraordinary world to grow up in: not only did it have deep respect for the traditions of European learning, but it was filled with intellectual passions—above all the passion for a just society. And it was a world filled with the immigrants' sense of America—of American history as a process by which the good society might at last be realized. . . . I was swept up in all sorts of socialist and radical ideas, and I believed that modern art and modern history had come to be very much related. ("Interview," 99)

During Kazin's adolescence and young manhood, the conjunction of literature and radicalism gave rise to a new possibility, one that eventually came to fruition in the autobiography. "What young writers of the Thirties wanted was to prove the literary values of our experience, to recognize the possibility of art in our own lives, to feel that we had moved the streets, the stockyards, the hiring halls into litera-ture—to show that our radical strength could carry on the experimental impulse of modern literature" (*Starting Out*, 15). In their work, Clifford Odets and James T.

Farrell gave glimpses of the new terrain that was opening up for literary representation. Radicalism at home, both literary and political, was dialectically related to radicalism on a worldwide scale. The Spanish Civil War, traumatic watershed of a whole generation, brought to Kazin a personal illumination about how he might make his contribution to Literature as a Jew.

Everything in the outside world seemed to be moving toward some final decision, for by now the Spanish Civil War had begun, and every day felt choked with struggle. It was as if the planet had locked in combat. In the same way that unrest and unemployment, the political struggles inside the New Deal, suddenly became part of the single pattern of the struggle in Europe against Franco and his allies Hitler and Mussolini, so I sensed I could become a writer without giving up my people. The unmistakable and surging march of history might yet pass through me. There seemed to be no division between my effort at personal liberation and the apparent effort of humanity to deliver itself. . . . Wherever I went now, I felt the moral contagion of a single idea. (*Starting Out*, 82–83)

The first fruit of this "single idea" was *On Native Grounds*, the literary history of modern American prose. Then came the disillusionment of the Brest-Litovsk Treaty, the shock of the Holocaust, the postwar hysteria that climaxed in the witchhunts of the McCarthy era. The 1930s were over, and the hidden Jewish background surged to the fore.[21]

Yet Kazin's "return," like that of the other New York Intellectuals, could never be that of the Prodigal Son. Judaism as a creed and religious community had never held him, and the Jewish culture represented by Brownsville could be redeemed only through literature. The adult writer returned to the scene of childhood to sift through his confused emotions. "Yet as I walk those familiarly choked streets at dusk and see the old women sitting in front of the tenements, past and present become each other's faces; I am back where I began" (6). This is all verbal sleight-of-hand. The adult narrator will leave Brownsville, whereas the poor Jews and newly arrived Blacks cannot. "Even the Negroes who have moved into the earliest slums deserted by the Jews along Rockaway Avenue have been infected with the damp sadness of the place and slouch along the railings of their wormy wooden houses like animals in a cage" (7). But in spite of the evident poverty that precludes any real "return," Kazin effects a rehabilitation of immigrant culture in a style that is manifestly "literary": the poverty and the squalor are aestheticized; Jewish gangsters and *machers* are left out of the account; Kazin repeatedly performs verbal arias on the tiny respites of beauty that are available even to the dispossessed. "[A] moment, only a moment, watching the evening crowd of women gathering at the grocery for fresh bread and milk. But between my mother's pent-up face at the window and the winter sun dying in the fabrics—'Alfred, see how beautiful!'—she has drawn for me one single line of sentience" (71).

The other mode Kazin could have drawn on to represent life in the ghetto was the comic one, but comedy and autobiography have rarely mixed well. The New York Intellectuals took themselves too seriously to welcome such treatments of a background about which they felt so ambivalent; furthermore, the modernist aesthetic seemed fundamentally hostile to Borscht Belt humor. Thus they were not inclined to champion novels that did not treat ghetto conditions with high seriousness. Daniel Fuchs's *Summer in Williamsburg* (1934) and Arthur Granit's *Time of the Peaches* (1959) were left to languish in the obscurity to which they quickly fell after their publication. The once popular *Haunch, Paunch and Jowl* (1923) by Samuel Ornitz was also ignored. If the New York Intellectuals had occasion to write about precursors to the authors of the Jewish-American Renaissance, they much preferred to mention Delmore Schwartz, Isaac Rosenfeld, or even Michael Gold. Henry Roth's *Call It Sleep* (1931) was eventually elevated to the ranks of a "rediscovered masterpiece," partially through the efforts of Kazin himself, because it did conform to the high seriousness of a literary calling.

Thus Kazin's autobiography came freighted with all the moral gravity and self-consciousness that the sternest gatekeepers of modernism could ask for. But it works, and to see how it works, I propose a comparison of a paragraph from *Walker* with an analogous passage from *The Time of the Peaches*. Although the setting is Brownsville during the Depression, a period just slightly later than the one portrayed in Kazin's book, the two communities are as far away from one another as Lilliput is from the London of Blake's poem quoted in *Walker*'s epigraph. Before Granit plunges into his story—such as it is—he has the narrator introduce his community.

When I was a child, Brownsville existed in a large enclave, the outer borders of which I was only dimly aware. Surrounded by the Negro violence of the Bedford-Stuyvesant district, the Nazi "gemutlichkeit" of Ridgewood, the Slav solemnity of East New York, the middle-class gentility of East Flatbush and the garbage dumps of Carnasie, Brownsville was a self-contained world in its own right. For miles and miles, as far as the eye could see, five hundred thousand Jews were packed away in block after block of monstrously constructed tenements. It seemed as if someone had deliberately said, "What, they're Jews! Let's put them in this lost area of the world where they can go mad and we can forget about them."

So large was this Brownsville enclave, it appeared as if all the world was Jewish; and if one were not, there was something definitely wrong. I was a Jewish prisoner in a ghetto cage who did not realize he was imprisoned. After all, as one gets accustomed to a prison, doesn't he see bars in front of the spectators' faces? . . .

They say cultures are "assimilated"; but I know they are destroyed, both from the inside and outside, just as my beautiful world of Brownsville was destroyed, even in America where the least of all the anti-Semitisms exists; and if the culture is Jewish, you can be assured, the destruction is deliberate. (9–11)

Granit presents a prosaic and contradictory portrait. Is Brownsville a "ghetto cage" or a "beautiful world"? The quasi-sociological descriptions of the neighborhoods surrounding Brownsville indicate the diversity of American reality without bringing that diversity into a significant relationship with the Jewish community: Negroes, Nazis, the middle class—all simply the Other. They play no significant role in the story that follows. The real division for the Jewish consciousness that informs the book is the traditional one between Gentiles, who hold all the power, and Jews, who are their victims. But even this definition is compromised by America, "where the least of all the anti-Semitisms exists." The confusion of the final paragraph is particularly obvious. Is the assimilation of the Jewish community in America a deliberate destruction? If the assimilation of the immigrant communities results in a general rise of wealth and status for their children, what's so bad about the disappearance of the ghetto?

Kazin's *Walker* grapples much more successfully with the moral complexity of the ghetto because it describes the beautiful aspects of the vanishing immigrant culture: socialist millennialism, the peace of the Sabbath, the intimacy of the family circle. "Socialism would be one long Friday evening around the samovar and the cut-glass bowl laden with nuts and fruits, all of us singing *Tsuzamen, tsuzamen, ale Tsuzamen!*" (61). Kazin's description of Brownsville comprehends the ambivalence of double consciousness.

> We were the end of the line. We were the children of the immigrants who had camped at the city's back door, in New York's rawest, remotest, cheapest ghetto, enclosed on one side by the Carnasie flats and on the other by the hallowed middle-class districts that showed the way to New York. "New York" was what we put last on our address, but first in thinking of the others around us. They were New York, the Gentiles, America; we were Brownsville—*Brunzvil*, as the old folks said—the dust of the earth to all Jews with money, and notoriously a place that measured all success by our skill in getting away from it. So that when poor Jews left, even Negroes, as we said, found it easy to settle on the margins of Brownsville, and with the coming of spring, bands of Gypsies, who would rent empty stores, hang their rugs around them like a desert tent, and bring a dusty and faintly sinister air of carnival into our neighborhood. (12)

Kazin makes the physical geography of Brooklyn reflect its social geography. Only a few stops from the terminus at New Lots, Brownsville was literally the end of the line—at that time the IRT. The "hallowed, middle-class districts" show the way to New York both physically and metaphorically, for New York represents "making it," escaping the poverty and provincialism of the ghetto. The we/they division of traditional Jewish consciousness is explicitly invoked, but nuanced by the realization that one can escape "Jewishness" by rising into the middle class. The curse here is not Jewishness but poverty. When the Jews leave, Negroes take their place. The hierarchies are clearly established, delineated both geographically and socially. In descending order: Gentiles, alrightniks ("Jews with money"), poor Jews, Negroes. Anticipating the insights of Bakhtin (who was not yet known in the

West), Kazin places Gypsies at the bottom of the list because they are not only transient but hint at a "carnivalesque" scale of values that would overturn the hierarchy altogether. This possibility is too frightening to be taken seriously, and so Kazin, who has risen in the hierarchy, perceives the muffled threat as "faintly sinister."

If *A Walker in the City* has won for itself a central position in Jewish-American literature, it is not only because it is a typical second-generation memoir but because its style conveys that situation in all its complexity. Kazin's autobiography announces itself as a work of literature by consciously inserting itself into the Great Tradition, and then successfully appropriates prose modernism for the representation of Jewish-American experience. In his remarks on the "Under Forty" symposium, Kazin said, "When I read a novel by an American Jew that is at least as grounded in the life it rejects as Farrell's *Studs Lonigan* or Dreiser's *Sister Carrie*, I shall believe in the empirical fact of our participation" (10). Seven years later, at the opening of the Jewish-American Renaissance, Kazin produced just such a piece of writing.

In spite of the American invitation to assimilate, Jewish identity persists. The dialectical movement between two poles of reference over the short history of Jewish presence in the New World and the even shorter history of unrestricted professional entry into American society have created models of discourse and the emergence of dominant themes that are the preconditions of a tradition. Though not based upon Antin's *Promised Land* or Cahan's *Rise of David Levinsky*, Kazin's *Walker in the City* shares the same themes and sociological conditions as its unrecognized ancestors. By consciously assimilating these themes and conditions to the Great Tradition, Kazin has given these topoi of Jewish-American writing a place in American literature and American autobiography. *A Walker in the City* establishes itself for its beautiful rendering of an American paradox: the escape from a provincial community that will bring in its wake the longing for what has been escaped. This paradox is not unique to the Jews in America, but that Kazin has expressed it in Jewish terms makes his autobiography a landmark of the Jewish-American tradition.

Why was it always them and us, Gentiles and us, alrightniks and us? Beyond Brownsville was all "the city," that other land I could see for a day, but with every next day back on the block, back to the great wall behind the drugstore I relentlessly had to pound with a handball. Beyond was the strange world of Gentiles, all of them with flaxen hair, who hated Jews, especially poor Jews, had ugly names for us I could never read or hear without seeing Pilsudski's knife cold against our throats.[22] To be a Jew meant that one's very right to existence was always being brought into question. Everyone knew this—even the Communists summer nights on Pitkin Avenue said so, could make the most listless crowd weep with reminders of what they were doing to us in Fascist Poland, Romania, Hungary. It was what I had always heard in the great *Kol Nidre* sung in the first evening hours of the Day of Atonement, had played on my violin for them Friday evenings in the dining room whenever I felt lost and wanted to show them how much I loved them through and through, would suffer loyally with them. Jews were Jews; Gentiles were Gentiles. The line between them had been drawn for all time. What had my private walks into the city to do with anything! (99)

But of course, the private walks, the search for America, the epiphany on the Brooklyn Bridge had everything to do with it. Whitman and Yom Kippur, Emerson and the pogroms of the Pale, Clifford Odets and Rosa Luxemburg—all these nourished Kazin's life, forming the basis of his autobiography, which has, in turn, carried its influences into the turbulent currents of the tributary that feeds both the American Merrimac and the waters of Babylon.

Transformations
in the
Promised
Land

I am simply saying that a device is a device, but that it also has consequences: once invented it takes on a life, a reality of its own. So in one century, men invoke the device of religion to cloak their conquest. In another, race. Now, in both cases you and I may recognize the fraudulence of the device, but the fact remains that a man who has a sword run through him because he refuses to become a Moslem or a Christian—or who is shot in Zatembe or Mississippi because he is black—is suffering the utter reality of the device. And it is pointless to pretend that it doesn't exist—merely because it is a lie!

Lorraine Hansberry, *Les Blancs*

Journey
to the
West

Literature is a big sea full of many fish. I let down my nets and pulled.
I'm still pulling.

Langston Hughes, *The Big Sea*

In one of the most famous poems to emerge from the Harlem Renaissance, provocatively titled "Heritage," Countee Cullen ponders his relationship to the land of his ancestors. "What is Africa to me?" he repeatedly asks in iambic tetrameter. Concluding that he must keep his association with Africa remote and unreal if he is not to be undone by Black anger and Black emotion, he underscores the point with an intertextual reference to a line of poetry from the French renaissance:

What is last year's snow to me,
Last year's anything?

The allusion to François Villon's famous refrain, "Mais òu sont les neiges d'antan?"[1] would not have escaped anyone who was familiar, as Cullen himself was, with the poetry of the Western tradition. Such knowledge, the modernists held, was the necessary stock in trade of the poet who aspired to immortality. Five years before Cullen published "Heritage," T. S. Eliot had enshrined such a pronouncement in the 1920 essay, "Tradition and the Individual Talent." Tradition, he wrote, invokes a historical sense that involves a perception not only of the pastness of the past but of

169

its continued presence. "The historical sense compels a man to write not merely with his own generation in his bones, but with a feeling that the whole of the literature of Europe from Homer and within it the whole of the literature of his own country has a simultaneous existence and composes a simultaneous order" (49). Eliot's reference points are primarily Western and national. He is neither interested in nor aware of ethnic imperatives, an ideological blind spot that would affect ethnic writers of succeeding decades who made modernism their literary touchstone.

Yet even in the first decades of the century, American thinkers who advocated cultural pluralism or the inevitability of racial expression dissented from Eliot's modernist view of literary tradition as a Eurocentric structure. Anglo-Saxon artists and thinkers, Horace Kallen wrote in "Democracy Versus the Melting-Pot," are dominant but express no ethos, no vision of a collective identity, whereas the "expression in appropriate form of the national inheritance" of the various minorities is "their chief spiritual asset" (*Culture and Democracy*, 105). Indeed a necessary corollary of the essentialist argument outlined in the previous chapter was the contention that ethnic artists could only produce ethnic art. On this point Jewish authors like Kallen and Lewisohn were in agreement with the *négritude* ideologues, such as Léopold Senghor. In spite of his mainstream contributions to American philosophy, Kallen proclaimed, "the book written by me is a Jewish book and is, first of all and at its source, an extension and development of the cultural creative process represented by the fathers that begot, the mothers that bore us even to the remotest antiquity and will" (qtd. in Ratner 76).

Such early pronouncements by Jewish writers—going very much against the tide of the dominant assimilationism within the secular Jewish community—were theoretical and polemical. Until the 1950s there was no significant corpus of Jewish-American literature in English, and that produced in Yiddish made little impact upon the national consciousness. The set of questions concerning the relation of a minority literature to the Western tradition was first significantly debated by the literary figures of the Harlem Renaissance. There too it was a parochial matter— most Americans viewed the art produced by African Americans as exotic or bizarre— but in the writings of Langston Hughes, Countee Cullen, Jean Toomer, and Claude McKay issues of literary influence and audience arose out of a complex and accomplished body of work.

The polemic between George Schuyler and Langston Hughes rehearsed in June 1926 in the pages of *The Nation* defined the positions that were to be adopted by artists and critics of other American minorities: literature as ethnic expression vs. literature as a universal (read, "Western") statement of common humanity. Schuyler, in his provocatively titled essay, "The Negro-Art Hokum," conceded that Black art was present in Africa but claimed that to suggest it also existed in America was "self-evident foolishness" (qtd. in Jemie 97–98). The African-American musical styles, he argued, are not racial expression but folk art, similar to the productions of any peasant group. The self-conscious productions of the middle class were "identical in kind with the literature, painting and sculpture of white Americans: that is, [they show] more or less evidence of European influence" (97–98). In terms of an African-American literary tradition, Schuyler echoed the opinions of such earlier Black writers as Paul Laurence Dunbar and Charles Chesnutt.

The following week Hughes published his rebuttal to Schuyler, "The Negro Artist and the Racial Mountain," which was recognized as a seminal essay by the Black Arts Movement. Opening his argument with a discreet reference to Cullen's repeated insistence that he saw himself as "a poet, not a Negro poet," Hughes explained that the mountain of his title was a metaphor for the urge within the race toward Whiteness, an urge that blocked the creation of a true Negro art in America. Citing the art of the common people as authentic racial expression, Hughes advocated the creation of a Black middle-class art, one that would replace "that old whispering 'I want to be white' hidden in the aspirations of his people, to 'Why should I want to be white? I am a Negro—and beautiful!" (180).

But if artists accepted their identification with an ethnic group as primary in the creation of their art, what was their relation to the Great Tradition of the modernist masters? The simple answer—common before the fragmentation of Enlightenment culture in the latter half of the twentieth century—was that ethnic writers enjoyed the dual heritage of double consciousness: Western literature on the one hand and a rich supply of folk expression on the other. But another question arises that was rarely asked of the writers of the first half-century: what was the relation of the ethnic artist to the literary tradition of his or her own people—not the oral material of folk tales, spirituals, sermons, and Chassidic parables, but the previous novels, poems, and stories of those who had written before there was a recognizable ethnic movement? Did Langston Hughes claim kinship with Paul Laurence Dunbar?[2] Was Michael Gold aware of the novels of Abraham Cahan or Anzia Yezierska? In the creation of imaginative literature, those Black and Jewish writers who chose to write in an ethnic vein (not all did so) either applied the forms and models of Western literature to a description of their milieu (the strategy of Countee Cullen, Jean Toomer, Ludwig Lewisohn, and Charles Reznikoff) or reproduced folk materials and nonstandard dialects (the path chosen by Sterling Brown, Zora Neale Hurston, Anzia Yezierska, and Henry Roth). Some writers—James Weldon Johnson and Bernard Malamud—used different strategies for different works. But although Malamud wrote many of his stories in a Yiddishized English, there is no indication that he owes any debt to Anzia Yezierska, Henry Roth, or Clifford Odets, who produced their own versions of the dialect. In like manner Zora Neale Hurston seems unaware of the previous narratives in Black English written by Charles Chestnutt (*The*

Conjure Woman, 1889). When Melvin Tolson produced the figures of his Harlem Gallery, he drew his inspiration from Pound and Eliot, not Langston Hughes or Claude McKay. The literary lodestar for Henry Roth in the creation of his masterpiece, *Call It Sleep*, was James Joyce, not Michael Gold. In a celebrated exchange from the early 1960s between Ralph Ellison and Irving Howe, the African American novelist drew a pregnant distinction between his literary kin and those from whom he drew his inspiration. As part of his repudiation of Wright, Ellison tells Howe:

> [P]erhaps you will understand when I say he did not influence me if I point out that while one can do nothing about choosing one's relatives, one can, as artist, choose one's "ancestors." Wright was, in this sense, a "relative"; Hemingway an "ancestor." Langston Hughes, whose work I knew in grade school and whom I knew before I knew Wright, was a "relative"; Eliot, whom I was to meet only many years later, and Malraux and Dostoievsky and Faulkner, were "ancestors." (*Shadow and Act*, 140)

Ellison, like Wright, was aware of African-American writing but neither drew his inspiration from it nor recognized it as a tradition. "[T]he notion of an intellectual or artistic succession based upon color or racial background," he writes in a sly thrust at Howe's refusal to identify himself as Jewish in his writing, "is no less absurd than one based upon a common religious background" (127).

Ellison, Wright, and Kazin are symptomatic transitional figures in the evolution of the ethnic writer because all were aware of their literary "relatives" to a degree unprecedented by their precursors, and all chose their "ancestors" from the Great Tradition. They were literary assimilationists in spite of their involvement with ethnic material, but their refusal to acknowledge their literary kin as ancestors was not grounded in ignorance, as might have been the case with their precursors, but in refusal. As we saw in chapter 4, Wright repudiated the writing of the Harlem Renaissance and Kazin had nothing good to say about the Jewish-American prose writers he encountered in his research for *On Native Grounds*. Ellison was the last African-American writer of importance to articulate this position before the victory of cultural nationalism in the 1960s. In "The World and the Jug" he made the link explicit between the social construction of ethnic identity and its literary ramifications. "It is not skin color which makes a Negro American but cultural heritage as shaped by the American experience, the social and political predicament; a sharing of that 'concord of sensibilities' which the group expresses through historical circumstance and through which it has come to constitute a subdivision of the larger American culture" (*Shadow and Act*, 131). Arguing against Howe's contention that the African-American writer could only create protest literature because he or she was so dominated by his or her caste status, Ellison raked Howe (and Wright) over the coals for recognizing nothing positive in Black American culture and for assuming that the sociological reality was all that counted. Amending the statement of James Baldwin that one writes "out of one thing only-one's own experience," Ellison adds, "one's own experience as understood and ordered through one's knowledge of self, culture and literature" (110–11). Wright serves Ellison as an example, for, as Ellison points out and as *Black Boy* makes clear, Wright was as much a product of his reading as of the South. And Ellison tells his own rosary of intellectual heroes while living in Macon County, Alabama: Marx, Freud, Eliot, Pound, Stein, and Hemingway.

But because Wright had been so lionized by the White literary establishment— a best-selling novelist and anointed spokesman of the Negro—subsequent African-American writers could not remain in ignorance. They had to incorporate his influence in their writing, either by emulation (Robert Bone describes a whole school of Richard Wright imitators) or repudiation. When both James Baldwin, with early essays published in *Partisan Review*,[3] and Ralph Ellison, through his satire of the Communist Party and his revision of *Native Son*'s blindness motif in *Invisible Man*, killed the literary father in the best Bloomian manner, a self-conscious African-American literary tradition was born.

Jewish-American literature produced no writer of similar stature until the advent of Saul Bellow. Yet because of the more assimilated position of American Jews, a self-conscious literary tradition was neither imposed from the outside nor accepted from within, and subsequent writers, such as Edward Wallant, Cynthia Ozick, and Chaim Potok did not have to do battle with Bellow's legacy in the same manner. During the 1950s, the ambiguous position of the American Jews actually facilitated their intellectual entry into the mainstream: African Americans were allowed only to speak for other Blacks, but American Jews cast themselves successfully in the role of Marginal Man. As Leslie Fiedler made clear in his essays of that time, the Jewish writer's ineffable Jewishness effected his or her imaginative entry into American literature, but the recognition given to Malamud, Bellow, and Philip Roth also bore out Isaac Rosenfeld's old claim "that whatever contributions Jewish writers may make to American literature will depend on matters beyond their control as writers" (qtd. in Richman 20).

This observation held equally true for African-American writing. The confluence of the revival of Black nationalism, feminism, and the wave in African independences in the 1960s initiated a far-reaching recovery of African-American texts and a rehabilitation of forgotten masterpieces: *Narrative of the Life of Frederick Douglass* (1845; reissued 1960), *Incidents in the Life of a Slave Girl* (1861; reissued 1969), *Cane* (1921; reissued 1969), and *Their Eyes Were Watching God* (1937; reissued 1969). Between 1966 and 1989, Equiano's *Narrative* was anthologized twice in its entirety, brought out once in an abridged edition, and twice in full reeditions.

The cultural nationalism of the Black Arts movement not only encouraged the tendency toward ethnic identification through art; it also engendered an effort to cut Black literature away from the Western tradition. "The Black Aesthetic," Addison Gayle Jr. wrote in a 1971 anthology of the same name, "is a corrective—a means of helping black people out of the polluted mainstream of Americanism" (xxiv). Jewish-American intellectuals never attempted to clear such a space for themselves. Eldridge Cleaver wrote that in spite of the universality of human experience, "a black man, unless he has become irretrievably 'white-minded,' responds with an additional dimension of his being to the articulated experience of another black" (97). Speaking for Black women writers, Alice Walker found her best sustenance in the productions of other women, especially Black women, championing the neglected writings of Zora Neale Hurston into a fantastic popular and critical renaissance. "We are a people," she wrote in her foreword to Robert Hemenway's 1977 biography of Hurston. "A people do not throw their geniuses away" (92). Finally the African-American critics created theoretical systems based on this specifically racial approach. Borrowing the poststructuralist strategies that allowed them to challenge the centrality of the Western canon, critics such as Robert Stepto, Houston Baker, and Henry Louis Gates Jr. constructed an African-American tradition that was just as complex, self-aware, and as constantly engaged in intertextual dialogue as Eliot's Tradition. "Black writers also read each other," Gates wrote in *The Signifying Monkey*, "and seem intent on refiguring what we might think of as key canonical topoi and tropes received from the black tradition itself" (xxii). The work of these critics, impressive in its range and conceptual creativity, helped make the field of African-American literary criticism (supplemented from the feminist ranks with the dazzling emergence of Black women writers) a legitimate specialization in English departments around the country.

By contrast, Jewish-American literary criticism remained weak and parochial, except where it benefited from feminist energy (in the rediscovery of Anzia Yezierska, for example) or inclusive versions of multiculturalism.[4] Literary critics of Jewish extraction—most notably the graduates of the *Partisan Review* crowd—occupied influential positions within the American intelligentsia and, but for the traditional American-Jewish unwillingness to make loud ethnic claims, they could have done a great deal to promote a self-conscious literary tradition. However, as Henry Louis Gates Jr. was later to observe, "Few definitions of tradition escape the racism, essentialism, or nationalism often implicit in rubrics such as 'African' or 'Jewish' or 'Commonwealth' literature" (120). Philip Rahv, Lionel Trilling, Alfred Kazin, Irving Howe, and Leslie Fiedler all wrote of Jewish-American books and on Jewish-American authors, but—with the partial exception of Howe and Fiedler—none were interested in staking their reputation on a Jewish-American tradition. All owed their primary allegiance to the Western canon of their modernist masters. Hence the dazzling postwar emergence of Jewish-American authors—superstars of the mainstream publishing scene in the 1950s and 1960s—never received for itself any appellation of ethnic affiliation. Few critics spoke of a "Jewish Renaissance" or a "New York Renaissance," although Bellow, Malamud, Mailer, Singer, and Roth were much more household names than had been Langston Hughes, Countee Cullen, or Jean Toomer during the Harlem Renaissance.[5] In his introduction to a Malamud anthology published in 1979, Rahv stated flatly, "the American-Jewish writers do not in the least make up a literary faction or school," and called the idea of such a school "ignorant and even malicious" (vii).

There were occasional breaches in the wall of ethnic silence. It was the Jewish critics Kazin, Fiedler, and Harold Ribalow who were responsible for the resurrection of the forgotten masterpiece *Call It Sleep*, although they praised the novel more for its mastery of modernist techniques than for its portrayal of the immigrant Jewish milieu. *Partisan Review* launched Isaac Bashevis Singer's career in English by commissioning Bellow to translate "Gimpel the Fool." Irving Howe increased his considerable fame as an editor and translator of Yiddish literature. Leslie Fiedler published a remarkable monograph called *The Jew in the American Novel*, which should have been a seminal text for the creation of Jewish-American criticism, but neither academia nor the public was interested in a Jewish literary tradition per se, and the book, published by a small ethnic press, languished in obscurity.

One thing Fiedler made evident in his study was that Jewish-American novelists wrote of their condition as Jews as filtered through their understanding of literature, i.e., the Western mainstream. They were not responding to one another, making intertextual references, or self-consciously revoicing the themes of their Jewish-American "relatives." Such claims—certainly admissible since the time of Wright—were to become the stock in trade of the postmodern African-American critics who were to make their reputations and that of African-American literary criticism in the 1980s, but the Jewish-American writers and critics had their moment when the Eliot version of the tradition—still Western, still "universal," and still monolithic—remained unchallenged.

Yet there were grounds for such an approach. Philip Roth was the first Jewish-American writer to derive his sense of identity from an ethnic literary tradition. In a provocative reading of this tradition, "Imagining Jews," he speaks of his creation, Alexander Portnoy, as a stand-in for his generation. "Like the rest of us, he too has read Saul Bellow, Bernard Malamud, and Norman Mailer" (*Reading Myself and Others*, 242). And in his portrayal of his literary *döppelganger*, Nathan Zuckerman, Roth limns the psychology of a young writer whose ethnic identity is passionately reawakened through the stories of a literary elder, E. I. Lonoff.

I "analyzed" Lonoff's style but kept to myself an explication of the feelings of kinship that his stories had revived in me for our own largely Americanized clan, moneyless immigrant shopkeepers to begin with, who'd carried on a *shtetl* life ten minutes' walk from the pillared banks and gargoyled insurance cathedrals of downtown Newark; and what is more, feelings of kinship for our pious, unknown ancestors whose Galician tribulations had been only a little less foreign to me, while growing up securely in New Jersey, than Abraham's in the Land of Canaan. (*The Ghost Writer*, 13)

But there weren't enough Zuckermans to create the intellectual environment in which a Jewish-American tradition might thrive. Even the criteria for inclusion in such a tradition—not a problem with African-American writers, for whom the "one-drop rule" applied in matters literary as well as sociological—were never staked out with much enthusiasm. To what extent could Nathaniel West's *Miss Lonelyhearts*, Arthur Miller's *Death of a Salesman*, and Allen Ginsberg's "Howl" be considered works of Jewish-American literature?[6] When Allen Guttman tried to include Ginsberg in a line of radical, nonreligious Jewish writers tracing its ancestry back to Emma Goldman, he ran into such trouble with the cultural topography of identification that he openly admitted:

It is the Jewishness rather than the Americanness of Allen Ginsberg (and Abbie Hoffman and Jerry Rubin and a great many others associated with the New Left) that seems problematical. Child of a family that had already converted from Judaism to Communism, he has become a guru whose benevolent visage beams from uncounted dormitory walls. In "Kraj Majales," he proclaimed himself a "Buddhist Jew" . . . . His comic failure to communicate with Judge Julius Hoffman [during the Chicago Seven Trial], who evidently decided that his testimony was a sign of madness, represents a gap that is more religious than generational. It is inevitable that Allen Ginsberg and Julius Hoffman have been and will continue to be identified as Jews, but anyone who attempts to discuss them as if they shared the same faith deserves a citation for the contempt of common sense. (176–77)

Guttman committed the same error as Ellison did in his reply to Howe when he implied that Jewish identity was based in religion, and his final appeal to "common sense" was unconsciously ironic since it was the philosophy of the Enlightenment that discouraged a serious examination of Jewish identity in America. The tradeoff for full civic participation in Enlightenment society was the relinquishing of a claim to any other than a religious (hence "private") status. During the postwar period of Jewish entry into the American mainstream, the emphasis à la Will Herberg (*Protestant-Catholic-Jew*) was on Jewish identity as a harmless religious creed with no national content. Since African Americans were specifically excluded from Enlightenment principles for most of American history, the definition of a "Negro" had been the subject of continuous debate, and subsequent determinations had not only social but legal consequences. In the tortuous career of minority relations in America, the Black's long history of caste status created a literary tradition that was easily recognizable and available for any number of ideological uses. Jewish-American literature has yet to emancipate itself.

Yet one question, in terms of our study, remains paramount for both traditions: to what extent do ethnic writers consciously refigure the tropes (Gates's "talking book," for example) of their predecessors? Is Wright aware that his autobiography recapitulates the driving quest for literacy and freedom of the slave narratives? Does Kazin know that his *yiddishe mama* and his rejection of Jewish literacy have their counterparts in earlier Jewish-American novels? If the answer is "no"—as is likely the case—then what are we to make of these parallels? Does continuity (or change) of an ethnic status as reflected by its writers translate into a coherent literary tradition? The question becomes more difficult to answer after these traditions have become self-consciously literary, which is why Wright and Kazin make good endpoints for the assimilationist assumptions that conditioned the ethnic autobiographer's self-image from the Enlightenment on down. From here on, we shall expand the scope of our definition of Black and Jewish beyond the national. And, as we shall see, the question of religion—or, more precisely, conversion—figures into each of these traditions in a fundamental way.

The first Black autobiographies of the eighteenth century—Britton Hammon, Ottobah Cugoano, Equiano, John Marrant, Ukasaw Gronniosaw, David George, and Boston King—all proclaimed the Christianity of their protagonists. John Marrant, David George, and Boston King were Baptist and Methodist ministers who spread the gospel in Canada, Africa, and New England. In *Narrative of the Uncommon Suffering and Surprizing Deliverance of Briton Hammon, A Negro Man . . .* (1760), the loyal slave employs biblical references and quotations, constantly thanking the Lord and praising His Providence for delivering him from the dangers posed by the Spaniards and Indians. Gronniosaw presents himself as a Christian pilgrim on a providential journey through life's trials and tribulations, thereby earning praise in Cugoano's antislavery tract, *Thoughts and Sentiments. . . .* Though Gronnisaw was poor, Cugoano wrote, "he would not have given his faith in the Christian religion, in exchange for all the kingdoms of Africa" (22).

The reason for the early Black embrace of Christianity is not difficult to understand. Christianity, as we saw in chapter 2, provided Blacks with an ideology that not only legitimized their claims to humanity within a Western framework, but also, as Angelo Costanzo notes, "partially eliminated the idea from the slave's mind that he was only a physical commodity" (20). Thus early Black autobiography found in the spiritual autobiographies known to their authors or their amanuenses a model for interpretive organization. Everything was viewed in the light of God's providence. Equiano ends his narrative by declaring: "I early accustomed myself to look at the hand of God in the minutest occurrence, and to learn from it a lesson of morality and religion; and in this light every circumstance I have related was, to me, of importance" (178).

Equiano's conversion was as heartfelt and as central to his autobiographical project as were his antislavery motives. He describes a period of extended spiritual anguish, well after he has gained his freedom, and in his uncertainty as to whether he is to be ultimately damned or saved, he is only held back from suicide by the thought that in taking his own life he assures his damnation (141). Like other spiritual autobiographers, conversion is what gives Equiano's life shape and meaning. "I was sensible of the invisible hand of God, which guided and protected me, when in truth I knew it not" (143). Equiano's narrative, like those of Gronniosaw, Marrant, George, and King, takes on the conventional shape of the spiritual autobiography: the recall of life in darkness, the splendor of conversion, and the description of life in the knowledge and service of God. Because Christianity was not part of the sub-Saharan heritage, Blacks underwent conversion as a rite of passage into Western society. Conversion served Black autobiographers as a means of establishing their credentials for consideration as legitimate participants in Western civilization. Thus for early Black autobiography, Christianity was the *sine qua non* of a valid subjectivity, and conversion was its most dramatic treatment.

But Christianity was not the only way station of note on the Black journey to the West.

These words of my master were like a voice from heaven to me: in an instant all my trepidation was turned into unutterable bliss, and I most reverently bowed myself with gratitude, unable to express my feelings, but by the overflowing of my eyes, and a heart replete with thanks to God. . . . As I was leaving the house I called to mind the words of the Psalmist, in the 126th Psalm, and like him, "I glorified God in my heart, in whom I trusted." (100)

This passage describes not Equiano's revelation, which occurred several years later and which we have already quoted, but his reaction to the order of his Quaker master, Robert King, to seek out the Secretary at the Register Office of Monserrat and get his manumission papers drawn up. In spite of its religious imagery, this hosannah springs from the secular mutation that becomes an essential element of the slave narrative: the acquisition of freedom. "Regardless of how they invoked the rhetoric of conversion, the authors of slave narratives generally told two stories: their reception of grace and their achieving liberation from legal bondage" (Dorsey 81). In both cases a transformation occurs that gives meaning to all that comes before and after. The secular conversion of the slave narrative maintains the tripartite organization of the spiritual autobiography:

| life of sin | conversion | life of mission |
| life of bondage | escape/manumission | life of freedom |

The life histories of Gronniosaw, Equiano, George, and King are both spiritual autobiographies and slave narratives; that of Marrant, who was never a slave, describes only his religious conversion.

The last Black autobiography of the eighteenth century, Venture Smith's "Narrative," inaugurates the pattern with which contemporary audiences are more much familiar: the secular slave narrative. Smith's amanuensis divides his narrative into three chapters corresponding to the tripartite structure outlined above. Chapter 1 chronicles his separation and captivity; chapter 2 describes his adult life of bondage in the United States until, through hard work and thrifty habits, he is able to purchase his freedom; and chapter 3 portrays his rise in the business world, and the success that allows him to buy the freedom of his friends and family.

As Christianity took on a distinctive coloration and special functions within the African-American community, conversion no longer served the purpose of legitimizing the Black in the eyes of his or her White counterparts. Instead it became another link in the chain of belonging to the Black community. And as the slave narrative developed in nineteenth-century America in response to the Abolitionist agenda, the secular conversion was brought to the fore at the expense of the spiritual. The most famous example of this slave narrative conversion—echoing but faintly the rhetoric of its religious prototype—is the scene in the *Narrative of the Life of Frederick Douglass* (1845) in which, as the author says to his reader, "You have seen how a man was made a slave; you shall see how a slave was made a man" (294). Hired out as a field hand to a planter with a reputation as a slave-breaker, Douglass finally engages in a long physical fight in which he emerges the victor. "I felt as I never felt before," he writes. "It was a glorious resurrection, from the tomb of slavery, to the heaven of freedom. My long-crushed spirit rose, cowardice departed, bold defiance took its place; and I now resolved that, however long I might remain a slave in form the day had passed forever when I could be a slave in fact" (299).

With the demise of the slave narrative, African-American autobiography entered a quiescent phase of forty years. When it reemerged, the religious aspects of the tradition were even less in evidence. The path laid out by Washington's *Up From Slavery*, that of the Black Horatio Alger who triumphs through hard work and virtue, was ideologically out of joint with a time in which the whole effort of White America seemed bent on depriving the Blacks of economic and social opportunity. As we have seen in chapter 4, African-American autobiography once again found its literary and political vocation with the advent of *Black Boy*. Previous autobiographies by W. E. B. Du Bois, James Weldon Johnson, Langston Hughes, and Zora Neale Hurston had been too individualistic, too faithful a recreation of the extraordinary lives of extraordinary men and women. They could not be read as representative narratives. For all of Wright's ambition and talent, his fanatical individualism and overt rejection of racial identification, the story he tells of his growing-up years—the broken homes, the omnipresent hunger, the unremitting hostility of White society, the thwarted emotions and repressive religiosity—was part of a story shared by millions of others. His explicit intention in writing the autobiography was to portray the environment, as he understood it in its sociological sense, of the Jim Crow South. "I wrote the book to tell a series of incidents strung through my childhood," Wright declared in a magazine article of 1945, "but the main desire was to render a judgment on my environment" (qtd. in Fabre 252). The desire to "render judgment" reforges the broken links to the long-out-of-print slave narratives. This strategy, once it had been rediscovered, would be adopted with great success by James Baldwin, Claude Brown, Maya Angelou, and—most notably—Malcolm X, who revived the theme of spiritual conversion in Black autobiography from a startlingly different perspective.

Wright's autobiography, though more successful than other postslavery accounts in its choice of narrative strategy, did share a significant theme with its predecessors—the false spiritual conversion. Johnson, Hughes, and Wright all relate episodes in which they were forced as children, through social and family pressure, to fake a spiritual redemption. Though Johnson's attitude toward the event is somewhat bantering and nonchalant, both Hughes and Wright experience their forced conversions as traumatic. Hughes cries for the second-to-last time in his life "because I couldn't bear to tell [Auntie Reed] that I had lied, that I had deceived everybody in the church, that I hadn't seen Jesus, and that now I didn't believe there was a Jesus any more, since he didn't come to help me" (*The Big Sea*, 21). In *Black Boy*, Richard, following his mother into the Methodist church because of his desire for society, is emotionally blackmailed into a baptism he does not want. "This business of saving souls had no ethics; every human relationship was shamelessly exploited. In essence, the tribe was asking us whether we shared its feelings; if we refused to join the church, it was equivalent to saying no, to placing ourselves in the position of moral monsters" (170).

In the nineteenth-century slave narrative, the secular conversion of liberation subordinated or substituted for spiritual conversion. In the twentieth century, spiritual conversion was often seen as a retrograde element in the autobiographer's narrative of ascent. Yet with the substitution of peonage and ghettoization for formal slavery, how could secular conversion manifest itself where no formal act of manumission was possible? Middle-class autobiographers such as Johnson and Du Bois did not feel the need for conversion, either spiritual or secular. Langston Hughes, who bounced back and forth between the middle and the lower class, had adumbrated a solution in *The Big Sea* but did not cast his eventual choice of artistic vocation into the form of a conversion narrative.

As Wright had brought naturalism into African-American fiction, so he married the secular conversion of Black autobiography with the modernist religion of Art. He introduces his scene of transformation when the boy Richard is clandestinely told his first fairy tale.

[Ella] whispered to me the story of Bluebeard and His Seven Wives and I ceased to see the porch, the sunshine, her face, everything. As her words fell upon my new ears, I endowed them with a reality that welled up from somewhere within me. She told how Bluebeard had duped and married his seven wives, how he had loved and slain them, how he had hanged them up by their hair in a dark closet. The tale made the world around me be, throb, live. As she spoke, reality changed, the look of things altered, and the world became peopled with magical presences. My sense of life deepened and the feel of things was different, somehow. Enchanted and enthralled, I stopped her constantly to ask for details. My imagination blazed. The sensations the story aroused in me were never to leave me. (47)

Richard is describing his first encounter with fiction. Apprehensively whispered to him by a Black schoolteacher living in his grandmother's home, the tale is angrily interrupted by Granny, a Seventh Day Adventist of the narrowest creed, who shouts, "I want none of that Devil stuff in my house!" (47). Like coitus interruptus, the truncated tale only whets Richard's appetite for more. And though his mother echoes Granny's warning that Richard will burn in hell, the story affects the child on an even deeper level.

They read my insistence as mere obstinacy, as foolishness, something that would quickly pass; and they had no notion how desperately serious the tale had made me. They could not have known that Ella's whispered story of deception and murder had been the first experience in my life that had elicited from me a total emotional response. No words or punishment could have possibly made me doubt. I had tasted what to me was life, and I would have more of it, somehow, some way. (48)

Richard has discovered an ingress to a richer, more heightened existence than what he finds in "reality." The creative imagination allows Richard to develop into something other than a Southern "nigger." The uses of this faculty are varied but serve a simultaneously protective and nurturing function: superstition in response to a barren childhood (83), violent fantasies of racial revenge (84), writing as an antidote to the intellectual poverty of religion (132) and school (182), reading as a cultural transfusion from other worlds (273).

As Horace Porter notes, "*Black Boy* . . . can be read as a portrait of the artist as a young man" (316). Although Richard's imagination—his ability to conceive of a fuller, freer existence—provides an occasional escape from his reality, it also brings him into sharper conflict with it: anxiety, unanswered questions, rebellion. Furthermore he finds no kindred spirits and grows increasingly isolated as he matures. His refusal to submit to unjust punishment causes him to fight most desperately with Aunt Addie and Uncle Tom. His will to resist spiritual and moral violation brings him into conflict with his grandmother and his principal. By the time he graduates from ninth grade, he is isolated at school, a pariah to his family (his mother excepted), bitterly proud and misunderstood.

Richard's attitudes endanger him in the White world of the South. Pride, integrity, imagination—all of this must be masked on pain of death. Up until he begins working for Whites, Richard has been able to overcome and defy the repressive forces of his society. But the agents of these forces were other Blacks, and Richard could get away with his defiance. Now another education must begin, another set of realities must be confronted that militate against an accession to cultural freedom and creativity. Because Richard has not learned the lessons of submission vis-à-vis his own race, the process of learning them in the White world is an agonizing one. In spite of his imagination and intelligence, Richard is beaten (the car ride), terrorized (run off the job at the optical company), manipulated (the fight with Harrison), humiliated (all of the above), turned into a criminal (bootlegging, burglary, the box-office fraud), and almost brutalized into surrender. "I had once tried to write, had once reveled in feeling, had let my crude imagination roam, but the impulse to dream had been slowly beaten out of me by experience" (272). Chapters 9 through 13 make for some of the most horrifying reading in American letters.

Black Boy does not describe an uninterrupted ascent to freedom. Though the book does not break cleanly into two parts, there are two stories of development here: the formation of an artist and the education of a Jim Crow "nigger." The *künstlerroman* is again taken up in chapters 13 and 14. Wright discovers Mencken, the modern novel, and the social criticism of contemporary authors. The youthful conversion to Writing blazes anew, bringing with it a transformation.

> It would have been impossible for me to have told anyone what I derived from these novels, for it was nothing less than a sense of life itself. All my life had shaped me for the realism, the naturalism of the modern novel, and I could not read enough of them. . . . In buoying me up, reading also cast me down, made me see what was possible, what I had missed. My tension returned, new, terrible, bitter, surging, almost too great to be contained. I no longer felt that the world about me was hostile, killing; I *knew* it. A million times I asked myself what I could do to save myself, and there were no answers. (274)

The rhetoric of darkness and salvation come naturally enough to the sensitive young man trying to free himself from the burden of Jim Crow strictures and perceptions. His first solution—the flight North—is the classic one of the slave narrative, but unlike in the slave narrative, Literature becomes the North Star that guides his steps to freedom.

For Black autobiography, first there was the Word, and the Word became Literature. As Peter Dorsey writes, "conversion accounts are frequently semimystical exercises in intertextuality," and this holds true not only for Wright's secular conversion but for Equiano's religious one. (Equiano first beholds the light of his salvation while reading Acts 4:12.) Both Black autobiographers refigure the famous conversion scene in Augustine's *Confessions*, in which the tortured seeker experiences his transformation as a consequence of reading Paul's *Epistles*, an act embarked upon after hearing a child cry, *"tolle lege, tolle lege"* [take up and read]. "By interacting with one form of sacred literature, the successful believer was able to construct another" (Dorsey, 22). And so, Equiano becomes a Protestant; Wright becomes an author; and both produce foundational texts of the Black tradition.

In the foundational texts of secular Jewishness, however, religious conversion could play no such role. Heinrich Heine noted accurately enough that such a conversion provided the ticket of entry into Western culture, but it also represented the exit door from Judaism. Christianity had so long cast the Jew in the role of the Other that some kind of abstention from the religion of the oppressor was at the core of Jewish identity—even the identity of assimilated Jews. The Jew who converted to Christianity was by most definitions—except for the racial ones of Nazism—no longer Jewish. Religious conversion could not play the midwife in the Jew's birth into Western culture as it had with the Black. That role was assumed by modernity.

Modernity came to the Jews well after the seventeenth century inaugurated the quarrel between the Ancients and the Moderns, thereby disseminating the concept of modernity (though not yet the word) in intellectual discourse. What seemed modern then (mostly the idea of scientific inquiry) hardly seems so today, and, in fact, the term "modern," though still in current usage, is so subjective and slippery that it seems to retain its validity as a label only when its meaning remains vague. Up until recently, "Modern" was now, of our time, that period to which we still belonged.[7] Obviously different senses and schemas of periodization assign differing starting dates to the modern period, but what they all had in common was that they extended to the present. For the European historian, modernity evolved out of the Italian Renaissance,[8] but for other people in other parts of the world, modernity was something imposed by the West through cultural and economic imperialism. Thus for the Black populations of Africa, the harbingers of modernity—the slave trade, colonialism, the New World communities—announced themselves as tragedies and cataclysms. Jewish entry into the modern period seemed much more benign, initiated as it was by the haskalah, Revolutionary emancipation, and the promise of eventual acculturation. But the political anti-Semitism of the latter part of the nineteenth century—also a modern phenomenon—culminated in a tragedy of such proportions that no Jew could ever regard his or her participation in the modern age as a legacy of unmixed blessings. As the historian Roger Seltzer writes, "The modern nation-state offered Jews an opportunity for fraternal belonging to the citizenry of the lands where they lived, just as the modern economy offered them the opportunity to move into a wider range of occupations and professions. But modern developments also threatened Jewry with disintegration and dissolution, while Jewish distinctiveness and stereotyping made them vulnerable to new forms of discrimination and mass hatred" (515).

For generations of orthodox Jews, from the eighteenth century onward, modernity hovered just beyond the Jewish horizon—as scientific ideas in non-Jewish tongues, as natural and speculative philosophy, as forbidden books on secular knowledge, as social, political, and literary intercourse with Gentiles in French, German, and Russian. Maimon was among the first to describe his conversion to modernity and its consequences. When he masters German sufficiently to read "an old work on Optics and Sturm's *Physics*," he paints the experience in transformative language. "After I had studied these books thoroughly, my eyes were all at once opened. I believed that I had found a key to all the secrets of nature, as I now knew the origin of storms, of dew, of rain, and such phenomena. I looked down with pride on all others, who did not yet know these things, laughed at their prejudices and superstitions, and proposed to clear up their ideas on these subjects and to enlighten their understanding" (107–8). Like Equiano's experience of Christian salvation, Maimon's conversion to modernity is largely an intertextual phenomenon. In his autobiography Maimon is uninterested in or incapable of presenting a Rousseauean life of the sentiments, but even he approaches an eighteenth-century "enthusiasm" when describing his first encounter with German philosophy. Having rescued a copy of Wolff's *Metaphysics* from a fate as wrapping paper in a butter shop, Maimon found himself "in raptures" at the first reading. "Not only this sublime science in itself, but also the order and mathematical method of the celebrated author . . . all this struck a new light in my mind" (213). The consequences of such a conversion are predictable: Maimon can no longer follow the laws of Judaism. The process whereby he eventually leaves Jewish society altogether is a gradual one. His tactlessness and fidelity to the truth as he sees it soon earn for him a reputation as an atheist and freethinker. When asked during his travels to pronounce the traditional blessing over the cup of wine, he refuses with the explanation that it is impossible for him "without manifest aversion, to say prayers which I regarded as a result of an anthropormorphic system of theology" (246).

Not all conversions to modernity were effected with such rapidity and relative ease. The Russian Jewish writer Moses Lob Lilienblum charted a much more difficult itinerary in the most important autobiography of the nineteenth century written in Hebrew, *Hattot Ne'urim* [The Sins of Youth], first published in 1876. Educated and raised in a traditional home, Lilienblum grew up stuyding the Talmud and rabbinical literature. Married at fourteen to an eleven-year-old girl from Wilkomir, Lilienblum moved in with his in-laws and was soon able to study independently. Although conservative by nature, as he confesses several times, he found himself responding to those commentators on the Torah who eschewed elements of the supernatural that were not directly part of the holy narrative. Slowly he found his way to the haskalah through the Hebrew writings of Nachman Krochman, "the Mendelssohn of Galicia," and the poetry of the Lebensohns. In 1868 at the age of twenty-five, Lilienblum completed a long essay titled "Orhot Ha-Talmud" [The Ways of the Talmud] in which he tried to demonstrate that traditional Judaism must be reformed "to unite religion with life." As a Talmudic scholar, he attempted to prove by the Talmud itself that such changes had always been made. "Do not stop your ears to the voice of one who loves his people and his religion and speaks to you," Lilienblum pleaded with the rabbis (qtd. in Zinberg, *Haskalah at Its Zenith*, 215). The response of the Wilkomir community was to brand the reformer a heretic. Their unremitting hostility eventually drove Lilienblum to Odessa, where he planned to take up secular studies and, if possible, enter the university as a student. As Lilienblum became more radical in his views, he passed from the reformist tenets of the haskalah to doubting the authority of the Talmud and finally of the Torah itself. He thus found himself without religion, a fact that pained him greatly.

The Russian Hebrew writer Mordecai Ze'ev Feierberg produced a fictional version of the loss of faith experienced by so many Jews of the nineteenth century in his novella *Le'an* [Whither?] of 1899. *Le'an* chronicles the inner life of Nachman, the son of "a brilliant rabbi and a saintly Jew," who shows promise of being a Talmudic prodigy. But Nachman is troubled in his pious study; not only is he drawn to the sap of life as represented by his response to the natural world, but he notices that he is practically alone in the *beit midrash*. "The synagogue . . . was deserted. All the boys had gone off to school. And he? Here he still sat with his books and his aging father" (162).

The schools, which played the role of Pied Piper to the Jewish youth, were government-sponsored public schools established to "Russify" the Jewish populations, which, it was hoped, would counter the effects of Polish nationalism. (The Czarist empire had just stifled a Polish revolution in 1863; the following year several dozen Jewish institutes, called Rabiner schools, were opened.) Nachman resists the secular call of the Rabiner school, but in reaction to the emotional and intellectual repression dictated by the life of a Talmud scholar, he falls from belief and secretly acquires Russian and German in order read the texts of the West. "A new world was opened to him. The books of the great minds in which he now immersed himself behind the closed doors of his room worked a revolution in his entire being. The Talmud and its commentaries, the various compilations of Codes, the old study house with its books—all now perished inside him. In their place lived Spinoza, Kant, Darwin, Buckle, and Spenser. Their books held him spell-bound. He thought and lived nothing else" (191–92). Unfortunately for Nachman, the epistemological revolution brought about by the conversion to modernity leads only to melancholia and early death. Nothing for him can replace the loss of faith. But with others, for whom, like Nachman, "[t]he new books had dispatched the old" (193), modernity offered new, sometimes specifically Jewish, forms of faith: haskalah, positivism, Zionism, socialism. Lilienblum himself, after the pogroms of 1881, became a publicist for Jewish nationalism, agitating in both Hebrew and Russian for the colonization of Palestine. In 1899 he published another autobiographical piece, *The Way Back*, which "ends with a ressurection to life; Lilienblum has been quickened from the slumber of alienation and renunciation and given a vocation of leadership in the life of the people, which has itself been reinspirited with an idea of renewed possibility" (Mintz 32).

Not all the fallen Jewish youth went the way of Zionism, as was illustrated in Abraham Cahan's *Bleter Fun Mein Leber* [Pages from my Life], written in Yiddish and first published in 1926. Like Maimon and Lilienblum, Cahan was brought up with the male ideal of pious observance and a life devoted to Talmudic study, but his path in modernity led to socialism and America. His grandfather had been a rabbi, his father a *melamed* and unsucessful innkeeper. Growing up in Vilna, a historic center of Jewish learning, Cahan was aware that just beyond the horizon, the haskalah writings were part of a new thought-structure for the Jews. "My father feared and respected the world he shared with his orthodox, pious friends," he wrote. "But he was irresistibly drawn to the secular books printed in Hebrew and he dreamed of helping me to become an 'educated man' according to worldly standards" (33). During the course of Cahan's *chedar* studies, his father makes the "astounding proposal" that his son enroll in a Rabiner school. His friends eventually dissuade him from his decision because, as Cahan writes, "To send a youngster to the Rabiner school could only mean 'to turn him into a goy'" (47). In 1877, at the age of fourteen, Cahan took the modernizing initiative himself and entered the newly founded Vilna Teacher's Institute, a normal school for Jewish teachers in which Yiddish was prohibited. During the course of his struggle to understand natural phenomena—the same topics that instantly transformed Maimon into a *maskil*—he collapses the two stages of the revelation of secular knowledge and moment of apostasy into one. One Saturday as he stood admiring the window of an engraver's shop, "everything suddenly became clear to me."

I rushed home and opened [my geography textbook] at once. There it was—day and night and winter and summer—all clear! I was ecstatic. So profound and yet so simple! What other mysteries of the universe and of nature could I unravel with scientific explanations? And what did such explanations do to man's concept of God?

   The excitement within me grew. My brain was in a whirl. Mysteries were problems for which I had not yet discovered the simple answers. But that did not mean there were no simple answers. I was overwhelmed by new questions—about God and His miracles. The answers came easily. Clearly, there were no mysteries! There was no God! (88–89)

Shortly afterwards comes the conversion to socialism, and it too is described in the autobiography in terms of a textual revelation as he reads his first underground pamphlet. "I will never forget that moment. I felt it as a turning point in my life" (142). Soon Cahan thinks of himself no longer as a Russian Jew, a man bound to tradition and blocked by prejudice, but as a member of the worldwide community at its most humane and progressive.

As these life stories illustrate, the Jewish journey to the West not only entailed a loss of faith in traditional Judaism, it often led to a substitute secular ideology—Deism and haskalah in the eighteenth century, socialism and Zionism in the nineteenth century, Marxism and modernism in the twentieth. But in America the pattern is truncated. No autobiographies of American Jews dwell on the loss of religion. The internal community had no power to hold the young protagonists within the Jewish fold, and, for the second generation, the message to assimilate came most powerfully from the immigrant parents themselves. Jewish-American autobiography doesn't narrate the conversion to modernity—that battle has already been fought. Instead it concentrates upon the discovery of a secular vocation.

Kazin's spiritual flight from Brownsville described in *A Walker in the City* is facilitated by his constant reading of what he calls "alien books." In this regard Kazin uses books to transport himself out of the Jewish ghetto in a manner somewhat similar to Wright's cultural transfusions while enduring his life in the South. "I read as if books would fill my every gap, legitimize my strange quest for the American past, remedy my every flaw, let me in at last into the great world that was anything just out of Brownsville" (172). *Walker* too is a portrait of the writer as a young man, and for Kazin—as for Delmore Schwartz, Henry Roth, Irving Howe, and so many others—literature proffered the spiritual nourishment that Judaism, as a spent ideological force, was not expected to provide. "[I]t puzzled me that no one around me seemed to take God very seriously. We neither believed nor disbelieved. He was our oldest habit" (46).

Curiously enough—and this appropriation brings our discussion of conversion full circle—the young Kazin becomes far more excited by the New Testament than by the Old. But it is not Christianity that lights his fire; he is no religious convert waiting to fall into the arms of the Church. Rather, he is turned on by the beauty of the language, the Bible as Literature, and he compares his exaltation in the life of Jesus to his reading Sir Thomas Browne, Henry Vaughn, William Blake, Walt Whitman, and Ernest Hemingway. When he does move to the content, he embraces Jesus as a left-wing Jewish poet-intellectual.

Surely I had been waiting for him all my life—our own Yeshua, misunderstood by his own, like me, but the very embodiment of everything I had waited so long to hear from a Jew—a great contempt for the minute daily business of the world; a deep and joyful turning back into our own spirit. It was *he*, I thought, who would resolve for me at last the ambiguity and the long ache of being a Jew. . . .

I had recognized him immediately, and all over: . . . that furious old Jewish impatience with *Success*, with comfort, with eating, with the rich, with the whole shabby superficial fashionable world itself. . . .

Yeshua, our own Yeshua, the most natural of us all, the most direct, the most enchanted, and as he sprang up from the heart of poor Jews, all the dearer to me because he could now return to his own kind: *and the poor have the gospel preached to them*. (161–63)

Ethnicity
and Its
Discontents

One belongs to an ethnic group in part involuntarily,
in part by choice.

—*Michael Novak,* The Rise of the Unmeltable Ethnics

Throughout this study, I have been positing a structural equivalence between Black
and Jewish identity which I have subsumed under the rubric of ethnicity. This
structural equivalence can be seen in the utility of paradigms developed within one
ethnic discourse as applied to another. Many Jewish intellectuals would recognize
their dilemma in the concept of double consciousness developed by Du Bois to describe Black subjectivity. Similarly, the typology developed by Robert Stepto for
Black narratives applies equally well to Jewish ones, indeed to numerous ethnic
narratives. Elaborating on the way double consciousness has been expressed in the
lives and writings of African Americans, Stepto lays out a typology of ascent and
immersion that, as we shall see, admirably describes the experience of many Jews.
In brief, Stepto's approach suggests that any "outsider" group, whether ethnic or
racial, faces similar challenges within the American social context.

Before we define Stepto's paradigm more specifically and discuss its wider ap-
plicability, it is necessary to understand the ways "race" and "ethnicity" have been
used in the twentieth century. So far I have used the term "ethnic" to cover the consciousness of both Blacks and Jews. Although in the past thirty years "ethnicity"

has frequently been substituted for "race" in common parlance, since the 1980s this usage has come under some criticism. Alan Wald castigates what he calls the "ethnicity school" for erasing the distinction between European ethnic groups who came here as voluntary immigrants and minorities of color who were brought here as slaves (African Americans) or conquered by force (Native Americans, Hispanic Americans). "Most damaging for the ethnicity school has been the charge that, in theorizing cultural difference, it privileges the category of ethnicity, relegating 'race' to a mere feature of some ethnic groups" ("Theorizing Cultural Difference," 22). E. San Juan Jr. further claims that the use of ethnicity as a category helps to maintain the racist status quo in America by purposely eliding race. "'Ethnicity' is the official rubric to designate the phenomenological plurality of peoples ranked in a hierarchy for the different allocation and distribution of resources" (15). According to San Juan, racial categories foreground actual power relations in America in a way that ethnic categories do not. "[Ethnicity theory] ignores power imbalances since racism occurs in situations of domination and subordination" (67).

How then does one characterize the structural equivalence I am positing between Black and Jewish identity vis-à-vis the Enlightenment West? While the above criticisms hold true for a narrowly American perspective, the theoretical paradigms of "internal colonialism" or "racial minority" are compromised by the same diasporic considerations that subvert national boundaries. Blacks are not a displaced minority in South Africa, even though there were parallels between apartheid and segregation. In most of sub-Saharan Africa, the vast majority of Blacks have never been much exercised by White racism. (African writers and intellectuals who have been educated by or have resided in the West complain about it, but their experience doesn't reflect the reality of their compatriots.) To take another non-American example, French Jews are much more likely to feel like a persecuted minority in their national culture, where anti-Semitism and memories of the Holocaust are still powerful, than are the African Americans in France who have chosen voluntary exile. Then there is the example of the Sephardic Jews who were expelled from many Arab countries after the establishment of Israel, not because of any "racial" difference—they were physically indistinguishable from their neighbors—but because of a religious and cultural difference that became politicized by a European movement they had nothing to do with. Finally there are the *falashas,* the Black Jews of Ethiopia taken into Israel on humanitarian grounds during the famine of the 1970s, who certainly bear the burden of racism (as do the Sephardim) in Israel. If race and ethnicity are social constructs, as critics of the ethnicity school freely admit, they suffer the vagaries of any social construct in the real world. They are resistant to theoretical purity, and the wider the area of inquiry—global as opposed to national—the muddier the categories become.

For the purposes of this study, I will continue to use "ethnicity" to characterize the psychological similarity between Blacks and Jews. While acknowledging the hierarchical difference in status between the two minorities in America, I have also emphasized throughout this study the common ground Enlightenment attitudes have created. In this regard, American ideologies and practice are but a local manifestation of Western attitudes. Consequently, although it is undoubtedly more accurate to maintain the distinction between racial and ethnic consciousness when comparing Blacks and Jews in America, I have found it most useful to subsume the two under the rubric of "ethnicity" in the context of the Enlightenment West.

With this as prologue, let us take a little tour of the term's past usage. "Ethnicity" the noun is of recent coinage, but the adjective "ethnic" comes freighted with a revealing double heritage. "Ethnic" began its known life as a Greek word, *ethnikos* "nation." From there it entered Late Latin as *ethnicus* and made its way into Middle English in the variant "heathen." "Ethnic" itself first appeared in English in the fifteenth and sixteenth centuries with the meaning "Pertaining to nations not Christian or Jewish," therefore "Gentile, heathen, pagan." This insider/outsider connotation remained even when the first use of "ethnic" grew obsolete and the word was adapted by the race-conscious nineteenth century to the more modern usage that has entered the language. "Ethnic" also possessed a descriptive meaning—one that hailed back to the neutral Greek term. In scientific discourse—in such terms as "ethnology" and "ethnogeny"—the suffix "ethno-" could be used simply as a combining form meaning "race" or "people." Everyone belonged to a race, so the insider/outsider dichotomy was not necessarily present in all uses of the term. However, ethnology first developed as a study of so-called primitive cultures, and the hierarchical valence present in the now obsolete religious meaning (i.e., not one of the saved) reasserted itself in the prefixes of "ethnobotany" and "ethnomusicology." In 1886 a gentleman named Lightfoot brought out the prejudicial nature of the term most succinctly when he wrote, "Heresies are at best ethnic, truth is essentially catholic"—the latter, of course, being Lightfoot's synonym for "universal" ("Ethnic," in *Oxford English Dictionary*).

In the liberal scientific discourse of the twentieth century, however, the term "ethnic group" came to be preferred over "race" as a way of dealing with human typologies. As early as 1936, zoologist Julian Huxley and ethnologist A. C. Haddon wrote:

The reader is now in a position to appreciate the fundamental difference between the term "race"—for which we prefer to substitute the term "ethnic group"—as misapplied to man. With certain rare and special exceptions . . . the races of animals do not wander from their normal habitats. . . . Stability in the habits of animals is an important and basic factor in the formation of races, or "sub-species," as zoologists usually call them. (*We Europeans*, 132)

People, by contrast, were far too mobile to maintain any sort of "racial" purity—assuming that such an Edenic condition ever existed. "Any systematic descriptive account of existing peoples must therefore include many mixed and intermediate groups of which the ethnic position and affinities are a matter of inference" (133). With this caveat, Huxley and Haddon nonetheless attempt a classification of European ethnic groups based on "hair in the first rank" combined with skin color and form of the nose. Acknowledging the liberal scientific lead of William Ripley in his *Races of Europe* (1900), the two Englishmen preface their discussion of the Jews with an astonishingly on-target description.

The Jews can rank neither as nation nor even as ethnic unit, but rather as a socio-religious group. . . . Like many other groups its members are held together partly by external pressure of various kinds, partly by a long historic memory, partly by a sense of common suffering, partly by a religion. These factors, acting through long ages, have produced a common consciousness which is relaxed when the pressure is relaxed and intensified with the reverse process. (*We Europeans*, 147)

In the United States, however, "ethnic" retained is original connotation of Otherness, and "ethnic group" came to be defined by sociologists as a minority group differentiated from the majority by national origin or cultural background. W. Lloyd Warner and Leo Srole's groundbreaking *Social Systems of American Ethnic Groups* (1945) reported on a study of "the Irish, French Canadians, Jews, Italians, Armenians, Greeks, Poles and Russians" in "a small industrial community in New England" named—just so no one should forget the dominant cultural matrix—Yankee City (1).

Many scholars and "lay people" now refer to African Americans as an ethnic group, but they were excluded from the study because, in the American mid-century, the term applied to White subdivisions of humanity as opposed to racial subdivisions. As Warner and Srole wrote, "The cultural traits of the ethnic group, which have become symbols of inferior status, can be and are changed in time; but the physical traits which have become symbols of inferior status are permanent" (285).

Once the notion of "White" Otherness had established itself as a sociological convention, it was not long before the noun "ethnicity" appeared on the scene. The *Oxford English Dictionary* marks the first usage in a 1953 *American Scholar* article by the sociologist David Riesman. Shortly after its coinage, however, the term "ethnicity"—and the idea it represented—underwent another significant change: ethnicity now referred to the distinctive characteristics of all minority groups in America regardless of race. Milton Gordon's definition serves as an example drawn from sociology.

When I use the term "ethnic group," I shall mean by it any group which is defined or set off by race, religion, or national origin, or some combination of these categories. I do not mean to imply that these three concepts mean the same thing. They do not. Race, technically, refers to differential concentrations of gene frequencies responsible for traits which, so far as we know, are confined to physical manifestations such as skin color or hair form; it has no intrinsic connection with cultural patterns and institutions. Religion and national origins, while both cultural phenomena, are distinctly different institutions which do not necessarily vary concomitantly. However, all these categories have a common social-psychological referent, in that all of them service to create, through historical circumstances, a sense of peoplehood. (27–28)

"Ethnicity" came to be associated primarily with American minorities of color. A 1976 anthology compiled by Cortés et al. was titled *Three Perspectives on Ethnicity in America: Blacks, Chicanos, and Native Americans.*

This change in meaning reflected a significant shift in the way mainstream and minority cultures related to one another. The cultural and political upheavals of the 1960s resulted in a challenge to melting pot ideology that modified the self-assessment of American minority groups even after the time period's more extreme manifestations (the Black Panthers, the Jewish Defense League) lost credibility with the mainstream.

Black Americans pioneered the way. The Black Power movement, drawing on the political victories and moral high ground captured by the civil rights struggle, claimed a leadership in American left-wing ideology that no minority group had ever before possessed. Mainstream American culture as represented by what was then known as "the Establishment" was under attack, and African Americans had the longest and best organized tradition of criticism. "The Movement is really a search for the moral equivalent of Blackness," a white SNCC (Student Non-Violent Coordinating Committee) worker was quoted as saying in a 1966 study (quoted in Newfield, 29). Black styles of self-naming, revolutionary action, cultural nationalism, and ideological criticism were adopted by other minority groups alienated from the mainstream. When White college students, forced into an oppositional stance by the threat of being drafted into the unpopular Vietnam War, joined the chorus of criticism and challenge, the crossover success of Black ideology left an unparalleled stamp on American thinking. As Morris Dickstein wrote in his book on the sixties, "the struggle for black rights can be said to have ignited the first phase of the politics of confrontation. Later, as the integration ideal gave way to nationalism, the group militance of the blacks spread to students, women, and homosexuals, as well as to other ethnic groups including the Jews" (156).

During the political tumult of the 1960s, ethnicity was transformed from the recalcitrant dross of the melting pot to a high point of integrity in the cesspool of American civilization. It became a matter of honor for the most oppressed of American minorities to cast off the names they had previously borne and choose for themselves ones that reflected their rightful status in the inchoate multiculturalism of the time. Indians called themselves Native Americans; Mexican-Americans adopted the term "Chicano"; Negroes became Blacks and Afro-Americans.[1] As Talcott Parsons noted in his liberal way, this double change in nomenclature achieved two contradictory aims: with Afro-American "symmetry is established between the definition of blacks as an ethnic group and other white Americans," while Black "very explicitly accentuates the racial focus of the identity . . . as somewhat distinguishable from the greater relative importance of the cultural component in the case of the principal white ethnic groups" (72).[2]

Shortly after the rise and success of Black Power, White groups who felt threatened by expanding Black opportunity and its imposition (as they perceived it) under the patronage of the federal government also underwent a resurgence of ethnic identification. The most vocal of these White ethnics—Polish Americans, Italian Americans, Irish Americans (many of whom voted for George Wallace in his openly racist Presidential campaign of 1972)—were no friends to the version of American ethnicity preached by the minorities of color. "The new black ethnicity is reformist in thrust," Harvard sociologist Martin Kilson wrote in a 1975 anthology, "while the new white ethnicity is conservative" (262). Although his statement ignored the prominent revolutionary rhetoric of the Black Power movement (Amiri Baraka would have laughed at the idea of reforming the Amerikan system), he was reasonably accurate in his characterization of the resurgent White ethnics. Michael Novak gave this neo-ethnic conservatism its most intellectual and articulate formulation in his 1972 book, *The Rise of the Unmeltable Ethnics*, in which he revived Kallen's arguments of 1915. "When a person thinks, more than one generation's passions and images think in him. Below the threshold of the rational or the fully conscious, our instincts and sensibilities lead backwards to the predilections of our forebears" (Novak 32). Like the Romantics and essentialists before him, Novak finds the legacy of the Enlightenment unnourishing. "The rise in ethnic consciousness today is also due to disillusionment with the universalist, too thinly rational culture of professional elites" (32).

The Jewish response to this rise was complex and contradictory. Resurgence in the other communities, though articulated by their intellectuals, was fueled by the fear and anger endemic to the blue-collar workforce and lower classes. By the 1970s, 80 percent of American Jews had risen to the middle class; many of them now belonged to the professional and liberal elites deplored by conservatives and their ethnic supporters. Furthermore, liberalism had for generations constituted the American Jews' principal political response to the opportunity to integrate into the larger society. The decline of anti-Semitism and the lowering of informal social barriers in the postwar era testified to the acceptance and, from the Jewish standpoint, success of the liberal outlook. With the social and political upheavals of the 1960s, however, radical versions of ethnicity proposed by activists of color on the Left and the conservative formulations of blue-collar ethnics (the White Excluded) on the Right challenged the Enlightenment legacy. Working- and lower-middle-class Jews who had failed to make the move out of the inner city often allowed themselves to be caught up by the reactionary temper of the newly bellicose "White" ethnics. Many assimilated Jews who had lost all sense of ethnic identification also swung into the conservative camp, prominently represented by such figures as Nixon's Secretary of State, Henry Kissinger, and Reagan ideologue Irving Kristol. When *Commentary* editor Norman Podhoretz joined a mid-sixties intellectual trend later labeled "neo-conservative," he found as allies in his battles with the New Left such prominent Jewish intellectuals as S. M. Lipset, Nathan Glazer, and Daniel Bell.

Liberal *alrightniks*, still the majority, found themselves faced with a novel situation, summed up from a Jewish perspective in a 1983 article in the *Encyclopedia Judaica*.

Used to regarding themselves as belonging to the "have-nots," Jews were surprised and dismayed to find that groups lower down the economic ladder, whose battle also they thought they had been fighting, looked upon them as "haves" whose entrenched position was standing in the way of their own legitimate aspirations.

This turn in inter-group relation took place against a background of urban decay in areas in which important Jewish communities had lived. In addition to crime and violence in the streets, Jews found themselves plagued by the wider problems of school integration, quotas, low-income housing, ethnic rights, and inter-group relations, as well as by anti-Semitism. This situation faced the Jews with contradictions which made them highly uncomfortable. Their traditional liberalism had made them accustomed to the posture of strong supporters of the underdog; they were now suddenly forced to defend their own status, their neighborhood, their safety and the adequate education of their children, finding themselves all too often, and much to their dismay, on the same side as segregationists and reactionaries. Having fought for a society from which discrimination would be eliminated, they found that society proposed to discriminate in favor of the groups lower down the ladder; now the priority given to the black and Puerto Rican populations along with other minority groups, forced them to consider themselves on occasions as a minority, and surprisingly, a neglected one. There were strong feelings of anger, of being at a disadvantage, of frustration, of a new insecurity. (Tempkin 605)

Although Jews were (once again) disproportionately overrepresented in the ranks of the New Left, most Jews who maintained institutional or religious affiliations kept their distance and chose not to emulate the militant ethnicity of radical Black, Hispanic, and Native American activists. Like their predecessors, third- and fourth-generation Jews did not press for political recognition as an ethnic group, but many experienced a renewal of identification expressed in activities and values derived from tradition and reshaped by American modernity: widespread observance of Passover, Chanukah, and the high holidays; religiously derived rites of passage (*bar* and *bat mitzvahs*, marriages, funerals); visits to Israel; a near-consensual commitment to Jewish and Israeli survival. Manifestations of ethnic revival in elite activities were also striking: the *havurah* movement of small, self-motivated communities of worship; Jewish Political Action Committees; advances in Jewish learning and intellectual life, including the establishment of Judaic studies in the university curriculum; even the numerically insignificant but culturally unexpected converts to Orthodoxy (the *baalei teshuva*) from the ranks of assimilated Jews.

The remarkable thing about the renewal of Jewish identification was that it carried little political valence. By contrast, Black pride had risen from the crucible of racial segregation that had been legal within the living memories of those who held their fists in the air. They smoldered with righteous anger. Analogous manifestations of ethnic assertion—cultural nationalism, the creation of Kwanzaa, interest in and identification with the politics of Africa, Malcolm X and the rise of the Black Muslims—streaked across the sky like lightning, briefly illuminating scenes of utopia and apocalypse. Black nationalism caught fire in a counterculture that never asked the question, "Is it good for the Jews?" Those Jews who participated in the New Left—Abbie Hoffman, Jerry Rubin, Todd Gitlin—checked their claims to Jewish ethnicity at the door. Class analysis and Third World perspectives were criteria of authenticity, and by the time New Left thought had crystallized around the image of Israel as a Western outpost of imperialism and racism—a 1975 U.N. resolution condemned Zionism as the latter—the damage was irreversible. An anti-Israeli stance allowed the expression of anti-Jewish sentiment; the weed had popped up again in spite of official sanction. (Racism, however, had never gone away—was barely coming to public consciousness—and facile condemnations of African dictators were later to serve an analogous function in its acceptable expression.)

Major public confrontations between Blacks and Jews occurred: the battle over the Ocean Hill-Brownsville school district (1968), the protest of the Forest Hills Jews over the construction of low-income housing in their neighborhood (1972), the Supreme Court *Bakke vs. University of California* decision (1978), Black presidential hopeful Jesse Jackson's "Hymietown" remark (1988), the Crown Heights killings (1991), the transformation of Black nationalism with the rise of Louis Farrakhan as a charismatic leader. Amiri Baraka read and published poems with a violent anti-Semitism unapologetically displayed (1961–67); Bernard Malamud wrote *The Tenants* (1971), which ends with an anguished Black writer being stabbed in the head by an equally anguished Jewish writer getting his balls cut off.

How then can we apply the term "ethnicity" to cover two entities—no matter how ideologically constructed—at such loggerheads? The term, as we have seen, has become inherently ambiguous. It is both universal and parochial, inclusive and exclusive of multiracial definition, in opposition to and dependent upon conventional thinking, externally imposed and internally accepted. The reality is more complex than the term that describes it, for ethnicity has not only its prelapsarian stage but—for a significant minority—a postmodernist one as well.

The "ethnic" similarities between Blacks and Jews can be seen in relation to Stepto's paradigm of ascent and immersion described below. Although Stepto developed his paradigm to describe the experience of African Americans, it applies equally well to Jews who did not share the underlying "racial" assumptions of the texts Stepto analyzes. In fact, it is both useful and instructive to note that the earliest "Black" autobiographies written in English did not themselves share those assumptions. Little in the first two of these autobiographies conclusively identifies the protagonists as Black. If this information were not provided on the title page, the reader would not otherwise know. The reason for this is not hard to see. Nothing reaches publication and dissemination without an ideological and commercial foundation. The abolition movement of the third quarter of the eighteenth century provided the context and opportunity for the appearance of the first slave narratives. However, neither the *Narrative of the Uncommon Suffering and Surprising Deliverance of Briton Hammon* (1760) nor the *Narrative of the Lord's Wonderful Dealings with John Marrant, a Black* (1785) were written as slave narratives. If they had been, the protagonist's ethnicity would have been central to the conventions of the genre. The stories of Hammon and Marrant were published as captivity narratives, a popular eighteenth-century form detailing the adventures of Western protagonists among the heathen tribes of the New World. Since the central character of the captivity narrative was by definition *not ethnic* (in the early sense of the term discussed above), his Blackness was of peripheral interest. John Sekora writes of Hammon's narrative that the text itself contains no reference to his Blackness (100), and Henry Louis Gates Jr. acknowledges that Marrant "narrated his story with almost no references to black people outside of his family" (142). Slave narrative by its very nature required an examination of the role of the Black in the world as a person of color, but the point of the captivity narrative was to illustrate how superior everything in the West—including slavery—was to Indian savagery. As Sekora writes of the genre, "From its beginnings the captivity had provided a theologically as well as physically useful version of manifest destiny" (95).

Hammon's narrative not only fulfilled the ideological imperative of the captivity tale in its fast-moving thirteen pages; it reinforced the comforting notion that every man has his place on the Great Chain of Being and should be grateful for it. Life for Hammon outside of service to his master is a purgatory of Indian captivity, involuntary servitude and arbitrary imprisonment in Havana, and a precarious living in English capitalism. By the time his master reenters Hammon's life on a boat bound for New England, the lost servant is more than ready to resume his position. The narrative is an autobiographical equivalent of one of the earliest poems in English published by a Black, Jupiter Hammon's "Verses from the Kind Master to the Dutiful Servant" (1778). No mention is made of an amanuensis, but Hammon's tale is as plain of ornament as an Amish piece of furniture. "As my Capacities and Condition of Life are very low," he tells the reader, "it cannot be expected that I should make those Remarks on the Sufferings I have met with, or the kind Providence of GOD for my Preservation, as one in a higher Station" (3). Thus Hammon (or his ghostwriter) gives up any attempt to interpret his life. Hammon's lot is defined not by his ethnicity but by his condition: he is a hewer of wood and a drawer of water. Neither he nor anyone else is conscious of his color because providence dictates his station in life, and others, including Whites, also occupy low positions. When he escapes from Cuba on a British man-o'-war, the captain refuses the Spanish demand for his return because he said "he could not answer it, to deliver up an *Englishman* under *English* Colours" (11).

The Marrant pamphlet is a more sophisticated production. Marrant's amanuensis, the Reverend W. Aldridge, hews to the ideological imperative of the captivity narrative when he writes that Marrant "arrives among the Cherokees, where gross ignorance wore its rudest forms, and savage despotism exercised its most terrifying empire" (Marrant, *Narrative*, iv), but Marrant's view of his captors is slightly more charitable. "When they recollect, that the white people drove them from the American shores, the [Indian] nations have often united, and murdered all the white people in the back settlements which they could lay hold of, man, woman, and child" (29–30). More importantly, Marrant's story is primarily cast as a conversion narrative, falling into its tripartite structure of life-in-darkness→conversion →life-as-one-saved. Marrant describes his early childhood as a free Black in the South who becomes a master of the violin and the French horn. The only slavery he mentions in the text is his self-description at thirteen as one "devoted to pleasure and drinking iniquity like water; a slave to every vice suited to my nature and to my years" (9). The conversion scene is dramatically rendered and, since Marrant was not destined to become an author, occurred not as a result of reading but from the charismatic preaching of the Reverend George Whitefield. No Christian conversion can be without intertextual content, however, and it is appropriate, given the context of this study, that the injunction that throws Marrant speechless and senseless upon the ground with the force of revelation is "Prepare to meet thy GOD, O Israel" (11). Marrant's new life, however, puts him at odds with his society and family. Everyone declares him crazy, and he undergoes such persecution that he decides to go off into the wilderness. Eventually he meets with an Indian hunter who takes care of him and teaches him his language. When they visit the Cherokees, Marrant is seized and sentenced to death. God effects a miraculous deliverance once Marrant begins to pray in Indian language. Marrant soon converts the Cherokee king and becomes a trusted adviser. Eventually, however, Marrant feels the need to move on and visits the Creek, Catawar, and Housaw Indians (29–30). Homesick, Marrant finally returns to civilization, where he is not even recognized by his own family until he reveals himself. Having passed the test as one of the saved, Marrant can now rejoin society without further impediment.

Hammon's narrative is structured around the folktale morphology of separation→testing→reintegration. Before his departure from his master, he has no past, no family, no previous life. After reuniting with his master, who joyfully tells him that "[he] was like one arose from the Dead," there is only the pamphlet itself. Hammon's *Narrative* displays a minimally Christian consciousness and an uncritical acceptance of the British status quo—elements it shares with Marrant's. *Narrative of the Lord's Wonderful Dealings* is much richer in its Christian allusion, its subordination of the folktale morphology to the requirements of the conversion narrative, and its elaboration of the captivity tale. Lacking in both are all the elements of the slave narrative that were to set the conventions of African-American autobiography: no description of life in racial bondage, no struggle for literacy, and, most importantly, no obvious color consciousness.

Yet such an internalized consciousness could be read in Marrant's *envoi*. Positing Christianity as the universal ideology that could transform the heathen nations, Marrant prays for the success of his anticipated missionary activities in Nova Scotia in a language both revelatory and typological: "That strangers may hear of and run to Christ; that Indian tribes may stretch out their hands to God; that the black nations may be made white in the blood of the Lamb; that vast multitudes of hard tongues, and of a strange speech, may learn the language of Canaan, and sing the song of Moses, and of the Lamb" (37–38). If Black nations were to be made white, the blood of the Lamb was just the first ablution in a series of ideological conversions whose guiding spirit was not so much Christ as John Locke, Horatio Alger, and Booker T. Washington.

Stepto, in his seminal study of African-American narrative, *From Behind the Veil*, clearly understands the impetus behind such attempts to enter the American mainstream. While he concentrates on writers who conceived of their situation in racial terms, his powerful and suggestive theory casts light on the "ethnic" similarity between Blacks and Jews. Stepto proposes two potentially interlocking paradigmatic myths as typologies for certain classics of Black American prose: the myth of ascent and the myth of immersion. In the archetypal ascent narrative, an "enslaved" figure in an oppressive environment makes a journey through the acquisition of (Western) literacy to "the least oppressive structure afforded by the world of the narrative," a level of freedom in which "he or she has gained sufficient literacy to assume the mantle of an articulate survivor." Stepto quickly points out that the survivor, in order to inhabit this new space of greater freedom, has to be willing to forsake "familial or communal postures" and thus runs the risk of ending up alone or alienated. This triggers the rise of the immersion narrative, "an expression of a ritualized journey" back to the ghetto, the South, the forsaken community, the wisdom of the elders. The immersion narrative ends with the questing figure "in or near the narrative's most oppressive social structure but free in the sense that he [or she] has gained or regained sufficient tribal literacy to assume the mantle of an articulate kinsman." Stepto then explains that the articulate kinsman has had to forsake the individual mobility of the denizen of the mainstream for "a posture of relative stasis in the most oppressive environment, a loss that is only occasionally assuaged by the newfound balms of group identity" (167).

These two paradigmatic narratives offer fine structures for the organization of ethnic autobiography. Whereas the novel can often have more protagonists than the narrative of the questing figure, autobiographies, almost by definition, do not. The classics of African-American autobiography—*The Life of Frederick Douglass, Up From Slavery, Black Boy, The Autobiography of Malcolm X*—yield easily to the analysis of ascent and immersion, as do a number of lesser known Jewish texts.

Before embarking upon this inquiry, I would like to make an additional distinction in Stepto's masterly description. There are several versions of ascent, several styles of immersion. There is ascent and acceptance of Enlightenment norms and there is ascent and alienation not only from "enslaved" community but from the mainstream as well. Both *Black Boy* and *Up from Slavery* are ascent narratives, and yet what a world of sensibility lies between them! Immersion too has its political, cultural, and religious styles. The questing figure may only adopt one in his or her return, giving that narrative an entirely different tonality than other tales of immersion.

Up from Slavery's acceptance of the Protestant ethic as the path of virtue leading to its inevitable reward is no less fervid than Mary Antin's celebration of her Americanization in *The Promised Land*. Antin wrote her autobiography as a success of American immigration, the story of a Russian Jewish girl whose intelligence and literary gifts blossomed under the liberal showers of democracy. "It required no fife and drum corps, no Fourth of July procession, to set me tingling with emotion," she writes (196). Simply the blessings of being an American were enough. There is a certain price that other members of her family—those not so fortunate or gifted—have to pay for coming to the New World. Her older sister must work to help support the family and, since she therefore never receives an education, is condemned to a limited life. Her father, a man who fell away from his training as a rabbi, never proved himself a successful businessman, leading a precarious economic existence both in Russia and America. In his Promised Land he has known only struggle and disappointment. "[T]he American flag," his daughter wrote in a classical reference, "could not protect him against the pursuing Nemesis of his limitations" (202). Her mother, who had come from a background of some comfort and privilege, was borne down by ill health and the drudgery of life in the Boston slums, an environment Antin describes as "a rubbish heap of damaged humanity" (286–87). Like a Horatio Alger heroine, Antin finds her way to recognition and acceptance—with a generous dollop of transcendentalism—through grit, sensitivity, and talent. One of the chapters is entitled "A Kingdom in the Slums" because Antin's real home was the library, Latin High School, and the wider world of Boston society to which she had access because of her talent for friendship. "It would have been amazing if I had stuck in the mire of the slum," she writes. "By every law of my nature I was bound to soar above it, to attain the fairer places that wait for every emancipated immigrant" (356). Pity the rest of her family did not reach such a blessed state.

Booker T. Washington too believes fervently in the gospel of individual merit and its righteous reward. He makes the Weberian link between hard work and worldly profit that Antin is too literary and transcendental to have in her purview. Washington's self-portrait as the ex-slave who built himself an empire of social good and influence in the heart of the South is iconic in African-American literature. It is a thoroughly American story, hewn directly from the rock of Enlightenment liberalism. "My experience is that there is something in human nature which always makes an individual recognize and reward merit, no matter under what colour of skin merit is found" (111).

Washington's story is one of ascent with a vengeance. Starting out with a living memory of conditions under slavery, Washington passes his adolescence in the grinding industrial poverty of a West Virginia mining town and only succeeds in escaping the mire of damaged lives by virtue of the vision he is vouchsafed as a child. "The picture of several dozen boys and girls in a schoolroom engaged in study made a deep impression upon me, and I had the feeling that to get into a schoolhouse and study in this way would be about the same as getting into paradise" (32). (This is as close to religious imagery as Washington gets. We've gone well beyond Christian conversion as the portal to Western civilization.) The stations upon the Way of Ascent are narrated and referred back to: the heroic struggle for education, the nights under the sidewalk in Richmond, the test of the broom, the sound education of Hampton Institute, and the miraculous creation of a Black college built upon its principles—"Tuskegee, the myth of uplift," as Stepto calls it (35). All the rewards that flow to the astonished and modest protagonist are the result of his ceaseless work for the well-being of others. His success as a public speaker, his growing national reputation, his honorary Harvard degree, President McKinley's visit to Tuskegee—all these tributes to Washington's success and character give him the platform from which to preach what Du Bois termed "a gospel of Work and Money" (*The Souls of Black Folk*, 246). He proves to be an accomplished orator and, in his wildly successful Atlanta Exposition speech of 1895, he voices a free-market theory of race relations that gives comfort to Whites both North and South. The following passage is a remarkable balancing act of submission and certainty that the race shall ultimately triumph.

The wisest among my race understand that the agitation of questions of social equality is extremist folly, and that progress in the enjoyment of all the privileges that will come to us must be the result of severe and constant struggle rather than of artificial forcing. It is important and right that all the privileges of the law be ours, but it is vastly more important that we be prepared for the exercises of these privileges. The opportunity to earn a dollar in a factory just now is worth infinitely more than the opportunity to spend a dollar in an opera-house. (*Up from Slavery*, 149)

Antin has no need to develop a political philosophy of being Other. Anti-Semitism had not yet developed into a shaping force on the American landscape. Her oppression as a Jew—the segregation, the systematic injustice, the pogroms, the demonization by the Russian Orthodox Church (again the blood libel)—all that was part of the Old World, life within the Pale. America will accept her as an emancipated immigrant. "Steadily as I worked to win America, America advanced to lie at my feet" (358). Antin's Jewish literary mentor, Emma Lazarus, had given poetic voice to such melting pot idealism in the final lines of the famous poem at the Statue of Liberty's base:

> *Give me your tired, your poor,*
> *Your huddled masses yearning to breathe free,*
> *The wretched refuse of your teeming shore,*
> *Send these, the homeless, tempest-tossed to me:*
> *I lift my lamp beside the golden door.*

But it was Booker T. Washington who pronounced the work ethic that was the presumed ticket of entry into America. "Success is to be measured not so much by the position that one has reached in life as by the obstacles which he has overcome while trying to succeed" (50).

Up from Slavery solidified Washington's reputation as *the* Negro Leader, and it has gone through numerous reeditions. *The Promised Land* did extremely well upon publication, selling 85,000 copies, but then fell into obscurity until the feminist revival. (It was republished in 1980 as part of a series of autobiographies of American women.) Both texts were influential as liberal briefs for the immigrant and the African American; both had their detractors. Having no explicit political philosophy outside of open immigration, Antin's book could only be criticized on ethnic grounds, and such criticism would have to come from a Jew who not only felt himself to be intensely Jewish, but also felt compelled to comment on a secular book. Ludwig Lewisohn, well into his period of return, fulfilled those requirements in a mid-century survey of Jewish-American literature in which he criticized *The*

Promised Land as facile and superficial. With weary pessimism, Lewisohn wrote that the motifs of Antin's book—its ignorance of and unconcern for "all that was glorious and sacred in [the] ancestral tradition"—led to "morbid lengths of self-degradation" by second-generation Amercan Jews "raging against their residual Jewishness" ("A Panorama," 4).

The cry of protest against Washington's philosophy also had ethnic origins, but as the terms of debate were explicitly political, so was the tenor of the response. Du Bois weighed in quickly with his famous chapter on Washington in *The Souls of Black Folk* (1903). "The attitude of an imprisoned group may take three main forms," he wrote: "a feeling of revolt and revenge; an attempt to adjust all thought and action to the will of the greater group; or, finally a determined effort at self-realization and self-development despite environing opinion" (244). Washington clearly voiced the second tendency. Men of the Talented Tenth, representing the third course of action, had to demand for their people the right to vote, civic equality, and the education of their youth according to ability. Then there were the spiritual descendants of Toussaint L'Overture, Gabriel Prosser, Denmark Vesey, and Nat Turner, who would criticize Washington from a racial standpoint, those who "hate the white South blindly and distrust the white race generally, and so far as they agree on definite action, think that the Negro's only hope lies in emigration beyond the borders of the United States" (Du Bois, *Souls of Black Folk*, 247).

Washington does not distrust the White race; Antin is proud to count her friends among the Boston elite. Both believe in the gospel of the toothbrush, the myth of uplift, the promise of America. Like other autobiographers of ascent and acceptance, their lives are testaments to the reality of opportunity, the triumph of hard work and individual merit, the Enlightenment belief in the perfectibility of the human condition. But Du Bois pointed out other tendencies, other responses to what even Washington admitted as "the ostracism and sometimes oppression of my race" (190). For many who had risen from the Black Belt, the *shtetl*, the ghetto, the slum, success in America led not to a harmonizing of its contradictions but to a heightened criticism, a decisive alienation.

Ludwig Lewisohn was the first Jewish-American writer to give voice to this alienation in autobiographical form. "No one has spoken out in America," he wrote in his prologue, about the Babbitry and anti-Semitism of American culture, but *Up Stream* would do its part (10). Born into a culturally assimilated Berlin Jewish family, as a child Lewisohn was brought to America by his parents and raised mostly in Charleston, South Carolina. His father, an unsuccessful small businessman, rejected Jewish traditions and declared himself a secularist and democrat. Though his mother was the educated daughter of a rabbi, she followed her husband's apostasy and encouraged her only son to become a Methodist in order to ease his entry into the American scene. Lewisohn accepted the ideology of assimilation and wrote that "at the age of fifteen, I was an American, a Southerner and a Christian" (77).

In this regard, Lewisohn's early experience parallels that of W. E. B. Du Bois, who recounted his story of ascent and alienation in the 1940 volume *Dusk of Dawn*. Growing up in the small Northern community of Great Barrington, Massachusetts, Du Bois escaped the harsher aspects of racism at the beginning of Reconstruction, but he could never imagine—as Lewisohn did—that his ethnic origins would be ignored by the larger American society. Nonetheless, Du Bois wrote, "in general thought and conduct I became quite thoroughly New England" (18–19).

Both Lewisohn and Du Bois trained to become college professors, Lewisohn at Columbia, Du Bois at Fisk, Harvard, and Berlin. Having grown up with caste consciousness, Du Bois had no illusions about making his way in a White academic establishment. By the time he attended Harvard as an undergraduate, he neither sought out nor desired the company of his White classmates. In other regards, however, Du Bois describes himself as a product of his nineteenth-century education. "I was blithely European and imperialist in outlook; democratic as democracy was conceived in America" (32). In fact, Du Bois acknowledged, "one consideration alone saved me from complete conformity with the thoughts and confusions of then current social trends; and that was the problems of racial and cultural contacts" (26–27). The life goal he conceived for himself during this period, though racially oriented, was methodologically appropriated from the ideology of the Enlightenment. "I was determined to make a scientific conquest of my environment, which would render the emancipation of the Negro race easier and quicker" (32).

Lewisohn's ambitions were more literary, and his illusions as to how far his fellow Americans would let him assimilate more profound. After four years of study at the College of Charleston, he graduated with honors at the age of nineteen with an M.A. in English literature. (His master's thesis, serialized in the *Sewanee Review*, was a study of Matthew Arnold.) At Columbia's doctoral program in English literature, the implacable anti-Semitism of Anglo-American academia hit him like a thunderbolt. Troubled by his inability to obtain financial support from the English Department for his studies, he sent an "impassioned" letter to his advisor, who replied in writing, "It is very sensible of you to look so carefully into your plans at this juncture, because I do not at all believe in the wisdom of your scheme. A recent experience has shown me how terribly hard it is for a man of Jewish birth to get a good position" (122). Walking about the New York streets afterward in a daze, the young scholar entered a bakery to buy something to eat, "and, catching sight of myself in a mirror, noted with dull objectivity my dark hair, my melancholy eyes, my unmistakably Semitic nose. . . . An outcast. . . . A sentence arose in my mind which I have remembered and used ever since. So long as there is discrimination, there is exile. And for the first time in my life my heart turned with grief and remorse to the thought of my brethren in exile all over the world . . . " (123). And so the turn toward ethnicity was taken, in Lewisohn's case, as an initial response to American discrimination. He was not so far removed in this—although it comes at a later point in his life—from the source of Du Bois's racial consciousness.

Living with my mother's people I absorbed their culture patterns and these were not African so much as Dutch and New England. The speech was an idiomatic New England tongue with no African dialect; the family customs were New England, and the sex mores. My African racial feeling was then purely a matter of my own later learning and reaction; my recoil from the assumptions of the whites; my experience in the South at Fisk. But it was none the less real and a large determinant of my life and character. I felt myself African by "race" and by that token was African and an integral member of the group of dark Americans who were called Negroes. (115)

Du Bois alludes to his experience with cultured Blacks in the South, which gave him a point of entry into an ethnic identification that was based upon an assumption of equality with other races—the ideology of the 1899 essay "On the Conservation of the Races," which I briefly examined in chapter 4. In that regard, Du Bois had experienced something of a "return," but it was immersion within the context of a caste status that could not be escaped, and although it left its residue upon his subsequent writings—most notably *The Souls of Black Folk*—his conscious intellectual framework remained conditioned by the universalist thinking of the Enlightenment. This caused him to work unremittingly for the NAACP for twenty-four years and later to move toward Marxism.

Lewisohn, by contrast, had not yet effected any sort of return by the time he wrote *Up Stream*. That would only come later in the course of his European exile in the 1920s. Although English literature was maintained as an Anglo-American preserve, Lewisohn's knowledge of German and German literature eventually landed him a berth in the German Department of Ohio State University. There he remained until America's entrance into World War I in 1917. Then, as H. L. Mencken observed in his favorable review of *Up Stream*, "It was now the German, not the Jew, who went upon the chopping block" (436). As a proponent of German culture, Lewisohn struggled against the prevailing chauvinism that, he believed, would negate German contributions to literature, philosophy, and the arts. By the time he was asked to leave his teaching position, he had completely converted to the "bohemian" stance taken by the writers he names in his epilogue: Edgar Lee Masters, Theodore Drieser, and Sinclair Lewis. "And I, in my own small and dusty way, was the eternal outcast, rebel, the other—thinking one—guilty before the herd, guiltless in the dwelling places of the permanent, breaker of taboos, creator of new values, doomed to defeat on this day in this little grimy corner of the universe, invincible and inextinguishable as a type. Shall I ever conquer the real estate broker?" (215). Convinced that American culture was a materialist wasteland, Lewisohn turned away from the very ideology so passionately propounded by the likes of Mary Antin and Emma Lazarus. "The doctrine of assimilation, if driven home by public pressure and official mandate, will create a race of unconscious and spiritual helots" (240). By the end of his autobiography, Lewisohn finds himself in sympathy with only a handful of equally "realistic" writers and intellectuals. His ethnicity affords him as yet no solace in the face of Philistine America; it provides only the first of several shocks that force him to look upon the ugly and banal American soul.

Du Bois also found himself increasingly alienated from the country of his birth as he continued along his path. First, however, he was drawn out of the ivory tower of his professorship at Atlanta University in the first years of the twentieth century by the increasing barbarism American Whites practiced upon those of his race. "One could not be a calm, cool, and detached scientist while Negroes were lynched, murdered and starved" (67). From 1910 to 1934, Du Bois reigned as editor-in-chief of *The Crisis*, the national periodical of the NAACP, where he composed influential editorials on all aspects of the racial question, both domestic and international.[3] As he wrote in his autobiography, "the National Association for the Advancement of Colored People was able to organize one of the most effective assaults of liberalism upon prejudice and reaction that the modern world has seen" (226–27); but once Du Bois began moving beyond liberal ideology, he had to break ranks with his former allies, eventually resigning his editorship of *The Crisis*. In line with a diasporic, pan-Africanist perspective he developed and promoted in contrast to the minority American purview of his NAACP coworkers, Du Bois embraced Marxist insights concerning the brutal economic organization and false consciousness of capitalism. "[T]he essential difficulty with the liberalism of the twentieth century was not to realize the fundamental change brought about by the world-wide organization of work and trade and commerce" (288–89). When he finally came to the hard-bitten conclusion that African Americans had to spend their best energies organizing and developing themselves within rather than battling against the intractable realities of legally sanctioned segregation, Du Bois found himself far closer to the thinking of the Communist Party of the 1930s than of the NAACP at any time. Seven years after resigning editorship of *The Crisis*, at age seventy-two, he published *Dusk of Dawn*. Advocating a "planned and deliberate recognition of self-segregation on the part of colored people" (200)—an unpopular position both inside the Black community and within a nation gearing up for its fight against fascism—the autobiography of one of the greatest African Americans of the twentieth century was all but ignored upon its publication.

In spite of its racial preoccupations—the book is subtitled "An Essay toward an Autobiography of a Race Concept"—*Dusk of Dawn* offers no hope of return to an African idyll and finds little solace in the folk culture of Black America. "Negro self-criticism recognizes a perfectly obvious fact and that fact is that most Negroes in the United States today occupy a low cultural status; both low in itself and low as compared with the national average in the land" (179). Race consciousness became not a source of pride but a veil, to take up the famous metaphor of *The Souls of Black Folk*, counterpoised between the Self and the World. "Racial identity presented itself as a matter of trammels and impediments as 'tightening bonds about my feet' . . . I saw the race problem was not as I conceived, a matter of clear, fair competition, for which I was ready and eager. It was rather a matter of segregation, of hindrance and inhibitions, and my struggles against this and resentment at it began to have serious repercussions upon my inner life" (130).

Both Lewisohn and Du Bois end their autobiographies as "articulate survivors," to use Stepto's phrase, but they are lone voices crying in the wilderness. As Stepto intimated, the narrative of ascent set the stage for the narrative of immersion. Both men were to make their journeys deeper into ethnic identity (this latter characterization oversimplifies Du Bois's complex and ever-evolving position, but he died in Africa as a citizen of Ghana), but these journeys were taken after the publications of the two autobiographies discussed above. It was not the lot of either man to write his narrative of immersion in any memorable fashion. (Both produced further autobiographical writings, but these subsequent productions lacked the structure and interest of their earlier efforts.) Indeed, immersion itself was not to become fashionable until the ideological breakup of the sixties. Then Black Power, the Six Day War, *The Autobiography of Malcolm X*, and the increasing enthronement of the Holocaust paved the way for the autobiographies of Paul Cowen and Leslie Alexander Lacy.

Gestures of immersion were not new to the autobiographies of Blacks and Jews published prior to the sixties. In *Here I Stand* (1958), Paul Robeson wrote of his discovery of Africa while in London, "the center of the British Empire," during the 1920s. "That discovery, which has influenced my life ever since, made it clear that I would not live out my life as an adopted Englishman, and I came to consider that I was an African" (33). Ben Hecht devotes many pages to his activities as a publicist and fundraiser for the Irgun in *A Child of the Century* (1954). Meyer Levin, a half-generation behind Hecht and aware of his example, wrote an autobiography, *In Search* (1950), that recorded his harrowing journey to the heart of the Holocaust as an Army reporter and his activities in Israel as a Zionist. The most famous discussions of immersion, of course, are those of *The Autobiography of Malcolm X* (1965), in which Malcolm details his odyssey from Malcolm Little to Detroit Red to Malcolm X to, finally, El-Hajj Malik El-Shabazz. "You don't even know who you are," his brother tells him during a prison visit, the first successful effort by his family to convert him to the Nation of Islam. "You don't even know, the white devil has hidden it from you, that you are a race of people of ancient civilizations, and riches in gold and kings. You don't even know your true family name, you wouldn't recognize your true language if you heard it. You have been cut off by the devil white man from all true knowledge of your own kind" (255). These life stories, however, were not purely narratives of immersion. Like Antin and Washington, Lewisohn and Du Bois, these autobiographers started their journeys either from a lower-middle-class background (Meyer Levin, Malcolm X) or unavoidably aware of their ethnic identity (Ben Hecht, Paul Robeson). Not having come from a background of privilege, their accession to the status of writer, journalist, international spokesperson, and activist was also a narrative of ascent. Malcolm X's description of his studies in prison—his painstaking acquisition of new vocabulary from a dictionary, for example—is as impressive as the autodidacticism of Solomon Maimon or Booker T. Washington. (Indeed, much of the dynamism of *The Autobiography of Malcolm X* comes from its ever-widening circles of ascent and immersion.) The pure narrative of immersion would have to come from the children of the assimilated Jews and the Black bourgeoisie, men and women who grew up in the aftermath of parental ascent and who finally rejected the melting pot myth of American success. Even Antin contemplates such a possibility as she muses upon the persistence of Jewish identity. "Perhaps [my grandchildren] may have to testify that the faith of Israel is a heritage that no heir in the direct line has the power to alienate from his successors" (248–49).

Paul Cowan, a writer for the *Village Voice* who began his journey toward Orthodox Judaism at the age of thirty-six, would have fervently seconded this speculation. Born in 1940, Cowan grew up the son of a powerful media executive. His father, Louis Cowan, was the president of CBS-TV in the mid-fifties, helping to define such prominent products of American popular culture as "The Quiz Kids," "Stop the Music," and "The $64,000 Question." Sent to Choate, an Episcopalian prep school, and then gaining admittance to Harvard, Paul prepared for an American elite that would accept him on condition that he continue down the path of assimilation forged by his forebears. His maternal grandfather, a mail-order magnate born a Reform Jew, died a Christian Scientist in the wealthy Chicago suburb of Kenilworth. Louis Cowan, though never denying his Jewish origins, changed his name from Cohen, sent his children to Christian prep schools as part of their training for the power elite, and celebrated Christmas and Easter in the secularized American manner. "In those years," Cowan writes of his childhood, "I barely knew what a Passover seder was. I didn't know anyone who practiced archaic customs such as keeping kosher or lighting candles on Friday night. Neither my parents nor I ever mentioned the possibility of a bar mitzvah" (3).

Leslie Alexander Lacy, born in 1937, also grew up the child of privilege, although his upper-class world was the segregated one of the South before the Civil Rights era. His father, an African-American physician, provided a luxurious standard of living for his family first in Franklin, then in Shreveport, Louisiana. "Thanks to my father's money, influence, motivation, and stupefying illusions of greatness for me, I had grown up behind a beautiful mask of Negro respectability" (8). Lacy was sent to the Palmer Memorial Institute, a Black prep school he viciously satirizes as a bastion of snobbism and bourgeois inculcation. Insulated from the company of lower-class African Americans, Lacy grew up passively accepting the values of his class and training. To a certain extent, wealth also protected him from the harsher aspects of Southern racism, although occasionally an evil smell would penetrate the perimeter of privilege. Educated to live in the enduring contradiction of a Black bourgeoisie whose dignity could be violated at will be any White person, Lacy observed his father being questioned and humiliated by a deputy sheriff after a minor traffic accident. "His manhood was not city wide," he wrote. "Everything else was temporary, and you adjusted to it without making it a part of your conscious existence. If you were intelligent, like my father, you could play tricks with your mind. If you were poor, you beat your wife. In either case, it was all in a day's work" (57).

As a segregated institute, Palmer kept White racism from its confines and promoted proper (i.e., "White") behavior as the best way to advance in life. Cowan was not similarly protected in his mainstream prep school, and he experienced numerous shocks to his psyche. "For the first two years I was at Choate, 1954 and 1955, I felt I was walking through a human minefield of anti-Semitism. Later, when I was more self-possessed and poised, the bigotry that so many people there displayed disgusted me so much that I decided I never wanted to become part of their crowd" (10). Like Lewisohn in the face of similar rejection, Cowan adopted the stance of the bohemian rebel, identifying with Noel Airman in Herman Wouk's 1955 best seller, *Marjorie Morningstar* (110), and taking as his adult role models the American realists John Steinbeck, John Dos Passos, and James Agee (158). He strove to get into Harvard because it was a place he equated with freedom from bigotry. Although Harvard fulfilled his dreams of assimilationist utopia, he found he could not entirely submerge the tormenting memories of Choate even while studying the literature of Puritan New England. A reading of Norman Mailer's story "The Time of Her Time" brought him to the conclusion that he was a passive Jew, and during his senior year he went to Israel to be "among the bravest of my own people." "Within weeks of my arrival there, an explosion had taken place in my consciousness. I could never have imagined the new ways, woven into the details that most Israelis take for granted, that I learned to obtain the sense of identity, the sense of pride, that I had sought throughout my adolescence" (104). But the "return," such as it was, was not a spiritual one and remained an episode. Cowan maintained no significant tie with Israel—he certainly didn't become a Zionist like Meyer Levin—and, like his fictional contemporary, Alexander Portnoy, he found himself attracted to blonde *shikses*, "my passport to the America I wanted to discover" (112). Plagued by the double consciousness of all American minorities, what he really wanted—and what he soon found—was a blond *shikse* who would accept his Jewish atavism.

Lacy also chose to go to college in New England (Tufts University), not because he expected it to be free of bigotry but because he considered "Negro" colleges to be inferior. Once in a mainstream educational institution, however, he underwent the kind of culture shock that Cowan had earlier experienced at Choate. "My land down South, my huge home and spacious yard, my colored servants, my wealth, fine speech, a special kind of security and faith in the future had not served me, not prepared me for the white world I was expected to deal with" (83). Constantly aware of his color, racial stereotypes, and his status as a minority in an overwhelmingly White world, Lacy was continually anxious, and eventually developed an ulcer. "I looked and functioned rather normally. I simply felt inferior. . . . Nothing at the Boston colleges gave substance to my being" (83).

Moving out to Los Angeles to live with his divorced mother, Lacy continued his education at the University of Southern California. There he embarked upon a friendship with a Jewish woman by the name of Judy. She eventually enrolled him in the socialist ranks of the 1950s, and he found himself participating in protests against capital punishment and the nuclear arms race. "I never knew that there was so much wrong with the world. It was like the falling of jail walls from my mind" (112). Eventually he and Judy became lovers, his first sexual experience. Like Cowan, Lacy overcame his sexual anxiety in the arms of a woman he perceived as coming from the culture of power. The Jewish woman was to the Black man what the blonde *shikse* was to the Jewish man.

Somewhat later, Paul and Rachel Cowan also became radicalized. Paul did civil rights work in the South during the summers of the early 1960s and functioned as a community activist on Chicago's South Side while attending the University of Chicago as a graduate student. When Paul and Rachel married in 1965, he learned that he was about to be drafted, which prompted both of them to join the Peace Corps for a two-year stint in Ecuador. Disillusioned by racist and colonialist attitudes they found in both the Peace Corps and the U.S. government, the Cowans returned to New York ready to participate in the antiwar movement. As a journalist for the *Village Voice*, Cowan wrote about some of the signal events of the decade. His involvement with the New Left led to an association with Catholic radicals that was rewarding both professionally and personally, but which brought him up short when he realized that he was fundamentally an outsider because of their repeated insistence that their actions stemmed from their religious beliefs. "I'd helped poor blacks in the South and in Chicago; worked with poor people in South America; taken some risks to resist the war. But if any religious ideology had instructed me to do those things, it was my mother's post-Holocaust world view. It certainly wasn't any belief in Jesus. Suddenly, I felt excluded from my friends' inviting culture" (142).

As the sixties drew Lacy into its ideological whirlpool, the young Black man from Louisiana began to distance himself from the world of White radicalism. "The political culture of the left I knew was unequivocally Jewish, or very much influenced by Jews," he writes (118). After leaving USC with an M.A. in political science, Lacy went to study law at Hastings College in San Francisco. At first he worked with the Socialist Workers Party, but he also heard for the first time the rhetoric of Black Power as articulated by Donald Ramsey and Donald Warden, founders of an organization of Black graduate students at the University of California. "The white left . . . had not achieved its predicted victory over capitalism, and besides, I thought I had had enough of its pussy, poetry, and politics. I still believed in socialism, but I also felt a need to assert my blackness" (115).

Then came immersion with a vengeance, one that was fully supported by the radical culture in which he moved. "'We are Blacks,' [Warden] shouted with a passion. 'We are from Africa, brought here as slaves. They—the Whites—called us Negroes, nigger boy, colored. But we are Blacks, people of African descent, Afro-Americans. In Africa we had our own language, culture, God; and that's where we were free.'" (108). As Lacy grew more confused over his divided loyalties, he decided to follow the example of W. E. B. Du Bois, a man who was "black and radical, and in [whose] life was the back-and-forth political pattern which was beginning to characterize mine" (120). Lacy went "back" to Africa and joined the contingent of African-American supporters of the Pan-Africanist leader, Kwame Nkrumah of Ghana. "William Edward Burghardt Du Bois had been the intellectual and political model of many in my generation," (154) Lacy wrote in his chapter entitled "Dusk of Dawn," a chapter in which he recounted his meeting with the Old Man two days before Du Bois's death at the age of ninety-five.

Lacy had by this time acquired an African-American girlfriend. He was in Africa to work the White man out of his consciousness, to come to an emotional as well as an intellectual belief that Black was beautiful. Essentialist notions floated through the ideological ether, and even Lacy hit an uncharacteristically *négritude* note.

The people of "Negro" Birmingham and every other black community which I had passed through in the South . . . had forgotten about the things I was seeing and hearing. They no longer spoke this language or carried this culture from generation to generation. But the spirit or character—something about the black people on these Accra streets—gave me, and also Eve, a feeling of belonging which I had only gotten in America from the dusky people who could still remember loud laughter, lack of European "refinement," festival nights and days, the bend of a black woman's buttocks; what Léopold Sédar Senghor had seen in Harlem, "humming with noise, with stately colours and flamboyant smells," saying to New York, "Let the black blood flow in your blood that it may rub the rust from your still joints, like an oil of life." (139)

By contrast, Cowan had to inch his way toward immersion in a religious culture that was in no way supported by the political dogmas of the Left. Chaim Potok's novel *The Chosen* (1967) made "the Orthodox Jewish world seem like a compellingly attractive, secure place" (145), mitigating the negative stereotypes offered by Wouk and Mailer. The wish was father to the deed, and Cowan made the journey to the Lower East Side to do a *Voice* article on "Jews Without Money, Revisited." Although he had immersed himself in other communities for journalistic research, "I had never felt the depths of personal connection to those communities that I did to the people I met in the Vladeck courtyards or in *shul* during the days before Tisha B'Av" (152).[4] As Paul moved cautiously toward greater observance, Rachel started a school for the New York Havurah to assure that something "more substantial and durable" of Jewish tradition would be passed on to their two children. After his parents died in a hotel fire, Cowan fell under the influence of a charismatic rabbi. "His example imbued the values my parents had passed on to me with a sense of history and an intensity of religious feeling that made them seem far more durable than anything I had found in the secular world" (195). Paul converted to Orthodox Judaism; as a third-generation feminist, Rachel could only come as far as the Conservative brand. *An Orphan in History* concludes with a description of the *bat mitzvah* ceremony their daughter has decided to celebrate. And so the autobiography ends in full immersion; the protagonist has brought not only himself but his family to the transcendent world of Judaism.

Lacy, unfortunately, does not find "The Political Kingdom" of Ghana to be a Black utopia. Nkrumah's government is corrupt, ideological, capricious, and dictatorial. Lacy eventually makes a place for himself as a student and lecturer at the University of Ghana in Legon, but he describes the African-American community around Nkrumah as "black bodies in exile" (167). Although the visit of Malcolm X briefly provides a unifying influence, the African-American community is dependent upon Nkrumah's power. As political life in Ghana proves less satisfying, Lacy gains a greater familiarity with African culture, and he has a final revelation that heals his White-imposed inferiority complex. Looking at the face of a young market woman, "I discovered that a black face is really beautiful. Its meaning screamed inside of my skull, healing my wounds, relaxing my anger" (232). The fall of Nkrumah soon sends Lacy to Nigeria, but the outbreak of the civil war there directs his thoughts homeward, and, four years after his arrival, he ends his "exile in Mother Africa" (236). "I discovered that trying to belong, to be saved, was at best ritualistic and misleading, covering over my disintegration rather than bringing to myself some reasonable kind of order. I was a being of reaction, a confused black creature trying to stabilize a painful neurosis without knowing, except in general terms, what had made me sick . . . " (238–39).

Lacy experienced a disillusionment with immersion—his political variant—that Cowan never had to confront. There are certainly paths of Black spiritual immersion—Pentecostalism, voodoo, the Nation of Islam—but the pan-Africanist version, born of the sixties, died with the sixties. Still, Lacy ends his ironically titled

Rise and Fall on a positive note. If his contemporaries failed to bring about the revolution, then their task is to pursue reform for the future generations who *will* organize a revolutionary Black culture.

Just as there are Black forms of religious immersion, so there are political modes of affirming Jewish identity. The century that witnessed the Holocaust and the birth of the state of Israel offered many opportunities, both exhilarating and terrifying, to strengthen an attenuating Jewishness. "This is a book about being a Jew," Meyer Levin begins his autobiography, but there is little in it about religion (9). Levin constructs his sense of identity from his shamefaced desire to escape the immigrant culture of his parents, his excitement and participation in the building of Jewish Palestine, and his firsthand discovery of the Nazi concentration camps immediately after the liberation. Like the Black forms of political identification, Jewish secular identity draws its vocabulary and iconography from a history of oppression, an international outlook, and a political discourse conducted in the language of the Enlightenment.

Forms of spiritual and religious immersion, however, require the acquisition of a specialized knowledge (Malcolm X must present a summary of Elijah Muhammad's teachings if his autobiography is to be accessible to outsiders) and, in the case of Judaism, an extensive ritual language. "I have been called to the *bimah* on Saturday morning and holy days for an *aliyah* and watched as the *baal korei* chants from the open Torah scroll. I have carried the scroll on Simchat Torah and on Saturday mornings I have lifted the Torah while the congregation sang "*V'zot ha-torah asher sam Moshe lifnay b'nai Yisrael al pi Adonai b-yad Moshe*" (28). So writes Julius Lester in his autobiography, *Lovesong: Becoming a Jew* (1988).

Lester's story of immersion is particularly apposite to our discussion because he first came to public notice as a writer with the publication of the 1968 manifesto, *Look Out, Whitey! Black Power's Gon' Get Your Mama!* Born the son of a Black Methodist minister in 1939, Lester grew up in the segregated South of Lacy's childhood. He discovered that he had a Jewish great-grandfather, but this knowledge made no perceptible impact at the time. At Fisk University, he rebelled against the bourgeois inculcation of its training and borrowed his style of rejection from the Beat generation. Determined to follow an artistic vocation, he went to New York City after graduation to become a writer and folk singer. Soon he met and married a Jewish student, Joan Steiner, who accelerated his political radicalization. Drawn into the civil rights movement as a folk singer, Lester underwent the same political evolution from civil rights to Black Power as did the SNCC (the Student Non-Violent Coordinating Committee), his sponsoring organization. Lester recorded two albums of original folk songs and achieved brief notoriety as the host of a New York City radio show, "The Great Proletarian Cultural Revolution," when he aired the reading of a poem written by a Black student that began:

Hey, Jew boy, with that yarmulke on your head
You pale-faced Jew boy—I wish you were dead.
I can see you Jew boy—no you can't hide
I got a scoop on you—yeh, you gonna die.

In the first skirmish of the war between American Blacks and Jews that opened nationwide with the struggle for community control of schools in the Brownsville section of New York City, Lester found himself dazed and confused by the virulence of the emotion he had tapped on both sides. The United Federation of Teachers filed a complaint against the sponsoring station with the Federal Communications Commission, and by the time the controversy was over, Lester was "anathema to Jews across the country" (65).

At the end of the 1960s, Lester found himself disenchanted with radical politics and his role in them. "I had started out to be the black James Joyce and had almost become a revolutionary hack writer" (*All Is Well*, 176). Not only did he find his artistic aspirations unmet by the demands of revolutionary politics but, even more important, he felt keenly that he had neglected his spirituality. The disintegration of his first marriage prompted an active spiritual quest that confirmed the importance of God to his sense of self.[5]

In 1971 he joined the newly created Department of Afro-American Studies at the University of Massachusetts in Amherst. Eight years later, Andy Young, the African-American ambassador to the U.N. appointed by President Carter, resigned his post because of secret meetings held with a Palestine Liberation Organization representative in defiance of official U.S. policy. Lester wrote a widely circulated and controversial article for the *Village Voice* in which he excoriated Black leadership for treating "Jews as scapegoats again" (127). This initiated simultaneously an alienation from Black ideology and a rapprochement with the Jewish community. A course offering on Blacks and Jews gave Lester an opportunity to study and teach Jewish history, prompting his first desire to convert. With the death of his father in 1981 the last emotional obstacle fell, and Lester began the process of instruction in Hebrew language and liturgy that was a prerequisite for formal conversion. His 1983 induction into Reform Judaism was followed a year later by circumcision. In 1984, as a result of a controversy over the alleged anti-Semitic cast of remarks made by James Baldwin during a university lecture, Lester transferred from the Department of Afro-American to the Department of Judaic studies. By 1986, his second wife (neither Black nor Jewish) had also converted to Judaism. Lester's autobiography of immersion, like Cowan's, ends on a ritual note, with Lester standing in a synagogue singing Jewish liturgical music. "All those years I sang folk songs, spirituals, blues, work songs, and always knew that something was absent, that as much as I loved spirituals, I was not wholly present when I sang them. . . . It is this music my voice was meant to sing. It is this music of praise and love that releases my soul into my voice" (243–44).

Lester makes clear from the essentialist assumptions behind his discussion of his "real" identity that his conversion to Judaism is not the embrace of an alien tradition but an immersion into his soul's belonging. As a child he identified more with Shylock than with the African-American role models presented to him in the segregated schools of Kansas City. During a sabbatical year in 1979, he found himself deeply moved and depressed by readings in Holocaust history and awoke one morning trying to say, "*Sh'ma Yisrael.*" Though Lester can scarcely deny that he is Black—nor does he wish to—he treats his Blackness as a social construction and his Jewishness as an essentialist one. "I am no longer deceived by the black face which stares at me from the mirror," he writes in the prologue. "I am a Jew" (1). Once he begins to feel as a Jew, every new incident that pits Blacks and Jews against one another only attenuates his political commitment to a Black identity. "If blackness is synonymous with unthinking and blind loyalty to the race, regardless of what any of its members do," he muses after presidential candidate Jesse Jackson referred to New York as "Hymietown" in what he thought was an off-the-record conversation with a Black reporter, "then I am not black" (209).

Discussing the persistence and renewal of ethnic identification in the 1970s, sociologist Herbert Gans endeavored to provide an explanatory model that would account for such a phenomenon while maintaining the melting pot ideology (rechristened "straight-line theory") still favored by the mainstream intellectual community. The concept he came up with was "symbolic ethnicity," an ethnic identification that serves as a leisure-time activity and loses its relevance to earning a living or regulating family life. Symbolic ethnicity, Gans writes, "is characterized by a nostalgic allegiance to the culture of the immigrant generation, or that of the old country; a love for and a pride in a tradition that can be felt without having to be incorporated in everyday behavior" (9). Although he recognizes "ethnic groups who still continue to make tiny bumps and waves in the line" (Black nationalists and orthodox Jews, for example) and "rebel converts to sacred and secular ways" (presumably the likes of Malcolm X and Paul Cowan), Gans predicts the eventual disappearance of an ethnicity based upon ancestral origin. What Gans fails to recognize as a proponent of straight-line theory is that new, made-in-America ethnicities are created that are not based on close ties to immigrant experience or Old Country culture, but upon current communities and American ethnic experience that, in the case of African Americans, extend farther back than that of the Pilgrims. Still, symbolic ethnicity nicely covers the stance of many Americans who acknowledge and act upon their ethnicity without making it the defining element of their lives. Symbolic ethnicity would explain why Edna Ferber entitled her autobiography *A Peculiar Treasure* (1939), a biblical allusion to the Jewish background she never wrote about as a bestselling author and playwright.[6] Symbolic ethnicity would explain why Ben Hecht, Hollywood's highest-paid screen writer of the 1940s, would agree to become to become a spokesperson for the Irgun, Jewish freedom fighters (or terrorists, depending on one's politics) in British Palestine. In *A Child of the Century* (1954), Hecht humorously attributes his participation in the "lunatic project . . . to drive the British and six of their satellite Arab countries out of Palestine" to an ancestral Jewish pirate who had taken boyhood possession of his soul. "I would rather that David, Saul or Solomon had taken up residence in me. But my spooky mariner is good enough to keep my soul alive with the whoop of Jewish destiny" (79). Symbolic ethnicity allows those Jews who have ascended into the American mainstream to maintain a Jewish identity while leading public and professional lives that make little reference to that identity. American Jews obviously have greater latitude to practice symbolic ethnicity than do African Americans, but individuals can be found even among the latter who would claim that the ties of race are obsolete and best forgotten.

Ben Hecht, whose novel *A Jew in Love* (1931) has been described as a translucent exercise in Jewish self-hatred, makes for fascinating study in ethnic identification, for his interior conflicts are made manifest through both his art and his action. In *A Child of the Century*, his ambivalence toward his Jewish identity—and the fact that it seems to have no influence on his success as a writer—comes out through humor, sentimental portraits of his family, and lighthearted sacrilege. An example of the latter is the title of a short chapter, "The Lord Is—How Many?" The anecdote he uses in this chapter to illustrate his agnosticism will also serve to introduce the autobiographies of those who find themselves at ethnicity's far horizon.

> I am reminded of a Negro I saw hanged in the Cook County Jail in Chicago. He was a dentist and had grown a little vague about things while awaiting execution. He stood on the gallows in a medical frock coat, his wing collar missing (a décolleté required by circumstances), and smiled oddly at the audience gaping at his last moments. Though the rope was around his neck, he was not entirely certain where he was or what was happening. Before springing the trap, the sheriff at his side inquired of the doomed dentist, as was tradition, if he had anything to say.
>
> The man with the rope around his neck smiled and answered in a faraway, polite voice, "Not at this time." (11–12)

Although Hecht identifies the protagonist as a Negro, his ethnicity makes no difference to the import of the story. The joke is in the dentist's befuddlement, and the fact that he is Black neither adds to nor detracts from that fact. It is a detail that adds verisimilitude but brings with it no sociological resonance.

There are autobiographers who write their own life stories as if their ethnic origins should be as incidental as this to where the real action is. These are writers moving beyond ethnicity—still recognizable because of a self-confessed ethnic origin but fundamentally not interested in talking about it. Actress Lauren Bacall and science fiction writer Samuel Delaney will serve as our examples.

Lauren Bacall, born Betty Persky, was famous by the age of twenty for her screen portrayal of frank sexuality and her liaison with her costar, Humphrey Bogart, which turned into a domestic, twelve-year marriage. She proved, after Bogart's death, to be a durable actress, going on to a stage career capped by a Tony award for her role in the musical *Applause*. Bacall's autobiography, *By Myself* (1978), is about her professional life and her search for satisfying male companionship. She favored high-profile lovers, featuring Frank Sinatra and Jason Robards Jr., as well as admitting to a crush on Adlai Stevenson.

Bacall's overt remarks about Jewishness focus mostly on the "nice Jewish girl" upbringing that imposed a Victorian set of morals upon the relationships between men and women. Yet her attitude toward Jewishness is potentially complex, filled with the same contradictions spoken of at greater length by Alfred Kazin and Leslie Fiedler. In the beginning, Bacall harbored Jewish self-hatred. As early as sixteen, when she was starting her modeling career, she resented the discussions of disbelief among the other models when they learned of her ethnicity: "and I resented being Jewish, being singled out because I was, and being some sort of freak because I didn't look it. Who cares? What is the difference between Jewish and Christian? But the difference is there—I've never really understood it and I spent the first half of my life worrying about it" (39). Many times, for Bacall, being Jewish was a source of pain. She feared that her Hollywood mentor, Howard Hawks, might have been anti-Semitic. Deep into her affair with Bogart, she asked him if it mattered to him that she was Jewish (148). When Bogart's third wife, Mayo, found out about their affair, she called Bacall a "Jewish bitch" (161). Her reaction to her first glimmer of professional success, when she landed a speaking part in a Broadway-bound show, is telling: "It wasn't so bad to be a little Jewish girl, now was it?" (64).

But then there are all the *haimischkeit* values. The people she loved the most steadfastly, besides Bogart, were her family members: her mother, her grandmother, her Uncle Charlie. This aspect of her Jewishness comes out most clearly in the passage in which she speaks about how her Old Country grandma would react to news of a romance between her and the costar of her first picture. "As far as her values went, Bogie had nothing going for him—he was too old for me, he'd had three wives, he drank, he was an actor, and he was Goyim" (145). The only Yiddish word in the whole autobiography is quoted (ungrammatically, in the plural) in the context of Grandma's values. Yet Bacall does use it, finds she needs it in this one case. Later when she discusses the christening of their first child, she finds she doesn't share Bogart's assumption that being Jewish could only be a disadvantage. "I, with my family-ingrained Jewish background, bucked it—it felt too strange to me.

True, I didn't go to synagogue, but I felt totally Jewish and always would" (275). Finally, in the valedictory pages of the book, she becomes enthusiastic about her ethnic background. "Going back through my life until now, the Jewish family feeling stands strong and proud, and at last I can say I am glad I sprang from that" (505). The possibility of an immersion narrative glimmers in the background, but as she wrote of her straitened childhood in Brooklyn, "everything I fantasized about had nothing to do with everything I lived" (3). Bacall turned her life into the movies, and Jewishness had no place in that fantasy.

Samuel Delaney presents us with a more intellectual scenario in the autobiography of his apprenticeship years, *The Motion of Light in Water: Sex and Science Fiction Writing in the East Village, 1957–1965*. Best known for an impressive string of successful science fiction novels, most notably *Dahlgren* (1975), Delaney has produced a sizable and complex oeuvre, including autobiographies, pornographic novels, and essays on language and science fiction. *The Motion of Light in Water* appeared in 1988 and its approach to autobiographical representation through writing is, as Craig Werner points out, "grounded in a specifically post-modernist sense of the irresolvable nature of self, life, and writing" (94). As postmodernist memoir, Delaney's book is necessarily multivoiced; the author inhabits several subject positions. Pondering the complex nature of his identity in the wake of a nervous breakdown, he writes:

> *A black man . . . ?*
> *A gay man . . . ?*
> *A writer . . . ? (212)*

None of these identities is definitive; all are problematic. The memories he associates with these three subjectivities are revealing. Concerning his formation as a writer, he speaks of a crippling handicap, undiagnosed during his years of schooling. "Because, at the time, I had no word—dyslexia—for all this, the difficulty, embarrassment, and pain connected with writing could somehow be set aside, not spoken of; placed, if not outside language, then into the same area of private speech into which I put all my sexual experiences" (217).

Delaney's experiences as a gay man, the next topic of his meditation, are also rich in difficulty, embarrassment, and pain. *Motion* spends far more time and energy on the protagonist's exploration of gay sex and its associated sensibility than on any well-worn observations about being Black in America. Still revealing a bit of internalized homophobia, the "gay man" of Delaney's list is associated with the nelly organist who played in his father's Harlem funeral parlor. "Herman had a place in our social scheme—but by no means an acceptable place, and certainly not a place I wanted to fill" (220). Groping for an acceptable identity in the era before the Stonewall Riots of 1969 marked the beginnings of gay liberation, Delaney describes his many sexual encounters with men without being able to place them within a larger social context. When he divulges his homosexuality in group therapy, he discovers that all previous public discussions of the subject—the pejorative "clinical" analyses of the psychologists and the anguished confessional novels of Gore Vidal, André Gide, and James Baldwin—are inadequate. "When you talk about something openly for the first time . . . for better or worse, you use the public language you've been given. It's only later, alone in the night, that maybe, if you're a writer, you ask yourself how closely that language reflects your experience. And that night I realized that language had done nothing but betray me" (247). While Delaney has plenty of postmodernist insights concerning the radical indeterminacy of language in conveying interior experience, especially that experience which finds no reflection in public discourse, his discussion of Black identity in this context is surprisingly meager. He says nothing about how language distorts or betrays his experience as a Black man, and his association with the "black man" portion of his triadic identity is with a friend of his father's, Mr. Henson. What makes Mr. Henson notable is not any achievement of his as a "race man" but the fact that he had been part of Admiral Peary's expedition to discover the North Pole. Mr. Henson is presented as living proof that being Black presents no insuperable obstacle to nonethnic achievement. "My parents wanted me to know that this humble man, this great man, this valiant man who'd first set foot on the North Pole was black, was real, and lived in Harlem like I did . . . and they hoped, as did a lot of other black parents, that I just might make the mental leap: therefore I too could do something memorable in the world" (223).

Blackness for the protagonist of *Motion* is never much of an issue. Even though the historical period covered in the autobiography coincides with the greatest upheaval of U.S. race relations in the twentieth century, none of this enters Delaney's bohemian world of the East Village. In 1961, at the age of nineteen, he and his Jewish girlfriend, Marilyn Hacker, marry in Michigan because of the restrictive age-of-consent and miscegenation laws in other states; but this holdover from the era of legalized caste status occasions no outburst of indignation or meditation on the deforming nature of racial categories on internal experience. Delaney is light enough to pass for White, and although he never denies his ethnic origins, neither does he revel in them. His concerns are far more private—his unconventional sexuality, the complex relationship he has with his wife (where racial difference never seems to be an issue)—and his artistic pursuits, folk singing and science fiction writing, are equally removed from ethnic influence.[7] In the East Village of the 1960s, he has chosen one of the few enclaves in America where race doesn't seem to matter.

Like Bacall, however, and like all recognizably ethnic writers, Delany retains his trace of double consciousness: he draws his epigraph from Equiano's *Narrative*.

If, then, the following narrative does not appear sufficiently interesting to engage general attention, let my motive be some excuse for its publication. I am not so foolishly vain as to expect from it either immortality or literary reputation. If it affords any satisfaction to my numerous friends, at whose request it has been written, or in the smallest degree promotes the interests of humanity, the ends for which it was undertaken will be fully attained, and every wish of my heart gratified. Let it therefore be remembered that, in wishing to avoid censure, I do not aspire to praise.

The passage elegantly offers two different *raisons d'être* for the autobiography: the request of friends and "the interests of humanity." Delaney seems to appropriate similar justifications for his own autobiography, but the passage of two centuries has made a difference. There is no equivalent for Delaney of the eighteenth-century abolition movement. Delaney is able to publish his autobiography because he is a successful writer; his reputation itself is a commodity in twentieth-century capitalism. He is also a theoretically informed and practicing postmodernist; one could hardly expect an unproblematic acceptance of past racial "stances" (victim, rebel, survivor, kinsman). What we get mostly, however, is silence. Yet the ironic act of postmodernist quotation is not ironic in Delaney's epigraph. It is the book's most visible link to ethnic identity. Now Equiano's *Narrative* is recognized as fountainhead for the rich tradition of Black autobiography into which *The Motion of Light in Water* might insert itself. The act of literary kinsmanship has become almost ornamental. It is an act of symbolic ethnicity.

Conclusion

Being a Jew, I would always be in opposition.

—Sigmund Freud

"Enlightenment is totalitarian," Max Horkheimer and Theodor Adorno wrote in *The Dialectic of Enlightenment* (6). The Frankfurt School theoreticians posited in their book that the Enlightenment represented a philosophy of total integration that subsumed everything under a tyrannical rationality, splitting subject and object, man and nature, signified and signifier, art and science into bounded, self-contained realms. On the level of philosophy, they criticized the Enlightenment for begging the philosophical question, perceiving in a disenchanted nature only what reason would allow and surrendering all human and supernatural dimensions to mere factuality.

What appears to be the triumph of subjective rationality, the subjection of all reality to logical formalism, is paid for by the obedient subjection of reason to what is directly given. What is abandoned is the whole claim and approach of knowledge: to comprehend that given as such; not merely to determine the abstract spatiotemporal relations of the facts that allow them to be grasped, but to conceive of them as the superficies, as mediated conceptual moments that come to fulfillment only in the development of their social, historical, and human significance (27).

Written from a Marxist perspective during a period when, as they say, "the end of the Nazi terror was within sight" (ix), *The Dialectic of Enlightenment* presents itself

221

as a foundational critique of totalitarianism. Not surprisingly, wherever they turned—to fascist Germany, to the Stalinist Soviet Union, or to capitalist America—Horkheimer and Adorno saw the tyrannical heritage of Enlightenment philosophy.

Horkheimer and Adorno's book, first published in German in 1944, did not spark a widespread critique of the Enlightenment at the time, but the writings of the Frankfurt School, and especially the interventions of Herbert Marcuse from within the American academic establishment, eventually did so through the cultural revolution of the 1960s. As Satya P. Mohanty notes, their judgment that the Enlightenment was totalitarian "revealed the deep anxiety many intellectuals in our times have felt about the founding age of modern criticism" (1). Yet the Enlightenment *Weltanschauung* was not totalitarian, despite the contradiction between its political ideals and specific practices—slavery and government-sanctioned anti-Semitism, to name but two—that invalidated its claims to universality. Even on a philosophical level, the Enlightenment was not as totalizing as Horkheimer and Adorno made out. We need only turn to the philosophical allegory with which Solomon Maimon ends his autobiography to illustrate the point.

This "final chapter," as Maimon calls it, is titled "The Merry Ball: A Page from the Diary of My Friend." One need not be an Oedipus, to paraphrase the author, to figure out that "my friend" is Maimon himself.

In attendance at the merry ball are all the great philosophers of history. To make sure the reader doesn't miss any of the allusions, Maimon provides footnotes explaining that Monsieur Pl. is Plato, Monsieur Ar. is Aristotle, Py. is Pyrrho, *und so weiter*. These would-be cavaliers are all competing for the attention of the Lady Metaphysics, who is invisible, though her "gossipy chambermaid," Physics, is not. Among the old cavaliers are the Greeks from Pythagoras to Pyrrho. All these revelers dance (philosophize) in a way that's peculiar to each: Pythagoras makes his steps conform to geometrical shapes, Aristotle writes a book on the art of dance, and so on. Finally we arrive at Monsieur Pyrrho, who doesn't believe the lady is attainable and claims that "das Tanzen sei schon an sich als eine gute Motion der Gesundheit zuträglich" [dancing was in and of itself emotion suitable to good health] (319). Then the moderns have their turn, and "diese tanzten zwar mit mehr Geschmack und Grazie, aber mit nicht besserem Erfolgen alse die vorigen" [although they danced with more taste and grace, they did not enjoy any greater success than the previous men]. The old debates were taken up again, and except for several insignificant changes (i.e., Kant's *Critique of Pure Reason*), "es bleib alles" [everything remained as before]. Finally, "einer der Gescheitesten" [one of the more shy ones], driven to speak by these "Donquixoteries," claims that the lady is a figment of everyone's imagination. (Though no letters or footnotes are provided, I believe

Hume is intended here.) This creates a storm of controversy, and the cavaliers divide into two parties based on the status of their belief in the Lady's existence.

Mein Freund . . . der dabei zugegen war, mischte sich auch darein. Er gab nicht nur der Meinung von der Nonexistenz der Dame seinen völligen Beifall, sondern behauptete auch, daß man ein guter Kavalier sein könne, ohne sich in eine solche Gehirngeburt zu verlieben, und foderte beide Parteien heraus, ihre Behauptungen wider seine Gegengründe zu verteidigen. (319)

[My friend who was attendance also got mixed up in all this. He not only accepted the opinion of those who doubted the existence of the Lady, he also maintained that it was possible to be a good cavalier without falling for this imaginary Lady and demanded both parties defend their positions against his counter-arguments.]

The role Maimon assigns to himself at the philosophical ball is of particular interest. Like Hume, he subscribes to a radical doubt; like Pyrrho, he believes in the dance for its own sake. How can one be a metaphysician without believing in metaphysics? Maimon challenges both sides to defend their position against his arguments. He is the critic who brings about a refinement of the systems. For, as he reveals in the final pages of the autobiographical narrative, all philosophies are relative.

I had been an adherent of all philosophical systems in succession, Peripatetic, Spinozist, Leibnitzian, Kantian, and finally Skeptic; and I was always devoted to that system, which for the time I regarded as alone true. At last I observed that all these systems contain something true, and are in certain respects equally useful. But . . . the difference of philosophical systems depends on the ideas which lie at their foundation in regard to the objects of nature, their properties and modifications, which cannot, like the ideas of mathematics, be defined in the same way by all men, and [be] presented *a priori*. . . . (288)

This may sound modern for 1793, but the attack on the concept of universality had already begun in the Enlightenment. Both Hume and Rousseau placed visible boundary markers on the supposedly illimitable domain of Reason. There are shadows of experience the Enlightenment itself can only point to. Hume's negative limitation of reason centered on an attack on causality itself; Rousseau presented his through emotion: "Feelings can only be described in terms of their effects," he writes in Book Three of *The Confessions* (105). Through personal experience (autobiography as philosophy), Rousseau learned that feeling is just as original and significant a side of life as the intellect. Furthermore, for Rousseau feeling is at the base of the intellect: "My feelings rose with the most inconceivable rapidity to the level of ideas" (328). These are the words he uses to describe the famous inspiration that assailed him on the road to Vincennes, the same inspiration that launched him on his career as a celebrated and controversial writer.

Initiating one line of the tradition I have investigated in this book, Solomon Maimon also used his autobiography as a basis for his philosophy. He is a Kantian who doesn't believe in *a priori* categories, a metaphysician who doesn't believe in metaphysics, a Jew who doesn't believe in Jehovah. Is it presumptuous to propose that Maimon was disposed to critique Enlightenment philosophy and its universalist pretensions because of his Jewish background? That is the thesis of John Murray Cuddihy's *Ordeal of Civility*, which presents Marx, Freud, and Claude Lévi-Strauss as intellectual rebels against Gentile norms of thought and behavior. "The genius of all the intellectual giants of the Jewish Diaspora has deep if 'hidden' connections with their being consciously and deliberately, albeit helplessly, social pariahs" (233), Cuddihy writes in yet another description of double consciousness.

Blacks too were skeptical of Enlightenment norms, which they perceived as European, American, or "White." The Black tradition of dissent expressed itself powerfully in vernacular forms such as music and folktales, amply illustrated in Gates's *Signifying Monkey*, and so eschewed the debate with European high culture carried out by Kafka, Freud, and Jacques Dérrida. As Craig Werner points out in his discussion of Charles Chesnutt, African-American literature early on showed a tendency to deconstruct American categories, but the subversions carried out in *The Conjure Woman* (1899) and "Baxter's Procrustes" were not recognized as such at the time (5–26). Eventually, the profound African-American distrust of the "White" epistemology surfaced in a novel that everyone hailed as a masterpiece—Ralph Ellison's *Invisible Man*. Ellison's critique of language (and racial categories) anticipated its poststructuralist theoretical elaboration by a generation. Ellison casts his critique in the form of a surrealistic African-American sermon heard on the lowest level of a marijuana-induced reverie.

"Brothers and sister, my text this morning is the 'Blackness of Blackness.'"
And a congregation of voices answered: "That blackness is most black, brother most black . . ."
"In the beginning . . ."
"At the very start," they cried.
". . . there was blackness . . ."
"Preach it . . ."
". . . and the sun . . ."
"The sun, Lawd . . ."
". . . was bloody red . . ."
"Red . . ."
"Now black is . . ." the preacher shouted.
"Bloody . . ."
"I said black is . . ."
"Preach it, brother . . ."
". . . an' black ain't . . ."
"Red, Lawd, red: He said it's red!"

"Amen, brother . . ."
"Black will get you . . ."
"Yes, it will . . ."
"Yes, it will . . ."
". . . an' black won't . . ."
"Naw, it won't!"
"It do . . ."
"It do, Lawd . . ."
". . . an' it don't."
"Halleluiah . . ."
". . . It'll put you, glory, glory, Oh my Lawd, in the WHALE'S BELLY."
"Preach it, dear brother . . ."
". . . and make you tempt . . ."
"Good God a-mighty!"
"Old Aunt Nelly!"
"Black will make you . . ."
"Black . . ."
". . . or black will un-make you."
"Ain't it the truth, Lawd?" (9–10)

But where is "the truth" in this welter of call-and-response, contradiction, and Alice-in-Wonderland rhyming? As Gates writes, "Ellison parodies here the notion of essence, of the supposedly natural relationship between the symbol and the symbolized" (236).

Twenty years before Dérrida mesmerized American literature departments with his demonstration that the gap between signified and signifier made the Saussurean sign (and thus language, narrative, and meaning) radically indeterminate, Ellison provided an overtly deconstructionist text from the Black experience. As Mohanty writes, "postmodernist constructivism may be defined most basically as the idea that all of those epistemological norms which were so dear to the Enlightenment— rationality, objectivity, and truth—are no more than social conventions, historically variable and hence without claim to universality" (11).

What followed the cultural revolution of the sixties and the subsequent embrace of poststructuralism in academia was a theoretical valorization of "minority" (or marginal) experiences the Enlightenment had previously ignored: feminism, gay liberation, Black studies, Asian-American studies, Latino studies. All of this was predicated on demystifying Enlightenment assumptions. Robert Elliot Fox sees it as a process of cultural archeological excavation rather than as a destruction of old idols.

One of the things that recent feminist and minority scholarship has done is to decode our American expression in order to reveal the multiplicity of codes operating below its homogenized level of broadcast. This is the reason Ralph Ellison's *Invisible Man* can speak for us on the "lower registers"—for it is there, in America's cultural subconscious, that all different inputs are joined. The silences of the "text" of our American experience at last have been broken open and made to "speak" as a result of the recovery operations that feminist and minority scholars in particular have undertaken. (22)

What is deconstructed here is Horkheimer and Adorno's myth of Enlightenment as a totalitarian structure. Fox challenges the idea that American culture was ever such a tightly woven entity.

Yet there is an irreconcilable difference between Enlightenment thought and contemporary versions of multiculturalism. "Human" universality and ethnic particularism will always find themselves in opposition. That is why double consciousness proved to be, ultimately, so corrosive to the dominant culture. Jews and Blacks were among the first to proffer the critique of Enlightenment universalism that is now a standard component of the postmodernist disciplines enumerated above. However, acceptance within academia does not constitute victory. The cultural revolution of the sixties made a space for minority discourse, but it certainly did not dismantle American political culture of the last two centuries. Metaphors of the melting pot and ideologies of a "color-blind" society are still powerful. And the inevitable conservative backlash has met with some success in what is currently known as "the culture wars." Allan Bloom's attack on higher education, *The Closing of the American Mind* (1987), is an example of a defiantly unreconstructed Enlightenment text.

Still, the era of Enlightenment hegemony in America is over—at least on the cultural level. One effect, for Blacks and Jews alike, has been a strengthening of diasporic consciousness. The cultural criticism of Gates, Houston Baker, and Robert Elliot Fox has definitively established the links between African and African-American expression. Judaic studies have developed differently from other minority disciplines because the diasporic components (Judaism, Hebrew, Zionism) have always been so powerful, but international developments—specifically the Six Day War and its aftermath—have only strengthened American Jewish awareness of its links to Israel.

For most American Jews, the oppression symbolized by Egypt is kept alive by ritual, memory, and a continuing diasporic consciousness. African Americans have no Passover, nor is the memory of oppression generations removed from their experience. Yet they too are no longer in Egypt. Perhaps the majority of American Jews believe they have finally arrived in the Promised Land, whereas most African Americans see themselves, at best, as belonging to the Wilderness generations. Yet these symbolic landscapes can be no more than suggestive. Israel's Promised Land is the Palestinian's Egypt; the patriarch's household is the wife's prison; the Black and Jewish bourgeoisie cooperate or confront one another in homes and institutions cleaned and maintained by the working poor of all colors. Appeals to ethnicity itself can mask the workings of oppression.

Where does the Flight from Egypt lead? This may be the final deconstruction, for the myth itself shows that an ethnicity coming into its own has blood on its hands. Will we learn from the mistakes of the Enlightenment or will we continue to take violent possession of a Land we believe is ours by divine right?

And the Lord spake unto Moses in the plains of Moab by Jordan near Jericho, saying,

Speak unto the children of Israel, and say unto them, When ye are passed over Jordan into the land of Canaan:

Then ye shall drive out all the inhabitants of the land from before you, and destroy all their pictures, and destroy all their molten images, and quite pluck down all their high places.

And ye shall dispossess the inhabitants of the land, and dwell therein, for I have given you the land to possess it. (Numbers 33.50–53)

Perhaps we can learn to do without such a God. Then we can dare to envision a world where no part of humanity will again have to slave in Egypt's shadow.

Notes

Introduction

1. Cf. Exodus 12:14: "You shall keep this day as a day of remembrance, and make it a pilgrim-feast, a festival of the Lord; you shall keep it generation after generation as a rule for all time."

2. Cf. Amos 3:2: "You only have I chosen among all the families of the earth."

3. Qtd. in Pluchon 24: "Tous les hommes, en sortant des mains de la nature naissent libres." Translation mine.

4. "[Le sieur Mendès] reproche à tous les Nègres d'être fourbes et menteurs. Les malheureux, qu'il poursuit pourraient faire le même reproche à la Nation juive, et le parallèle ne lui serait peut-être pas favorable." Translation mine.

5. "On entend un véritable réquisitoire contre les Juifs, individus inhumains et barbares, ennemis de la vraie religion; on lit une dissertation philosophique sur le caractère contre nature de la servitude, et sur la bonté morale des Noirs." Translation mine.

6. "How is it," Samuel Johnson wrote, "that we hear the loudest yelps for liberty among the drivers of Negroes?" (454).

Chapter 1

1. Cf. Sloan 318: "Buffon places the probable origin of 'le premier peuple digne de porter ce nom' in central Asia, with the rise of China as the presumed first great civilization. . . . With Buffon in the *Epoques* presuming a gradual historical progression in response to the gradual cooling of the earth . . . the southward shift of optimal conditions of temperature are, by implication, the cause of the technological, intellectual, and cultural achievements and the presumed superiority of the European peoples."

2. Sephardic Jews had come to Western Europe via North Africa, Spain, and Portugal.

228

They benefitted from years of tolerance under Muslim rule. Ashkenazi Jews, by contrast, had been inhabitants of Eastern and Central Europe for centuries. They had often suffered at the hands of ignorant and rapacious Christians.

3. In his original draft, Jefferson included the slave trade in his list of indictments against George III ("He has waged cruel war against human nature itself, violating its most sacred rights of life and liberty in the persons of a distant people who never offended him"), but the Southern delegates to the Continental Congress refused to sign until the clause was excised.

4. Cf. David Brion Davis, *The Problem of Slavery in Western Culture* (348–49) for his theory on the origin of "a new ethic of benevolence" in the English-speaking world.

5. Cf. Poliakov, *History of Anti-Semitism* 166: "In the second half of the eighteenth century, most fashionable German dramatists—Iffland, Kotzebue, the two Stephanies—were putting 'good Jews' on the stage, while translators of many foreign plays were inserting them, in order to adapt the original version to contemporary taste."

6. Cf. Seeber 173–80.

7. Jews were seen as tremendously procreative, which explained in part the attempts by the various polities in which they had settled to control their increase. Physiocrats argued that the more people there were to work the land, the richer the state. The logic of physiocratic thinking was that Jews should be permitted to multiply at will but that their economic activity should be redirected toward manufacturing and agriculture.

8. Forty years earlier, however, the relation between Parliament and the populace in terms of progressive ideology was reversed. In 1753 Parliament passed a Naturalization Bill to simplify procedures for the naturalization of the Jews and to permit them to acquire land. Dubbed by pamphleteers as the Jew Bill, this legislation, which had passed both houses of Parliament without difficulty, triggered an explosion of popular protest that included but was not limited to petitions from all sections of the population, church sermons, and pamphlets predicting a Jewish takeover of the country. Six months after its publication, the government had to repeal the unpopular law. At that time, Britain's Jewish population was numerically insignificant. Cf. Poliakov, *History of Anti-Semitism*, 36: "The furious and ephemeral anti-Jewish explosion of 1753 . . . proved that medieval hatreds and terrors persisted in the hearts of the English population."

9. It also provided for the expulsion of all Jews from the colonies, forbade Protestants from public worship, and barred non-Catholics from any post of police command or plantation manager.

10. Montesquieu writes in his ironic defense of slavery, "It is impossible to assume that these people are men because if we assumed they were men one would begin to believe that we ourselves were not Christians" (250).

11. *Cursory Remarks upon the Reverend Mr. Ramsay's Essay on the Treatment and Conversion of African Slaves in the Sugar Colonies* (1785).

12. *Apology for Negro Slavery: The West-India Planters Vindicated from the Charge of Inhumanity* (1786).

13. François Hell, *Observations d'un alsacien sur l'affaire présente des Juifs d'Alsace* (1779).

14. Napoleon's representative to the Assembly, Count Molé, opened the Assembly with these words: "It is His Majesty's wish that you become Frenchmen, and it is for you to decide whether you accept this title or to reflect that you renounce it if you do not make yourself worthy of it" (qtd. in Mahler 64).

Chapter 2

1. Of the five workingmen killed in the Boston Massacre of 1770, one was a journeyman, one was an apprentice, one was a ropewalker, and two were sailors, including a half-black, half-Indian runaway slave from the Bahamas by the name of Crispus Attucks.

2. Moses Hadas edited a severely abridged version of the 1888 translation in 1967, called *Solomon Maimon, An Autobiography* (New York: Schocken Books, 1947), but this too is a rare find.

3. These are (1) Thomas Bluett, *Some Memoirs of the Life of Job, the Son of Solomon the High Priest of Boonda in Africa; Who was a Slave about Two Years in Maryland; and afterwards being brought to England, was set free and sent to his native land in the year 1734;* (2) *The Declaration and Confession of Jeffrey, A Negro, who was executed at Worchester, October 17, 1745, for the murder of Mrs. Tabitha Sanford, at Mendon, the 12th of September Preceeding;* and (3) *The Life and Dying Speech of Arthur, A Negro Man, Who was executed at Worchester, October 20, 1768 for a rape committed on the Body of one Deborah Metcalf.*

4. Cf. Potkay and Burr 128.

5. A cunning critic could make deconstructionist hay with the *Paradise Lost* quotes, in which the lot of the West Indian slaves is underscored by a passage describing the fallen angels in hell and a quote of defiance from Satan himself—a curious choice for a devout Christian.

6. One of John Marrant's sermons, delivered in Boston, was printed and sold in 1789. Since there is, again, a disparity between the "rough English" of Marrant's unedited *Journal* and the polished sentences of the pamphlet, scholars speculate that Prince Hall, Boston founder of Black Masonry, edited the sermon before its publication. Cf. Potkay and Burr 74.

7. However, Mahler makes clear that Mendelssohn's objections to the language were more political than aesthetic. Cf. Mahler 162: "The motive of social prestige was all the more emphasized by the fact that, like many other of his enlightened contemporaries, Mendelssohn continued to conduct his personal correspondence with intimate friends and family in Yiddish." Within a few decades, however, Yiddish actually died out in German Jewry apart from isolated expressions and phrases.

8. Zinberg 30. In fact, a *maskil* from Metz, Isaiah Berr Bing, published a Hebrew translation of the work in Berlin in 1786.

9. The Calvinist pastor Basnage published his *Histoire des Juifs, depuis Jésus Christ jusqu'à présent* (1706) in Holland, the first work ever produced that tried to apply the rules of historical criticism to the subject. In the introduction to the second edition, Basnage related with pride that the Jews themselves accepted his work because he had been an impartial historian. The book caused a sensation throughout scholarly Europe.

10. Quoted in Zinberg 30.

11. As a matter of historical record, Equiano could not have seen Whitefield when and where he said he did because the preacher was in England at that time. He probably heard him during one of his trips to Savannah, Georgia, where the minister had founded an orphanage.

12. Cf. Richardson 10: "Despite Whitefield's personal popularity as a preacher, his theological views did not endure in Methodism. His separation from the Wesleys meant that he played little if any part in the subsequent development of Methodism. . . . Whitefield was a great preacher, but he left little or nothing in the way of an organized movement."

13. Cf. *Equiano's Travels: His Autobiography*. This abridgment in the highly influential African Writers Series has become the mostly widely known version of the *Narrative* in Africa and Great Britain.

Chapter 3

1. Fishberg's use of the term "environment" refers to nurture rather than nature. Confusing though it may be, it is reflective of the shift in twentieth-century scientific thinking away from the latter to the eventual triumph of the former as the predominant component of human development.

2. The detail about the assimilated Jew losing his soul is particularly prescient and unexpected, given Park's assimilationist beliefs. By contrast, as we shall see, Park doesn't appear to believe that Blacks have a soul worth saving.

3. It was Wirth who brought the influence of the Chicago School of sociology to bear in Wright's writings. Wirth's wife, Mary, met Richard as a caseworker for the Wright family in 1933 and helped him obtain work during the Depression. Wright heard Wirth lecture at the John Reed Club, and later, as Wright was doing the research for *Twelve Million Black Voices*, he asked Wirth to provide him with a program of reading in sociology. Wright was also friends with Horace R. Cayton, Wirth's Black research associate. When Cayton and another Black Chicago sociologist, St. Clair Drake, published their massive study of Chicago's South Side, *Black Metropolis* (1945), Wright provided the introduction, in which he wrote, "it was from [the] scientific facts [of men like the late Robert E. Park, Robert Redfield, and Louis Wirth] that I absorbed some of the quota of inspiration necessary for me to write *Uncle Tom's Children* and *Black Boy*" ("Introduction," xvii–xviii).

4. Published in a climate of opinion that saw eventual assimilation into an American mainstream as the inevitable and worthiest goal for all minorities, Herskovits's book did not gain significant attention or influence until its republication in 1958.

5. The *Protocols* first appeared in 1905 as part of a book, printed by the government press, by a Russian mystic, who presented them as extracts of the 1897 World Zionist Congress. Exposure of the hoax came in 1921 when a *London Times* correspondent noticed that almost half of the *Protocols* was a direct plagiarism of a satire on Napoleon III by a French lawyer named Maurice Joly. This, of course, did not deter the anti-Semites, who published the *Protocols* in every European language for decades thereafter. They still circulate in Arabic translation today.

6. Cf. Feingold III: "So attuned was the Reconstructionist approach to the needs of secularizing Jews that one can say most American Jews were Reconstructionists without knowing it."

Chapter 4

1. "Le communism est comme la pointe de la flamme républicaine et le prodigieuse température révolutionnaire de la France mûrit, avant l'heure, le prolétariat européen." Translation mine.

2. Cf. Klehr II: "The Comintern had defined the first period as one of revolutionary upsurge and the Second Period—from 1923 to 1928—as an era of capitalist stabilization."

3. Although, as William Maxwell shows in *New Negro, Old Left* (1999), the position of Black intellectuals on the left was more complex than has sometimes been thought, Blacks remained generally unimpressed with Communist propaganda.

4. In his 1942 evaluation of Wright's novel, Alfred Kazin characterized this analysis as "crude Stalinist homilies" (*On Native Grounds*, 301).

5. Other historians of the period (Alexander Bloom, for example) have either accepted this Jewish definition of the group or have used the term to include the non-Jewish participants

as well. I have followed the more inclusive example of Alan Wald, who makes the point that "upwardly mobile Jews comprised a disproportionate number of intellectuals involved in all radical movements in New York in the 1930s" (Wald 9).

6. Rosenfeld's wife was Kazin's secretary at *The New Republic*. Rosenfeld had grown up in Chicago along with Bellow, and it was through Rosenfeld that Kazin made the latter's acquaintance.

7. The indeterminacy of Equiano's "nationality" has allowed his autobiography to be claimed by African-American literature, Afro-British literature, and African literature. Maimon has been described in written commentaries as a Polish Jew, a Lithuanian Jew, and even a Russian Jew.

8. One need only look at the history of Israel and Rwanda to see how problematic the "triumph" of nationalism has turned out to be for Blacks and Jews.

9. "The last time I saw our kitchen this clearly was one afternoon in London at the end of the war, when I waited out the rain in the entrance to a music store" (Kazin, *Walker in the City*, 51).

10. It is almost shocking that Howe should write of a Polish pogrom three years after the end of the Holocaust when he wishes to cite an example of European barbarism toward the Jews. In his "intellectual autobiography," Howe writes: "By 1946 it was impossible not to know, and sensitive people often fell into a shared numbness, a blockage of response, as if to put aside the anguish that was lying in wait." Cf. *A Margin of Hope*, 249.

11. It took a *goyische* critic, Edmund Wilson, to propose that Agnon receive the prize.

12. Black street culture retained some nationalist strains, but from the 1930s, when the Communist Party assumed a position of leadership, to the 1960s with the advent of the Black Arts Movement, Black nationalism was a decidedly secondary theme among African-American writers and intellectuals.

13. "In the United States, we fight for a real application of the Constitution, which is not the case in African nations. We fight to become part of a civilization we accept. We do not oppose the West: we want the effective application of Western principles of freedom" (Wright, "Interview," 201–2).

14. "The great dichotomy, the underlying ideological schism that dominates the Negro social outlook in America, is that of integrationism vs. all trends that reflect nationalism, separatism or ethnic group identity. Negro integrationists become pro-Marxist Communist, and Negro Marxist-Communists become pro-integrationist because for Negro Integrationists, Marxism lends a radical flavor to integrationism which in itself is not revolutionary in essence" (Cruse, *Crisis of the Negro Intellectual*, 263).

15. When Hansberry's play, *The Sign in Sidney Brustein's Window*, opened in 1964, she denied in an interview with *The New York Times* that *Raisin in the Sun* was ever a Negro play. "Some persons ask how it is that I have 'left the Negro question' in the writing of this latest play. I hardly know how to answer as it seems to me that I have never written about 'the Negro question.' *A Raisin in the Sun*, for instance, was a play about an American family's conflict with certain of the mercenary values of its society, and its characters were Negroes" (qtd. in Cruse 282-283).

16. Both Ralph Ellison and Robert Stepto propose readings of the above passage that mitigate its harshness.

17. Robert Stepto, in an Oedipal move, suggests that the passage in *Black Boy* quoted above "can be easily read as yet another strident attempt by Wright's persona to condemn and obliterate the haunting image of his father" (*From Behind the Veil*, 158).

18. Wright echoes Lukacs's distinction between critical and naturalistic realism when he criticizes the writing of the Harlem Renaissance for not portraying African-American life with an awareness of "the concepts that move and direct the forces of history today" ("Blueprint," 321).

19. In an article on Paul Goodman, Taylor Stoehr accuses Kazin of "fondling his memories of life in Brownsville like an old roué" (72).

20. Cf. Kazin, "The Self as History: Reflections on Autobiography," 31–32: "What I have tried to write in *A Walker in the City, Starting Out in the Thirties, New York Jew*, is personal history, a form of my own influenced by the personal writings of Emerson, Thoreau, Whitman."

21. Cf. Silvers,"Alfred Kazin: The Critic as Creator": "What was astonishing to me [when *On Native Grounds* came out in 1942] was the sense I got from the reviewers that, working quite by myself, I had done a cultural history of an age that was passing. For by that time we were well into the war and had seen the Soviet-Nazi alliance come and go, and it was just beginning to be clear that the leftist idealism of the book, and its grand historical design, expressed the confidence of a period that had ended. Now it has become altogether clear" (99).

22. In the Poland reconstituted after World War I by the Treaty of Versailles, where three and a half million Jews still lived, Poles looked on unassimilated Jews as strangers and proceeded to squeeze them out of the national economy. During the war with Russia in 1919, 30,000 Jews were reported killed by Polish armies, and sporadic assaults continued even after the peace. When General Pilsudski came to power in 1926, overt anti-Semitic violence ended, but the policy of impoverishment called the "cold pogrom" rendered tens of thousands of Polish Jews destitute.

Chapter 5

1. "Ballade des dames du temps jadis."

2. In fact, Hughes exhibits a precocious sense of a Black literary tradition in his autobiography, *The Big Sea* (1940), where he states that he wrote his early poems after the manner of Carl Sandburg and Paul Laurence Dunbar. Later on, when his materialistic father challenged him to name a "colored" author who made money from his writing, Hughes replied, "Alexander Dumas."

3. *Partisan Review* published "Everybody's Protest Novel" in June 1949 and "Many Thousands Gone" in the November-December issue of 1951. Both essays were reprinted in *Notes of a Native Son*.

4. In my investigation of Jewish-American autobiography, I was struck by the paucity of critical material. Whereas African-American autobiography staggers under the weight of countless articles and book-length studies, I have uncovered only three articles to date that discuss in a theoretical manner American-Jewish autobiography as a genre.

5. Literary historian Louis Harap does refer to the 1950s as the "Jewish Decade" (21–51). On the other hand, Robert Alter is quick to debunk the idea of a "so-called renaissance of American Jewish literature" (*After the Tradition*, 35–45).

6. Allen Guttman states categorically that "West, Miller, and Salinger are nominally Jews, but they are in no important sense Jewish writers" (*The Jewish Writer in America*, 13). Two years earlier, a study of Jewish-American novelists, *Radical Sophistication* by Max Schultz, contained full chapters devoted to the writings of West and Salinger.

7. Postmodernism, of course, has successfully supplanted "modern" as the temporal marker for contemporary discourse. Even "modern" has come to seem quaint.

8. Cf. "Modern" in Raymond Williams, *Keywords: A Vocabulary of Culture and Society*, 174: "A conventional contrast between ancient and modern was established in the Renaissance; a middle or medieval period was not fully defined until [the seventeenth century]."

Chapter 6

1. According to a compilation of Gallup Poll statistics, while only 19 percent of African Americans favored the term "Black" in 1969, that figure grew to nearly 66 percent three years later (Kilson 246).

2. Julius Lester wrote of the latter change in nomenclature, "Even the redefining of ourselves as 'black' places us closer to those people called white, because we, too, now claim race as identity" (*Lovesong*, 45).

3. Cf. *Dusk of Dawn*, 303: "I think I may say without boasting that in the period from 1910 to 1930 I was a main factor in revolutionizing the attitude of the American Negro toward caste. My stinging hammer blows made Negroes aware of themselves, confident of their possibilities and determined in self-assertion. So much so that today common slogans among the Negro people are taken bodily from the words of my mouth."

4. A comparison of this remark to Lacy's *négritude* passage quoted above brings out an interesting contrast between Jewish and Black cultural literacy. While the Westernized Black has created a diasporic Black culture that is essentially a child of the modern age, the Jewish diaspora has been kept alive by traditionalists.

5. At this point, Lester wrote his first autobiography, *All Is Well* (1976), in which one finds no trace of any incipient Jewish identity.

6. In Exodus 19, Yahweh tells Moses on Mount Sinai, "Ye have seen what I did unto Egyptians, and how I bare you on eagles' wings, and brought you unto myself. Now therefore, if ye will obey my voice indeed, and keep my covenant, then ye shall be a peculiar treasure unto me above all people: for all the earth is mine" (Exodus 19:4–6).

7. Delaney's comment on an early science fiction classic, *Starship Troopers* by Robert Heinlein, is revealing in this context. Cf. *The Jewel-Hinged Jaw*, 94: "Heinlein, in the midst of a strophe on male make-up, generates the data that the first person narrator, with whom we have been traveling now through two hundred and fifty-odd pages (of a three-hundred-and-fifty page book) is non-caucasian. . . . What remains with me, nearly ten years after my first reading of the book, is the knowledge that I have experienced a world in which the placement of the information about the narrator's face is proof that in such a world much of the race problems had, at least, dissolved."

Works Cited

Acholonu, Catherine Obioanufu. *The Igbo Roots of Olaudah Equiano: An Anthropological Research*. Owerri, Nigeria: Afa Publications, 1989.

Adams, Francis D., and Barry Sanders. "Introduction." In *Three Black Writers in Eighteenth Century England*, 1–16. Belmont, Calif.: Wadsworth Publishing Co., 1971.

Allison, Robert J. "Introduction." In *The Interesting Narrative of the Life of Olaudah Equiano Written by Himself*, 1–26. The Bedford Series in History and Culture. Boston and New York: St. Martin's Press, 1995.

Alter, Robert. *After the Tradition: Essays on Modern Jewish Writing*. New York: E. P. Dutton, 1969.

———. "The Education of Alfred Kazin." *Commentary* 65, no. 6 (June 1978): 44–51.

Altmann, Alexander. *Moses Mendelssohn: A Biographical Study*. University: The University of Alabama Press, 1973.

Andrews, William L. *To Tell a Free Story: The First Century of Afro-American Autobiography, 1760–1865*. Chicago: University of Illinois Press, 1986.

Anstey, Roger. *The Atlantic Slave Trade and British Abolition, 1760–1810*. London: Macmillan, 1975.

Antin, Mary. *The Promised Land*. 1911. New York: Arno Press, 1980.

Arendt, Hannah. *Rahel Varnhagen, The Life of a Jewish Woman*. Trans. Richard and Clara Winston. 1957. Baltimore and London: The Johns Hopkins University Press, 1997.

Atlas, Samuel. *From Critical to Speculative Idealism: The Philosophy of Solomon Maimon*. The Hague: Martinus Nijhoff, 1964.

Augustine, Saint, Bishop of Hippo. *Confessions*. Trans. Rex Warner. New York: New American Library, 1963.

Bacall, Lauren. *By Myself*. New York: Ballantine Books, 1978.

Bach, H. I. *The German Jew: A Synthesis of Judaism and Western Civilization, 1730–1930*. London: Oxford University Press, 1984.

Baeck, Leo. *This People Israel: The Meaning of Jewish Existence.* Trans. Albert H. Friedlander. New York: Holt, Rinehart and Winston, 1955.

Baldwin, James. *Notes of a Native Son.* Boston: Beacon Press, 1955.

———. "Princes and Powers." 1957. In *Collected Essays,* 143–69. New York: Literary Classics of the United States, 1998.

Barker, Anthony J. *The African Link: British Attitudes to the Negro in the Era of the Atlantic Slave Trade, 1550–1807.* London: Frank Cass, 1978.

Barthes, Roland. "Myth Today." In *A Barthes Reader,* ed. Susan Sontag, 93–149. New York: Hill and Wang, 1982.

Beiser, Frederick C. *The Fate of Reason: German Philosophy from Kant to Fichte.* Cambridge: Harvard University Press, 1987.

Bell, Daniel. "Reflections on Jewish Identity." In *The Ghetto and Beyond,* ed. Peter I. Rose, 465–76. New York: Random House, 1969.

Benedict, Ruth, and Gene Weltfish. *The Races of Mankind.* New York: Public Affairs Committee, Inc., 1943.

Bennet, Lerone Jr. *Before the Mayflower: A History of Black America.* 1961. New York: Penguin Books, 1988.

Berman, Paul. "The Other and the Almost the Same." In *Blacks and Jews: Alliances and Arguments,* 1–28. New York: Dell, 1994.

Bloom, Alexander. *Prodigal Sons: The New York Intellectuals and Their World.* New York: Oxford University Press, 1986.

Blumenbach, Johann. *Decas collectionis suae cranorum diversarum gentium illustrata.* Göttingen: I. C. Dietrich, 1790–1820.

Blyden, E. W. *Christianity, Islam and the Negro Race.* 1887. Edinburgh: Edinburgh University Press, 1967.

Bone, Robert. *The Negro Novel in America.* New Haven, Conn.: Yale University Press, 1958.

Bontemps, Arna. "The Slave Narrative: An American Genre." In *Great Slave Narratives,* vii–xix. Boston: Beacon Press, 1969.

Boyarin, Daniel, and Jonathan Boyarin. "Diaspora: Generation and the Ground of Jewish Identity." *Critical Inquiry* 19 (1993): 693–725.

Brawley, Benjamin. "Every Race Has a Peculiar Genius." In *Black Nationalism in America,* ed. John H. Bracey Jr. et al., 327–31. New York: Bobbs-Merrill, 1970.

Brown, Claude. *Manchild in the Promised Land.* New York: The Macmillan Company, 1965.

Buhle, Paul. *Marxism in the United States: Remapping the History of the American Left.* London: Verso, 1987.

Cahan, Abraham. *The Education of Abraham Cahan.* Trans. Leon Stein et al. Philadelphia: The Jewish Publication Society of America, 1969.

Cappetti, Carla. *Writing Chicago: Modernism, Ethnography, and the Novel.* New York: Columbia University Press, 1993.

Carson, Clayborne. "Black-Jewish Universalism in the Era of Identity Politics." In *Struggles in the Promised Land: Toward a History of Black-Jewish Relations in the United States,* ed. Jack Salzman and Cornel West, 177–93. New York and Oxford: Oxford University Press, 1997.

———. "Blacks and Jews in the Civil Rights Movement: The Case of SNCC." In *Bridges and Boundaries: African Americans and American Jews,* ed. Jack Salzman et al., 36–49. New York: The Jewish Museum, 1992.

Cassirer, Ernst. *The Philosophy of the Enlightenment.* Trans. Fritz Koelln and James Pettegrove. 1932. Boston: Beacon Press, 1961.

Chesnutt, Charles W. *The Marrow of Tradition*. 1901. Ann Arbor: University of Michigan Press, 1969.

Chinosole. "Tryin' to Get Over: Narrative Posture in Equiano's Autobiography." In *The Art of Slave Narrative: Original Essays in Criticism and Theory*, ed. John Sekora and Darwin T. Turner, 45–54. Macomb, IL: Western Illinois University Press, 1982.

Chyet, Stanley F. "The Political Rights of the Jews in the United States: 1776–1840." In *Critical Studies in American Jewish History*, vol. 2, 27–88. New York: Ktav, 1971.

Clark, Kenneth B., "Candor About Negro-Jewish Relations." In *Bridges and Boundaries: African Americans and American Jews*, ed. Jack Salzman et al., 91–98. New York: The Jewish Museum, 1992.

Cleaver, Eldridge. *Soul on Ice*. New York: Dell, 1968.

Clifford, James. *Routes: Travels and Translations in the Late Twentieth Century*. Cambridge: Harvard University Press, 1993.

Cobb, Martha K. "The Slave Narrative and the Black Literary Tradition." In *The Art of Slave Narrative: Original Essays in Criticism and Theory*, ed. John Sekora and Darwin T. Turner, 36–44. Chicago: Western Illinois University Press, 1982.

Committee on Civil Rights. "A Program of Action: The Committee's Recommendations." In *Civil Rights and African Americans: A Documentary History*, ed. Albert P. Blaustein and Robert L. Zangrando. Evanston, Ill.: Northwestern University Press, 1991.

Coon, Carleton Stevens. "Have the Jews a Racial Identity?" In *Jews in a Gentile World*, ed. Isacque Graeber and Steuart Henderson Britt, 20–37. New York: Macmillan, 1942.

Cooney, Terry A. *The Rise of the New York Intellectuals: Partisan Review and Its Circle*. Madison: The University of Wisconsin Press, 1986.

Cortés, Carlos E. et al. *Three Perspectives on Ethnicity in America: Blacks Chicanos, and Native Americans*. New York: G. P. Putnam's Sons, 1976.

Costanzo, Angelo. *Surprizing Narrative: Olaudah Equiano and the Beginnings of Black Autobiography*. New York: Greenwood Press, 1987.

Cowan, Paul. *An Orphan in History: Retrieving a Jewish Legacy*. Garden City, N.Y.: Doubleday, 1982.

Cox, Oliver. *Caste, Class and Race: A Study in Social Dynamics*. 1948. New York: Monthly Review Press, 1959.

Cruse, Harold. *The Crisis of the Negro Intellectual*. 1967. New York: Quill, 1984.

Cuddihy, John Murray. *The Ordeal of Civility: Freud, Marx, Lévi- Strauss, and the Jewish Struggle with Modernity*. New York: Basic Books, 1974

Cugoano, Ottobah. *Thoughts and Sentiments on the Evil and Wicked Traffic of the Slavery and Commerce of the Human Species by Ottobah Cugoano, A Native of Africa*. 1787. Ed. Paul Edwards. London: Dawsons, 1969.

Daiches, David. "Brownsville Idyll." Rev. of *A Walker in the City* by Alfred Kazin. *Commentary* 11 (1952): 604–5.

Daiches, Salid. "Solomon Maimon and His Relation to Judaism." *The Jewish Review* 5, no. 26 (1914): 142–72.

Davis, David Brion. *The Problem of Slavery in Western Culture*. Ithaca, N.Y.: Cornell University Press, 1966.

Day, Thomas. *The Dying Negro, A Poetical Epistle from a Black, Who shot himself on board a vessel in the river Thames; to his intended Wife*. Holborn: W. Flexney, 1774.

Delaney, Samuel *The Motion of Light in Water*. New York: New American Library, 1988.

———. *The Jewel-Hinged Jaw*. Elizabethtown, N.Y.: Dragon Press, 1977.

Delany, Paul. *British Autobiography in the Seventeenth Century.* London: Routledge & Kegan Paul, 1969.

Dickstein, Morris. *Gates of Eden: American Culture in the Sixties.* New York: Basic Books, 1977.

Dorsey, Peter A. *Sacred Estrangement: The Rhetoric of Conversion in Modern American Autobiography.* University Park: The Pennsylvania State University Press, 1993.

Douglass, Frederick. *Narrative of the Life of Frederick Douglass.* 1848. In *The Classic Slave Narratives,* ed. Henry Louis Gates Jr., 243–331. New York: New American Library, 1987.

Drescher, Seymour. *Capitalism and Antislavery: British Mobilization in Comparative Perspective.* Oxford: Oxford University Press, 1987.

Dubnow, S. M. *History of the Jews in Russia and Poland from the Earliest Times Until the Present Day.* Vol. 2. Trans. I. Friedlander. Philadelphia: The Jewish Publication Society of America, 1918.

Du Bois, W. E. B. *Dusk of Dawn.* 1940. New York: Schocken Books, 1968.

———. "On the Conservation of Races." In *Black Nationalism in America,* ed. John H. Bracey Jr. et al., 250–62. New York: Bobbs-Merrill, 1970.

———. *The Souls of Black Folk.* 1903. In *Three Negro Classics,* ed. and introduced by John Hope Franklin, 206–389. New York: Avon Books, 1965.

Edwards, Paul. Introduction. In Olaudah Equiano, *The Interesting Narrative of Olaudah Equiano or Gustavus Vassa, the African,* v–lxxxi. London: Dawsons of Pall Mall, 1969.

Edwards, Paul, and David Dabydeen. Introduction. In *Black Writers in Britain: 1760–1890,* ed. Paul Edwards and David Dabydeen, ix–xv. Edinburgh: Edinburgh University Press, 1991.

Edwards, Paul, and James Walvin. *Black Personalities in the Era of the Slave Trade.* Baton Rouge: Lousiana State University Press, 1983.

Eisen, Arnold M. *Galut: Modern Jewish Reflection of Homelessness and Homecoming.* Bloomington: Indiana University Press, 1986.

Eisenstein-Barzilay, Isaac. "The Treatment of the Jewish Religion in the Literature of the Berlin Haskalah." *Proceedings of the America Academy for Jewish Research* 24 (1955): 39–68.

Eliot, T. S. *The Sacred Wood: Essays on Poetry and Criticism.* 1920. London: Methuen & Co., 1953.

Ellison, Ralph. *Going to the Territory.* New York: Random House, 1986.

———. *Invisible Man.* New York: Random House, 1952.

———. *Shadow and Act.* New York: Random House, 1964.

Equiano, Olaudah. *The Interesting Narrative of the Life of Olaudah Equiano or Gustavus Vassa, the African.* 1789. In *The Classic Slave Narratives,* ed. Henry Louis Gates Jr., 1–182. New York: New American Library, 1987.

Eze, Emmanuel C., ed. *Race and the Enlightenment, A Reader.* Cambridge, Mass.: Blackwell Publishers, 1997.

Fabre, Michel. Introduction. In *Richard Wright Reader,* ed. Ellen Wright and Michel Fabre, vii–xx. New York: Harper & Row, 1978.

———. *The Unfinished Quest of Richard Wright.* Trans. Isabel Barzun. New York: William Morrow & Co., 1973.

Feierberg, M. Z. *Whither? and Other Stories.* Trans. Hillel Halkin. Philadelphia: The Jewish Publication Society of America, 1973.

Feingold, Henry L. *A Time for Searching: Entering the Mainstream, 1920–1945.* The Jewish People in America, vol. 6. Baltimore: The Johns Hopkins University Press, 1992.

Fiedler, Leslie. "The City and the Writer." Rev. of *A Walker in the City* by Alfred Kazin. *Partisan Review* 19, no. 2 (1952): 238–41.

———. "What Can We Do about Fagin?" *Commentary* 7 (1949): 411–18.

Fishberg, Maurice. *The Jews: A Study of Race and Environment*. New York: Charles Scribner's Sons, 1911.

Fox, Robert Elliot. *Masters of the Drum: Black Lit/oratures Across the Continuum*. Westport, Conn.: Greenwood Press, 1995.

Franklin, John Hope. *From Slavery to Freedom: A History of Negro Americans*. 1947. New York: McGraw-Hill, 1988.

Frazier, E. Franklin. *The Negro Family in the United States*. 1939. Chicago: University of Chicago Press, 1966.

Fryer, Peter. *Staying Power: The History of Black People in Britain*. London: Pluto Press, 1984.

"Galut." *Encyclopaedia Judaica*, 1971 edition.

Gans, Herbert J. "Symbolic Ethnicity: The Future of Ethnic Groups and Cultures in America." *Ethnic and Racial Studies* 2, no. 1 (1979): 1–20.

Gates, Henry Louis Jr. *The Signifying Monkey: A Theory of Afro-American Literary Criticism*. New York: Oxford University Press, 1988.

Gayle, Addison Jr. *Richard Wright: Ordeal of a Native Son*. New York: Doubleday, 1980.

———. ed. *The Black Aesthetic*. New York: Doubleday, 1971.

Gibson, Donald B. "Richard Wright: Aspects of His Afro-American Literary Relations." In *Critical Essays on Richard Wright*, ed. Yoshinobu Hakutani, 82–90. Boston: G. K. Hall, 1982.

Gill, Brendan. Rev. of *A Walker in the City*, by Alfred Kazin. *The New Yorker*, 17 November 1951, 180.

Gilroy, Paul. *The Black Atlantic: Modernity and Double Consciousness*. Cambridge: Harvard University Press, 1993.

Gordon, Milton M. *Assimilation in American Life: The Role of Race, Religion and National Origins*. New York: Oxford University Press, 1964.

Gossett, Thomas F. *Race; The History of an Idea in America*. Dallas, Texas: Southern Methodist University Press, 1963.

Graetz, Heinrich. *History of the Jews*, vol. 5. 1895. Philadelphia: The Jewish Publication Society of America, 1949.

Granit, Arthur. *The Time of the Peaches*. New York: Abelard- Schuman, 1959.

Grant, Madison. Introduction. In Lothrop Stoddard, *The Rising Tide of Color*. New York: Charles Scribner's Sons, 1920.

Gronniosaw, Ukawsaw. *The Black Prince; being a narrative of the most remarkable occurrences and strange vicissitudes exhibited in the life and experience of James Albert Ukasaw Gronniosaw, an African prince, as was related by himself*. Ed. Hannah More. 1770. Salem, N.Y.: Dodd & Ramsey, 1809.

———. *A Narrative of the Most Remarkable Particulars in the Life of James Albert Ukawsaw Gronniosaw, An African Prince, Written by Himself*. In *Black Atlantic Writers of the 18th Century: Living the New Exodus in England and the Americas*, ed. Adam Potkay and Sandra Burr, 23–63. New York: St. Martin's Press, 1995.

Guttman, Allen. *The Jewish Writer in America: Assimilation and the Crisis of Identity*. New York: Oxford University Press, 1971.

Haley, Alex. *The Autobiography of Malcolm X*. London: Penguin Books, 1965.

Hammon, Briton. 1760. *A Narrative of the Uncommon Sufferings and Surprizing Deliverance of Briton Hammon, a Negro Man, Servant to General Winslow of Marshfield, in New England*. 1760. Fairfield, Wash.: Ye Galleon Press, 1994.

Harap, Louis. *In the Mainstream: The Jewish Presence in Twentieth Century American Literature, 1950s-1980s*. New York: Greenwood Press, 1987.

Hazard, Paul. *European Thought in the Eighteenth Century: From Montesquieu to Lessing.* Trans. J. Lewis May. London: Hollis & Carter, 1954.

Hecht, Ben. *A Child of the Century.* New York: Simon and Schuster, 1954.

Hempton, David. *Methodism and Politics in British Society, 1750–1850.* Stanford, Calif.: Stanford University Press, 1984.

Hertzberg, Arthur. *The French Enlightenment and the Jews.* New York: Columbia University Press, 1968.

Higham, John. *Send These To Me: Immigrants in Urban America.* Baltimore: The Johns Hopkins University Press, 1975.

Horkheimer, Max, and Theodor Adorno. *The Dialectic of Enlightenment.* Trans. John Comming. 1947. New York: Herder and Herder, 1972.

Howe, Irving. "Black Boys and Native Sons." In *Critical Essays on Richard Wright,* ed. Yoshinabu Hakutani, 39–47. Boston: G. K. Hall, 1982.

———. "The New York Intellectuals." In *The Decline of the New,* 211–265. New York: Harcourt, Brace & World, 1970.

———. "The Lost Young Intellectual." *Commentary* 2, no. 4 (1946): 361–67.

———. *A Margin of Hope: An Intellectual Autobiography.* New York: Harcourt, Brace, Jovanovich, 1982.

———. *A World More Attractive: A View of Modern Literature and Politics.* New York: Horizon Press, 1963.

———. *World of Our Fathers.* New York: Simon & Schuster, 1976.

Hughes, Langston. *The Big Sea.* 1940. New York: Hill and Wang, 1993.

———. "The Negro Artist and the Racial Mountain." In *The Black Aesthetic,* ed. Addison Gayle Jr., 175–81. New York: Doubleday, 1971.

Huxley, Julian, and A. C. Haddon. *We Europeans: A Survey of "Racial" Problems.* London: Harper & Brothers, 1936.

Jacobs, Melville. "Jewish Blood and Culture." In *Jews in a Gentile World,* ed. Isacque Graeber and Steuart Henderson Britt, 38–55. New York: Macmillan, 1942.

James, C. L. R. *The Black Jacobins: Toussaint L'Ouverture and the San Domingo Revolution.* 1938. London: Allison & Busby, 1980.

JanMohamed, Abdul R., and David Lloyd. "Toward a Theory of Minority Discourse: What Is To Be Done?" In *The Nature and Context of Minority Discourse,* ed. Abdul JanMohamed and David Lloyd, 1–16. Oxford: Oxford University Press, 1990.

Jemie, Onwuchekwa. "Hughes' Black Esthetic." In *Critical Essays on Langston Hughes,* ed. Edward J. Mullen, 95–120. Boston: G. K. Hall, 1986.

"The Jewish Writer and the English Literary Tradition: A Symposium, Part II." *Commentary* 8 (October 1949): 361–70.

Johnson, Samuel. *Taxation No Tyranny.* 1775. In *The Yale Edition of the Works of Samuel Johnson.* Vol. 10, *Political Writings.* Ed. Donald J. Greene, 411–54. New Haven, Conn.: Yale University Press, 1977.

Jones, LeRoi. *Black Magic: Collected Poetry, 1961–1967.* New York: Bobbs-Merrill, 1969.

Jordan, Winthrop D. *White Over Black: American Attitudes towards the Negro, 1550–1812.* 1968. Baltimore: Penguin Books, 1969.

Juares, Jean. *La Constituante.* Vol. 1 of *Histoire socialiste de la revolution française.* Paris: Editions sociales, 1968.

Jurt, Joseph. "Condorcet: l'idée de progrès et l'opposition à l'esclavage." In *Condorcet: mathé-*

maticien, économiste, philosophe, homme politique, ed. Pierre Crépel and Christian Gilain, 385–95. Paris: Minerve, 1989.

Kallen, Horace. *Culture and Democracy in the United States.* New York: Boni & Livewright, 1924.

———. *Judaism at Bay: Essays Toward the Adjustment of Judaism to Modernity.* New York: Bloch Publishing, 1932.

Karl, Frederick R. *Modern and Modernism: The Sovereignty of the Artist 1885–1925.* New York: Atheneum, 1985.

Katz, Jacob. *Out of the Ghetto: The Social Background of Jewish Emancipation, 1770–1870.* Cambridge: Harvard University Press, 1973.

———. *Tradition and Crisis: Jewish Society at the End of the Middle Ages.* Trans. Bernard Dov Cooperman. New York: New York University Press, 1993.

Kaufman, Jay. "Thou Shalt Surely Rebuke Thy Neighbor." In *Black Anti-Semitism and Jewish Racism,* ed. Nat Hentoff, 69. New York: Schocken, 1970.

Kaufman, Jonathan. *Broken Alliance: The Turbulent Times Between Blacks and Jews in America.* New York: Penguin, 1988.

Kazin, Alfred. *Bright Book of Life.* Notre Dame, Ind.: University of Notre Dame Press, 1971.

———. Interview. In *Creators and Disturbers: Reminiscences by Jewish Intellectuals of New York,* ed. Bernard Rosenberg and Ernest Goldstein, 194–209. New York: Columbia University Press, 1982.

———. "The Jew as Modern Writer." *Commentary* 41, no. 4 (1966): 37–41.

———. *New York Jew.* New York: Random House, 1978.

———. *On Native Grounds.* 1942. Garden City, N.Y.: Doubleday & Co., 1956.

———. "The Self as History: Reflections on Autobiography." In *The American Autobiography: A Collection of Critical Essays,* ed. Albert E. Stone, 31–43. Englewood Cliffs, N.J.: Prentice-Hall, 1981.

———. *Starting Out in the Thirties.* Boston: Little, Brown & Co., 1962.

———. *A Walker in the City.* 1951. New York: Grove Press, 1958.

Kempton, Murray. *Part of Our Time: Some Ruins and Monuments of the Thirties.* New York: Simon and Schuster, 1955.

Kilson, Martin. "Blacks and Neo-Ethnicity in America." In *Ethnicity: Theory and Experience,* ed. Nathan Glazer and Daniel Moynihan, 236–66. Cambridge: Harvard University Press, 1975.

King, Marthin Luther Jr. *A Testament of Hope: The Essential Writings of Martin Luther King.* Ed. James Melvin Washington. San Francisco: Harper & Row, 1986.

Kinnamon, Keneth. *The Emergence of Richard Wright: A Study in Literature and Society.* Urbana: University of Illinois Press, 1972.

Klehr, Harvey. *The Heyday of American Communism: The Depression Decade.* New York: Basic Books, 1984.

Kristol, Irving. "How Basic is 'Basic Judaism'? A Comfortable Religion for an Uncomfortable World." *Commentary* 5, no. 1 (1948): 27–34.

Lacy, Leslie Alexander. *The Rise and Fall of a Proper Negro.* New York: Macmillan, 1970.

Lascelles, E. C. P. *Granville Sharp and the Freedom of Slaves in England.* London: Oxford University Press, 1928.

Lester, Julius. *All Is Well.* New York: William Morrow, 1976.

———. *Lovesong: Becoming a Jew.* New York: Henry Holt, 1988.

Levin, Meyer. *In Search, an Autobiography*. New York: Horizon Press, 1950.

Lewis, David Levering. "Parallels and Divergences: Assimilationist Strategies of Afro-American and Jewish Elites from 1910 to the Early 1930s." In *Bridges and Boundaries: African Americans and American Jews*, ed. Jack Salzman et al., 17–35. New York: George Braziller, 1992.

Lewisohn, Ludwig. *A Jew Speaks: An Anthology of Ludwig Lewisohn*. New York: Harper & Brothers, 1931.

———. "A Panorama of a Half-Century of American Jewish Literature." *Jewish Book Annual* 9 (1950–51): 3–10.

———. *Up Stream: An American Chronicle*. New York: Horace Liveright, 1922.

Linebaugh, Peter, and Marcus Rediker. "The Many-Headed Hydra: Sailors, Slaves, and the Atlantic Working Class in the Eighteenth Century." *Journal of Historical Sociology* 3, no. 3 (September 1990): 225–52.

Lipset, Seymour Martin, and Earl Raab. *The Politics of Unreason: Right-Wing Extremism in America, 1790–1970*. New York: Harper & Row, 1970.

Low, Alfred D. *Jews in the Eyes of the Germans: From the Enlightenment to Imperial Germany*. Philadelphia: Institute for the Study of Human Issues, 1979.

Lynd, Robert, and Helen Lynd. *Middletown, A Study in American Culture*. New York: Harcourt, Brace and Co., 1929.

Mahler, Raphael. *A History of Modern Jewry: 1780–1815*. London: Vallentine, Mitchell & Co., 1971.

Maimon, Salomon. *Salomon Maimons Lebensgeschichte von ihm selbst geschrieben und Herausgegeben von Karl Philipp Moritz*. Ed. Zwi Batscha. 1792. Reprint, Frankfurt am Main: Inself Verlag, 1984.

———. *Solomon Maimon: An Autobiography*. Trans. J. Clark Murray. London: Gardner, Paisley, 1888.

Marrant, John. *A Narrative of the Lord's Wonderful Dealings with John Marrant, a Black*. 1785. The Garland Library of Narratives of North American Indian Captivities, vol. 17, iii–38. New York: Garland Publishing Inc., 1978.

Martin, Gaston. *Histoire de l'esclavage dans les colonies françaises*. Paris: Presses Universitaires de France, 1948.

Mauriac, François. Foreword. In *Night*, by Elie Wiesel, vii–xi. Trans. Stella Rodway. New York: Hill & Wang, 1960.

Maxwell, William J. *New Negro, Old Left: African-American Writing and Communism Between the Wars*. New York: Columbia University Press, 1999.

Mencken, H. L. "Dream and Awakening." Rev. of *Up Stream* by Ludwig Lewisohn. *The Nation* 114 (April 12, 1922): 436.

Mendelsohn, Moses. *Jerusalem and Other Jewish Writings*. Trans. and ed. Alfred Jospe. New York: Schocken Books, 1969.

Minkin, Jacob. *The World of Moses Maimonides with Selections from His Writings*. New York: Thomas Yoseloff, 1957.

Mintz, Alan. *"Banished from Their Father's Table": Loss of Faith and Hebrew Autobiography*. Bloomington: Indiana University Press, 1989.

Mohanty, Satya P. *Literary Theory and the Claims of History*. Ithaca, N.Y. and London: Cornell University Press, 1997.

Montesquieu, Charles de Secondat, baron de. *The Spirit of the Laws*. Trans. Anne Cohler et al. Cambridge: Cambridge University Press, 1989.

"Moses Mendelssohn." *The Universal Jewish Encyclopedia*, 1904 edition.

Murphy, Beatrice M. *Pulse* 3 (1945): 32–33.

Murray, Albert. *The Omni-Americans: New Perspectives on Black Experiences and American Culture.* New York: Outerbridge & Dienstfrey, 1970.

Myrdal, Gunnar. *An American Dilemma: The Negro Problem and Modern Democracy.* New York: Harper & Brothers, 1944.

Naison, Mark. *Communists in Harlem during the Depression.* Urbana: University of Illinois Press, 1983.

Newfield, Jack. *A Prophetic Minority.* New York: Signet, 1966.

Novak, Michael. *The Rise of the Unmeltable Ethnics: Politics and Culture in the Seventies.* New York: Macmillan, 1972.

Ottley, Roi. *New World A-Coming.* Boston: Houghton Mifflin, 1943.

Ottobah, Cugoano. *Thoughts and Sentiments on the Evil and Wicked Traffic of the Slavery and Commerce of the Human Species . . . by Ottobah Cugoano, A Native of Africa.* 1787. Ed Paul Edwards. London: Dawsons, 1969.

Padmore, George. *Pan-Africanism or Communism.* 1956. New York: Doubleday, 1971.

Padover, Saul K. Introduction. In *Confessions and Self-Portraits: 4600 Years of Autobiography,* xiii–xx. New York: John Day, 1957.

Park, Robert E. *Race and Culture.* Glencoe, Ill.: The Free Press, 1950.

Parsons, Talcott. "Some Theoretical Considerations on the Nature and Trends of Change of Ethnicity." In *Ethnicity: Theory and Experience,* ed. Nathan Glazer and Daniel Moynihan, 53–83. Cambridge: Harvard University Press, 1975.

Pluchon, Pierre. *Nègres et Juifs au XVIIIe siècle.* Paris: Editions Tallandier, 1984.

Podhoretz, Norman. *Making It.* New York: Harper & Row, 1967.

Poliakov, Leon. *The Aryan Myth: A History of Racist and Nationalist Ideas in Europe.* Trans. Edmund Howard. London: Sussex University Press, 1974.

———. *The History of Anti-Semitism,* vol. 3. Trans. Miriam Kochan. New York: Vanguard, 1975.

Popkin, Richard H. "The Philosophical Basis of Eighteenth-Century Racism." In *Racism in the Eighteenth Century,* ed. Harold E. Pagliaro, 245–56. Studies in Eighteenth-Century Culture 4. Cleveland: The Press of Case Western Reserve University, 1973.

Porter, Horace A. "The Horror and the Glory: Wright's Portrait of the Artist in *Black Boy* and *American Hunger.*" In *Richard Wright: Critical Perspectives Past and Present,* ed. Henry Louis Gates Jr. and K. A. Appiah, 316–27. New York: Amistad, 1993.

Potkay, Adam, and Sandra Burr, eds. *Black Atlantic Writers of the 18th Century: Living the New Exodus in England and the Americas.* New York: St. Martin's Press, 1995.

Raboteau, Albert. *Slave Religion.* New York and Oxford: Oxford University Press, 1980.

Rahv, Philip. Introduction. *A Malamud Reader,* ed. Philip Rahv. New York: Farrar, Straus and Giroux, 1967.

Ratner, Sidney. "Horace M. Kallen and Cultural Pluralism." In *The Legacy of Horace M. Kallen,* ed. Milton R. Konvitz, 48–63. Rutherford, N.J. : Fairleigh Dickinson University Press, 1987.

Redding, Saunders. "The Negro Writer and His Relationships to His Roots." In *The American Negro Writer and His Roots: Selected Papers from the First Conference of Negro Writers, March, 1959,* 1–7. New York: The American Society of African Culture, 1960.

Richardson, Harry V. *Dark Salvation: The Story of Methodism as It Developed Among Blacks in America.* Garden City, N.Y.: Doubleday, 1976.

Richman, Sidney. *Bernard Malamud.* Twayne United States Authors Series 109. New York: Twayne Publishers, 1966.

Robeson, Paul. "The Culture of the Negro." In *Black Nationalism in America*, ed. John H. Bracey Jr. et al., 331–47. New York: Bobbs-Merrill, 1970.

———. *Here I Stand.* Boston: Beacon Press, 1958.

Rosenfeld, Alvin H. "Inventing the Jew: Notes on Jewish Autobiography." In *The American Autobiography: A Collection of Critical Essays*, ed. Albert E. Stone, 133–56. Englewood Cliffs, N.J.: Prentice-Hall, 1981.

Roth, Philip. *The Ghost Writer.* New York: Farrar, Straus and Giroux, 1979.

———. *Reading Myself and Others.* New York: Farrar, Straus and Giroux, 1975.

Rousseau, Jean-Jacques. *The Confessions.* Trans. J.M. Cohen. London: Penguin Books, 1953.

Samuels, Wilfred D. "Olaudah Equiano (Gustavus Vassa)." In *Afro-American Writers Before the Harlem Renaissance*, 123–29. Vol. 50 of *The Dictionary of Literary Biography*. Detroit: Bruccoli Clark, 1986.

Sancho, Ignatius. *The Letters of the Late Ignatius Sancho, an African.* Ed. Paul Edwards. London: Dawsons, 1968.

Sandiford, Keith A. *Measuring the Moment: Strategies of Protest in Eighteenth-Century Afro-English Writing.* London: Associated University Presses, 1988.

San Juan Jr., E. *Racial Formations/Critical Transformations: Articulations of Power in Ethnic and Racial Studies in the United States.* Atlantic Highlands, N.J. and London: Humanities Press, 1992.

Schmidt, H. D. "The Terms of Emancipation 1781–1812." In *Leo Baeck Institute Year Book 1*, 28–47. London: East and West Library, 1956.

Schultz, Max. *Radical Sophistication.* Athens, Ohio: Ohio University Press, 1969.

Schwartz, Delmore. *In Dreams Begin Responsibilities and Other Stories.* Ed. James Atlas. New York: New Directions, 1978.

Seeber, Edward. *Anti-Slavery Opinion in France During the Second Half of the Eighteenth Century.* Baltimore: The Johns Hopkins University Press, 1937.

Sekora, John. "Red, White, and Black: Indian Captivities, Colonial Printers, and the Early African-American Narrative." In *A Mixed Race: Ethnicity in Early America*, ed. Frank Shuffelton, 92–104. New York: Oxford University Press, 1993.

Seltzer, Robert M. *Jewish People, Jewish Thought: The Jewish Experience in History.* New York: Macmillan, 1980.

Sharpton, Al. *Go and Tell Pharaoh.* New York: Doubleday, 1996.

Shapiro, Edward S. *A Time for Healing: American Jewry since World War II.* The Jewish People in America, vol. 5. Baltimore: The Johns Hopkins University Press, 1992.

Shirley, Walter. Preface. In *A Narrative of the Most Remarkable Particulars in the Life of James Albert Ukawsaw Gronniosaw, An African Prince, Written by Himself.* Ed. Hannah Moore. 1770. In *Black Atlantic Writers of the 18th Century: Living the New Exodus in England and the Americas*, ed. Adam Potkay and Sandra Burr, 75–76. New York: St. Martin's Press, 1995.

Shyllon, Folarin. "Olaudah Equiano: Nigerian Abolitionist and First National Leader of Africans in Britain." *Journal of African Studies* 4, no. 4 (1977–78): 433–51.

Silvers, Robert B. "Alfred Kazin: The Critic as Creator." *Horizon* 4, no. 6 (1962): 98–103.

"The Slave Trade." In *Encyclopedia of African-American Culture and History*, 1996 edition.

Sloan, Phillip R. "The Ideal of Racial Degeneracy in Buffon's *Histoire Naturelle.*" In *Racism in the Eighteenth Century*, ed. Harold E. Pagliaro, 293–321. Studies in Eighteenth-Century Culture 4. Cleveland: The Press of Case Western Reserve University, 1973.

Smith, Venture. "A Narrative of the Life and Adventures of Venture, A Native of Africa: But Resident above Sixty Years in the United States of America. Related by Himself." In *Early Negro Writing*, ed. Dorothy Porter, 538–83. Boston: Beacon Press, 1971.

Steinberg, Stephen. *The Ethnic Myth: Race, Ethnicity and Class in America*. Boston: Beacon Press, 1981.

Stepto, Robert. *From Behind the Veil: A Study of Afro-American Narrative*. Urbana: University of Illinois Press, 1979.

Stoddard, Lothrop. *The Rising Tide of Color Against White World Supremacy*. New York: Charles Scribner's Sons, 1920.

Stoehr, Taylor. "Paul Goodman and the New York Jews." *Salmagundi* 66 (1985): 50–103.

Sypher, Wylie. *Guinea's Captive Kings: British Anti-Slavery Literature of the Eighteenth Century*. Chapel Hill: The University of North Carolina Press, 1942.

Tempkin, Sefton D. "United States of America." *Encyclopedia Judaica Decennial Book, 1973–1982*. Jerusalem: Keter Publishing House, 1983.

"Under Forty: A Symposium on American Literature and the Younger Generation of American Jews." *Contemporary Jewish Record* 7, no. 1 (1944): 3–36.

Wald, Alan. *The New York Intellectuals: The Rise and Decline of the Anti-Stalinist Left from the 1930s to the 1980s*. Chapel Hill: University of North Carolina Press, 1987.

———. "Theorizing Cultural Difference: A Critique of the Ethnicity School." *MELUS* 14 (summer 1987): 21–33.

Walker, Alice. *In Search of Our Mothers' Gardens*. New York: Harcourt, Brace, Jovanovich, 1983.

Walzer, Michael. *Exodus and Revolution*. New York: Basic Books, 1985.

Warner, W. Lloyd, and Leo Srole. *The Social Systems of American Ethnic Groups*. Yankee City Series 3. New Haven, Conn.: Yale University Press, 1945.

Washington, Booker T. *The Future of the American Negro*. Boston: Smally, Maynard and Co., 1899.

———. *Up from Slavery*. 1901. In *Three Negro Classics*, ed. John Hope Franklin, 24–205. New York: Avon Books, 1965.

Waxman, Meyer. *The History of Jewish Literature*, vol. 3. New York: Thomas Yoseloff, 1936.

Weinberg, Meyer. *Because They Were Jews: A History of Antisemitism*. New York: Greenwood Press, 1986.

Wener, Eric. *Mendelssohn: A New Image of the Composer and His Age*. Trans. Dika Newlin. New York: The Free Press of Glencoe, 1963.

Werner, Craig. *Playing the Changes: From Afro-Modernism to the Jazz Impulse*. Chicago: University of Illinois Press, 1994.

Whaley, Joachim. "The Protestant Enlightenment in Germany." In *The Enlightenment in National Context*, ed. Roy Porter and Mikulas Teich, 106–117. Cambridge: Cambridge University Press, 1981.

Williams, Raymond. *Keywords: A Vocabulary of Culture and Society*. New York: Oxford University Press, 1976.

Wirth, Louis. *The Ghetto*. Chicago: The University of Chicago Press, 1928.

Wright, Richard. *12 Million Black Voices: A Folk History of the Negro in the United States*. New York: Viking, 1941.

———. *American Hunger*. New York: Harper & Row, 1977.

———. *Black Boy: A Record of Childhood and Youth*. 1945. New York: Harper & Row, 1966.

———. *Black Power: A Record of Reactions in a Land of Pathos*. 1954. New York: Harper & Row, 1995.

————. "Blueprint for Negro Writing." In *The Black Aesthetic*, ed. Addison Gayle Jr., 333–45. Garden City, N.Y.: Doubleday, 1971.

————. "Interview with Richard Wright: *L'Express*/1960." In *Conversations with Richard Wright*, ed. Keneth Kinnamon and Michel Fabre, 201–7. Jackson: University Press of Mississippi, 1993.

————. "Introduction." In *Black Metropolis*, St. Clair Drake and Horace Clayton, xvii–xviii. New York: Harcourt and Brace, 1945.

————. "The Literature of the Negro in the United States." In *White Man, Listen!* 1957. New York: Harper Collins, 1995, 71–110.

————. *Native Son.* 1940. New York: Harper & Row, 1966.

————. "Tradition and Industrialization." In *White Man, Listen!* 1957. New York: Harper & Row, 1995, 45–69.

Yudkin, Leon Israel. *Jewish Writing and Identity in the Twentieth Century.* London: Croom Helm, 1982.

Zinberg, Israel. *The Berlin Haskalah.* Trans. Bernard Martin. Vol. 8 of *The History of Jewish Literature.* Cincinnati, Ohio: Hebrew Union College Press, 1976.

————. *Haskalah at Its Zenith.* Trans. Bernard Martin. Vol. 12 of *The History of Jewish Literature.* Cincinnati, Ohio: Hebrew Union College Press, 1978.

Index